The Challenge of the Left Opposition (1923-25)

LEON TROTSKY

THE CHALLENGE OF THE LEFT OPPOSITION (1923~25)

Edited with an introduction
by Naomi Allen

Pathfinder Press, New York

First Edition, 1975

Pathfinder Press, Inc.
410 West Street
New York, N.Y. 10014

CONTENTS

LEON TROTSKY was born Lev Davidovich Bronstein in 1879 in the Ukraine. His first arrest for revolutionary activity was in 1898. He was exiled to Siberia, but escaped to collaborate with Lenin on *Iskra* in London in 1902. He broke with Lenin the following year at the time of the split between Bolsheviks and Mensheviks, was briefly aligned with the Mensheviks, but in 1904 broke with them and began a decade-long effort to reunite the Russian Social Democratic Labor Party. During the 1905 revolution he was the leader of the St. Petersburg Soviet and developed his theory of permanent revolution. He was again exiled to Siberia and again escaped. He was part of the tiny minority in the socialist movement who refused to support their governments in World War I. When the February revolution broke out in 1917 he was in New York, but he arrived back in Russia in May, joined the Bolshevik Party, was elected to its Central Committee, and in October was the leader of the Petrograd Soviet and the chief organizer of the Bolshevik insurrection. As the first commissar of foreign affairs, he headed the Soviet delegation to negotiate a peace with Germany at Brest-Litovsk. As commissar of war (1918-25) he created the Red Army and led it to victory through three years of civil war and imperialist intervention. He was a member of the Politburo of the Russian Communist Party from its formation until 1926, and of the Executive Committee of the Communist International from 1920 to 1927. He formed the Left Opposition in 1923 to fight for the preservation of Leninist internationalism and proletarian democracy. Defeated by the Stalin faction, he was expelled from the party in 1927, exiled first to Siberia in 1928 and then to Turkey in 1929. In 1933 he abandoned his efforts to reform the Communist International and called for the creation of a new International. He viewed his work on behalf of the Fourth International, founded in 1938, as the most important work of his life. In his final exile he was hounded from country to country by both the Stalinists and the fascists. He lived in Turkey until 1933, France until 1935, Norway until 1936, and Mexico until his death in August 1940 at the hands of a Stalinist assassin.

Preface

This volume is the first in a series of the writings of Leon Trotsky on the Communist Left Opposition in the Soviet Union from the time of its founding in the autumn of 1923 to 1929, when Trotsky was forcibly expelled from the USSR. Its purpose is to present, as Trotsky presented them, the ideas of the Left Opposition on the main issues in dispute during this crucial period of Soviet history. Several of the pieces collected here were published in English in the 1920s but have been out of print for decades, or have been reissued only in pamphlet form. Others are translated from the Russian for the first time and in some cases have not been published previously in any language, since under the conditions of the factional struggle in the Soviet Union the views of the Oppositionists were more and more prevented from receiving a hearing among the ranks of the communist movement, either domestically or internationally.

This collection will make available for the first time a full presentation of the major tenets of the Opposition's program, which will be a useful resource for students of early Soviet history or those trying to investigate the most far-reaching antagonism in the communist movement.

During his final exile starting in 1929, Trotsky wrote extensively about the degeneration of the Russian revolution (see in particular his major work on the subject, *The Revolution Betrayed,* written on the eve of the first Moscow show trial in 1936). The present volume, while it lacks the advantage of hindsight, compensates for that by presenting the central issues as they emerged in the course of the struggle.

This series is not a documentary history of the Left Opposition. It is limited to Trotsky's writings and speeches and does not attempt to reckon with the vast quantity of material produced both by Trotsky's cothinkers and by his opponents. Although the scope of this project is limited to Trotsky's contributions to the

13

inner-party struggle, his central position in the leadership of the
Opposition, his prolific output, and the consistency of his critique
over the succeeding decades prevent this limitation from becoming a handicap.

The present volume covers the initial period of the Left Opposition from its formation until the end of 1925—when, in the wake
of the Leningrad Opposition's defeat at the Fourteenth Party
Congress, Trotsky considers the prospect of a United Opposition
with Zinoviev and Kamenev.

For the convenience of the reader an exposition of the major
events of these two years has been included in the introduction.
Explanatory notes, a list of abbreviations and unfamiliar terms,
a bibliography, and a list of Trotsky's other writings may be
found at the back of the book. An editorial note preceding each
selection explains its source and gives other information about
the translation, editing, etc. Wherever possible we have replaced
Trotsky's citations of Russian texts with references to the standard English translation. These and any other editorial interpola-
tions are given in square brackets.

This project could not have been successful without the kind
permission of the Harvard College Library to examine, translate,
and publish material in the open section of the Trotsky archives.

N.A.

Introduction

When the Bolsheviks established the Soviet Republic in October 1917, they ushered in a new era of world history. The first socialist revolution marked the beginning of the end for the capitalist system, which held the entire world in its grip. It meant the start of economic construction on a rational, planned basis for the benefit of the overwhelming majority of people in Russia and in the nations subjugated by tsarism. Workers and oppressed peoples all over the world regarded the Russian revolution as an example to be emulated. It had brought into being a new society that had long been dreamed of but never before realized in life.

It was not immediately apparent, either to participants or to observers, what was going wrong when the Soviet Republic along with the Russian Communist Party began to show signs of degeneration. Even Lenin, whose personal role in the formation and early years of the Soviet state was central, did not at first fully grasp what was happening. Stalinism was a new phenomenon, and in its early stages, while Lenin was alive, it was impossible to foresee what it would become. Lenin was, however, the first to come to grips with it and to organize a struggle against it—the last struggle of his life. To preserve the state monopoly of foreign trade and the right of self-determination of non-Russian nationalities, and to prevent the growth of a privileged bureaucratic caste in the party and state, Lenin offered to form a bloc with Trotsky, and asked Trotsky to defend their common views at the Twelfth Party Congress scheduled for April 1923.* In December 1922 and January 1923 Lenin wrote a series of notes designed to be read to the congress, which came to be known as his "Testament," pointing out that "Stalin . . . has unlimited authority concentrated in his hands, and I am not sure whether he will always be capable of using that authority with sufficient caution. . . ." The Testa-

---

*Lenin's last efforts to reverse the growth of a privileged bureaucratic cast in the party are documented in **Lenin's Fight Against Stalinism,** by Lenin and Trotsky (Pathfinder Press, 1975).

ment called for the removal of Stalin from the post of general secretary and his replacement by a comrade "more tolerant, more loyal, more polite, and more considerate to the comrades, less capricious, etc." The Testament was suppressed by the Stalinists and was not published in the USSR until 1956. Shortly before the Twelfth Congress Lenin suffered a stroke that left him paralyzed and speechless until his death in January 1924. In Lenin's absence, Trotsky hesitated to open fire at the Twelfth Congress, fearing that his move would be interpreted as a bid for the position of Lenin's successor, and hoping that Lenin would recover sufficiently to lead the struggle in person. He may also have been deceived by the maneuvers of Stalin, who readily accepted all of Trotsky's amendments to resolutions in order to keep him from launching a direct public attack on the bureaucracy.

The bourgeois world, which had viewed with the utmost hostility the gains the Soviet people had made through their revolution, was quick to announce that the degeneration of the revolutionary party and state was proof that power corrupts and that the seeds of corruption had been sown by Lenin and only reaped by Stalin. The Stalinists, who had played lesser parts in the revolution but were the protagonists of the revolution's decline, muddied the waters by insisting that their regime was the faithful continuation of Lenin's. And the voice of the Left Opposition, like the voice of all opposition after it, was largely silenced.

The struggle between the Left Opposition and what was to become the Stalinist faction, far from being a petty dispute over theoretical intangibles or a power struggle between individuals, involved crucial historic issues which retain their relevance in any contemporary discussion of foreign or domestic policy in the workers' states, or of revolutionary strategy in the colonial or imperialist countries.

The main issue at the outset was the bureaucratization of the Russian Communist Party and the Soviet state, and the accompanying suppression of democracy in the party and the state, as well as in the working class as a whole. This was central because it exercised a decisive effect on all the other questions that were under debate in the Soviet Union, from Trotsky's personal role in the leadership, to the pace of industrialization, the attitude toward revolutionary upheavals in other lands, and the degree of democratic rights needed in the period of the transition from capitalism to socialism. Time would reveal a great unifying theme in these apparently little-related issues: How could the Soviet working class retain in its hands the power it had won, when the summits of party and state came to be more and more dominated by a conservatized, privileged bureaucratic elite? Was capitalism to be overturned only to be replaced by another system of authoritarian minority rule?

Of all the Bolshevik leaders, only Lenin and Trotsky saw the danger at its outset. Lenin was dead before the struggle was fully in the open. Trotsky succeeded in rallying the revolutionary core of the Communist Party; but in an overwhelmingly peasant country isolated by a hostile capitalist world this proved insufficient, and the movement he had initiated with Lenin went down to defeat. Both the Soviet Union and the world socialist movement paid a terrible price for that defeat.

Domestically, the victory of Stalinism in the Soviet Union meant the immense toll in human suffering caused by the forced collectivization of agriculture and the crash industrialization program in the thirties. This included the artificial famine in the Ukraine in 1932, in which five to six million peasants died when the grain they had harvested for their own subsistence was seized for export; the crushing of the rights of the non-Russian nationalities in the Soviet Union; the destruction in the great purges of the thirties of the entire generation of revolutionists that had worked with Lenin to make the October Revolution, as well as the leadership of the Red Army; the disorganization of Soviet military power on the eve of World War II and the failure to prepare militarily for Hitler's invasion; continuing economic mismanagement; and the denial of even those civil liberties that are enjoyed by the populations of the imperialist democracies.

Internationally, the price of bureaucratic supremacy in the Soviet Union was the turning back of the world revolution on every front for an entire historic period. Instead of a revolutionary foreign policy, the Kremlin advanced a policy of conciliation with imperialism ("peaceful coexistence") that required the sacrifice of revolutionary activity both in the imperialist countries and in the colonial world. The result was a series of unnecessary defeats that gave imperialism a new lease on life, enabling it to survive into the nuclear era, where it can threaten the very existence of life on earth.

As long as the Stalinist bureaucracy maintains its grip on the Soviet state it will continue to do everything in its power to prevent the spread of revolution abroad and the development of proletarian democracy in the USSR. Without these two factors, the building of a truly socialist society of equality, abundance, and freedom in the Soviet Union is impossible.

Thus the historical significance of the struggle of the Left Opposition comes into focus. For what the Left Opposition accomplished on an international scale, despite its defeat in the USSR, was to preserve for future struggles the program of revolutionary Marxism and the best traditions of Bolshevism at a time when they were in danger of being obliterated.

*   *   *

By late 1923, when this volume begins, the Soviet Republic was six years old. It had weathered in its short history a series of dramatic social convulsions such as have spelled the downfall of older and more experienced regimes. But it had not emerged unscathed from the catastrophes of world war, civil war, blockade, and famine. The difficulties that would be encountered during peacetime construction were in large measure the consequences of the social dislocations of the preceding years.

First among these dislocations was World War I. By 1917, the ill-fed, poorly trained and equipped tsarist forces, under an incompetent and corrupt general staff, had sustained massive casualties in their confrontation with the more modern German army. Because most of the soldiers had been drafted from among the peasantry, agriculture was in disarray. The railroads wore out, and industrial production declined. The war exacerbated the already difficult life in tsarist Russia beyond endurance.

With the country ground down by more than three years of warfare, the first official act of the new Soviet government in November 1917 was to sue for peace with Germany. It was not until March 1918 that peace was finally concluded, on terms that were exceedingly unfavorable to the Soviet Republic. But even then the work of peacetime reconstruction could not begin, for in the summer of 1918 civil war was launched by pro-tsarist, pro-capitalist White Guard forces backed by money, munitions, and troops from the Allied governments. By this time the Russian armies had dissolved, and the task of preparing the defense of the Republic fell to Trotsky; as commissar of war, he had to build the Red Army from the ground up. The civil war raged back and forth for almost three years over several fronts.

War is an expensive undertaking even for a prosperous country. For Soviet Russia it was an exercise in achieving the impossible.

From an economy that had already suffered the ravages of war and revolution, the Bolsheviks had to extract the means to defend the workers' state. That was the period of "war communism," which required the subordination of the economy to the military needs of the government. Industry, already tottering on the verge of collapse, was nationalized; the part that could still function was directed into producing war materiel. Private trade was prohibited. Since few manufactured goods existed for the peasants to buy, trade between town and countryside broke down. Armed detachments were sent to the countryside to requisition food for the army and city dwellers. The peasants retaliated by hoarding their surpluses and refusing to plant more than they needed for their own consumption. Thus only a short time after they had hailed the October Revolution for distributing the land, the peasants came into bitter conflict with the measures the revolution was forced to resort to for survival.

The condition of the workers in the cities was even worse. The young Russian working class, which had had the power and the militancy to sweep the revolution to victory only a few years before, was decimated and dispersed by the civil war. Those who had escaped death or mutilation at the front had left the cities to escape starvation. In 1921, when the civil war drew to a successful conclusion, the two major cities of Russia, Moscow and Petrograd, had only one-half and one-third of their former inhabitants, respectively, and even those populations were starving. Money had lost its value, and wages, when paid at all, were often paid in kind. Russia's national income was only one-third and industrial output less than one-fifth their prewar levels. Agriculture was largely wrecked. The low point in the fortunes of the Soviet Republic was reached when drought, sandstorms, and an invasion of locusts brought acute famine to thirty-six million people in 1921. The effort to stay alive became the preoccupation of the great majority.

The catastrophic decline of industry and the dispersal and destruction of the proletariat between 1918 and 1921, on the one hand, and the estrangement if not downright hostility of the peasantry, on the other, would have a long-range effect on the relative weight of both classes in the economy and consequently on the future measures of the Soviet state. The peasants had reluctantly permitted the confiscation of their crops as long as there was a threat of tsarist restoration and loss of their newly acquired lands. With the victory of the revolution in the civil war the peasantry became less and less willing to sacrifice for the benefit of the economy as a whole. By early 1921 peasant unrest had produced violent outbreaks in many parts of the country.

Just as the inability of the bourgeoisie to hold the loyalty of the peasant masses had been a decisive factor in the success of the revolution in 1917, the question of whether the Bolsheviks would be able to hold their loyalty was the central one in the debates over policy after the civil war. Although the antagonism between city workers and peasants became more sharply pronounced in the grain crisis of 1923 and the accompanying dispute over how to solve it, it was clear well before then that the transition to socialism in a predominantly peasant country would hinge on the peasants' support for the workers' state.

At the Tenth Congress of the Russian Communist Party in March 1921 Lenin insisted on the centrality of this problem: "In such a country [with a minority of industrial workers and a vast majority of small farmers] a socialist revolution can triumph only on two conditions. First, if it is given timely support by a socialist revolution in one or several advanced countries. As you know, we have done very much indeed in comparison with the past to bring about this condition, but far from enough to make it a reality.

"The second condition is agreement between the proletariat, which is exercising its dictatorship, that is, holds state power, and the majority of the peasant population" [*Collected Works,* Vol. 32, "Report on the Substitution of a Tax in Kind . . ." (March 15, 1921), p. 215].

International revolution and a working relationship with the peasantry were themes that Lenin would return to repeatedly.

From 1914 on, the Bolsheviks had expected that the world war would act as the detonator of proletarian revolutions in the West. This was not an unfounded theoretical assumption. At the war's end, Europe was shaken by a wave of rebellion unmatched since the revolutions of 1848. In Hungary and Bavaria short-lived soviet governments were actually established in 1919. In 1920, the Red Army met and defeated a Polish assault and chased the retreating armies into Poland, where an insurrection appeared imminent. In Czechoslovakia, Romania, and Italy, majorities had left the reformist Socialist parties to form Communist parties allied with the Communist International. In Northern Italy the workers had occupied the factories and called for a workers' government.

The Second World Congress of the Communist International, meeting in 1920 in the midst of these events, was optimistic. The

Russian delegates, in particular, felt that the day was near when food, machinery, technological advisers, and industrial credits would be extended by the victorious workers of Europe to the Russian workers, who had had to stand alone against the bourgeoisie at such great expense in human suffering and economic destruction.

But the European revolution was defeated on every front, either through the treachery of the mass social democratic organizations or through the inexperience of the young Communist parties, most of whose members had their origins in the social democracy and had not had an opportunity to absorb the lessons of the Russian revolution. The Hungarian and Bavarian soviets were crushed. The Polish uprising failed to materialize. The Italian Communist Party hesitated and finally failed to try to take power at the crucial moment. The German party exhausted its resources during 1920 in a series of confrontations with the social democratic government, which had murdered the revolutionists Karl Liebknecht and Rosa Luxemburg the previous year. By the end of 1920, the Bolsheviks recognized that the setbacks to the revolutionary forces in Europe had given a respite of uncertain duration to the capitalist system, that the revolutionary wave had given way to a period of capitalist stabilization. At the top of the agenda for European communists was no longer the imminent seizure of power but rather the broadest possible defense of the workers' rights against a systematic attack by a frightened but victorious bourgeoisie. The communists were only a minority of the working class. Through the united front tactic they now sought to join forces with the social democratic majority for a common struggle against reaction—and in the process to win to communism those workers who still remained loyal to the reformist social democracy.

Similarly, a policy of domestic retrenchment was called for. The adoption of the New Economic Policy (NEP) in March 1921 was an attempt to secure an alliance between the peasantry and the working class that would see the Soviet state through the period of enforced isolation until the victorious revolution of the Western proletariat came to its aid. The NEP was a domestic measure of retrenchment that corresponded to the tactics of the Comintern designed to deal with the delay in the world revolution. Its purpose was to reverse the growing estrangement of the peasantry from the proletarian state by improving the standard of rural life—chiefly by permitting the peasantry to market its grain at

unregulated prices, to earn money with which to buy manufactured goods in the cities. This would in turn provide the peasantry with an incentive to produce larger crops than it needed to
feed itself. Forced confiscation of the agricultural surpluses was
to be replaced by a progressive tax in kind; the restoration of
private trade between city and countryside through the free market would permit an accumulation of capital; the capital could be
channeled into industry. Thus a revival of agriculture would
prime the industrial pump as well, and in that respect would hold
out a long-term promise for the reconstruction of the Soviet economy as a whole. Since foreign loans and aid were by and large
ruled out—the capitalist governments abroad were not enthusias-
tic about contributing to the viability of a socialist system and
preferred to speculate on its collapse so that they would be able to
invest on their own terms—the accumulation of capital to rebuild
the economy would have to be accomplished within the framework of the Soviet economy itself.

Without the war and civil war it might have been possible to
use the steady growth of agriculture to subsidize the industrialization of Russia. But after the civil war the peasant was in no
condition—and in no mood—to tolerate that. So the effort to
revive the economy, while restoring the flow of food into the
cities, in fact took place largely at the expense of industry, and
thus of the city proletariat.

From the autumn of 1921 onwards, more and more industrial
enterprises were cut off from state credits and supplies of raw
materials; instead of working under a single economic authority
they competed with one another, with the result of increasing
chaos and waste. At the same time, demand for consumer goods
among the peasants, because of the 1921 famine, proved unexpectedly low, which interfered with the delivery of grain to the
cities; and the specter of industrial unemployment once again appeared in the cities. While the NEP had an immediate salutary
effect on agriculture and the condition of the peasant, the problems of the industrial worker remained unsolved. By 1922 the
harvest had reached 75 percent of its prewar level, but industry
had recovered only to 25 percent, and even that figure was
mainly for light industry. Heavy industry remained stricken, and
as a result those areas of light industry that depended on raw
materials or replacement parts were threatened with stagnation.
The soviets, the political organs of the workers, which had assumed power only four years earlier, were being drained of
independent content and becoming rubber stamps for the govern-

ment bureaucracy. Thus the proletariat, its economic power undermined by the disorganization of industry, had virtually ceased to play a political role.

From the first days of the NEP, disagreements had arisen within the party over how much to take from the villages for the reconstruction of industry. The Central Committee majority, whose spokesmen at this time were Rykov and Sokolnikov, was inclined to pressure industry, by withholding credits, to reduce prices to a level that put goods within the reach of the peasantry. The majority moved to assist the peasant further by reducing agricultural taxes. In their scheme, the market, which had permitted the limited recovery that had already taken place, was to continue functioning freely so as to allow the peasant sector to prosper. Industry would recover more gradually on the basis of peasant demand for its products and state subsidies would be determined by the profitability of the enterprise. Just how far supporters of the majority were willing to go in relying on the forces of the market may be seen from their attempt in December 1922 to dismantle the state monopoly of foreign trade—an attempt blocked by Lenin.

Faced with the urgent need to avert mass starvation and get the wheels of the economy rolling again, the Communist Party had moved in unison to institute the NEP. The successful harvest of 1922 set the countryside on the road to recovery. But in the summer of 1923 the revival of agriculture at the expense of industry began to have an effect on prices that came to be known as the "scissors" effect from the appearance of the phenomenon on a graph: the simultaneous rise of industrial prices and fall of agricultural prices. Trotsky had pointed to this phenomenon in his "Theses on Industry," presented to the Twelfth Party Congress in April 1923; but his warning had been ignored in the hope that the market would automatically correct the price disparity and that, in any event, it would not grow more severe. However, the crisis continued to intensify, and on October 1 the scissors opened to their widest point.

Industry faced a sales crisis. Manufactured goods lay unsold in the warehouses. Unemployment rose, and wages were cut or paid irregularly. At this juncture, the government sharply curtailed credits to industry, a measure that was supposed to force industrial concentration and higher efficiency, and consequently lower prices. But its immediate effect was to intensify the industrial crisis, particularly the problems of unemployment and wage payments.

The minority in the Central Committee, which after October 1923 was called the Opposition, was led by Trotsky, Preobrazhensky, and Pyatakov. They maintained that the first successes of the NEP should be consolidated by a comprehensive plan for the industrialization of the country, based on state subsidies to hasten industrial recovery and development. If heavy industry were helped to become rationalized and concentrated, the prices of manufactured goods would reflect that improvement by dropping. If it were not assisted, the boom in light industry (producing consumer goods) would be short-lived and even agriculture would suffer from the lack of equipment and farming tools. Credits directed to heavy industry should be guided by a long-range economic plan rather than the short-range criterion of profitability.

The debate over a single plan for the entire nationalized sector of the economy also goes back to the origins of the NEP. The inauguration of the NEP had diverted the party's attention from the theoretically sound idea of an economic plan, which was universally accepted under war communism, to the more immediate problem of reviving the market economy. The successes of the NEP had been achieved by resorting to capitalist methods and institutions within the framework of the workers' state; but the NEP was intended to assist not in the rebirth of capitalism in Russia but in the resuscitation of the economy so that the work of socialist construction could go forward. However, as early as 1923 the private sector was accumulating capital and expanding while the nationalized sector was working at a loss.

Trotsky pointed out that nationalization of heavy industry provided a tremendous advantage to the workers' state; to require competition not only between the nationalized sector and the privately owned sector of the economy but also among the enterprises of the nationalized sector was to relinquish a major weapon in the struggle to overcome capitalist property relations. Furthermore, there was a political necessity for serious planning at an early date: reviving industry would have as its corollary reviving the industrial proletariat, putting it back on its feet after the economic blows it had received, and enabling it to exercise political power.

The State Planning Commission (Gosplan) had been constituted at the same time as the NEP, but chiefly, it appears, as a vestige of war communism. It was limited to an advisory role with respect to the administrative problems of individual enterprises, and it had no authority to act to coordinate the various sectors of the nationalized economy or to establish a schedule of priorities.

Trotsky met with little success in his campaign to make Gosplan into an agency that could administer an economic plan on a national scale, a campaign he carried on from the earliest days of the NEP. After repeatedly resisting Trotsky's proposal for an overall plan to be administered by Gosplan, Lenin began to rethink his position on this question. On December 27, 1922, he dictated a note to the Politburo recommending a policy along the lines of Trotsky's proposals for Gosplan. But the Politburo refused to publish Lenin's note, and his new thinking on the question was hushed up. Trotsky raised the issue at the Twelfth Congress in April 1923, in his "Theses on Industry." Although his "Theses" were adopted by the congress, none of his recommendations were put into effect. He returned to the theme repeatedly in the articles and letters printed here; but it was not until the end of the decade, under the pressure of inescapable necessity, that the party turned to planning as a serious economic tool.

*　　　*　　　*

Why did October 1923 represent a turning point in the development of the disputes in the party? The answer to this question cannot be found in an examination of the conditions prevailing in the Soviet Union alone at that time, or in a study of the development of the inner-party dispute. It is necessary to look beyond the borders of the Soviet Union, to the international situation, to understand why, in October 1923, Trotsky and forty-six prominent party members took the step of demanding an open discussion in the Communist Party of the differences within the Central Committee.

Internationalism was a fundamental characteristic of the Left Opposition from its inception. While this was in sharp contrast with the emerging narrow nationalism of the budding Stalin faction, it was rooted in the most basic theoretical conclusions of Marxism: socialism could exist only as a world society with an international division of labor; and even a serious beginning of the construction of a planned economy in a national segment of a future world society required a developed industry and a skilled, numerically substantial working class. Both Lenin and Trotsky had concluded that a socialist *revolution* was possible in a country that lacked such material prerequisites, but that such a revolution could only be a holding action with a brief lifetime if it were not relieved by aid from a successful revolution in the advanced nations. This traditional Marxist view was proven to be essentially correct, with one modification: in the absence of both the material prerequisites of socialist construction and of aid from the West, the Russian Revolution did not fall back all the way to its capitalist starting point; instead, it stabilized for a whole period just short of that by throwing up the parasitic Stalinist caste. Trotsky understood that the key to defeating the incipient bureaucracy was to spread the revolution, and that this was a life-and-death matter both for the Soviet working class and for the world communist movement.

In 1920, as described above, the Bolsheviks had recognized that the postwar revolutionary wave had receded and an era of capitalist stabilization had begun. This, however, did not suggest that further upheavals in the world revolution would not take place, or that they need not occupy themselves with problems of the communist movement in other countries. It did suggest that they had to take emergency domestic measures (the NEP) to attempt to survive until a new wave of revolution would sweep Europe, which might lead to the establishment of workers' power in one or more advanced industrialized nations. The capitalist system had stabilized itself on the basis of the defeat of the postwar upheavals; but such stability, the Bolsheviks knew, could not be long-lived.

A revolutionary development did occur in Germany in 1923. A victim of the Versailles system, according to which the victors of World War I exacted reparations from the vanquished nations, Germany by 1923 was drained and exhausted. When it was late with reparations payments in January 1923, France invaded the Ruhr valley and established an occupation force there. This triggered a nationwide policy of passive resistance against the occupiers and against the whole Versailles system. In its early stages, the resistance campaign was led and organized by the bourgeois parties; Communist deputies in the Reichstag initially even voted against the government's call for passive resistance. However, as the campaign began to take its toll of the country's social and economic life, the bourgeois parties began to vacillate and the communists swung into the leadership and began to gather forces.

Throughout the spring and summer the crisis intensified, with inflation becoming so severe that wages were meaningless and money more useful as fuel than as a means of exchange. The workers, resenting the hardships of inflation and unemployment, surged to the banner of the communists. German party declarations began to speak of the imminence of a revolutionary showdown.

What happened next can only be understood in the light of the history of the German party and of the transformation being wrought in the Soviet party leadership and consequently in the Comintern.

In March 1921, the German party, under the direction of the Hungarian Comintern representative Bela Kun, had called the workers to arms and proclaimed an insurrection against the government, in response to sporadic clashes with the police. Communist workers, without any preparation and with little popular support, fought for a week with government forces. As the fighting died down, the party's Central Committee called for a general strike, which only further isolated the communists from their fellow workers. The results of the "March action" were heavy casualties and massive arrests, as well as a catastrophic decline in membership. That summer, the Third World Congress of the Comintern characterized the March action as a putsch and condemned the ultraleftism that had brought the German communists to an unprepared uprising in isolation from the masses of the working class. The congress adopted the united front tactic for the European parties, urging them to turn their attention to the effort to win the masses of workers away from the reformist social democracy and to the banner of communism, and to avoid further adventurist steps.

The March action had demonstrated the futility of spontaneous, unprepared uprisings by a minority of the workers without the support of the majority. However, having burned their fingers once in the fire of insurrection, the German leadership falsely extended the ban on putschism to cover the very idea of insurrection. When the revolutionary crisis mounted in Germany in the summer of 1923, and the masses of workers threw their support behind the Communist Party and its call for a workers' Germany; when the bourgeoisie, hesitating and unsure of itself, failed to take any measures to solve the social crisis or assume leadership of the massive discontent; the party leadership did not recognize the situation for what it was and failed to mobilize the party and the working class for the seizure of power or to make technical preparations for an insurrection.

Disagreements arose within the Russian Politburo, which had been watching the German events closely, over an assessment of the events and a strategy for dealing with them. Radek, who was in Germany, reported his fears that the German party was heading for another abortive insurrection. Zinoviev, at the head of the Comintern, urged bold action but—just as he had done in Russia in 1917—balked at the idea of an insurrection. Stalin did not believe that the situation was revolutionary and wrote that the Germans should be "restrained." Trotsky had become convinced that the situation was revolutionary and that the party should set a date for the insurrection and begin preparing for it; it should mobilize the workers for the seizure of power and rid itself of its fatalism. His article "Is It Possible to Fix a Definite Schedule for a Counter-Revolution or a Revolution?," written in September 1923, was the first of several articles that answered the contention that the insurrection would occur without conscious planning.

In October the Politburo finally agreed to urge the Germans to set a date for the insurrection. Once the date had been set, the German party, backed by Zinoviev, began frantically to prepare for it, and formed a coalition government in Saxony. But by October the upsurge had begun to wane. Passive resistance had been officially ended on September 26. The German party's paper was banned. The economy began to come under control again, and the initiative passed back into the hands of the bourgeoisie. The government demanded that the Saxony rebels capitulate by October 21, and then attacked. On the defensive, the party called for a general strike. When there was no response, Brandler, the party leader, called off the insurrection. A small uprising in Hamburg was crushed in forty-eight hours.

Heinrich Brandler was blamed for the defeat to save the reputations of those who had told him what to do. This was the first example of what later became a common practice—designating scapegoats to explain away defeats. Furthermore, the Comintern refused to admit that the revolution had failed and the movement was on the decline, and continued to speak about the "eve of the German revolution" as late as 1925, referring to the October 1923 defeat as an episode.

Trotsky was convinced that the German revolution had failed because of the errors of the leaderships of both the German and the Russian parties. They had waited too long and had hesitated when decisive action was necessary. He wrote the essay "Lessons of October" under the influence of his conviction that until the experience of the Bolshevik Party in the Russian revolution was thoroughly absorbed by communists throughout the world, the same political errors that had proved catastrophic in Germany would continue to lead revolutions to disaster.

The defeat of the German revolution in 1923 was a grave setback for the Soviet people; it reinforced their isolation and condemned them to go it alone for an indefinite time. The fate of the Russian revolution had always been closely linked to that of the German revolution in the minds of the Bolsheviks; now the hope that the German proletariat would soon come to their aid was dashed. To Trotsky and the Left Opposition, the failure of the German revolution dictated a decisive change in the terms of the dispute within the Russian party. No longer was it possible to shut one's eyes to the bureaucratization of the party apparatus, the dangers of adaptation to the peasantry, the infringements on proletarian democracy, in the expectation that the spread of proletarian revolution in the West would make the conditions of Soviet power in Russia more favorable and help to solve the problems arising from backwardness, poverty, and isolation. Now these problems would have to be tackled. First and foremost, the problem of the regime in the party had to be settled, because it was the chief obstacle to the solution of all the other problems that faced the Soviet Republic. That was the reason Trotsky decided to mount a public attack on the policies of the Politburo majority—led at this time by Zinoviev, Kamenev, and Stalin— with his two letters to the Central Committee in October 1923.

What had changed in the Soviet Union in October 1923 that led to the formation of the Left Opposition were the prospects for an immediate international solution to the crisis of state and party policy. Like the NEP two and a half years earlier, the formation of the Left Opposition was an effort to improve the Soviet state's chances of holding out until the next wave of proletarian revolution—this time apparently to be postponed for some time. The existence of an organized Opposition would resist the free expansion of the bureaucracy, subject it to criticism, and perhaps retard its development long enough to keep intact the roots of the proletarian dictatorship until conditions for its existence improved.

*   *   *

The Rise of a Privileged Bureaucracy

Alongside the debate over economic questions that occupied the attention of the party during this period, and with an increasing influence on that debate, an alarming change began to be observable in the character of the governing party: from an association of revolutionists it was turning into the instrument of a privileged bureaucracy with a conservative social program. What was occurring was a shift in the relative weights of the peasantry and the proletariat, the twin pillars of the Soviet system, to the detriment of the proletariat. This shift was reinforced by the defeat of the international revolution.

The dispersal and declassing of large sections of the proletariat during the civil war have been described above. At the heart of the industrialization controversy was the problem of reconstituting the proletariat as a viable class that could exercise power in its own name and provide political and economic direction to the peasantry. But the reassertion of the peasants and independent traders was accompanied by a corresponding waning of the political power and self-confidence of the proletariat. The NEP compounded the problem by producing an increased stratification in the countryside, where the strengthening of capitalist property relations and the operation of the free market led to the growth of exploiting layers: a class of rich peasants (kulaks), independent traders, and speculators (Nepmen).

The alliance between the workers and the peasants was an indispensable prerequisite for the survival of the Soviet state once the international revolution proved to be delayed. But the efficacy of the alliance between the two classes depended on the ability of the proletariat, through its state apparatus, to lead the peasantry toward socialism. But the proletariat was prostrate, apathetic, and exhausted.

The decline of the proletariat and the rise of the bureaucracy coincided with the consolidation and expansion of the Soviet state apparatus. In a country of profound cultural backwardness, including widespread illiteracy, the skills for administering state or industry were rare. When the Soviet government was first formed, it had to rely on great numbers of former officials of the tsarist state who could read and write and who knew the rudiments of administration. This need became all the greater in view of the widespread desertion of the Soviet Republic by the bulk of the intelligentsia and later by the other Soviet parties—the Left Mensheviks and the Left Social Revolutionaries. To convince the skilled administrators to stay, the Soviet government was forced to offer them material incentives, allowing them a standard of living considerably exceeding that of the masses of Soviet citizens. The privileged governmental bureaucracy, with its alien and hostile class outlook, was a source of infection; at the same time, it was an indispensable apparatus of organization. Furthermore, what was true of the Soviet state was equally true of the Red Army and of Soviet industry, where former tsarist army officers and factory managers had to be offered bonuses for their services.

Lenin had recognized the inherent danger of the Soviet bureaucracy practically from the outset. In 1921, at the Tenth Party Congress, he said, "We do have a bureaucratic ulcer; it has been diagnosed and has to be treated in earnest. . . . We need to understand that the struggle against the evils of bureaucracy is absolutely indispensable, and that it is just as intricate as the fight against the petty-bourgeois element. The bureaucratic practices of our state system have become such a serious malaise that they are dealt with in our Party Programme, because they are connected with this petty-bourgeois element, which is widely dispersed" (*CW,* Vol. 32, "Report on the Political Work of the Central Committee . . ." [March 8, 1921], pp. 190-91).

During the period of war communism, Lenin had sought to counteract the danger of bureaucratism by ensuring that the soviets remained solidly controlled by revolutionists, usually workers and poor peasants, who would check the influence of careerists in every level of administration. But with the NEP, the character of the soviets began to change: in the rural areas, on the local level, more and more soviets were being captured by kulaks and used by them as an avenue to political influence and as a facade of legality for the growing exploitation of poor peasants; in the cities, the administration of industry was passing back into the hands of former bourgeois managers and specialists, who were acquiring unprecedented authority and influence.

In his effort to protect the party from the effects of the growing bureaucratism, Lenin in 1919 urged the creation of the People's Commissariat of the Workers and Peasants Inspection (Rabkrin), headed by Stalin until 1922. Rabkrin had the authority to inspect other commissariats to evaluate their functioning and take measures to cut through bureaucracy and inefficiency.

Simultaneous with the growth of the state bureaucracy, however, and partly drawing strength from it, was an even more ominous development: the growth of a bureaucratic tendency within the Communist Party itself.

Until 1917 the Bolshevik Party (which changed its name to Communist Party in 1918) had been a small, illegal group, well trained in the conspiratorial methods necessary under tsarism. During the revolution and civil war the membership tripled and quadrupled; by 1919 a quarter of a million people had joined. These members, recruited during the most difficult years of the revolution, were generally the most dedicated and selfless revolutionists, motivated not by the pursuit of personal gain but by determination to participate in the conquest and consolidation of Soviet power. The party's membership tripled again between 1919 and 1922, rising to 700,000, but by this time the character of the recruitment was changing. Careerists and self-seekers, anxious to ally themselves with those in power in the hope of securing their future job prospects, heavily outnumbered the revolutionists.

In addition, under the peculiar circumstances of the one-party government, the Communist Party began to attract to its ranks many people whose motivation was honest enough but whose political views had little in common with Bolshevism. By inclination and outlook they would have been disposed to join the other, more conservative parties that had participated in the first period of the Soviet regime—the Left Mensheviks and the Left Social Revolutionaries. But these parties no longer existed.

The non-Communist parties in the soviets, expecting the collapse of the new regime, had gone over to the counterrevolution during the civil war. They had supported the anarchist uprising at the Kronstadt naval garrison in 1921. But despite this and numerous other acts of outright sedition, they were permitted to function legally into 1922. They were finally banned—not, as the Stalinists later claimed, out of any principle of one-party rule, but as an extraordinary measure arising from a civil war in which the needs of Soviet democracy were forced to bow before the exigencies of defense. This was considered a temporary ban, instituted to prevent the collapse of the whole Soviet order at a time when its continued existence was in question. The result, however, was that the normal variety of outlets for political energies and sympathies was eliminated, and social antagonisms—which under ordinary circumstances would have been reflected in a struggle among political parties with different programs—were forced to refract themselves through the only legal party, the Communist Party. But around the same time, the

Tenth Party Congress in March 1921 banned factions within the party.

This was the first such ban in the eighteen-year history of Bolshevism; up to this time, party factions had functioned freely, even through the most dangerous days of the civil war. Heated discussions had been the norm before and during congresses; disparate groupings would vie with each other for the majority support that would make their line the official party policy.

This exceptional measure was taken to marshal every possible ounce of strength to resist the attack on the Soviet regime by the sailors at Kronstadt, in the face of open support for the Kronstadt rebellion in some quarters in the party. But even this measure had little in common with the monolithic suppression of dissent that later became the norm under Stalin. While prohibiting the formation of tight factions within the party which would circulate platforms and meet separately, the "Resolution on Party Unity" drafted by Lenin for the Tenth Party Congress guaranteed critics of official party policy the right to have their criticism heard by the entire party through a special discussion bulletin and through the holding of special symposiums; it stipulated only that such criticism could not be submitted for preliminary discussion to groups formed on the basis of "platforms." Even after the Tenth Party Congress members continued to exercise their rights to band together on specific issues and level attacks on the party leadership. Lenin himself was planning to organize a grouping on several issues shortly before his death. What was not permitted was the disruption of the party's unity in action. The ban on factions and on opposition parties was intended to last only until an improvement in the military security of the Republic permitted it to be lifted.

The flow of nonproletarians into the Communist Party during the NEP included a significant proportion of kulaks, factory managers, specialists, and other petty-bourgeois elements whose existence had been tolerated as a necessary evil for the country's recovery but who had not previously received the political status and endorsement of party membership. A similar phenomenon occurred when party members, seeking to fill the gaps in the economy caused by desertion or sabotage by former factory managers or state officials, took industrial or governmental positions; they thus came under the pressure of an alien class milieu.

As the conditions of the NEP led increasing numbers of nonproletarians into the party, the problem of privilege also infected the party functionaries, creating a layer that depended on the central apparatus of the party for appointments to salaried positions and access to the material privileges that kept its living standard above that of most of the population.

Stalin rose to prominence in the bureaucratized apparatus because he best represented its outlook: a narrow nationalist disdain for revolutionists in other countries, whose activities could prove costly to the Soviet state treasury and attract the hostile attention of imperialist military establishments; an exaggerated respect for established authority in the form of bourgeois governments; a contempt mingled with fear of the workers and their wrangling assemblies and councils; a love of solid comfort and unchallenged authority; and a sentimental romanticization of peasant life. These were not personal characteristics so much as social ones, representative of the new layer of petty-bourgeois apparatchiks who sought to protect their economic security by agreements with capitalism abroad and suppression of the working class at home.

By late 1922 the incipient bureaucratic caste, with Stalin at its head, had raised itself above the rank and file of the party, not to speak of the masses of workers and poor peasants, and was already functioning independently of them. Reinforced in its position by the deepening isolation of the Soviet Republic, which weakened the immediate practical appeal of proletarian internationalism, and unopposed by the exhausted and apathetic working masses, it by now included in its ranks former enemies of the October Revolution as well as the politically passive elements who had become party members for reasons of self-interest rather than political conviction.

It was at this time that Lenin, newly returned to activity after his first stroke, was horrified at the burgeoning bureaucracy in the party and took steps to organize a bloc with Trotsky against it. In January 1923 he openly launched his attack on bureaucratism in two articles on the functioning of Rabkrin—and, by clear implication, its head, Stalin. The Politburo attempted to suppress the sharper of these two articles. In March Lenin suffered another stroke, which ended his political activity.

Between December 1922 and January 1923, as Lenin was withdrawing from his work for the final time, the triumvirate of Stalin, Kamenev, and Zinoviev, all Old Bolsheviks from the prerevolutionary period, organized a secret faction whose purpose was to prevent Trotsky from having a majority in the Politburo.

This faction, which Trotsky called the "secret Politburo," consisted of every member of the Politburo except Trotsky (Stalin, Zinoviev, Kamenev, Rykov, Bukharin, and Tomsky) plus Kuibyshev, who was the chairman of the Central Control Commission. It met secretly to confront him as a bloc and to organize the struggle against him. This marked a definite shift—from the situation that had existed while Lenin was alive and well, in which factional alignments were temporary blocs around concrete proposals and issues, to a permanent power caucus in the highest body of the party, whose purpose was to preserve control in its hands regardless of the issues at stake. As first constituted, the triumvirate did not base itself on a program of principled agreement but on a secret mutual-assistance pact. Using a system of patronage, appointment, and punitive transfers, the triumvirs gained control of the national party apparatus during the year 1923. They created an army of local, province-level, and city-level secretaries personally loyal to them and increasingly beyond the democratic control of their constituencies.

The secretarial apparatus that the triumvirate developed to consolidate its control of the party not only bungled revolutionary situations abroad; it also refused to take any measures to strengthen the proletarian base of the workers' state against the rise of nonproletarian forces and the increasing influence of antirevolutionary pressures. It was an empirical social layer that preferred to accommodate an increasingly rich and powerful peasantry rather than take steps to curb its influence. This was expressed above all in the refusal to institute an economic plan and increase the pace of heavy industry, while the capitalist market relations in the countryside were permitted unrestrained growth. The chief theoretician of this adaptation to the peasantry was Bukharin. Under his slogan "Peasants, enrich yourselves" and Zinoviev's slogan "Face to the countryside" the government from 1924 on contributed to the growth of the kulaks and Nepmen through various concessions expanding the scope of the market economy (legalizing the leasing of land and the hiring of labor, tax reductions for prosperous peasants, etc.).

Trotsky's critique of Stalinism did not emerge all at once but developed over time as the nature of the Stalinist faction continued to define itself. The Left Opposition developed in response to the course of the ruling faction. Its demands in the early stages of the struggle were essentially for more freedom of discussion; for reversal of the trend toward universal appointment from the center; for strengthening industry, so the workers could become a weightier social force; for more workers in the party. Who formed the 1923 Opposition? The forty-six party members who addressed themselves to the Central Committee in October 1923 were almost all leading figures of the revolution and civil war and occupied important posts in the government or party. In addition to Pyatakov, the vice-chairman of the Council of the National Economy, and Preobrazhensky, one of the most talented economists of the period, they included Radek, an astute politician; Antonov-Ovseenko, a chief political commissar of the Red Army; Muralov, a leading military man; the gifted journalist Sosnovsky; Rakovsky, who had been head of the Bolshevik government in the Ukraine and a leading Soviet diplomat; and others who agreed on the necessity of economic reorganization and political democracy. But the group was not homogeneous; it included individuals who had little interest in the economic questions but valued inner-party democracy for its own sake. The forty-six were united at this stage by their dissatisfaction with the party regime and their conviction that a return to the norms of proletarian democracy would contribute to the solution of a great many of the party's ills.

The Sequence of Events

Trotsky opened his assault on the Central Committee's policies in his letter of October 8, 1923, which was quickly followed by the Platform of the Forty-six (see p. 397), which raised many of the same issues. The initial response of the bureaucratic faction was to threaten the dissenters with disciplinary reprisals and refuse to publish their statement. News of the Opposition spread, however, stimulating interest in the ideas of the dissidents, and on November 7 *Pravda* opened its columns to a discussion, inviting party members to contribute articles on the issues.

The response was overwhelming. *Pravda*'s circulation doubled. Cell after cell in the factories, army, and universities declared for the Opposition. In an attempt to coopt and contain the Opposition sentiment, the triumvirs resorted simultaneously to repression and concessions. Their critics were demoted and transferred. In violation of party statutes, the Central Committee of the Communist Youth, which overwhelmingly supported the Opposition, was dissolved by the General Secretariat of the party and replaced with a more obedient group. At the same time, the triumvirs prepared a special resolution whose exclusive purpose was to allow them to identify themselves with the sentiment for inner-party democracy and allay the suspicions aroused by the controversy among the membership. To be effective, they reasoned, this resolution had to be signed by Trotsky. Thus, on December 5, the New Course resolution, bearing Trotsky's amendments, was unanimously adopted by the Politburo (see p. 404).

Although he put his name to the Politburo's resolution, Trotsky feared that it was a paper concession the majority was trying to use to escape censure, like the concessions made in the resolutions at the Twelfth Party Congress. In a series of articles written for *Pravda* in December 1923, he elaborated on the themes of bureaucratic abuse and routinism, and the lack of rank-and-file initiative and independence. On December 8 he addressed an open letter to the party ranks urging them to guard the democracy of the party and charging the Old Guard (those who had been members before 1917 and now occupied the highest positions) with bureaucratic degeneration.

Trotsky's letter was greeted warmly in the party branches, but to no avail. In the course of the year 1923 Stalin and Zinoviev had already overhauled the party apparatus, replacing the elected secretaries of cells and districts with appointees loyal to the triumvirate. On December 15 an article by Stalin appeared in *Pravda* opening a campaign against the Opposition, attacking the forty-six, and trying to discredit Trotsky by referring to his pre-1917 disagreements with Lenin. Trotsky refused to conduct the discussion on the level of slander and character assassination, and his only reply was one sentence, published in *Pravda* on December 17: "I make no response to certain specific articles which have recently appeared in *Pravda*, since I think this better answers the interests of the party, and in particular the discussion now in progress about the New Course."

Stalin's article opened the floodgates for the anti-Trotskyist campaign. Its purpose was to divert the party's attention from the New Course discussion. The editors of *Pravda* published scores of articles attacking the Opposition but only occasional articles speaking for it, and then only after long delays. They also permitted the party press to be used to spread crude falsifications without allowing the Oppositionists to defend themselves. This of course became standard procedure after 1924; but in December 1923 it was a fresh abuse of power by the triumvirate and one the Opposition sharply called the Politburo to task for.*

---

*The following excerpts from a protest note of late December 1923, from

Stalin's control of the secretarial apparatus was sufficient to enable him to rig the elections to the Thirteenth Party Conference in January 1924, which was supposed to conclude the debate in the party. The Opposition's grass-roots popularity did not prevent its representation from being reduced at each successive level of voting. In Moscow province, although the apparatus never announced the vote totals in the party cells, the Opposition had 36 percent of the vote at the district level; this was reduced by half, to 18 percent, at the province level conference which elected delegates to the Thirteenth Conference. Ultimately the Opposition received only three delegates to the Thirteenth Party Conference, where no effort was made to answer its arguments except by insults and invective. Stalin's report to the conference was a concentrated attack on Trotsky, in which he threatened to suppress the Opposition through the provisions of the Tenth Congress resolution banning factions.

During the Thirteenth Conference, as during the open discussion the preceding November, Trotsky was ill and unable to take part. On his way to Sukhum, where he went to convalesce, he received the news of Lenin's death.

The triumvirs made use of Lenin's death to proclaim the so-called Lenin levy—they threw open the gates of the party to new members without the usual selection process, and between February and May 240,000 people joined, not only workers but also clerks, petty officials, careerists, and self-seekers of all varieties.

Trotsky, Radek, and Pyatakov to the Politburo, were published only in **Sotsialistichesky Vestnik,** a Menshevik emigre paper in Berlin, May 28, 1924:

"It is all too obvious that if the regime of fabrications prevailing in the party section of **Pravda** is not immediately discontinued, it cannot help but deal grave blows to the party, as a result of the disgusting activities that are being conducted against the party, although in the party's name. There is no point in talking about party democracy if falsifications can be substituted for party information with impunity. We demand:

"(1) the appointment of a commission to be given no more than twenty-four hours to investigate the allegations we have cited;

"(2) the immediate suspension of Comrades Nazaretyan and Sapronov from their **Pravda** posts;

"(3) the categorical statement that none of the comrades who give the commission the necessary information will be victimized by the party or meet any other kind of repression."

The commission was appointed, only to whitewash the entire affair. It was not long before **Pravda** ceased making even a pretense of acting as a forum for party discussions.

The ostensible purpose of the Lenin levy was to strengthen the proletarian composition of the party, as the Opposition had demanded; but the indiscriminate way it was done had the effect of dissolving the revolutionary core of the party in a mass of unassimilated human material, without experience or training but with the old habit of obeying orders. This gave Stalin's machine complete independence from the party. The Lenin levy was followed by another reshuffling of party functionaries, with most of the remaining revolutionists replaced by appointees who were creatures of the apparatus.

Trotsky returned to Moscow in May 1924 for the Thirteenth Congress, where he once again withstood a torrent of attacks and threats to make,a speech defending his actions over the past year and rejecting Zinoviev's demand that he "recant" his errors. (This was the first time that dissidents in the party were asked to disavow their ideas in order to escape censure; the demand for recantation would later be made of Zinoviev, as well as of virtually all those who joined in the clamor for Trotsky's recantation in 1924). The congress declared an end to the controversy that had begun with the publication of the New Course resolution. But it did not even begin to discuss or evaluate the recent momentous defeat in Germany.

*   *   *

Because of the intimate relationship between the Russian party and the Comintern, it was inevitable that the changing temper in the former should find its reflection in the latter. Stalin could not tolerate opposition in the International any more than he could at home. Between 1923 and 1924, aided by Zinoviev, the Comintern's president, he set out to remake the Comintern in the pattern of the Russian party. Using the authority and prestige that the Russians had earned in the eyes of foreign communists as pioneers of the socialist revolution, he was successful in dislodging the leaderships of national sections that were sympathetic to the Russian Opposition and replacing them with handpicked representatives who could be relied upon to support the Russian majority. By the time of the Thirteenth Party Congress in May 1924, this process was well under way. At the congress the leaders of all the European parties present except the French rose to add their voices to the shower of abuse rained upon Trotsky. A month later the Fifth World Congress of the Comintern opened in Moscow. Called the "Bolshevization" congress, its purpose was to consolidate the victory the triumvirate had won in the Russian party by extending it to the International. This victory was sealed by a policy of artificial splits in the Communist parties all over the world and expulsions of all Oppositionists and their sympathizers.

*   *   *

Under threat of disciplinary action, Trotsky was blocked from defending himself against the allegations being spread against him everywhere. But the bureaucracy was not yet strong enough to silence him entirely. In the autumn of 1924 a collection of his speeches and writings during the revolution was published as a volume of his *Collected Works*. The publication of the book, entitled *1917*, was particularly timely in that it exposed, for the benefit of the generation that had not yet reached political awareness in 1917, the lies that the triumvirs had been spreading about him and his activities before and during the revolution: that he had been a "semi-Menshevik," opposed to Lenin, etc.

But in addition Trotsky wrote a long preface for the volume, entitled "Lessons of October." The essay revealed the role of the present-day triumvirs during the two crucial turning points of the revolution (in April and October 1917). He went on to demonstrate that the same policies the triumvirs had followed in 1917 (when they, and not he, had opposed Lenin) had recently led to the disaster in Germany; and he argued that in order to avoid similar mistakes in the future, the real history of the Bolshevik Party and the Russian revolution had to be studied in detail and assimilated by the Russian party and by the Comintern. Finally, implicit in his argument is the point that the triumvirs, because of their actions in 1917, ought not to be entrusted with the leadership of the party, and certainly were not qualified to utter definitive pronouncements on Lenin and Leninism.

A few years later nobody in the Soviet Union could have had such a work as "Lessons of October" published legally and openly. But in 1924 the real Leninist tradition of free discussion was still strong and the bureaucracy had not yet learned how to subvert it fully.

The publication of "Lessons of October" triggered the second major anti-Trotskyist campaign, which exceeded the first in its ferocity and initiated the unrestrained falsification of history that later became so characteristic of Stalinist slander campaigns.

Two years later, when the triumvirate had splintered, Zinoviev and Kamenev revealed that they had invented "Trotskyism" to assist their struggle against Trotsky. Zinoviev even described their method: to relate Trotsky's pre-1917 differences with Lenin to new issues. And that was what they did. By clipping quotations out of context from Lenin's writings from 1904 on, they made it appear that Lenin's view of Trotsky was unambiguously negative. Conversely, they said that Trotsky had "overemphasized" the failure of the Old Guard to come along with Lenin in 1917 in order to discredit not the opponents of Lenin but the entire Leninist tradition. Everything possible was done and said to make it appear that a trend called "Trotskyism," the opposite of Leninism, really did exist, and that Trotsky had always been hostile to Bolshevism.

Assisting this campaign was the simultaneous process of deifying Lenin, begun with the embalming and public display of his corpse and rapidly moving on to a suprahistorical approach to his writings. The result was that "Leninism" in the hands of the triumvirs became a weapon of struggle against Lenin's policies.

The campaign in the press, directed by the triumvirate, ran all autumn and winter, and was accompanied by a mobilization of the party cells to pass resolutions denouncing Trotsky's actions, writings, and other heresies, and by a similar mobilization of the non-Russian sections of the Comintern.

Unlike the public controversy following the publication of the New Course resolution, the press was rigidly held in control by the triumvirate; nothing was published on the subject of "Trotskyism" but attacks on Trotsky.

*   *   *

By 1924 Soviet Russia had returned to normal diplomatic relations with most of its neighbors and had been recognized by most of the major European powers (the United States would not recognize the USSR until 1933). For the moment, the direct imperialist threat to the Soviet Republic's existence appeared to have abated, and an era of stability in the capitalist world had set in.

Between the formation of the triumvirate in late 1922 and the deliberate strangulation of the Spanish revolution in 1936, the Stalinist bureaucracy went through a process of consolidation and change. In its early stages, it appeared to be a tendency within the revolutionary movement with different ideas about how to build socialism in the Soviet Union and extend the revolution abroad. As it developed, however, it became identifiable as a distinct social group that defended interests separate from those of the working class, seeking above all to maintain and increase its privileges.

The bureaucratic degeneration of the Soviet leadership had a profound impact on the world revolution. By the thirties the Comintern had become an instrument of counterrevolution for the benefit of the Soviet government's diplomatic ties with the capitalist nations abroad. (Even at that late date, however, Stalin had to physically wipe out thousands of Old Bolsheviks and behead the Red Army to carry out his counterrevolutionary plans.) But in the twenties this policy had not yet jelled. The bureaucracy was still in the process of defining itself.

In the broad sense, the Stalinists began to reflect unconsciously the outlook of the nonproletarian elements that had permeated the party, and began to look for rationalizations of their new outlook in theoretical terms. Stalin's theory of socialism in one country, which was first promulgated in December 1924, was an attempt to free Soviet foreign policy from the program of international proletarian revolution. It asserted that the alliance of workers and peasants was, in and of itself, a sufficient guarantee against the dangers of capitalist restoration within the borders of the USSR. This was an instinctive turning away from foreign revolutionary entanglements, which had proved disappointing. It enabled the Stalin faction to justify its course toward the peasantry and to attack the Marxist evaluation of the peasantry as "Trotskyism"; it was also a theoretical consolation for the failure of the international revolution and a means of attacking the orientation toward it.

It was only after Lenin's death that any open challenge to internationalism could be made. Stalin launched it in 1924, under the guise of an attack on Trotsky's theory of permanent revolution. The two basic tenets of Trotsky's theory, elaborated in 1905, stipulated, first, that in tsarist Russia the proletariat could accomplish such bourgeois-democratic tasks as land reform by taking power and establishing a workers' and peasants' government—which would also begin to carry out socialist tasks; and second, that the Russian revolution would open the era of the world socialist revolution.

Prior to April 1917, Lenin had used a different formulation to summarize the expected development of the revolution. He agreed with Trotsky that the principal tasks of the revolution would be bourgeois-democratic. He agreed that the bourgeoisie was too reactionary and too subservient to tsarism to be entrusted with the leadership. He agreed also that the revolution would be likely to proceed to socialist tasks in the process of solving bourgeois-democratic ones. But he did not grant that this last was a necessary line of development. His slogan of a "democratic dictatorship of the workers and peasants" envisioned a nonbourgeois revolutionary coalition government composed of both workers' and peasants' parties. Since he thought the peasants could very well have a majority in such a government, he predicted that it might restrict its economic program to modernization of the capitalist economy for a considerable period after the seizure of power.

In April 1917 Lenin concluded that the only peasant party on the scene, the Social Revolutionary Party, was so hopelessly mired in the politics of bourgeois liberalism that the revolution could proceed only along the path outlined by Trotsky; that is, by combining bourgeois-democratic and socialist tasks under the leadership of the Bolshevik Party.

In this crucial turn in Lenin's thinking, he was opposed by virtually the entire Bolshevik leadership, which had been following the policy of critically supporting the bourgeois Provisional Government and its conduct of the war. In April 1917, Lenin had to overcome the resistance of the party's leadership before he could persuade the party to set its course for socialist revolution; and in October he had to lead the party against those who balked at the prospect of insurrection. Foremost among this section of the party leadership were Zinoviev and Kamenev. (Stalin opposed Lenin in April but followed him in October.) In 1924 these men revived, in the name of Leninism, a caricature of the "democratic dictatorship of the proletariat and peasantry" for use in the Comintern. It was a caricature because they included in their formula a force Lenin had never looked to as a progressive force—the liberal bourgeoisie. On the pretext of strengthening an international alliance of workers and peasants, Stalin, with Bukharin as his theoretician, left open the door to alliances with bourgeois parties with the aim of installing liberal bourgeois governments in power. This fundamental revision of Leninism would later bear bitter fruit in the defeats of the Chinese revolution of 1925-27 and the British general strike of 1926.

In its anticipation of the actual development of the Russian revolution, Trotsky's theory of permanent revolution had been remarkably accurate. By 1924 his essays on the subject had been reprinted and translated many times and were unchallenged as a statement of Bolshevik thinking. However, Trotsky had viewed it as a theory of the *Russian* revolution, and it was not until late 1927, under the influence of the events in China, that he became fully convinced that the theory was applicable to colonial and semicolonial countries in general. So when Stalin opened an attack on the theory of permanent revolution in December 1924, it was not part of a dispute over the theory's application to a current problem but rather an attempt to discredit Trotsky by raking up Lenin's prerevolutionary attacks on the theory of permanent revolution—attacks that had become obsolete in 1917.* Furthermore, in the popular mind "permanent revolution" suggested an indeterminate and chaotic period of upheavals and dislocations; and the triumvirs appealed to the popular exhaustion and longing for peace and quiet in their deliberate misrepresentation of the theory. They also accused Trotsky of pessimism and of readiness to write off the Soviet state's chances of survival.

Trotsky replied to the attacks on permanent revolution and clarified the historical terms of the controversy in his hitherto unpublished answer to the critics of "Lessons of October" entitled "Our Differences." But he considered these questions to be diversionary tactics at this time. He would not respond to Stalin's "theory" of socialism in one country until 1926. This serves to underline the point that the terms of the struggle in the Russian Communist Party changed as the struggle developed. Neither the scope of the differences, nor their implications, nor the nature of the Stalinist bureaucracy was completely clear in the early stages.

Once the triumvirs had secured control of the apparatus, they did not hesitate to extend the factional struggle to the party cells in the army. They submitted resolutions against Trotsky to the military cells, to a national conference of political commissars, and finally to the party fraction in the Revolutionary Military Committee over which Trotsky had presided since its formation. A plenum of the Central Committee was called for January 18, 1925, to discuss the "Trotsky question." Feeling that his position as Commissar of War had become untenable, Trotsky addressed a

---

*There is no evidence that Lenin actually read Trotsky's book on permanent revolution prior to the October Revolution. The only recorded criticisms of it in his writings refer to it only through the writings of Martov and Parvus and misrepresent Trotsky's actual position, which he had evidently not heard first-hand at that time.

letter to the plenum saying that "the interests of our cause demand my speedy release from the duties of chairman of the Revolutionary Military Committee." He explained why he had refrained from publishing his refutation of the slanders against him (it would only "intensify the controversy . . . and give it a more acute character") but why he could no longer remain silent. He offered, upon being relieved of the Commissariat of War, to take any assignment the Central Committee saw fit to give him.

Trotsky did not attend the plenum of the Central Committee which unanimously approved his ouster from the Revolutionary Military Committee while rejecting motions inspired by Zinoviev and Kamenev to expel him from the Politburo and the party. The Central Committee issued a lengthy resolution reiterating all the major charges against Trotsky and ending with six points: (1) threatening to expel him from the party unless he demonstrated "submission to party discipline, not only in words but also in deeds, and complete unconditional renunciation of every stand against Leninism"; (2) removing him from the Revolutionary Military Committee; (3) postponing a decision on his assignment and threatening to remove him from the Politburo and Central Committee if he made "new attempts to violate, or failed to carry out, the decisions of the party"; (4) ending the discussion; but (5) continuing the work of "enlightening" the party as to the anti-Bolshevik character of Trotskyism from 1903 to "Lessons of October"; and (6) extending the campaign against Trotskyism beyond the party and the party youth to the broad masses of workers and peasants.

Throughout the year 1925, the campaign to "enlighten" the party and the population as a whole continued unabated, although Trotsky was not permitted to defend himself or to participate in any way. The Opposition had ceased to function, under threat of expulsion. Its proponents, fearful of precipitating a showdown, avoided controversy; and Trotsky himself made no move that might provoke retaliations by the triumvirate. He still considered the Communist Party to be the revolutionary party, and thought that his place was inside it, trying to influence it in the direction he knew to be correct, whatever the obstacles. Only great historic events could prove it bankrupt and justify the construction of a new party. Furthermore, it would be much more difficult to influence the ranks of the party from the outside. For these reasons, the Opposition bided its time, waiting for more favorable circumstances to act.

In May 1925, after four months without an assignment,

Trotsky was appointed to serve on the Supreme Council of the National Economy under Dzerzhinsky. This was an attempt to distract him from political questions in favor of the technicalities of economic administration. He took the assignment seriously and threw himself into his work. Before long he was making studies of the comparative levels of Russian and European industry, using the figures he produced to substantiate his argument that only a unified plan would enable Soviet Russia to catch up with and surpass the capitalist West.

Up to this point he had been writing and speaking extensively about cultural problems of Soviet society—family relations, education, religion, art, alcoholism, youth, the press (see *Problems of Everyday Life, Women and the Family,* and *Leon Trotsky on Literature and Art*). In these popular articles and speeches he did not allude to the internal disputes in the party, which made it difficult for the bureaucracy to ban them; but their pronounced antibureaucratic emphasis made it possible for him to get a public hearing for at least part of the Opposition's views. Now he also began to write and speak frequently on the technical and scientific problems of socialist construction. It was in his capacity as an economist and as a partisan of planning that Trotsky wrote "Toward Capitalism or Socialism?" in August 1925, lauding the first appearance of control figures for the national economy issued by Gosplan for 1925-26. Trotsky considered the control figures an important step toward laying the groundwork for an economic plan. But even as he wrote "Toward Capitalism or Socialism?" the Council of Labor and Defense, under Kamenev's direction, was shelving the discussion.

The silencing of the Opposition did not prevent the contradictions between town and countryside from becoming ever more acute during the course of 1925. Differentiation in the countryside was becoming more pronounced. The conditions of the agricultural laborers and poor peasants worsened as the kulaks gathered increasing wealth and power into their hands. In 1925 fewer than 10 percent of the peasants produced more than half the marketable grain surpluses; by withholding them from the market they were creating food shortages in the towns; and by refusing to buy the overpriced industrial goods, they were creating new crises in industry and new disruptions in the lives of the industrial workers. The workers, again becoming restive and dissatisfied, took refuge in drunkenness and absenteeism. In the major industrial cities the dislocations were particularly acute.

In response to this crisis a new alignment began to develop in the Politburo. Zinoviev, head of the Leningrad party organization, and Kamenev, head of the Moscow organization, made themselves the spokesmen of the mood of industrial unrest, which was strongest in the major urban centers. They also drew back from Stalin's theory of socialism in one country, refusing, as early as April 1925, to allow it to be made official party doctrine. In public, however, they limited themselves to an attack on Bukharin, who since 1924 had become the major defender of the wealthy peasant and of basing Russia's industrial development on the growth of the peasant market. As a result, Stalin relied on an alliance in the Politburo with Bukharin and his supporters, Rykov and Tomsky, on the issue of socialism in one country, and to secure their loyalty he backed them cautiously on their policy toward the peasants; Zinoviev and Kamenev opposed the new ruling faction on both counts.

During the summer of 1925 Stalin worked to remove party functionaries loyal to Zinoviev and Kamenev and to replace them with his own followers. He succeeded in Moscow, but not in Leningrad.

The shake-up in the Politburo reached its climax at the Fourteenth Party Congress in December 1925, the first congress not preceded by a full and open discussion. An indication of the way the outcome of party elections was determined entirely by control of the secretarial apparatus is the fact that all the delegates from Leningrad supported the Leningrad Opposition while all those from Moscow supported the new majority.

At the congress, the fundamental issues at stake—socialism in one country, the course toward the peasantry, industrialization policy, planning—were heatedly debated. Zinoviev and Kamenev disclosed the unscrupulous and unprincipled measures which they and Stalin had used to crush the 1923 Opposition. Trotsky remained silent, taken by surprise at the rift in the triumvirate; but he began, with three articles written before and during the Fourteenth Congress (published in this volume for the first time), to consider the possibility of a bloc with Zinoviev and Kamenev and a renewal of open struggle in the party.

*   *   *

The subsequent volumes of this series will follow the struggle of the Trotskyist Opposition through its merger with the Leningrad Opposition of Zinoviev and Kamenev to form the United Opposition (1926-27); the defeat of the Chinese revolution and the British general strike; the publication of "The Platform of the Opposition," co-authored by Trotsky and Zinoviev; the Opposition's expulsion from the party in 1927 and the capitulation of the Zinovievists; the exile of the Oppositionists to Siberia in 1928; and Stalin's "left turn." For the purposes of this introduction, all that remains is to describe what became of the Russian Left Opposition.

In 1929, Stalin still did not feel strong enough to physically liquidate the Opposition. Instead, he forcibly exiled Trotsky to Turkey in order to decapitate the Opposition, and stepped up the persecution of Oppositionists. In the Soviet Union this meant prison and Siberian exile; abroad it meant further expulsions, ostracism, and, where the Stalinists were strong enough, beatings or even murders. But sending Trotsky out of the Soviet Union not only failed to close the chapter of opposition within the USSR; it opened a new chapter of opposition internationally. In virtually every country with a communist movement, expelled Oppositionists had formed organizations. Trotsky lost no time in establishing connections with these groups and constituting the International Left Opposition.

Until 1933 the International Left Opposition considered itself (and functioned as) a faction of the Comintern, determined to win the Comintern back to a revolutionary path. But when the German Communist Party allowed Hitler to come to power without a fight, and not one voice in the Comintern was raised to demand an evaluation of the sectarian policy that had permitted such a momentous defeat, Trotsky and his cothinkers concluded that the Comintern was dead as a revolutionary organization, and that it would be necessary to build a new, revolutionary, International.

The Fourth International was not actually founded until 1938. In the meantime, the victimization of Oppositionists in the Soviet Union and abroad became harsher. In his effort to wipe out every vestige of dissent and prepare the once-revolutionary party to turn its hands to the work of counterrevolution, Stalin staged three big Moscow frame-up trials, accusing the entire generation of Old Bolsheviks who had collaborated with Lenin of espionage, sabotage, and a conspiracy to restore capitalism. The chief defendants in all of these trials, in absentia, were Trotsky and his son Leon Sedov. In the course of these trials Stalin wiped out tens of thousands of Old Bolsheviks, both Right and Left Oppositionists, as well as independent-minded party members who had nothing to do with the Opposition, and workers who had run afoul of the apparatus in one way or another. In 1940 Trotsky fell victim to a Stalinist assassin in Mexico.

Born in a period of revolutionary defeats and reaction, the Fourth International survived persecutions such as few organizations have faced. Its ideas and its vitality were preserved by a small number of dedicated revolutionists during World War II and the years of Cold War reaction. In the renewed crises of capitalism since the mid-1960s the forces of the Fourth International have recorded an impressive growth, while world Stalinism has shattered along nationalist lines into a melange of warring factions. Trotskyism, which the Kremlin thought it had interred along with its founder, stands today as the continuation of revolutionary Marxism—in practice as well as theory—in the unfolding struggles that mark the decline of world capitalism.

Naomi Allen
December 1974

FIRST LETTER
TO THE CENTRAL COMMITTEE

October 8, 1923

NOTE: In the autumn of 1923 the economic crisis reached a peak, with the "scissors"—the disparity between high industrial prices and low agricultural prices—opening to their widest point in early October. Seeking to force industry to lower prices, the government withheld credit from the nationalized enterprises. The immediate result was widespread unemployment and desperation in the cities and, in August and September, a massive strike wave, with the participation of members of two ultraleftist groups of party members, the Workers' Group and the Workers' Truth. In September, the Central Committee of the Communist Party met to discuss the problems facing the country, and instituted a series of measures designed to come to the aid of the peasant, with a further curtailment of credit to industry and repressive measures against party members involved in the strikes. Felix Dzerzhinsky, who had headed a subcommittee on the political situation, reported on the strike wave and the participation in it of groupings of party members. There was special significance in this— Dzerzhinsky was also the head of the GPU, the political police, which had been used in the past to defend Soviet power against its enemies. Dzerzhinsky had recently reorganized the GPU; at issue was whether it would be granted the authority to intervene in the party itself against party members who opposed the line of the leadership.

Dzerzhinsky's report set the stage for Trotsky's letter to the Central Committee of October 8. In it Trotsky outlined the fundamental causes of the economic crisis and the measures that should be taken to alleviate it, alluding to Lenin's letter "Granting Legislative Functions to the State Planning Commission," which the Politburo had refused to publish. He opposed the actions taken by the Central Committee, which amounted to organizational measures designed to intimidate the voices of discontent in the party ranks while refusing to take any steps to eliminate the cause of their discontent. Trotsky further called for a return to party democracy to enable the party to perform the tasks before it. This was Trotsky's first move to take the discussion outside the Central Committee. Until this time he had restricted his efforts to ad hoc campaigns on individual issues. Now he declared his intention to exercise his right to bring his disagreements to the party rank and file.

Never published in the Soviet press, Trotsky's October 8 letter was partly quoted, partly paraphrased, and partly summarized in the Menshevik emigre paper Sotsialistichesky Vestnik *(Socialist Messenger), May 28, 1924. The translation for this volume by Marilyn Vogt follows the* Vestnik's *text exactly, although in certain cases it appears likely that emphasis was introduced by the* Vestnik *and not by Trotsky.—Ed.*

To the Central Committee and the Central Control Commission
  1. "One of the proposals of Comrade Dzerzhinsky's commission (on strikes and other matters) states that we must make it obligatory for party members who know about groupings in the party to inform the GPU, the Central Committee, and the Central Control Commission. It would seem that informing the party organizations of the fact that hostile elements are working within it is such an elementary duty for every party member that it should not be necessary to introduce a special resolution to that effect six years after the October Revolution. The very fact that there arose a need for such a resolution is a highly alarming symptom, along with others no less clear."

  Thus Trotsky begins his letter that initiated the recent discussion, and he continues: "The need for such a resolution means that: (a) illegal oppositional groupings have been formed in the party that may become dangerous to the revolution; (b) there exist such moods in the party as to permit comrades who know about such groupings to refrain from informing the party organizations about them.

  "Both these facts testify to an extraordinary deterioration of the situation within the party since the Twelfth Congress. . . . Many, many party members, by no means the worst, have felt the greatest alarm at the methods and procedures used in the preparations for the Twelfth Congress. . . ." However, six months of work by the new Central Committee has seen the intensified application of the techniques and methods used to organize the Twelfth Congress; and within the party this has resulted in the formation of openly hostile and embittered groupings as well as the presence of numerous elements who know about the danger these groups represent but do not report it. . . .

2. There are two reasons for the marked deterioration of the situation inside the party: (a) the fundamentally improper and *unhealthy regime within the party;* and (b) *the dissatisfaction* of the workers and peasants with the grave economic situation that has come about not only as a result of objective difficulties but also because of obvious radical mistakes in economic policy.

3. "The Twelfth Congress was assembled under the slogan of *smychka* [link, or bond, between workers and peasants, industry and agriculture]. As the author of the theses on industry, I pointed out to the Central Committee before the congress took place how very dangerous it would be if our economic task were presented to the Twelfth Congress in an abstract and agitational manner when the task was to call for 'a turn in the party's attention and resolve' toward concrete vital undertakings designed to lower the prime cost of state-produced goods."

4. The resolution on industry calls for a consolidation and strengthening of the State Planning Commission (Gosplan) and for it to be established as the leading planning body. It is extremely significant that after the Twelfth Congress, the Central Committee came into possession of a memorandum Comrade Lenin had written back at the time of his illness, in which he expressed the idea that Gosplan must be given legislative (or more accurately, binding administrative) powers. In fact, since the Twelfth Congress Gosplan has been moved still further into the background. . . . "To a greater extent than before the congress the most important economic questions are being decided by the Politburo in a hasty manner with no preliminary preparation and with no reference to an overall plan. . . ."

Trotsky further points out that on September 19 [1923] Rykov and Pyatakov introduced a memorandum in which they said that "some of the Politburo's decisions compel us to draw attention to the fact that under the existing circumstances the management of the state industries entrusted to us has become extremely difficult." Trotsky concludes this point with the words: "There is no economic leadership. *The chaos comes from the top.*"

5. Under this point, Trotsky indicated that one of the reasons for the current commercial and industrial crises is the "autarchic character of our *fiscal policy,* i.e., it is not subordinated to the general economic plan." And further: "This is best exemplified by the fact that the disparity between industrial and agricultural prices, which has increased at an enormous rate, is tantamount to the liquidation of the New Economic Policy because for the peasants—*the basis of the NEP*—it makes no difference why they cannot buy anything, whether it is because private trade has been banned by decree or because two boxes of matches cost as much as a pood [36 pounds] of grain." Pointing out that the drive for consolidation of industry runs up against "political" considerations at every step, Trotsky felt it was necessary to focus attention on one small part of the problem which, in his opinion, clearly illuminates the problem as a whole by showing what the party's economic leadership degenerates into "in the absence of a plan, a system, or a correct line of party policy."

"At the Twelfth Congress," Trotsky writes, "shocking abuses on the part of some party organizations were revealed in connection with commercial and industrial advertising. What did these abuses consist of? Essentially, that the party organizations, which are supposed to guide the economic agencies by instilling in them a higher degree of conscientiousness, precision, economy, and sense of responsibility, were in fact disorienting them by resorting to a most crude and profligate method of cheating the country. Instead of simply levying an industrial tax on an enterprise for the benefit of the party organizations, which would have been illegal but at least would have made real sense, they resort to *soliciting obligatory but senseless advertisements,* on which paper and typographical labor are subsequently wasted, etc. What is most scandalous is that the managers did not decide to resist this rapaciousness and depravity; but on the contrary, they pay for the half-page or page in some such publication as *Sputnik Komunista* [The Communist's Companion] in strict compliance with the order of the secretary of the province committee. If any manager dared oppose this procedure, i.e., showed a real understanding of party duty, he would forthwith be put on the list of those who do not recognize the 'party leadership' and would suffer all the ensuing consequences. . . . Only someone who totally failed to understand the meaning of correct economic management and a feeling of responsibility would look the other way when faced with this kind of 'economic leadership'. . . ."

7. The last plenum of the Central Committee set up a party

commission on curtailing overhead expenses and lowering prices. "But it is absolutely obvious that for the state agencies to *mechanically lower prices* in response to political pressures in most cases only enriches the middleman and has hardly any effect on the peasant market. . . . The very creation of a commission for lowering prices is eloquent and devastating proof of how a policy that ignores the importance of planned and manipulative adjustment is driven by the force of its own inevitable consequences *into attempts to command price in the style of war communism.* The one leads to the other, undermining the economy and not normalizing it.

8. "The appalling price disparity—with the added burden of a single tax, burdensome mainly because it doesn't conform to the existing economic relations—has again provoked *profound discontent among the peasantry.* This policy has affected the attitudes of the workers, both directly and indirectly. Finally, the changed moods among the workers have made inroads into the party. Opposition groupings have revived and grown. Their dissatisfaction has increased. Thus, for us, the *smychka* is working in reverse: from the peasantry—through the working class—to the party. Those who had not foreseen this earlier or who until recently closed their eyes to it, have received an adequate object lesson. . . ." The heart of the sharp conflict, both within the Politburo and on the eve of the congress, Trotsky states, is to be found in the attitudes toward the central problem: the rationalization of state industry and the closing of the scissors.

9. The Twelfth Congress indicated that one of the most important tasks of the new Central Committee was the careful individual selection of managers at all levels. The attention of the Orgburo [Organization Bureau] in selecting personnel, however, has been directed down an altogether different path. When decisions on appointments, dismissals, and transfers are made, members of the party are evaluated, above all, from the point of view of how much they may support or hinder the maintenance of the regime within the party, which, secretly and unofficially but all the more effectively, is being realized through the Orgburo and the Secretariat of the Central Committee. At the Twelfth Congress it was stated that the people on the Central Committee must be "independent." Today this word no longer needs any commentary.[1]* Since the congress, the General Secretariat has

---

*Notes begin on p. 414.

applied the criterion of "independence" in appointing province committee secretaries; and, continuing from the top down, in appointments all the way to the lowest party cell. This work of selecting the party hierarchy from among comrades whom the Secretariat considers independent in the sense of the word indicated above has developed with unprecedented intensity.

10. "Even during the harshest days of war communism, the *system of appointment within the party* was not practiced on one-tenth the scale it is now. The practice of appointing secretaries of province committees is now the rule. This creates for the secretaries a position that is essentially independent of the local organizations. In the event that opposition, criticism, or protests occur, the secretary, with the help of the center, can simply have the opponent *transferred.* At one of the meetings of the Politburo the announcement was made, with obvious satisfaction, that in cases where provinces are merged, the only question that interests the organizations involved is who will be the secretary of the unified province committee. The secretary, appointed by the center and thereby virtually independent of the local organizations, is in turn a source of subsequent appointments and dismissals within the province itself. Organized from the top down, the secretarial apparatus has, in an increasingly autonomous fashion, been gathering 'all the strings into its own hands.' The participation of the party ranks in the actual shaping of the party organization is becoming more and more illusory. Over the past year or year and a half a special *party secretary psychology* has been created, the main feature of which is the conviction that the secretary is capable of deciding any and all questions without being familiar with the substance of the matters involved. Quite often we observe cases in which comrades who have not shown any organizational, administrative, or other ability while in charge of Soviet institutions nevertheless begin to make economic and other decisions in a high-handed manner as soon as they set foot in the post of secretary. This practice is all the more harmful because it dissipates and kills any feeling of responsibility.

11. "The Twelfth Congress of the party took place under the aegis of democracy. Many of the speeches of that time made in defense of *workers' democracy* seemed to me exaggerated, and to a considerable extent demagogic, in view of the *incompatibility of* a fully developed *workers' democracy with the regime of a dictatorship.* But it was absolutely clear that the tight hold that characterized the period of war communism should yield to a livelier and broader party responsibility. However, the regime

which had essentially taken shape even before the Twelfth Congress and which, after it, was fully consolidated and given finished form, is much farther removed from workers' democracy than was the regime during the fiercest periods of war communism. The *bureaucratization of the party apparatus* has reached unheard-of proportions through the application of the methods of secretarial selection. Even in the cruelest hours of the civil war we argued in the party organizations, and in the press as well, over such issues as the recruitment of specialists, partisan forces versus a regular army, discipline, etc.; while now there is not a trace of such an open exchange of opinions on questions that are really troubling the party. There has been created a very broad layer of party workers, belonging to the apparatus of the state or the party, who have totally renounced the idea of holding their own political opinions or at least of openly expressing such opinions, as if they believe that the secretarial hierarchy is the proper apparatus for forming party opinions and making party decisions. Beneath this layer that refrains from having its own opinions lies the broad layer of party masses before whom every decision stands in the form of a summons or command. *Within this basic stratum of the party there is an extraordinary degree of discontent,* some of which is absolutely legitimate and some of which has been provoked by incidental factors. This discontent is not being alleviated through an open exchange of opinions in party meetings or by mass influence on the party organizations (in the election of party committees, secretaries, etc.), but rather it continues to build up in secret and, in time, leads to *internal abscesses.*"

12. At the Twelfth Congress a policy line favoring the "Old Bolsheviks" was officially adopted. On this point, emphasizing that the Old Bolshevik cadres are "the revolutionary leaven of the party and its organizational backbone," Trotsky agrees that they ought to occupy all the leading positions in the party. However, the system whereby they are appointed from the top represents a danger, all the more so because, in the appointment of secretaries, the "independence" referred to above still remains in effect. The growing discontent over this exclusive and self-contained apparatus of secretaries, who identify themselves with Old Bolshevism, can in the future have grave consequences for preserving the ideological hegemony of the Old Bolsheviks of underground days in the party of contemporary times.

13. "The Politburo's attempt to draw up *a budget based on the*

sale of vodka, i.e., to make the revenue of the workers' government independent of success or failure in economic construction, was an ominous symptom. Only resolute protest within the Central Committee and outside it checked this venture, which would have inflicted a savage blow not only to our economic work but to the party itself. However, the Central Committee has not to this day rejected the notion of legalizing vodka in the future. There is without question an inner connection between the separate and self-contained character of the secretarial organization—more and more independent of the party—and the tendency toward setting up a budget as independent as possible of the success or failure of the party's collective work of construction. The attempt to depict any negative attitude toward the legalization of vodka as virtually a crime against the party and the *removal from the central organ's editorial board* of a comrade who demanded freedom of discussion on this disastrous plan will remain forever one of the most disgraceful moments in the party's history."

Points 14 and 15 were devoted to criticizing the Politburo's decisions and measures with respect to the army and the higher institution in charge of it—the Revolutionary Military Committee. While, for understandable reasons, we will not go into the details of these criticisms (sometimes more than colorful) on this question, we will note that Trotsky writes: "At the recent plenum an attempt was made to put a group of Central Committee members, headed by Stalin, on the Revolutionary Military Committee. Only my protest, expressed in the most categorical fashion, kept the plenum from immediately implementing this measure." Trotsky, in addition, sets forth the history of how Lashevich and Voroshilov came to be members of the Revolutionary Military Committee, comparing the measures involved with the campaign, notorious at the time, against the Ukrainian Council of People's Commissars.[2]

Point 15 of the letter concludes with the following illustrative lines: "It is no wonder that in response to a reproach I directed at him to the effect that the real motives for the proposed changes in the Revolutionary Military Committee had nothing in common with the officially stated motives, Kuibyshev not only failed to deny that a discrepancy existed—and how could he, in fact, deny it?—but stated flatly to me: 'We consider it necessary to wage a struggle against you but we cannot declare you an enemy; this is why we must resort to such methods.'"[3]

Trotsky's letter concludes with points 16 and 17. "The party is entering perhaps the most crucial historical epoch carrying a heavy burden of mistakes on the part of its leading bodies. On the sixth anniversary of the October Revolution and on the eve of the revolution in Germany, the Politburo is obliged to discuss a draft resolution that says every party member must inform the party organizations and the GPU of illegal groupings within the party. It is perfectly obvious that such a regime and such an attitude toward the party within the party itself are incompatible with fulfilling the tasks that may, and by all indications will, confront the party if there is a revolution in Germany. Secretarial bureaucratism must be brought to an end. Party democracy must enjoy its rightful place—at least enough of it to prevent the party from the threat of ossification and degeneration. The rank and file of the party must express its dissatisfactions within the framework of party principles and the responsibilities of a party member. And it must have a real opportunity to construct the party's organizational apparatus in accordance with party regulations and above all in accordance with the entire purpose of our party. . . .

"The members of the Central Committee and the Central Control Commission know that while fighting resolutely and unequivocally within the Central Committee against the false policy, I have deliberately avoided submitting the struggle within the Central Committee to the judgment of even a very narrow circle of comrades: specifically, to those who, given any party course that was at all reasonable, would surely occupy a prominent place in the Central Committee and the Central Control Commission. I am compelled to state that my efforts over the past year and a half have yielded no results. This raises the danger that the party may be caught unawares by a crisis of exceptional severity; and in that case any comrade who saw the danger but failed to openly call it by name could be rightly accused by the party of placing form above content.

"In view of the situation that has developed, I think it is not only my right but my duty to make the true state of affairs known to every party member whom I consider to be sufficiently prepared, mature, self-restrained, and consequently capable of helping the party find a way out of this impasse without factional convulsions and upheavals."

SECOND LETTER
TO THE CENTRAL COMMITTEE

October 24, 1923

NOTE: On October 15, before the Politburo had answered Trotsky's October 8 letter, forty-six prominent party members issued a statement in support of his criticisms, calling for a conference of the Central Committee with those "most prominent and active party workers" who had voiced opposition to the Central Committee's course. The "Platform of the Forty-six" is reprinted as an appendix to this volume (p. 397).

In its reply to Trotsky's letter the Politburo accused him of "instigating a struggle against the Central Committee" and committing a number of mistakes that might "give rise to a real crisis in the party and a breach between the party and the working class." Without answering a single one of his arguments, it charged that his economic proposals were motivated by his eagerness to become "dictator of economic and military affairs." And finally, in an early attempt to distort history for factional purposes, the Politburo alluded to Lenin's former disagreements with Trotsky, not in answer to any of Trotsky's proposals but in order to discredit his ideas by casting aspersions on his past.

Trotsky's reply to the Politburo ignored its defamation of his character and set the record straight on Lenin's positions. Excerpts from both the Politburo's letter and Trotsky's second letter to the Central Committee of October 24, 1923, were published in Sotsialistichesky Vestnik, *May 28, 1924. The translation for this volume by Marilyn Vogt again follows the* Vestnik's *text.—Ed.*

We cite here the text of excerpts that are most characteristic of Trotsky's second letter to the Central Committee and the Central Control Commission.

. . . 2. "On attempts to involve Lenin's name in our disagreements." "The letter of the Politburo members attempts to draw Comrade Lenin's name into the present controversy, presenting the matter as if one side represents the continuation of Comrade Lenin's policies and the other a struggle against them. Attempts to depict the dispute in such a way, although in a more cautious and veiled manner, have been made more than once—both during the period of preparation for, and particularly after, the Twelfth Congress. Precisely because these attempts took the form of insinuations and oblique references, it was impossible to respond to them. And they were made as insinuations precisely because it was calculated that in such form they would not be answered. The present 'answer' from the members of the Politburo, which attempts to make the hints a little more concrete, reveals by the same token, as we will now see, how totally unfounded the hints are, and at the same time gives us an opportunity to refute them clearly and unequivocally. I will examine the disputed questions point by point, giving exact quotations and references to documents that are readily accessible for verification.

"(1) One of the central questions with regard to the economy has been and continues to be the question of the role of overall guidance in planning, i.e., the systematic coordination of the fundamental sectors of the state-run economy in the process of adapting them to the growing market. I have held and still hold the opinion that one of the most important causes of our economic crises is the absence of correct and uniform regulation from above. It is absolutely true that on the question of the organization of guidance in planning I had differences with Comrade Lenin. Lenin's authority has meant no less to me than to any other member of the Central Committee. But I believed then and I believe now that the party elects members of the Central Committee with the understanding that they will uphold in the Central Committee whatever they believe is right in any given instance.

"But how did Lenin himself resolve this question in his own mind? On July 2, 1923, the Politburo received from Nadezhda Konstantinovna Krupskaya [Lenin's wife] a special memorandum from Lenin, 'Granting Legislative Functions to the State Planning Commission,' dictated December 27, 1922. In this document Lenin writes the following: 'This idea was suggested by Comrade Trotsky, it seems, quite a long time ago. I was against it at the time, because I thought that there would then be a fundamental lack of co-ordination in the system of our legislative institutions. But after closer consideration of the matter I find that in substance there is a sound idea in it, namely: the State Planning Commission stands somewhat apart from our legislative institutions, although, as a body of experienced people, experts, representatives of science and technology, it is actually in a better position to form a correct judgement of affairs. . . . In this respect I think we can and must accede to the wishes of Comrade Trotsky, but not in the sense that specifically any one of our political leaders, or the Chairman of the Supreme Economic Council, etc., should be Chairman of the State Planning Commission' [Lenin, *Collected Works,* Vol. 36 (Moscow: Progress Publishers, 1966), pp. 598-99]. And in conclusion Lenin spoke out against having Gosplan's work be to consider specific, assigned tasks and in favor of its work being the type through which it could 'systematically . . . solve the whole range of problems within its ambit' [ibid., p. 602]. As we see, the problem is presented here with ample clarity and completeness.

"(2) Another economic question on which there were disagreements at the plenum of the Central Committee not long before the Twelfth Congress, and in which Lenin was involved, concerned the monopoly of foreign trade, that is, an issue which at the Twelfth Congress I referred to (without objection from anyone whatsoever) as one of the mainstays of the socialist dictatorship under conditions of capitalist encirclement. I have in my possession a rather extensive correspondence with Lenin on this question. I am citing here in full only Lenin's letter of December 13, 1922. It clearly shows how he regarded the problem."*

(3) Under this point Trotsky refers to the fact that Lenin had entrusted him with the defense of the Georgian case in the party's Central Committee.

"(4) One of the central questions is that raised by Lenin on the *reorganization of the Workers and Peasants Inspection* (Rabkrin) and the Central Control Commission. It is remarkable that even this question has been and continues to be portrayed as a topic of dispute between Lenin and me, when in fact this question, like the national question, presents the groupings within the Polit-

---

Vestnik did not quote the letter. The relevant section is as follows: "Dear Comrade Trotsky: . . . I think that you and I are in maximum agreement. . . . At any rate, it is my request that at the forthcoming plenum you should undertake the defence of our common standpoint on the unquestionable need to maintain and consolidate the foreign trade monopoly . . . " [*CW,* Vol. 45, "To L.D. Trotsky" (December 13, 1922), pp. 601-02].

buro in exactly the opposite light. It is absolutely true that I had
a very negative attitude toward the old Rabkrin. However, in his
article "Better Fewer, but Better," Lenin gave a more devastating
evaluation of the Workers and Peasants Inspection than I ever
would have done: 'The People's Commissariat of the Workers and
Peasants Inspection does not at present enjoy the slightest authority. Everybody knows that no other institutions are worse
organized than those of our Workers and Peasants Inspection,
and that under present conditions nothing can be expected from
this People's Commissariat' [*CW*, Vol. 33, "Better Fewer, but
Better" (March 2, 1923), p. 490]. If we recall who was at the head
of the Rabkrin for the longest period of time, it is not difficult to
understand at whom this description was aimed, as well as the
article on the national question.

"What was the Politburo's reaction, however, to Lenin's proposal that the Workers and Peasants Inspection be. reorganized?
Bukharin could not bring himself to publish this article, whereas
Lenin insisted it be published immediately. Nadezhda Konstantinovna Krupskaya informed me of the article by telephone and
requested that I intercede in order to hasten the article's publication. At the session of the Politburo that was quickly convened on
my request, all those present—Stalin, Molotov, Kuibyshev, Rykov, Kalinin, and Bukharin—*were not only against Lenin's plan
but were also against the publication of the article.* The objections
of the members of the Secretariat were particularly sharp and
categorical. In view of Lenin's persistent demands that he be
shown the article in print, Comrade Kuibyshev, future People's
Commissar of Rabkrin, proposed at this session that the Politburo print *one copy* of a special issue of *Pravda* with Lenin's
article in it to pacify him, *while at the same time concealing the
article from the party as a whole.* Comrade Kuibyshev, a former
member of the Secretariat, was appointed head of the Central
Control Commission. In place of a struggle against Lenin's plan
on the reorganization of Rabkrin, a plan was adopted whereby
Lenin's plan would be 'rendered harmless.' Did the Central Control Commission (under Kuibyshev's direction) thereby acquire
the attributes of an independent, impartial party institution,
upholding and maintaining the groundwork of party legality and
party unity against any excesses by the party administration? I
will not get into a discussion of this question at this point because
I presume that the answer is already quite clear.

"Such are the most instructive episodes of recent times regarding my 'struggle' against the policies of Lenin."

THE NEW COURSE

NOTE: The triumvirate refused to allow either the "Platform of the Forty-six" or Trotsky's two letters to be published or distributed to the party. Instead, they opened a campaign against the Opposition in the party cells, which had the counterproductive effect of arousing interest in the Opposition's ideas. Under pressure, the triumvirs opened a public discussion in the pages of Pravda *and other newspapers on the anniversary of the revolution, November 7. The response was so strong that the Politburo felt compelled to give token endorsement to the demands for party democracy, and on December 5 unanimously adopted the New Course resolution printed as an appendix on page 404 of this book.*

Trotsky followed this with a series of articles written for Pravda *during December 1923. One of the main accusations leveled against him, because of his support for industrialization, was that he "underestimated the peasantry." When his articles were published as a pamphlet entitled* The New Course *in early 1924, Trotsky included a proposal he had made to the Central Committee in February 1920, arguing that the system of forced requisitioning of foodstuffs from the peasants should be replaced by an agricultural tax, and that manufactured goods should be made available to the peasants so that they would be willing to sell their grain on the market. Trotsky's proposal was not accepted at the time it was made; only a year later, when the disaffection of the peasantry had reached crisis proportions, did the party adopt a similar program to the one Trotsky had proposed: it was called the "New Economic Policy."*

He also included in the collection an article by eight Young Communists defending him against the charge that he sought to "counterpose the youth to the old generation."

The New Course *was not published in English until 1943, in a translation by Max Shachtman. Except for corrections of trans-*

*lating errors or ambiguities and changes for stylistic consistency,
that version has been used here.—Ed.*

Preface

January 1924

This pamphlet appears after considerable delay: illness prevented me from publishing it sooner. But on the whole, the questions have only been broached in the discussion that has developed till now.

Around the questions concerning the internal regime of the
party and the economy of the country have risen clouds of dust in
the course of the discussion that often form an almost impene-
trable mist and badly blur the vision. But that will pass. The dust
clouds will disperse. The questions will stand out in their true
form. The collective thought of the party will gradually draw
what it requires from the debates, will reach maturity and become
more sure of itself. And thus the base of the party will widen and
its leadership will become more sure.

Herein lies the objective meaning of the resolution of the Central Committee on the "new course" of the party, no matter what
"reverse gear" interpretations are made of it. All the previous
work of purging the party, the raising of its political education
and its theoretical level, and finally the setting up of qualifications for party functionaries, can be crowned only by widening
and intensifying the independent activity of the entire party
collectivity. Such activity is the only serious guarantee against
all the dangers connected with the New Economic Policy and the
retarded development of the European revolution.

However, it is indubitable that the new course of the party can
only be a means and not an end in itself. For the coming period,
one may say that its weight and value will be determined by the
degree to which it helps us solve our principal economic task.

The administration of our state economy is necessarily centralized. The result has been, in the first instance, that questions and
differences of opinion on the central economic administration

have been confined to a narrow circle of persons. The thinking of
the party as a whole has not yet been brought to bear directly
upon the basic questions and difficulties of the planned management of the state economy. Even at the Twelfth Congress, questions concerning the planned management of the economy were
broached, at bottom, only formally. This is what explains in large
measure why the ways and means set down in the resolution of
this congress remain almost entirely unapplied up to recently,
and why the Central Committee was obliged the other day to pose
anew the question of the necessity of putting into operation the
economic decisions of the Twelfth Congress, particularly those
dealing with the Gosplan.

But this time too the decision of the Central Committee has
been met from different sides by skeptical reflections on the
Gosplan and on planned management in general. This skepticism has no creative thought, no theoretical depth, nothing serious behind it. And if this cheap skepticism is tolerated in the
party, it is precisely because the thinking of the party has not yet
broached clearly the questions of centralized, planned management of the economy. Yet the fate of the revolution depends
entirely upon the triumph of such management.

It is only in the last chapter that this pamphlet takes up the
question of planned management, and that on the basis of a
specific example which we did not select arbitrarily but which
was imposed upon us by the discussion inside the party. It is
hoped that at the coming stage, party thought will deal with all
these questions in a much more concrete fashion than now. To
follow the present economic discussion as a spectator— and that
is now my position—it would seem that the party has come back
a year late to work out again in a more critical manner the
decisions of the Twelfth Congress. It follows that the questions
that were, so to speak, the monopoly of a narrow circle of persons,
are gradually becoming the center of attention of the entire party.
For my part, I can only advise the comrades working on economic questions to study attentively the debates of the Twelfth Congress on industry and to link them, as they ought to be linked,
with the present discussion. I hope to be able to return soon to
these questions.

It must be recognized that in the course of the oral and written
discussion in the party, a vast quantity of "facts" and information have been put into circulation that have nothing in common
with reality and represent, to put it delicately, the fruit of fleeting

inspiration. We offer proof of this in our pamphlet. To resort to such "striking" means is at bottom to evidence a lack of respect for the party. And in my opinion, the latter should reply to these proceedings by a painstaking check of the quotations, figures, and facts put forward. That is one of the most important means of educating the party and of assuring one's own education.

Our party is mature enough not to have to take refuge in "dead calm" or in frenzied discussion. A more stable democratic regime in the party will assure our discussion the character it ought to have and will teach that only carefully verified data should be presented to the party. In this regard, the public opinion of the party ought to take shape by means of unrelenting criticism. The factory cells should check through their daily experience, both the data of the discussion and its conclusions. It would likewise be very useful for the youth in the schools to base their historical, economic, and statistical works upon a rigorous verification of the data circulated in the present discussion by the party, data on which the latter, tomorrow or the day after, will base its decisions.

I repeat: the most important acquisition the party has made and must preserve is that the principal economic questions, previously settled inside a very few institutions, have now become the center of attention of the party masses. Thus we are entering a new period. The clouds of dust stirred up by the discussion will disperse, the false data will be rejected by party thought, and the fundamental questions of economic organization will never again leave the horizon of the party. The revolution will gain by it.

L. Trotsky

P.S.—This pamphlet contains, in addition to the chapters published in *Pravda*, some new chapters, as follows: "Bureaucratism and the Revolution," "Tradition and Revolutionary Policy," "The 'Underestimation' of the Peasantry," "Planned Economy." As to the articles already published, I present them here without changing a word. That will enable the reader better to judge how their meaning has at times been and still is monstrously distorted during the discussion.

L.T.

Chapter 1
The Question of Party Generations

December 23, 1923

In one of the resolutions adopted during the discussion in Moscow, the complaint is made that the question of party democracy has been complicated by discussions on the relations between the generations, personal attacks, etc. This complaint attests to a certain mental confusion. Personal attacks and the mutual relations between generations are two entirely different things. To pose now the question of party democracy without analyzing the membership of the party, from the social point of view as well as from the point of view of age and political standing, would be to dissolve it into a void.

It is not by accident that the question of party democracy rose up first of all as a question of relations between the generations. It is the logical result of the whole evolution of our party. Its history may be divided schematically into four periods: a) the quarter of a century of preparation up to October, the only one in history; b) October; c) the period following October; and d) the "new course," that is, the period we are now entering. Despite its richness, its complexity, and the diversity of the stages through which it passed, the period prior to October, it is now realized, was only a preparatory period. October made it possible to check up on the ideology and the organization of the party and its membership. By October we understand the acutest period of the struggle for power, which can be said to have started approximately with Lenin's April Theses[4] and ended with the actual seizure of the state apparatus. Even though it lasted only a few months, it is no less important in content than the whole period of preparation, which is measured in years and decades. October not only gave us an unfailing verification, of a unique type, of the party's great past, but itself became a source of experience for the future. It was through October that the pre-October party was able for the first time to assess itself at its true worth.

The conquest of power was followed by a rapid, even abnormal, growth of the party. A powerful magnet, the party attracted not only workers with little consciousness, but even certain elements plainly alien to its spirit: functionaries, careerists, and political hangers-on. In this chaotic period, it was able to preserve its Bolshevik nature only thanks to the internal dictatorship of the Old Guard, which had been tested in October. In the more or less important questions, the leadership of the older generation was then accepted almost without challenge by the new members, not only by the proletarian ranks but also by the alien elements. The climbers considered this docility the best way of establishing their own position in the party. But they miscalculated. By a rigorous purging of its own ranks, the party rid itself of them. Its membership diminished, but its consciousness was enhanced. It may be said that this check-up on itself, this purge, made the post-October party feel itself for the first time a half-million-headed collectivity whose task was not simply to be led by the Old Guard but to examine and decide for itself the essential questions of policy. In this sense, the purge and the critical period linked with it are the preparation, as it were, of the profound change now manifesting itself in the life of the party, which will probably go down in its history under the name of *"the new course."*

There is one thing that ought to be clearly understood from the start: the essence of the present disagreements and difficulties does not lie in the fact that the "secretaries" have overreached themselves on certain points and must be called back to order, but in the fact that *the party as a whole is about to move on to a higher historical stage.* The bulk of the communists are saying in effect to the leaders: "You, comrades, have the experience of before October, which most of us lack; but under your leadership we have acquired after October a great experience which is constantly growing in significance. And we not only want to be led by you but to participate with you in the leadership of the class. We want it not only because that is our right as party members but also because it is absolutely necessary to the working class as a whole. Without our modest experience, experience which should not merely be taken note of in the leading spheres but which must be introduced into the life of the party by ourselves, the leading party apparatus is growing bureaucratic, and we, rank-and-file communists, do not feel ourselves sufficiently well-armed ideologically when confronting nonparty people."

The present change is, as I have said, the result of the whole preceding evolution. Invisible at first glance, molecular processes in the life and the consciousness of the party have long been at work preparing it. The market crisis gave a strong impetus to critical thought. The approach of the events in Germany set the party aquiver. Precisely at this moment it appeared with particular sharpness that the party was living, as it were, on two stories: the upper story, where things are decided, and the lower story, where all you do is learn of the decisions. Nevertheless, the critical revision of the internal regime of the party was postponed by the anxious expectation of what seemed to be the imminent showdown in Germany. When it turned out that this showdown was delayed by the force of things, the party put the question of the "new course" on the order of the day.

As often happens in history, it is precisely during these last months that the "old course" revealed the most negative and most insufferable traits: apparatus cliquism, bureaucratic smugness, and complete disdain for the mood, the thoughts, and the needs of the party. Out of bureaucratic inertia it rejected, from the very beginning, and with an antagonistic violence, the initial attempts to put on the agenda the question of the critical revision of the internal party regime.

This does not mean, to be sure, that the apparatus is composed exclusively of bureaucratized elements, or even less, of confirmed and incorrigible bureaucrats. Not at all! The present critical period, whose meaning they will assimilate, will teach a good deal to the majority of the apparatus workers and will get them to abandon most of their errors. The ideological and organic regrouping that will come out of the present crisis will, in the long run, have healthful consequences for the rank and file of the communists as well as for the apparatus. But in the latter, as it appeared on the threshold of the present crisis, bureaucratism has reached an excessive, truly alarming development. And that is what gives the present ideological regrouping so acute a character as to engender legitimate fears.

It will suffice to point out that two or three months ago the mere mention of the bureaucratism of the apparatus, of the excessive authority of the committees and the secretaries, was greeted by the responsible representatives of the "old course," in the central and local organizations, with a shrug of the shoulders or by indignant protestations. Appointment as a system? Pure imagination! Formalism, bureaucratism? Inventions, opposition solely for the pleasure of making opposition, etc. These comrades, in all sincerity, did not notice the bureaucratic danger they themselves represent. It is only under pressure from the ranks that they began, little by little, to recognize that there actually were manifestations of bureaucratism, but only somewhere at the organizational periphery, in certain regions and districts, that these were only a deviation in practice from the straight line, etc. According to them, bureaucratism was nothing but a survival of the war period, that is, a phenomenon in the process of disappearing, only not fast enough. It is not necessary to say how false this explanation and this approach to things are.

Bureaucratism is not a fortuitous feature of certain provincial organizations, but a general phenomenon. It does not travel from district to the central organization through the medium of the regional organization, but much rather from the central organization to the district through the medium of the regional organization. It is not at all a "survival" of the war period; it is the result of the transference to the party of the methods and the administrative manners accumulated during these last years. However exaggerated were the forms it sometimes assumed, the bureaucratism of the war period was only child's play in comparison with present-day bureaucratism which grew up in peacetime, while the apparatus, in spite of the ideological growth of the party, continued obstinately to think and decide for the party.

Hence, the unanimously adopted resolution of the Central Committee on the structure of the party has, from the standpoint of principle, an immense importance which the party must be clearly aware of. It would indeed be unworthy to consider that the profound meaning of the decisions reached boils down to a mere demand for more "mildness," more "solicitousness" toward the masses on the part of the secretaries and the committees, and to some technical modifications in the organization. *The resolution of the Central Committee speaks of a "new course," and not for nothing.* The party is preparing to enter into a new phase of development. To be sure, it is not a question of breaking the organizational principles of Bolshevism, as some are trying to have us believe, but of applying them to the conditions of the new stage in the development of the party. It is a question primarily of instituting healthier relations between the old cadres and the majority of the members who came to the party after October.

Theoretical preparation, revolutionary tempering, political experience—these represent the party's basic political capital, whose principal possessors, in the first place, are the old cadres of the party. On the other hand, the party is essentially a democratic organization, that is, a collectivity which decides upon its road by the thought and the will of all its members. It is completely clear that in the complicated situation of the period immediately following October, the party made its way all the better for the fact that it utilized to the full the experience accumulated by the older generation, to whose representatives it entrusted the most important positions in the organization.

On the other hand, the result of this state of things has been that, in playing the role of party leader and being absorbed by the questions of administration, the old generation accustomed itself to think and to decide, as it still does, for the party. For the communist masses, it brings to the forefront purely scholastic, pedagogical methods of participating in political life: elementary political training courses, examinations of the knowledge of members, party schools, etc. Thence the bureaucratism of the apparatus, its cliquism, its exclusive internal life, in a word, all the traits that constitute the profoundly negative side of the old course. The fact that the party lives on two separate stories bears within it numerous dangers, which I spoke of in my letter on the old and the young. By "young" I mean of course not simply the students but the whole generation that came to the party after October, the factory cells in the first place.

How did this increasingly marked uneasiness of the party manifest itself? In the majority of its members saying or feeling that: "Whether the apparatus thinks and decides well or badly, it continues to think and decide too often without us and for us. When we happen to display lack of understanding or doubts, to express an objection or a criticism, we are called to order, discipline is invoked; most often, we are accused of being obstructors or even of wanting to establish factions. We are devoted to the party to our very marrow and ready to make any sacrifice for it. But we want to participate actively and consciously in working out its views and in determining its course of action." The first manifestations of this state of mind unmistakably passed by unperceived by the leading apparatus, which took no account of it, and that was one of the main causes of the antiparty groupings in the party. Their importance should certainly not be exaggerated, but neither should their meaning be minimized, for they ought to be a warning to us.

The chief danger of the old course, a result of general historical causes as well as of our own mistakes, is that the apparatus manifests a growing tendency to counterpose a few thousand comrades, who form the leading cadres, to the rest of the mass, whom they look upon only as an object of action. If this regime should persist, it would threaten to provoke, in the long run, a degeneration of the party at both its poles, that is, among the party youth and among the leading cadres. As to the proletarian

base of the party, the factory cells, the students, etc., the character of the peril is clear. Not feeling that they are participating
actively in the general work of the party and not getting a timely
answer to their questions to the party, numerous communists
start looking for a substitute for independent party activity in the
form of groupings and factions of all sorts. It is precisely in this
sense that we speak of the symptomatic importance of groupings
like the "Workers' Group."

But no less great is the danger, at the other pole, of a regime
that has lasted too long and become synonymous in the party
with bureaucratism. It would be ridiculous, and unworthy ostrich
politics, not to understand, or not to want to see, that the accusation of bureaucratism formulated in the resolution of the Central
Committee is directed precisely against the cadres of the party. It
is not a question of isolated deviations in practice from the ideal
line, but precisely of the general policy of the apparatus, of its
bureaucratic tendency. Does bureaucratism bear within it a
danger of degeneration, or doesn't it? Anyone who denied it
would be blind. In its prolonged development, bureaucratization
threatens to detach the leaders from the masses; to bring them to
concentrate their attention solely upon questions of administration, of appointments and transfers; to narrow their horizon; to
weaken their revolutionary spirit; that is, to provoke a more or
less opportunistic degeneration of the Old Guard, or at the very
least of a considerable part of it. Such processes develop slowly
and almost imperceptibly, but reveal themselves abruptly. To see
in this warning, based upon objective Marxist foresight, an "out-
rage," an "assault," etc., really requires the skittish sensitivity
and arrogance of bureaucrats.

But, *in actuality,* is the danger of such degeneration really
great? The fact that the party has understood or felt this danger
and has reacted to it energetically—which was the specific cause
of the resolution of the Central Committee—bears witness to its
profound vitality and by that very fact reveals the potent sources
of antidote which it has at its disposal against bureaucratic
poison. There lies the principal guarantee of its preservation as a
revolutionary party. But if the old course should seek to maintain
itself at all costs by tightening the reins, by increasingly artificial selection, by intimidation, in a word, by procedures indicating a distrust of the party, the actual danger of degeneration of a
considerable part of the cadres would inevitably increase.

The party cannot live solely upon past reserves. It suffices that the past has prepared the present. But the present must be ideologically and practically up to the level of the past in order to prepare the future. The task of the present is to shift the center of party activity toward the masses of the party.

But, it may be said, this shifting of the center of gravity cannot be accomplished at one time, by a leap; the party cannot "put in the archives" the old generation and immediately start living a new life. It is scarcely worthwhile dwelling on such a stupidly demagogic argument. To want to put the old generation in the archives would be madness. What is needed is that precisely this old generation should change its orientation and, by doing so, assure in the future the preponderance of its influence upon all the independent activity of the party. It must consider the new course not as a maneuver, a diplomatic stroke, or a temporary concession, but as a new stage in the political development of the party. In this way, both the generation that leads the party and the party as a whole will reap the greatest benefit.

Chapter 2
The Social Composition of the Party

December 1923

The internal crisis of the party is obviously not confined to the relations of the generations. Historically, in a broader sense, its solution is determined by the social composition of the party and, above all, by the specific weight of the factory cells, of the industrial proletarians that it includes.

The first concern of the working class after the seizure of power was the creation of a state apparatus (including the army, the organs for managing the economy, etc.). But the participation of workers in the state, cooperative, and other apparatuses implied a weakening of the factory cells and an excessive increase of functionaries in the party, proletarian in their origin or not. That is the contradiction of the situation. We can get out of it only by means of substantial economic progress, a strong impulsion to industrial life, and a constant flow of manual workers into the party.

At what speed will this fundamental process take place? Through what ebbs and flows will it pass? It is hard to predict that now. At the present stage of our economic development, everything must of course be done to draw into the party the greatest possible number of workers at the bench. But the membership of the party can be altered seriously (so that, for example, the factory cells make up two-thirds of its ranks) only very slowly and only under conditions of noteworthy economic advance. In any case, we must still look forward to a very long period during which the most experienced and most active members of the party (including, naturally, those of proletarian origin) will be occupied at different posts of the state, trade union, cooperative, and party apparatuses. And this fact itself implies a danger, for it is one of the sources of bureaucratism.

The education of the youth necessarily occupies an exceptional place in the party, as it will continue to do. By using our workers' schools, universities, and institutions of higher learning to build the new contingent of intellectuals, which includes a high proportion of communists, we are detaching the young proletarian elements from the factory, not only for the duration of their studies but in general for their whole life: the working youth that have gone through the higher schools will in all probability be assigned, all of them, to the industrial, state, or party apparatus. This is the second factor in the destruction of the internal equilibrium of the party to the detriment of its basic cells, the factory nuclei.

The question of whether the communist is of proletarian, intellectual, or other origin obviously has its importance. In the period immediately following the revolution, the question of the profession followed before October even seemed decisive, because the assignment of the workers to this or that soviet function seemed to be a temporary measure. At the present time, a profound change has taken place in this respect. There is no doubt that the chairmen of the regional committees or the divisional commissars, whatever their social origin, represent a definite social type, regardless of their individual origin. During these six years, fairly stable social groupings have been formed in the Soviet regime.

So it is that at present, and for a fairly long period to come, a considerable part of the party, represented by the best-trained communists, is absorbed by the different apparatuses of civil, military, economic, etc., management and administration; another part, equally important, is doing its studying; a third part is scattered through the countryside where it deals with agriculture; the fourth category alone (which now represents less than a sixth of the membership) is composed of proletarians working at the bench. It is quite clear that the development of the party apparatus and the bureaucratization accompanying this development are engendered not by the factory cells, linked together through the medium of the apparatus, but by all the other functions that the party exercises through the medium of the state apparatuses of administration, economic management, military command, and education. In other words, the source of bureaucratism resides in the growing concentration of the party's attention and efforts upon the governmental institutions and apparatuses, and in the slowness of the development of industry.

Because of these basic facts and tendencies, we should be fully aware of the dangers of bureaucratic degeneration of the old cadres. It would be vulgar fetishism to consider that just because they have attended the best revolutionary school in the world, they contain within themselves a sure guarantee against any and all dangers of ideological narrowing and opportunistic degeneration. No! History is made by people but people do not always make history consciously, not even their own. In the last analysis, the question will be resolved by two great factors of international importance: the course of the revolution in Europe and the rapidity of our economic development. But to reject fatalistically all responsibility for these objective factors would be a mistake of the same stripe as to seek guarantees solely in a subjective radicalism inherited from the past. In the same revolutionary situation, and in the same international conditions, the party will resist the tendencies of disorganization more or resist them less, to the extent that it is more or less conscious of the dangers and that it combats these dangers with more or less vigor.

It is plain that the heterogeneity of the party's social composition, far from weakening the negative sides of the old course, aggravates them in the extreme. There is not and cannot be any other means of triumphing over corporatism, the caste spirit of the functionaries, than by the realization of democracy. By maintaining "calm," party bureaucratism disunites everyone and everything and deals blows equally, even if differently, to the factory cells, the industrial workers, the army people, and the student youth.

The latter, as we have seen, react in a particularly vigorous way against bureaucratism. Not for nothing did Lenin propose to draw largely upon the students in order to combat bureaucratism. By their social composition and their contacts, the student youth reflect all the social groups of our party as well as their state of mind. Their youthfulness and their sensitivity prompt them to give an active form immediately to this state of mind. As studying youth, they endeavor to explain and to generalize. This is not to say that all acts and moods reflect healthy tendencies. If this were the case, it would signify one of two things: either that all goes well in the party, or that the youth are no longer the mirror of the party. But neither is true. In principle, it is right to say that the factory cells, and not the institutions of learning, are our base. But by saying that the youth are our barometer, we give their political manifestations not an essential but a symptomatic value. A barometer does not create the weather; it is confined to recording it. In politics, the weather takes shape in the depth of the classes and in those spheres where they enter into contact with each other. The factory cells create a direct and immediate contact between the party and the class of the industrial proletariat, which is essential to us. The rural cells create a much feebler contact with the peasantry. It is mainly through the military cells, situated in special conditions, that we are linked with the peasants. As for the student youth, recruited from all the sections and strata of Soviet society, they reflect in their checkered composition all our merits and demerits, and it would be stupid not to accord the greatest attention to their moods. Besides, a considerable part of our new students are communists with, what is for youth, a fairly substantial revolutionary experience. And the more pugnacious of the "apparatchiks" are making a great mistake in turning up their noses at the youth. The youth are our means of checking up on ourselves, our replacements; the future belongs to them.

But let us return to the question of the heterogeneity of the groups in the party that are separated from each other by their functions in the state. The bureaucratism of the party, we have said and we now repeat, is not a survival of some preceding regime, a survival in the process of disappearing; on the contrary, it is an essentially new phenomenon, flowing from the new tasks, the new functions, the new difficulties, and the new mistakes of the party.

The proletariat realizes its dictatorship through the Soviet state. The Communist Party is the leading party of the proletariat and consequently of its state. The whole question is to realize this leadership without merging into the bureaucratic apparatus of the state, in order not to be exposed to a bureaucratic degeneration.

The communists find themselves variously grouped in the party and the state apparatus. In the latter, they are hierarchically dependent upon each other and stand in complex personal reciprocal relations to the nonparty mass. In the party, they are all equal in all that concerns the determination of the tasks and the basic working methods of the party. The communists working at the bench are part of the factory committees, administer the enterprises, trusts, and syndicates, are at the head of the Council of National Economy, etc. In the direction that it exercises over the economy, the party takes and should take into account the experience, observations, and opinions of all its members placed at the various rungs of the ladder of economic administration. The essential, incomparable advantage of our party consists in its being able, at every moment, to look at industry with the eyes of the communist machinist, the communist specialist, the communist director, and the communist merchant, collect the experiences of these mutually complementary workers, draw conclusions from them, and thus determine its line for directing the economy in general and each enterprise in particular.

It is clear that such leadership is realizable only on the basis of a vibrant and active democracy inside the party. When, on the other hand, the methods of the "apparatus" prevail, the leadership of the party gives way to administration by its executive organs (committee, bureau, secretary, etc.). As this regime becomes consolidated, all affairs are concentrated in the hands of a small group, sometimes only of a secretary, who appoints, removes, gives instructions, inflicts penalties, etc.

With such a degeneration of the leadership, the principal superiority of the party, its multiple collective experience, retires to the background. Leadership takes on a purely organizational character and frequently degenerates into order-giving and meddling. The party apparatus goes more and more into the details of the tasks of the Soviet apparatus, lives the life of its day-to-day cares, lets itself be influenced increasingly by it, and fails to see the forest for the trees.

If the party organization as a collectivity is always richer in experience than virtually any organ of the state apparatus, the same cannot be said of the functionaries taken as individuals. Indeed, it would be naive to believe that as a result of his title, a secretary unites within himself all the knowledge and all the competence necessary to the leadership of his organization. In reality, he creates for himself an auxiliary apparatus with bureaucratic sections, a bureaucratic machinery of information, and with this apparatus, which brings him close to the Soviet apparatus, he tears himself loose from the life of the party. And as a famous German expression puts it: "You think you are moving others, but in reality it is you who are moved."

The whole daily bureaucratic practice of the Soviet state thus infiltrates the party apparatus and introduces bureaucratism into it. The party, as a collectivity, does not feel its leadership, because it does not realize it. Thence the discontent or lack of understanding, even in those cases where leadership is correctly exercised. But this leadership cannot maintain itself on the right line unless it avoids becoming lost in paltry details, and assumes a systematic, rational, and collective character. So it is that bureaucratism not only destroys the internal cohesion of the party, but weakens the necessary exertion of influence by the latter over the state apparatus. This is what completely escapes the notice and the understanding of those who yell the loudest about the leading role of the party in its relations with the Soviet state.

Chapter 3
Groups and Factional Formations

December 22, 1923

The question of groupings and factions in the party has become the pivot of the discussion. In view of its intrinsic importance and the extreme acuteness that it has assumed, it demands to be treated with perfect clarity. Yet it is posed in a completely erroneous manner.

We are the only party in the country, and in the period of the dictatorship it could not be otherwise. The different needs of the working class, of the peasantry, of the state apparatus, and of its membership, act upon our party, through whose medium they seek to find a political expression. The difficulties and contradictions inherent in our epoch, the temporary discord in the interests of the different layers of the proletariat, or of the proletariat as a whole and the peasantry, act upon the party through the medium of its worker and peasant cells, the state apparatus, the student youth. Even episodic differences in views and nuances of opinion may express the remote pressure of distinct social interests and, in certain circumstances, be transformed into stable groupings; the latter may, in turn, sooner or later take the form of organized factions which, opposing themselves to the rest of the party, undergo by that very fact even greater external pressure. Such is the dialectic of inner-party groupings in an epoch when the Communist Party is obliged to monopolize the direction of political life.

What follows from this? If factions are not wanted, there must not be any permanent groupings; if permanent groupings are not wanted, temporary groupings must be avoided; finally, in order that there be no temporary groupings, there must be no differences of opinion, for wherever there are two opinions, people inevitably group together. But how, on the other hand, avoid differences of opinion in a party of half a million which is leading the country in exceptionally complicated and painful conditions? That is the essential contradiction residing in the very situation of the party of the proletarian dictatorship, a contradiction that cannot be escaped solely by purely formal measures.

The partisans of the "old course" who vote for the resolution of the Central Committee with the assurance that everything will remain as in the past, reason something like this: Just look, the lid of our apparatus has just scarcely been raised and already tendencies toward groupings of all sorts are manifesting themselves in the party. The lid must be jammed back on and the pot closed hermetically. It is this short-sighted wisdom that pervades dozens of speeches and articles "against factionalism." In their heart of hearts, the apparatchiks believe that the resolution of the Central Committee is either a political mistake that they must try to render harmless, or else an apparatus strategem that must be utilized. In my view, they are grossly mistaken. And if there is a tactic calculated to introduce disorganization into the party, it is the one followed by people who persist in the old orientation while feigning to accept respectfully the new.

It is in contradictions and differences of opinion that the working out of the party's public opinion inevitably takes place. To localize this process *only* within the apparatus, which is then charged to furnish the party with the fruit of its labors in the form of slogans, orders, etc., is to sterilize the party ideologically and politically. To have the party as a whole participate in the working out and adoption of the resolutions, is to promote temporary ideological groupings that risk transformations into durable groupings and even into factions. What to do? Is it possible that there is no way out? *Is it possible that there is no intermediate line between the regime of "calm" and that of crumbling into factions?* No, there is one, and the whole task of the leadership consists, each time that it is necessary and especially at turning points, in finding this line in a way that corresponds to the real situation of the moment.

The resolution of the Central Committee says plainly that the bureaucratic regime is one of the sources of factions. That is a truth which now hardly needs to be demonstrated. The old course was far indeed from "full-blown" democracy, and yet it no more preserved the party from illegal factions than the present stormy discussion which—it would be ridiculous to shut one's eyes to this!—may lead to the formation of temporary or durable groupings. *In order to avert this, the leading party bodies must heed the voices of the broad party masses and must not consider every criticism a manifestation of factionalism and thereby cause conscientious and disciplined party members to withdraw into closed circles and fall into factionalism.*

But doesn't this way of putting the question come down to a justification of Myasnikov and his partisans?[5] We hear the voice of higher bureaucratic wisdom. Why? In the first place, the phrase we have just emphasized is only a textual extract from the resolution of the Central Committee. Further, since when does an *explanation* equal a *justification?* To say that an abscess is the result of defective blood circulation due to an insufficient flow of oxygen, is not to "justify" the abscess and to consider it a normal part of the human organism. The only conclusion is that the abscess must be lanced and disinfected and, above all, the window must be opened to let fresh air provide the oxygen needed by the blood. But the trouble is that the most militant wing of the "old course" is convinced that the resolution of the Central Committee is erroneous, especially in its passage on bureaucratism as a source of factionalism. And if it does not say so openly, it is only out of formal considerations, quite in keeping with its mentality, drenched with that formalism which is the essential attribute of bureaucratism.

It is incontestable that factions are a scourge in the present situation, and that groupings, even if temporary, may be transformed into factions. But as experience shows, it is not at all enough to declare that groupings and factions are an evil for their appearance to be prevented. What is needed to bring this about is a certain policy, a correct course adapted to the real situation.

It suffices to study the history of our party, even if only for the period of the revolution, that is, during the period when the constitution of factions became particularly dangerous, to see that the struggle against this danger cannot be confined to a formal condemnation and prohibition of groupings.

It was in the fall of 1917 that the most formidable disagreement broke out in the party, on the occasion of the capital question of the seizure of power.[6] With the furious pace of events, the acuteness of the struggle immediately gave an extreme factional character to the disagreements: perhaps without wanting to, the opponents of the violent uprising in fact made a bloc with nonparty elements, published their declarations in outside organs, etc. At that moment, the unity of the party hung by a hair. How was the split to be averted? Only by the rapid development of events and their favorable outcome. The split would have taken place inevitably if the events had dragged along for several months, all the more so if the insurrection had ended in defeat. Under the firm leadership of the majority of the Central Committee, the party, in an impetuous offensive, moved over the head of the opposition, power was conquered, and the opposition, not very great numerically but qualitatively very strong, adopted the platform of October. The faction and the danger of a split were overcome at that time not by formal decisions based upon party statutes, but by revolutionary action.

The second great disagreement arose on the occasion of the Brest-Litovsk peace.[7] The partisans of revolutionary war then constituted a genuine faction, with its own central organ, etc. How much truth there is in the recent anecdote about Bukharin being almost prepared, at one time, to arrest the government of Lenin, I am unable to say. Generally speaking, this looks a little like a bad Mayne-Reed story or a communist Pinkerton tale. It may be presumed that the history of the party will take note of this. However that may be, the existence of a left communist faction represented an extreme danger to the unity of the party. To have brought about a split at the time would not have been difficult and would not have demanded of the leadership any great intellectual effort: it would have sufficed to issue a ban against the left communist faction. Nevertheless, the party adopted more complex methods: it preferred to discuss, to explain, to prove by experience, and to resign itself temporarily to the anomalous phenomenon represented by the existence of an organized faction in its midst.

The question of military organization likewise produced the constitution of a fairly strong and obdurate grouping, opposed to the creation of a regular army and all that flowed from it: a centralized military apparatus, specialists, etc.[8] At times, the struggle assumed extreme sharpness. But, as in October, the question was settled by experience, by the war itself. Certain blunders and exaggerations of the official military policy were attenuated, not without the pressure of the opposition, and that not only without damage but with profit to the centralized organization of the regular army. As to the opposition, it fell apart little by little. A great number of its most active representatives participated in the organization of the army in which, in many cases, they occupied important posts.

Clearly defined groupings were constituted at the time of the memorable discussion on the trade unions.[9] Now that we have the opportunity to embrace this entire period at a glance and illuminate it in the light of subsequent experience, we can record that the discussion in no way revolved around the trade unions, or even workers' democracy: what was expressed in these disputes was a profound uneasiness in the party, caused by the excessive prolonging of the economic regime of war communism. The entire economic organism of the country was in a vise. The discussion on the role of the trade unions and of workers' democracy covered up the search for a new economic road. The way out was found in the elimination of the requisitioning of food products and of the grain monopoly, and in the gradual liberation of state industry from the tyranny of the central economic managements. These historical decisions were taken unanimously and completely overshadowed the trade union discussion, all the more so because of the fact that following the establishment of the NEP, the very role of the trade unions themselves appeared in a completely different light and, several months later, the resolution on the trade unions had to be modified radically.

The longest-lasting grouping and, from certain angles, the most dangerous one, was the "Workers' Opposition."[10] It reflected, although distortedly, the contradictions of war communism, certain mistakes of the party, as well as the essential objective difficulties of socialist organization. But this time, too, we did not confine ourselves merely to a formal prohibition. On the questions of democracy, formal decisions were made, and on the purging of the party effective and extremely important measures were taken, satisfying what was just and healthy in the criticism and the demands of the "Workers' Opposition." And the main thing is that because of the decisions and the economic measures adopted by the party, the result of which was to bring about the disappearance of the differences of opinions and the groupings, the Tenth Congress was able to prohibit formally the constitution of factions, with reason to believe that its decisions would not remain a dead letter. But as experience and good political sense show, it goes without saying that by itself this prohibition contained no absolute or even serious guarantee against the appearance of new ideological and organic groupings. The essential guarantee, in this case, is a correct leadership, paying timely attention to the needs of the moment, which are reflected in the party; and flexibility of the apparatus, which ought not paralyze but rather organize the initiative of the party, and which ought not fear criticism or intimidate the party with the bugbear of factions (intimidation is most often a product of fright).

The decision of the Tenth Congress prohibiting factions can only have an auxiliary character; by itself it does not offer the key to the solution of any and all internal difficulties. It would be gross "organizational fetishism" to believe that whatever the development of the party, the mistakes of the leadership, the conservatism of the apparatus, the external influences, etc., a decision is enough to preserve us from groupings and from upheavals inherent in the formation of factions. Such an approach is in itself profoundly bureaucratic.

A striking example of this is provided for us by the history of the Petrograd organization. Shortly after the Tenth Congress, which forbade the constitution of groupings and factions, a very lively organizational struggle broke out in Petrograd, leading to the formation of two clearly antagonistic groupings. The simplest thing to do, at first glance, would have been to declare one of the groups (at least one) to be pernicious, criminal, factional, etc. But the Central Committee refused categorically to employ this method, which was suggested to it from Petrograd. It assumed the role of arbiter between the two groupings and succeeded, not right away, to be sure, in assuring not only their collaboration but their complete fusion in the organization. There you have an important example which deserves being kept in mind and might serve to light up some bureaucratic skulls.

We have said above that every important and lasting grouping in the party, to say nothing of every organized faction, has the tendency to become the expression of some social interests. Every *incorrect* deviation may, in the course of its development, become the expression of the interests of a class hostile or semi-hostile to the proletariat. But first of all this applies to bureaucratism. It is necessary to begin right there. That bureaucratism is an incorrect deviation, and an unhealthy deviation, will not, let us hope, be contested. This being the case, it threatens to lead the party off the right road, the class road. That is precisely where its danger lies. But here is a fact that is instructive in the highest degree and at the same time most alarming: those comrades who assert most flatly, with the greatest insistence and sometimes most brutally, that *every* difference of opinion, *every* grouping of opinion, however temporary, is an expression of the interests of classes opposed to the proletariat, do not want to apply this criterion to bureaucratism.

Yet the social criterion is, in the given instance, perfectly in place, for bureaucratism is a well-defined evil, a notorious and incontestably injurious deviation, officially condemned but not at all in the process of disappearing. Moreover, it is pretty difficult to make it disappear at one blow! But if, as the resolution of the Central Committee says, bureaucratism threatens to *isolate the party from the masses,* and consequently to weaken the class character of the party, it follows that the struggle against bureaucratism can in no case be identified in advance with some kind of nonproletarian influence. On the contrary, the aspiration of the party to preserve its proletarian character must inevitably generate resistance to bureaucratism. Naturally, under cover of this resistance, various erroneous, unhealthy, and harmful tendencies may manifest themselves. They cannot be laid bare except by a Marxist analysis of their ideological content. But to identify resistance to bureaucratism with a grouping which allegedly serves as a channel for alien influences is to be oneself the "channel" of bureaucratic influences.

Nevertheless, there should be no oversimplification and vulgarization in the understanding of the thought that party differences, and this holds all the more for groupings, are nothing but a struggle for influence of antagonistic classes. Thus, in 1920, the question of the invasion of Poland stirred up two currents of opinion, one advocating a more audacious policy, the other preaching prudence.[11] Were there different class tendencies there? I do not believe that anyone would risk such an assertion. There were only differences in the appreciation of the situation, of the forces, of the means. But the essential criterion of the appreciation was the same with both parties.

It frequently happens that the party is able to resolve one and the same problem by different means, and differences arise as to which of these means is the better, the more expeditious, the more economical. These differences may, depending on the question, embrace considerable sections of the party, but that does not necessarily mean that you have there two class tendencies.

There is no doubt that we shall have not one but dozens of disagreements in the future, for our path is difficult and the political tasks as well as the economic questions of socialist organization will unfailingly engender differences of opinion and temporary groupings of opinion. The political verification of all the nuances of opinion by Marxist analysis will always be one of the most efficacious preventive measures for our party. But it is this concrete Marxist verification that must be resorted to, and not the stereotyped phrases which are the defense mechanism of bureaucratism. The heterogeneous political ideology which is now rising up against bureaucratism can be all the better checked, and purged of all alien and injurious elements, the more seriously the road of the "new course" is entered upon. However, this is impossible without a serious change in the mentality and the intentions of the party apparatus. But we are witness, on the contrary, to a new offensive at the present time by the latter, which rejects every criticism of the "old course," formally condemned but not yet liquidated, by treating it as a manifestation of factional spirit. If factionalism is dangerous—and it is—it is criminal to shut your eyes to the danger represented by *conservative bureaucratic factionalism.* It is against precisely this danger that the resolution of the Central Committee is primarily directed.

The maintenance of the unity of the party is the gravest concern of the great majority of communists. But it must be said openly: If there is today a serious danger to the unity or at the very least to the unanimity of the party, it is unbridled bureaucratism. This is the camp in which provocative voices have been raised. That is where they have dared to say: We are not afraid of a split! It is the representatives of this tendency who thumb through the past, seeking out everything likely to inject more rancor into the discussion, resuscitating artificially the recollections of the old struggle and the old split in order to accustom imperceptibly the mind of the party to the possibility of a crime as monstrous and as disastrous as a new split. They seek to counterpose the party's need for unity and its need for a less bureaucratic regime.

If the party allowed itself to take this road, and sacrificed the vital elements of its own democracy, it would only succeed in exacerbating its internal struggle and in upsetting its cohesion. You cannot demand of the party confidence in the apparatus when you yourself have no confidence in the party. There is the whole question. Preconceived bureaucratic distrust of the party, of its consciousness and its spirit of discipline, is the principal cause of all the evils generated by the domination of the apparatus. The party does not want factions and will not tolerate them. It is monstrous to believe that it will shatter or permit anyone to shatter its apparatus. It knows that this apparatus is composed of the most valuable elements, who incarnate the greatest part of the experience of the past. But it wants to renew it and to remind it that it is *its* apparatus, that it is elected *by it* and that it must not detach itself from it.

Upon reflecting well on the situation created in the party, which has shown itself in a particularly clear light in the course of the discussion, it may be seen that the future presents itself under a double perspective. Either the organic ideological regrouping that is now taking place in the party along the line of the resolutions of the Central Committee will be a step forward on the road of the organic growth of the party, the beginning of a new great chapter—which would be the most desirable outcome for us all, the one most beneficial to the party, which would then easily overcome any excesses in the discussion and in the opposition, to say nothing of vulgar democratic tendencies. Or else the apparatus, passing over to the offensive, will come more and more under the power of its most conservative elements and, on the pretext of combatting factions, will throw the party backward and restore "calm." This second eventuality would be by far the most grievous one; it would not prevent the development of the party, it goes without saying, but this development would take place only at the price of considerable efforts and upheavals. For this method would only foster still more the tendencies that are injurious, disintegrative, and hostile to the party. These are the two eventualities to envisage.

My letter on the "new course" [see p. 123] had as its purpose to aid the party to take the first road, which is the most economical and the most correct. And I stand fully by the position in it, rejecting any tendentious or deceitful interpretation.

Chapter 4
Bureaucratism and the Revolution
(Outline of a Report
that the Author Could Not Deliver)

December 1923

1. The essential conditions which not only prevent the realization of the socialist ideal but are, in addition, sometimes a source of painful tests and grave dangers to the revolution, are well enough known. They are: a) the internal social contradictions of the revolution which were automatically compressed under war communism but which, under the NEP, unfold unfailingly and seek political expression; b) the protracted counterrevolutionary threat to the Soviet Republic represented by the imperialist states.

2. The social contradictions of the revolution are class contradictions. What are the fundamental classes of our country?—a) the proletariat, b) the peasantry, c) the new bourgeoisie with the layer of bourgeois intellectuals that covers it.

From the standpoint of economic role and political significance, first place belongs to the proletariat, organized in the state, and to the peasantry, which provides the agricultural products that are dominant in our economy. The new bourgeoisie principally plays the role of intermediary between Soviet industry and agriculture as well as among different parts of Soviet industry and the different spheres of agriculture. But it does not confine itself to being a commercial intermediary; in part, it also assumes the role of organizer of production.

3. Putting aside for the moment the question of the tempo of development of the proletarian revolution in the West, the course of our revolution will be determined by the comparative growth of the three fundamental elements of our economy: state industry, agriculture, and private commercial-industrial capital.

4. Historical analogies with the Great French Revolution (the fall of the Jacobins) made by liberalism and Menshevism for their own nourishment and consolation, are superficial and inconsistent. The fall of the Jacobins was predetermined by the lack of maturity of the social relationships: the left (ruined arti-

sans and merchants), deprived of the possibility of economic development, could not be a firm support for the revolution; the right (bourgeoisie) grew irresistibly; finally, Europe, economically and politically more backward, prevented the revolution from spreading beyond the limits of France.

In all these respects our situation is incomparably more favorable. With us, the nucleus as well as the left wing of the revolution is the proletariat, whose tasks and objectives coincide entirely with the tasks of socialist construction. The proletariat is politically so strong that while permitting, within certain limits, the formation by its side of a new bourgeoisie, it has the peasantry participate in the state power not through the intermediary of the bourgeoisie and the petty-bourgeois parties, but directly, thus barring to the bourgeoisie any access to political life. The economic and political situation of Europe not only does not exclude but makes inevitable the extension of the revolution over its territory.

So while, in France, even the most clairvoyant policy of the Jacobins would have been powerless to alter radically the course of events, with us, whose situation is infinitely more favorable, the correctness of a political line drawn according to the methods of Marxism will be for a considerable period of time a decisive factor in safeguarding the revolution.

5. Let us take the historical hypothesis more unfavorable to us. The rapid development of private capital, if it should take place, would signify that Soviet industry and commerce, including the cooperatives, do not assure the satisfaction of the needs of peasant economy. In addition it would show that private capital is interposing itself more and more between the workers' state and the peasantry, is acquiring an economic and therefore a political influence over the latter. It goes without saying that such a rupture between Soviet industry and agriculture, between the proletariat and the peasantry, would constitute a grave danger for the proletarian revolution, a symptom of the possibility of the triumph of the counterrevolution.

6. What are the *political* paths by which the victory of the counterrevolution might come about if the *economic* hypothesis just set forth were to be realized? There could be many: either the direct overthrow of the workers' party, or its progressive degeneration, or finally, the conjunction of a partial degeneration, splits, and counterrevolutionary upheavals.

The realization of one or the other of these eventualities would depend above all on the *tempo* of economic development. In case private capital succeeded, little by little, slowly, in dominating state capital, the political process would assume in the main the character of the degeneration of the state apparatus in a bourgeois direction, with the consequences that this would involve for the party. If private capital increased rapidly and succeeded in fusing with the peasantry, then active counterrevolutionary tendencies directed against the Communist Party would probably prevail.

If we set forth these hypotheses bluntly, it is of course not because we consider them historically probable (on the contrary, their probability is at a minimum), but because only such a way of putting the question makes possible a more correct and all-sided historical orientation and, consequently, the adoption of all possible preventive measures. The superiority of us Marxists is in distinguishing and grasping new tendencies and new dangers even when they are still only in an embryonic stage.

7. The conclusion from what we have already said in the economic domain brings us to the problem of the "scissors," that is, to the rational organization of industry and to its coordination with the peasant market. To lose time in this connection is to slow down our struggle against private capital. That is where the principal task is, the essential key to the problem of the revolution and of socialism.

8. If the counterrevolutionary danger rises up, as we have said, out of certain social relationships, this in no way means that by a rational policy it is not possible to parry this danger (even under unfavorable economic conditions for the revolution), to reduce it, to remove it, to postpone it. Such a postponement is likely, in turn, to save the revolution by assuring it either a favorable economic shift at home or contact with the victorious revolution in Europe.

That is why, on the basis of the economic policy indicated above, we must have a definite state and party policy (including a definite policy inside the party) aimed at counteracting the accumulation and consolidation of tendencies directed against the dictatorship of the working class and nurtured by the difficulties and failures of economic development.

9. The heterogeneous social composition of our party reflects the objective contradictions of the revolution's development, along with the tendencies and dangers flowing from it:

The factory nuclei, which assure the contact of the party with the essential class of the revolution, now represent one-sixth of the membership of the party.

In spite of all their negative sides, the cells in the soviet institutions assure the party its leadership of the state apparatus, which also determines the great specific weight of these cells. A large percentage of old militants take part in the life of the party through the medium of these soviet cells.

The rural cells give the party a certain contact (still very weak) with the countryside.

The military cells effect the contact of the party with the army, and by means of the latter, with the countryside too (above all).

Finally, in the cells in the educational institutions, all these tendencies and influences mingle and cross.

10. By their class composition, the factory cells are, it goes without saying, basic. But inasmuch as they constitute only one-sixth of the party and their most active elements are taken away to be assigned to the party or the state apparatus, the party cannot yet, unfortunately, lean exclusively or even principally upon them.

Their growth will be the surest gauge of the success of the party in industry and in the economy in general—and at the same time will be the best guarantee that it will retain its proletarian character. But it is hardly possible to expect their speedy growth in the immediate future. As a result, the party will be obliged in the next period to assure its internal equilibrium and its revolutionary line by leaning on cells of a *heterogeneous* social composition.

11. The counterrevolutionary tendencies can find support among the kulaks, the middlemen, the retailers, the concessionaires—in a word, among elements much more capable of surrounding the state apparatus than the party itself. Only the peasant and military cells might be threatened with a more direct influence and even a penetration by the kulaks.

Nevertheless, the differentiation of the peasantry represents a factor which will be of help to us. The exclusion of kulaks from the army (including the territorial divisions) should not only remain an untouchable rule but, what is more, become an important measure for the political education of the rural youth, the military units, and particularly the military cells.

The workers will assure their leading role in the military cells by politically counterposing the rural working masses of the army to the renascent stratum of the kulaks. In the rural cells, too, this counterposition applies. The success of the work will naturally depend, in the long run, upon the extent to which state industry succeeds in satisfying the needs of the countryside.

But whatever the speed of our economic successes may be, our fundamental political line in the military cells must be directed not simply against the Nepmen, but primarily against the renascent kulak stratum, the only historically conceivable and serious support for any and all counterrevolutionary attempts. In this respect, we need more minute analysis of the various components of the army from the standpoint of their social composition.

12. It is beyond doubt that through the medium of the rural and military cells, tendencies reflecting more or less the countryside, with the special traits that distinguish it from the town, filter and will continue to filter into the party. If that were not the case, the rural cells would have no value for the party.

The changes in mood that manifest themselves in the cells are a reminder or a warning to the party. The possibility of directing these cells according to the party line depends on the correctness of the general course of the party as well as upon its internal regime and, in the last analysis, on whether we come closer to solving or attenuating the problem of the "scissors."

13. The state apparatus is the most important source of bureaucratism. On the one hand, it absorbs an enormous quantity of the most active party elements and it teaches the most capable of them the methods of administration of people and things, instead of political leadership of the masses. On the other hand, it largely preoccupies the attention of the party apparatus, over which it exerts influence by its methods of administration.

That, in large measure, is the source of bureaucratization of the apparatus, which threatens to separate the party from the masses. This is precisely the danger that is now most obvious and direct. The struggle against the other dangers must under present conditions begin with the struggle against bureaucratism.

14. It is unworthy of a Marxist to consider that bureaucratism is only the aggregate of the bad habits of officeholders. Bureaucratism is a social phenomenon in that it is a definite system of administration of people and things. Its profound causes lie in the heterogeneity of society, the difference between the daily and the fundamental interests of various groups of the population. Bureaucratism is complicated by the lack of culture among the broad masses. With us, the essential source of bureaucratism resides in the necessity of creating and sustaining a state appara-

tus that unites the interests of the proletariat and those of the peasantry in perfect economic harmony, from which we are still far removed. The necessity of maintaining a permanent army is likewise another important source of bureaucratism.

It is quite plain that precisely the negative social phenomena which we have just enumerated and which now nurture bureaucratism could place the revolution in peril should they continue to develop. We have mentioned this hypothesis above: the growing discord between the state and peasant economy, the growth of the kulaks in the countryside, their alliance with private commercial-industrial capital: these would be—given the low cultural level of the toiling masses of the countryside and in part of the towns— the causes of the eventual counterrevolutionary dangers.

In other words, bureaucratism in the state and party apparatus is the expression of the most vexatious tendencies inherent in our situation, of the defects and deviations in our work which, under certain social conditions, might sap the foundations of the revolution. And, in this case as in many others, quantity will at a certain stage be transformed into quality.

15. The struggle against the bureaucratism of the state apparatus is an exceptionally important but prolonged task, one that runs more or less parallel to our other fundamental tasks— economic reconstruction and the elevation of the cultural level of the masses.

The most important historical instrument for the accomplishment of all these tasks is the party. Naturally, not even the party can tear itself away from the social and cultural conditions of the country. But as the voluntary organization of the vanguard, of the best, most active, and most conscious elements of the working class, it is able to preserve itself from the tendencies of bureaucratism much better than can the state apparatus. To do that, it must see the danger clearly and combat it without letup.

Thence the immense importance of the education of the party youth, based upon personal initiative, in order to serve the state apparatus in a new manner and to transform it completely.

Chapter 5
Tradition and Revolutionary Policy

December 1923

The question of the relationship of tradition and party policy is far from simple, especially in our epoch. More than once, recently, we have had occasion to speak of the immense importance of the theoretical and practical tradition of our party and have declared that we could in no case permit the breaking of our ideological lineage. It is only necessary to come to an agreement on what is meant by the tradition of the party. To do that, we must begin largely by the inverse method and take some historical examples in order to base our conclusions upon them.

Let us take the "classic" party of the Second International, the German social democracy. Its half century of "traditional" policy was based upon an adaptation to parliamentarism and to the unbroken growth of the organization, the press, and the treasury. This tradition, which is profoundly alien to us, bore a semi-automatic character: each day flowed "naturally" from the day before and just as "naturally" prepared the day to follow. The organization grew, the press developed, the cash box swelled.

It is in this automatism that the whole generation following Bebel took shape: a generation of bureaucrats, of philistines, of dullards whose political character was completely revealed in the first hours of the imperialist war. Every congress of the social democracy spoke invariably of the party's old tactics, consecrated by tradition. And the tradition was indeed powerful. It was an automatic tradition, uncritical, conservative, and it ended by stifling the revolutionary will of the party.

The war finished for good the "traditional" equilibrium of the political life of Germany. From the very first days of its official existence, the young Communist Party entered a tempestuous period of crises and upheavals. Nevertheless, throughout its comparatively short history may be observed not only the creative but also the conservative role of tradition which, at every stage, at every turn, collides with the objective needs of the movement and the critical judgment of the party.

As early as the first period of the existence of German communism, the direct struggle for power became its heroic tradition. The terrible events of March 1921 disclosed starkly that the party did not yet have sufficient forces for attaining its goal. It had to make a sharp about-face toward the *struggle for the masses* before recommencing the direct struggle for power.

This about-face was hard to accomplish, for it went against the grain of the newly formed tradition. In the Russian party, at the present time, we are being reminded of all the differences of opinion, even the most preposterous, that arose in the party or in its Central Committee in recent years. It would not hurt to recall also the principal disagreement that appeared at the time of the Third Congress of the Communist International. It is now obvious that the change achieved at that time under the leadership of Lenin, in spite of the furious resistance of a considerable part of the congress—at the start, a majority—literally saved the International from the destruction and decomposition with which it was threatened if it went the way of automatic, uncritical "leftism," which, in a brief space of time, had already become a hardened tradition.

After the Third Congress, the German Communist Party carried out, painfully enough, the necessary change. Then began the struggle for the masses under the slogan of the united front, accompanied by long negotiations and other pedagogical procedures. This tactic lasted more than two years and yielded excellent results. But at the same time, these new propaganda methods, being protracted, were transformed . . . into a new semi-automatic tradition which played a very serious role in the events of the last half of 1923.

It is now incontestable that the period running from May (beginning of the resistance in the Ruhr) or July (collapse of this resistance) to November, when General Seeckt took over power, was a clearly marked period of crisis without precedent in the life of Germany. The resistance that the half-strangled Republican Germany of Ebert-Cuno tried to offer against French militarism crumpled up, taking with it the pitiful social and political equilibrium of the country. The Ruhr catastrophe played, up to a certain point, the same role for "democratic" Germany that the defeat of the German troops played five years earlier for the Hohenzollern regime.

Incredible depreciation of the mark, economic chaos, general effervescence and uncertainty, decomposition of the social democracy, a powerful flow of workers into the ranks of the communists, universal expectation of an overthrow. If the Communist Party had abruptly changed the pace of its work and had profited by the five or six months that history accorded it for direct political, organizational, technical preparation for the seizure of power, the outcome of the events could have been quite different from the one we witnessed in November. There was the problem: the German party had entered the new, brief period of this crisis, perhaps without precedent in world history, with the ready methods of the two preceding years of propagandistic struggle for the establishment of its influence over the masses. Here a new orientation was needed, a new tone, a new way of approaching the masses, a new interpretation and application of the united front, new methods of organization and of technical preparation—in a word, a brusque tactical change. The proletariat should have seen a revolutionary party at work, marching directly to the conquest of power.

But the German party continued, at bottom, its propaganda policy of yesterday, even if on a larger scale. It was only in October that it adopted a new orientation. But by then it had too little time left to develop its dash. Its preparations were speeded up feverishly, the masses were unable to follow it, the lack of assurance of the party communicated itself to both sides, and at the decisive moment, the party retreated without giving battle.

If the party surrendered its exceptional positions without resistance, the main reason is that it proved unable to free itself, at the beginning of the new phase (May-July 1923), from the automatism of its preceding policy, established as if it was meant for years to come, and to put forward squarely in its agitation, action, organization, and tactics the problem of taking power.

Time is an important element of politics, particularly in a revolutionary epoch. Years and decades are sometimes needed to make up for lost months. It would have been the same with us if our party had not made its leap in April 1917 and then taken power in October. We have every reason to believe that the German proletariat will not pay too dearly for its omission, because the stability of the present German regime, above all because of the international situation, is more than doubtful.

It is clear that, as a conservative element, as the automatic pressure of yesterday upon today, tradition represents an extremely important force at the service of the conservative parties and deeply inimical to the revolutionary party. The whole strength of the latter lies precisely in its freedom from conservative traditionalism. Does this mean that it is free with regard to tradition in general? Not at all. But the tradition of a revolutionary party is of an entirely different nature.

If we now take our Bolshevik Party in its revolutionary past and in the period following October, it will be recognized that its most precious fundamental tactical quality is its unequaled ability to orient itself rapidly, to change tactics quickly, to renew its armament and to apply new methods, in a word, to carry out abrupt turns. Tempestuous historical conditions have made this tactic necessary. Lenin's genius gave it a superior form. This is not to say, naturally, that our party is completely free of a certain conservative traditionalism: a mass party cannot be ideally free. But its strength and potency have manifested themselves in the fact that inertia, traditionalism, routinism, were reduced to a minimum by a farsighted, profoundly revolutionary tactical initiative, at once audacious and realistic.

It is in this that the genuine tradition of the party consists and should consist.

The relatively strong bureaucratization of the party apparatus is inevitably accompanied by the development of conservative traditionalism with all its effects. It is better to exaggerate this danger than to underrate it. The undeniable fact that the most conservative elements of the apparatus are inclined to identify their opinions, their methods, and their mistakes with the "Old Bolshevism," and seek to identify the criticism of bureaucratism with the destruction of tradition, this fact, I say, is already by itself the incontestable expression of a certain ideological petrification.

Marxism is a method of historical analysis, of political orientation, and not a mass of decisions prepared in advance. Leninism is the application of this method in the conditions of an exceptional historical epoch. It is precisely this union of the peculiarities of the epoch and the method that determines that courageous, self-assured policy of *brusque turns* of which Lenin gave us the finest models, and which he illuminated theoretically and generalized on more than one occasion.

Marx said that the advanced countries, to a certain extent, show the backward countries the image of their future. Out of this conditional proposition an effort was made to set up an absolute law which was at the root of the "philosophy" of Russian Menshevism. By means of it, limits were fixed for the proletariat, flowing not from the course of the revolutionary struggle but from a mechanical pattern; Menshevik Marxism was and remains solely the expression of the needs of bourgeois society, an expression adapted to a belated "democracy." In reality, it turned out that Russia, joining in its economy and its politics extremely contradictory phenomena, was the first to be pushed onto the road of the proletarian revolution.

Neither October, nor Brest-Litovsk, nor the creation of a regular peasant army, nor the system of requisitioning food products, nor the NEP, nor the State Planning Commission, were or could have been foreseen or predetermined by pre-October Marxism or Bolshevism. All these facts and turns were the result of the independent, critical application of the methods of Bolshevism, marked by the spirit of initiative, in situations that differed in each case.

Every one of these decisions, before being adopted, provoked struggles. The simple appeal to tradition never decided anything. As a matter of fact, with each new task and at each new turn, it is not a question of searching in tradition and discovering there a nonexistent reply, but of profiting from all the experience of the party to find by oneself a new solution suitable to the situation and, by doing so, enriching tradition. It may even be put more sharply: Leninism consists of being courageously free of conservative retrospection, of being bound by precedent, purely formal references, and quotations.

Lenin himself not so long ago expressed this thought in Napoleon's words: *"On s'engage et puis on voit"* (start fighting and then see). To put it differently, once engaged in the struggle, don't be excessively preoccupied with canon and precedent, but plunge into reality as it is and seek there the forces necessary for victory, and the roads leading to it. It is by following this line that Lenin, not once but dozens of times, was accused in his own party of violating tradition and repudiating "Old Bolshevism."

Let us recall that the *otsovists*[12] invariably appeared under cover of defending Bolshevik traditions against Leninist deviation (there is some extremely interesting material on this score in *Krasnaya Letopis* [Red Chronicle], No. 9). Under the aegis of "Old Bolshevism," in reality under the aegis of formal, fictitious, false tradition, all that was routinist in the party rose up against Lenin's April Theses. One of our party's *historians* (the historians of our party, up to now, have unfortunately not had much luck) told me at the height of the October events: "I am not with Lenin because I am an Old Bolshevik and I continue to stand on the ground of the democratic dictatorship of the proletariat and the peasantry." The struggle of the "left communists" against the Brest-Litovsk peace and for revolutionary war likewise took place in the name of saving the revolutionary traditions of the party, in the name of the purity of "Old Bolshevism," which had to be protected against the dangers of state opportunism. It is needless to recall that the whole criticism by the "Workers' Opposition" consisted, at bottom, of accusing the party of violating the old traditions. Only recently we saw the most official interpreters of the party's traditions on the national question take a stand in distinct contradiction to the needs of party policy in this question as well as to Lenin's position.[13]

These examples could be multiplied, and any number of others could be cited, historically less important but no less conclusive. But what we have just said suffices to show that every time objective conditions demand a new turn, a bold about-face, and creative initiative, conservative resistance betrays a natural tendency to counterpose the "old traditions"—and what is called Old Bolshevism but is in reality the empty husk of a period just left behind—to new tasks, new conditions, new orientation.

The more ingrown the party apparatus, the more imbued it is with the feeling of its own intrinsic importance, the slower it reacts to needs emanating from the ranks and the more inclined it is to set formal tradition against new needs and tasks. And if there is one thing likely to strike a mortal blow to the spiritual life of the party and the doctrinal training of the youth, it is certainly the transformation of Leninism from a method demanding for its application initiative, critical thinking, and ideological courage, into a canon which demands nothing more than interpreters appointed for good and all.

Leninism cannot be conceived of without theoretical breadth, without a critical analysis of the material bases of the political process. The weapon of Marxist investigation must be constantly sharpened and applied. It is precisely in this that tradition consists, and not in the substitution of a formal reference or an accidental quotation. Least of all can Leninism be reconciled with ideological superficiality and theoretical slovenliness.

Lenin cannot be chopped up into quotations suited for every possible case, because for Lenin the formula never stands higher than the reality; it is always the tool that makes it possible to grasp the reality and to dominate it. It would not be hard to find in Lenin dozens and hundreds of passages which, formally speaking, seem to be contradictory. But what must be seen is not the formal relationship of one passage to another, but the real relationship of each of them to the concrete reality in which the formula was introduced as a lever. The Leninist truth is always concrete!

As a system of revolutionary action, Leninism presupposes a revolutionary sense sharpened by reflection and experience, which, in the social realm, is equivalent to the muscular sensation in physical labor. But revolutionary sense cannot be confused with demagogical flair. The latter may yield ephemeral successes, sometimes even sensational ones. But it is a political instinct of an inferior type. It always leans toward the line of least resistance. Leninism, on the other hand, seeks to pose and resolve the fundamental revolutionary problems, to overcome the principal obstacles; its demagogical counterpart consists in evading the problems, in creating an illusory appeasement, in lulling critical thought to sleep.

Leninism is, first of all, realism, the highest qualitative and quantitative appreciation of reality, from the standpoint of revolutionary action. Precisely because of this it is irreconcilable with flying from reality behind the screen of hollow agitationalism, with passive loss of time, with haughty justification of yesterday's mistakes on the pretext of saving the tradition of the party.

Leninism is genuine freedom from formalistic prejudices, from moralizing doctrinairism, from all forms of intellectual conservatism attempting to stifle the will to revolutionary action. But to believe that Leninism signifies that "anything goes" would be an irremediable mistake. Leninism includes the morality, not formal but genuinely revolutionary, of mass action and the mass party. Nothing is so alien to it as functionary arrogance and bureaucratic cynicism. A mass party has its own morality, which is the bond of fighters in and for action. Demagogy is irreconcilable with the spirit of a revolutionary party because it is deceitful: by presenting one or another simplified solution for the difficulties of the hour, it inevitably undermines the future and weakens the party's self-confidence.

Swept by the wind and gripped by a serious danger, demagogy easily dissolves into panic. It is hard to juxtapose, even on paper, panic and Leninism.

Leninism is warlike from head to foot. War is impossible without cunning, without subterfuge, without deception of the enemy. Victorious war cunning is a constituent element of Leninist politics. But at the same time, Leninism is a supreme revolutionary honesty toward the party and the working class. It admits of no fiction, no bubble-blowing, no pseudograndeur!

Leninism is orthodox, obdurate, irreducible, but it does not contain so much as a hint of formalism, canon, or bureaucratism. In the struggle, it takes the bull by the horns. To make out of the traditions of Leninism a supratheoretical guarantee of the infallibility of all the words and thoughts of the interpreters of these traditions, is to scoff at a genuine revolutionary tradition and transform it into official bureaucratism. It is ridiculous and pathetic to try to hypnotize a great revolutionary party by the repetition of the same formulas, according to which the right line should be sought not in the essence of each question, not in the methods of posing and solving this question, but in information . . . of a biographical character.

Since I am obliged to speak of myself for a moment, I will say that I do not consider the road by which I came to Leninism as less safe and reliable than the others. I came to Lenin fighting, but I came fully and all the way. My actions in the service of the party are the only guarantee of this: I can give no other supplementary guarantees. And if the question is to be posed in the field of biographical investigation, then at least it ought to be done properly.

It would then be necessary to reply to thorny questions: Were all those who were faithful to the master in the small matters also faithful to him in the great? Did all those who showed such docility in the presence of the master thereby offer guarantees that they would continue his work in his absence? Does the whole of Leninism lie in docility? I have no intention whatever of analyzing these questions by taking as examples individual comrades with whom, so far as I am concerned, I intend to continue working hand in hand.

Whatever the difficulties and the differences of opinion may be in the future, they can be victoriously overcome only by the party's collective thinking, checking up on itself each time and thereby maintaining the continuity of development.

This character of the revolutionary tradition is bound up with the peculiar character of revolutionary discipline. Where tradition is conservative, discipline is passive and is violated at the first moment of crisis. Where, as in our party, tradition consists of the highest revolutionary activity, discipline attains its maximum point, for its decisive importance is constantly checked in action. That is the source of the indestructible alliance of revolutionary initiative, of critical, bold elaboration of questions, with iron discipline in action. And it is only by this superior activity that the youth can receive from the old this tradition of discipline and carry it on.

We cherish the traditions of Bolshevism as much as anybody. But let no one dare identify bureaucratism with Bolshevism, tradition with officious routine.

Chapter 6
The 'Underestimation' of the Peasantry

December 1923

Certain comrades have adopted very singular methods of political criticism: they assert that I am mistaken today on this or that question because I was wrong on this or that question a dozen years ago. This method considerably simplifies the task.

The question of today needs to be studied in its own right and in its full contents. But a question raised several years ago has long since been exhausted and judged by history, and to refer to it again does not require great intellectual effort; all that is needed is memory and good faith.

But I cannot say that in this last respect all goes well with my critics. And I am going to prove it by an example from one of the most important questions.

One of the favorite arguments of certain circles during recent times consists of pointing out—mainly by indirection—that I "underestimate" the role of the peasantry. But one would seek in vain among my adversaries for an analysis of this question, for facts, quotations, in a word, for any proof.

Ordinarily, their argumentation boils down to allusions to the theory of the "permanent revolution," and to two or three bits of corridor gossip. And between the theory of the "permanent revolution" and the corridor gossip there is nothing, a void.

As to the theory of the "permanent revolution," I see no reason to renounce what I wrote on this subject in 1904, 1905, 1906, and later. To this day, I persist in considering that the thoughts I developed at that time, taken as a whole, are much closer to the genuine essence of Leninism than much of what a number of Bolsheviks wrote in those days.

The expression *"permanent revolution"* is an expression of Marx, which he applied to the revolution of 1848. In Marxist literature, naturally not in revisionist but in revolutionary Marxist literature, this term has always had citizenship rights. Franz Mehring employed it for the revolution of 1905-07. The permanent revolution, in an exact translation, is the continuous revolution, the uninterrupted revolution.

What is the political idea embraced in this expression? It is, for us communists, that the revolution does not come to an end after this or that political conquest, after obtaining this or that social reform, but that it continues to develop further and its only boundary is the socialist society. Thus, once begun, the revolution (insofar as we participate in it and particularly when we lead it) is in no case interrupted by us at any formal stage whatever. On the contrary, we continually and constantly advance it, in conformity, of course, with the situation, so long as the revolution has not exhausted all the possibilities and all the resources of the movement. This applies to the conquests of the revolution inside a country as well as to its extension over the international arena.

For Russia, this theory signified: what we need as a political goal is not the bourgeois republic, nor even the democratic dictatorship of the proletariat and peasantry, but a workers' government supporting itself upon the peasantry and opening up the era of the international socialist revolution.*

Thus, the idea of the permanent revolution coincides entirely with the fundamental strategic line of Bolshevism. It is understandable if this was not seen eighteen or fifteen years ago. But it is impossible not to understand and to recognize it, now that the general formulas have been verified by full-blooded historical context.

One cannot discover in my writings of that time the slightest attempt to leap over the peasantry. The theory of the permanent revolution led directly to Leninism and in particular to the April 1917 Theses.

These Theses, however, determining the policy of our party in

---

*See L. Trotsky, **Results and Prospects** [in **Permanent Revolution and Results and Prospects** (Pathfinder Press)].—L.T.

and throughout October, provoked panic, as is known, among a very large part of those who now speak only in holy horror of the theory of the "permanent revolution."

However, to enter into a discussion on all these questions with comrades who have long ago ceased to read and who live exclusively on the muddled recollections of their youth, is not a very easy thing to do; besides, it is useless. But comrades, and young communists in the first place, who do not weary of studying and who, in any case, do not let themselves be frightened either by cabalistic words or by the term "permanent," will do well to read for themselves, pencil in hand, the works of those days, for and against the "permanent revolution," and to try to get from these works the threads that link them with the October Revolution, which is not so difficult.

But what is much more important is the practice pursued during and after October. There it is possible to check up every detail. Needless to say, on the question of the political adoption by our party of the "Social Revolutionary" agrarian program, there was not a shadow of disagreement between Lenin and me. The same goes for the decree on land.

Regardless of whether our peasant policy has been right or wrong on some specific point, it never provoked any differences of opinion among us. It is with my active participation that our policy was oriented toward the middle peasant. The experiences and conclusions of our military work contributed in no small degree to the realization of this policy.

Besides, how was it possible to underestimate the role and importance of the peasantry in the formation of a revolutionary army recruited from among the peasants and organized with the aid of the advanced workers?

It suffices to examine our military political literature to see how permeated it was with the thought that the civil war is politically the struggle of the proletariat with the counterrevolution for influence over the peasantry, and that victory cannot be assured save by the establishment of rational relationships between the workers and the peasants, in an individual regiment, in the district of military operations, and in the state as a whole.

In March 1919, in a report sent to the Central Committee from the Volga region, I supported the necessity of a more effective application of our policy oriented toward the middle peasant, and against the inattentive and superficial attitude that was still current in the party on this question.

In a report prompted by a discussion in the Sengilei organization I wrote: "The temporary political situation—which may even last a long time—is nevertheless a much more profound social and economic reality, for even if the proletarian revolution triumphs in the West, *we will have to base ourselves in large measure, in the construction of socialism, upon the middle peasant and draw him into the socialist economy.*"

Nevertheless, the orientation toward the middle peasant in its first form ("show solicitude toward the peasants," "do not give them orders," etc.), proved inadequate. There was a growing feeling of *the necessity of changing the economic policy.* On the basis of my observations of the state of mind of the army and my declarations during my economic inspection trip in the Urals, I wrote to the Central Committee in February 1920: "The present policy of requisitioning food products according to the norms of consumption, of joint responsibility for the delivery of these products and of the equal distribution of industrial products, is lowering agricultural production and bringing about the atomization of the industrial proletariat, and threatens to completely disorganize the economic life of the country."

As a fundamental practical measure, I proposed to: "replace the requisitioning of surpluses by a levy proportionate to the quantity of production (a sort of progressive tax on agricultural income), set up in such a way that it is nevertheless more profitable to increase the acreage sown or to cultivate it better."

My text as a whole* represented a fairly complete proposal to go over to the New Economic Policy in the countryside. To this proposal was linked another, dealing with the new organization of industry, a less definitive and much more circumspect proposal, but directed on the whole against the regime of the "Centers," which was destroying all contact between industry and agriculture.[14]

These proposals were at that time rejected by the Central Committee; this, if you please, was the only difference of opinion on the peasant question. It is now possible to estimate variously the extent to which the adoption of the New Economic Policy was expedient in February 1920. Opinion may be divided on this matter. Personally, I do not doubt that we would have gained from it. At any rate, it is impossible to conclude from the docu-

---

*I am publishing the basic part of this document as an appendix to this chapter.—L.T.

ments I have just reported that I systematically ignored the peasantry or that I did not sufficiently appreciate its role.

The discussion on the trade unions grew out of the economic blind alley we had gotten into thanks to the requisitioning of food products and the regime of omnipotent "Centers." Could the "merging" of the trade unions into the economic organs have remedied the situation? Obviously not. But neither could any other measure remedy the situation so long as the economic regime of "war communism" continued to exist.

These episodic discussions were wiped out before the decision to resort to the market, a decision of capital importance which did not engender any difference of opinion. The new resolution devoted to the tasks of the trade unions on the basis of the NEP were worked out by Lenin between the Tenth and Eleventh Congresses and were, again, adopted unanimously.

I could adduce a good dozen other facts, politically less important, but all of which would refute just as flatly the fable of my so-called "underestimation" of the role of the peasantry. But is it after all really necessary and possible to refute an assertion so completely undemonstrable and based so' exclusively upon bad faith, or in the best case, upon a defective memory?

Is it true that the fundamental characteristic of international opportunism is the "underestimation" of the role of the peasantry? No, it is not. The essential characteristic of opportunism, including our Russian Menshevism, is the underestimation of the role of the *proletariat* or, more exactly, the lack of confidence in its revolutionary strength.

The Mensheviks founded their whole argument against the seizure of power by the proletariat on the enormous number of peasants and their immense social role in Russia. The Social Revolutionaries considered that the peasantry was created for the purpose of being under their leadership and, through them, to rule the country.

The Mensheviks, who at the most critical moments of the revolution made common cause with the Social Revolutionaries, judged that by its very nature the peasantry was destined to be the principal prop of bourgeois democracy, to whose aid they came on every occasion, by supporting either the Social Revolutionaries or the Cadets. Moreover, in these combinations the Mensheviks and the Social Revolutionaries delivered the peasantry bound hand and foot to the bourgeoisie.

It may be said, to be sure—and it would be entirely valid—that the Mensheviks underestimated the possible role of the peasantry *in comparison with the role of the bourgeoisie;* but still more did they underestimate the role of the proletariat in comparison with that of the peasantry. And it is from the latter underestimation that the former, which was derivative, flowed.

The Mensheviks categorically rejected as a utopia, as a fantasy, as nonsense, the leading role of the proletariat in relation to the peasantry, with all the consequences flowing therefrom—that is, the conquest of power by the proletariat supporting itself upon the peasantry. That is the Achilles' heel of Menshevism which, by the way, resembles Achilles only in its heel.

Finally, what were the principal arguments in our own party against the seizure of power before October? Did they really consist of the underestimation of the role of the peasantry? On the contrary, they consisted of an overestimation of its role in relationship to that of the proletariat. The comrades who opposed the taking of power alleged mainly that the proletariat would be submerged by the petty-bourgeois element, whose base was the multimillioned peasantry.

The term "underestimation" in itself expresses nothing, either theoretically or politically, for it is not a question of the absolute weight of the peasantry in history but of its role and its importance with reference to other classes: on the one side, the bourgeoisie; on the other, the proletariat.

The question can and should be posed concretely, that is, from the standpoint of the dynamic relationship of forces of the different classes. The question that has considerable political importance for the revolution (decisive in certain cases, but far from being everywhere identical) is that of knowing if, in the revolutionary period, the proletariat will draw the peasantry to its side and in what proportion.

Economically, the question that has immense importance (decisive in some countries like our own, but certainly not everywhere identical) is that of knowing in what measure the proletariat in power will succeed in harmonizing the construction of socialism with the peasant economy. But in all countries and under all conditions, the essential characteristic of opportunism resides in the overestimation of the strength of the bourgeois class and the intermediate classes, and in the underestimation of the strength of the proletariat.

Ridiculous, not to say absurd, is the pretension to establish some kind of universal Bolshevik formula out of the peasant question, valid for the Russia of 1917 as well as of 1923, for America with its farmers as well as for Poland with its big landed estates.

Bolshevism began with the program of the restoration of the small plots of land to the peasants, replaced this program with that of nationalization, made the agrarian program of the Social Revolutionaries its own in 1917, established the system of the requisition of food products, then replaced it with the food tax. . . . And we are nevertheless still very far from the solution of the peasant question, and we still have many changes and turns to make.

Isn't it clear that the practical tasks of today cannot be dissolved in the general formulas created by the experiences of yesterday? That the solution of the problems of economic organization cannot be replaced by a bald appeal to tradition? That it is not possible to determine the historic path by standing solely upon memories and analogies?

The capital economic task of the day consists of establishing between industry and agriculture, and consequently within industry, a correlation that would permit industry to develop with a minimum of crises, collisions, and upheavals; and assuring industry and state commerce a growing preponderance over private capital.

That is the general problem. It is divided into a series of partial problems: What methods should be followed in the establishment of a rational correlation between town and country, between transportation, finance, and industry, between industry and commerce? Which institutions are indicated to apply these methods? What, finally, are the concrete statistical data that make it possible at any given moment to establish the plans and economic calculations best suited to the situation? Every one, obviously, a question whose solution cannot be predetermined by any general political formula whatever. It is necessary to find the concrete reply in the process of construction.

What the peasant asks of us is not to repeat a correct historical formula of class relationships (*smychka,* etc.) but to supply him with cheaper nails, cloth, and matches.

We will succeed in satisfying these demands only by an increasingly exact application of the methods of registration, organization, production, sale, checking on work done, amendment, and radical change.

Do these questions bear a principled or programmatic character? No, for neither the program nor the theoretical traditions of the party have bound us, nor could they bind us, on this point, because of the lack of necessary experience and its generalization.

Is the practical importance of these questions great? Immeasurably. Upon their solution depends the fate of the revolution. In these circumstances, to dissolve every practical question, and the differences of opinion flowing from it, in the "tradition" of the party, transformed into an abstraction, means in most cases to renounce what is most important in this tradition itself: the posing and solving of every problem in its integral reality.

There ought to be an end to the jabbering about underestimating the role of the peasantry. What is really needed is to lower the price of merchandise for the peasants.

Appendix
The Fundamental Questions
of Food and Agrarian Policy
(A Proposal Made to the Central
Committee of the Party
in February 1920)

The seignorial and crown lands have been turned over to the peasantry. Our whole policy is directed against the peasants who possess a large area of land and a large number of horses (the kulaks). On the other hand, our food policy is based upon the requisitioning of the surpluses of agricultural production (above consumer norms). This prompts the peasant not to cultivate his land except for his family needs. In particular, the decree on the requisitioning of every third cow (regarded as superfluous) leads in reality to the clandestine slaughter of cows, the secret sale of the meat at high prices and the disorganization of the dairy products industry. At the same time, the semiproletarian and even proletarian elements of the towns are settling in the villages, where they are starting their own farms. Industry is losing its workers, and in agriculture the number of self-sufficient farms tends to increase constantly. By that very fact, the basis of our food policy, established on the requisitioning of surpluses, is undermined. If in the current year the requisitioning yields a greater quantity of products, it must be attributed to the extension of Soviet territory and to a certain improvement in the provisioning apparatus. But in general the food resources of the country are threatened with exhaustion, and no improvement in the requisitioning apparatus will be able to remedy this fact. The tendency toward economic decay can be combated by the following methods:

1. Replace the requisitioning of surpluses with a levy proportional to the quantity of production (a sort of progressive tax on agricultural income), set up in such a way that it is nevertheless more profitable to increase the acreage sown or to cultivate it better.

2. Institute a more rigorous correlation between the delivery to the peasants of industrial products and the quantity of grain furnished by them, not only by cantons and towns, but also by rural farms.

Have the local industrial enterprises participate in this task. Pay the peasants for the raw materials, fuel, and food products supplied by them, partly in products of industrial enterprises.

In any case, it is clear that the present policy—requisitioning food products according to norms of consumption, joint responsibility for delivery of these products, and equal distribution of industrial products—is lowering agricultural production and bringing about the atomization of the industrial proletariat, and threatens to completely disorganize the economic life of the country.

Chapter 7
Planned Economy (1042)

December 1923

In the present oral and written discussion, Order No. 1042 has suddenly, for no apparent reason, attracted attention.[15] Why?

How? Without doubt, the majority of party members have forgotten the significance of this mysterious number. I shall explain. It is the order of the Commissariat of Transport, of May 22, 1920, on the repairing of locomotives. Since then, it would seem, much water has flowed under railroad and other bridges. It would seem that there are now many questions more urgent than whether we correctly or incorrectly organized the repairing of locomotives in 1920. There exist many more recent planning instructions in metallurgy, machine construction, and especially agricultural machinery. There exists the clear and precise resolution of the Twelfth Congress on the meaning and tasks of planned management. We have the recent experience of planned production for 1923. Why, then, is it precisely now that a plan dating back to the period of war communism has reappeared, like the *deus ex machina,* to use an expression of the Roman theater?

It has come forward because behind the machine there were stage directors for whom its appearance was necessary for the climax. Who are these stage directors and why did they suddenly find themselves in need of Order No. 1042? It is entirely incomprehensible. You would have to believe that this order was found necessary by people in the toils of an irresistible concern for historical truth. Obviously, they too know that there are many other questions more important and more timely than the plan for repairing the rolling stock of the railroads, set up almost four years ago. But is it possible—judge for yourselves!—to go forward, to establish new plans, to be responsible for their correctness, for their success, without beginning by explaining to everyone, to every single, solitary person, that Order No. 1042 was a false order, which neglected the factor of the peasantry, despised the tradition of the party, and led to the forming of a faction? At first sight, 1042 seems to be a simple order number. But if you delve into the matter more deeply, you will see that the number 1042 is no better than the apocalyptic number "666," symbol of the ferocious beast. It is necessary to begin by smashing the head of the beast of the Apocalypse and then we shall be able to talk at leisure about other economic plans not yet covered by a four-year-old past. . . .

To tell the truth, I had no desire at first to take up the time of my reader with Order No. 1042. All the more so because the attacks directed at it boil down to subterfuges or to vague allusions aimed at showing that the people who use them know a lot more than they are saying, whereas in reality the poor creatures know nothing whatsoever. In this sense, the "accusations" against No. 1042 do not differ greatly from the 1041 other accusations. . . . Quantity is presumably to substitute here for quality. The facts are unscrupulously misrepresented, the texts are distorted, proportions are scorned, and the whole is dumped into a heap without order or method. In order to get a clear idea of the differences of opinion and the mistakes of the past, it would be necessary to reconstitute exactly the situation of the time. Do we have the spare time for it? And, if so, is it worthwhile, after having neglected so many other essentially false hints and accusations, to react to the reappearance of "Order No. 1042"?

Upon reflection, I told myself that it was necessary, for we have here a case, classic in its kind . . . of lightmindedness and bad faith in an accusation. The affair of Order 1042 did not occur in the ideological sphere, but was a material affair, in the field of production, and consequently was measured in figures and weights. It is relatively simple and easy to gather reliable information about it, to report actual facts; also, the use of simple prudence would have guided those who concern themselves with the subject, for it is fairly easy to show them that they are talking about something they do not know and do not understand. And if it turns out from this concrete, precise example that the *deus ex machina* is only a frivolous buffoon, it will perhaps help a number of readers to understand the staging methods behind the other "accusations," whose inanity is unfortunately much less verifiable than that of Order 1042.

I shall endeavor, in my exposition of the affair, not to confine myself to historical data and to link the question of Order 1042 to the problems of planned production and management. The concrete examples that I shall give will probably render the affair a little clearer.

Order 1042, concerning the repairing of locomotives and the methodical utilization toward this end of all the appropriate forces and resources of the railroad administration and the state, was worked out for a long time by the best specialists, who to this day occupy high posts in railroad management. The application of Order 1042 was actually begun in May-June, formally on July 1, 1920. The plan was the concern not only of the roundhouses of the railway lines but also of the corresponding plants of the Council of National Economy. We present below a comparative table, showing the realization of the plan, on the one hand by the railroad roundhouses, and on the other hand by the plants of the

Council of National Economy. Our figures are a reproduction of
the incontestable official data presented periodically to the Council of Labor and Defense by the Main Transportation Commission and signed by the representatives of the Commissariat of
Transport and the Council of National Economy.

REALIZATION OF ORDER NO. 1042
(Percentage of Realization of the Plan)

	Railroad Roundhouses	Plants of the Council of National Economy
1920		
July	135	40.5
August	131.6	74
September	139.3	80
October*	130	51
November	124.6	70
December	120.8	66
Total	129.7	70**
1921		
January	95	36
February	90	38
March	98	26
April	101	

(Emshanov was Commissar of Transport in 1921.)

Thus, thanks to the intensification of the work of the roundhouses of the Commissariat of Transport, it was possible beginning with October to increase by 28 percent the monthly norms of
production. In spite of this increase, the execution of the plan in
the second half of 1920 exceeded the established norm by 130
percent. During the first four months of 1921, the execution of the
plan was a little below 100 percent. But following that, under
Dzerzhinsky, matters lying outside the authority of the Commis-

---

*In view of the successes obtained in the execution of the plan, the
norms set were raised, beginning with October, by 28 percent.—L.T.

**In supplying the railroad roundhouses with material and spare parts,
the plants of the Council of National Economy accomplished only 30
percent of the program they had undertaken to achieve.—L.T.

sariat of Transport interfered with the execution of the plan: on the one hand, the lack of material and of supplies for the repair work itself, and on the other hand, the extreme insufficiency of fuel, which made impossible the utilization even of the available locomotives. As a result, the Council of Labor and Defense decided, in an order of April 22, 1921, to reduce considerably, for the balance of 1921, the repair norms on locomotives established in plan 1042. For the last eight months of 1921, the work of the Commissariat of Transport represented 80 percent and that of the Council of National Economy 44 percent of the original plan.

The results of the execution of Order 1042 in the first semester, the most critical one for transportation, are set forth in the following way in the theses of the Eighth Congress of Soviets, approved by the Political Bureau of the party's Central Committee:

"The repair program has thus acquired a precise temporal character not only for the railroad roundhouses, but also for the plants of the Council of National Economy working for transportation. The repair program, established at the cost of considerable labor and approved by the Main Transportation Commission, was nevertheless carried out in very different proportions in the railroad roundhouses (Commissariat of Transport) and in the plants (Council of National Economy): while in the roundhouses, major and minor repairs, expressed in units of average repair, *increased this year from 258 locomotives to more than 1,000, that is, four times,* this representing 130 percent of the fixed monthly program, the plants of the Council of National Economy supplied material and spare parts only in the proportion of *one-third of the program* established by the Commissariat of Transport in agreement with the two departments of the Main Transportation Commission."

But we see that after a certain time the execution of the norms set up by Order 1042 became impossible as a result of the shortage of raw materials and fuel. That is just what proves the order erroneous!—will say certain critics, who, by the way, have just learned this fact from reading these lines. They must be given the following answer: Order 1042 regulated the repairing of locomotives, but in no instance the production of metal and the mining of coal, which were regulated by other orders and other institutions. Order 1042 was not a universal economic plan, but only a transportation plan.

But was it not necessary, it will be asked, to harmonize it with the resources in fuel, in metals, etc.? Indisputably; and that is precisely why the Main Transportation Commission was created with the *participation on a parity basis of representatives of the Commissariat of Transport and the Council of National Economy.* The establishment of the plan took place according to the indications of the representatives of the Council of National Economy, who declared that they were in a position to supply such and such materials. Therefore, if there was an error in calculation, the fault is *entirely upon the Council of National Economy.*[16]

Perhaps, after all, that is what the critics meant to say? It is doubtful, very doubtful! The "critics" display the greatest solicitude for historical truth, but only on the condition that it sticks by them. Among these post factum critics there are, alas, some who bore the responsibility at the time for the stewardship of the Council of National Economy. In their criticisms, they simply made a mistake in address. That can happen. As extenuating circumstances, moreover, it should be pointed out that forecasts concerning the mining of coal, the production of metals, etc., were much more difficult to establish then than now. If the forecasts of the Commissariat of Transport on the repairing of locomotives were incomparably more exact than those of the Council of National Economy, the reason for it is—at least up to a certain point—that the administration of the railroads was more centralized and had greater experience. We readily acknowledge that. But that alters nothing in the fact that the error in evaluation was wholly attributable to the Council of National Economy.

This error, which necessitated the reduction of the norms of the plan but did not cause the abolition of the plan itself, testifies neither directly nor indirectly against Order 1042, which essentially bore the character of an orientation and carried provisions for periodic alterations suggested by experience. *The checking of a plan of production is one of the most important points in its realization.* We have seen above that the production norms of Order 1042 were raised, beginning with October 1920, by 28 percent, because the productive capacity of the roundhouses of the Commissariat of Transport proved to be greater, thanks to the measures taken, than had been supposed. We have likewise seen that these norms were strongly reduced, beginning with May 1921, as a result of circumstances beyond the control of the said Commissariat. But the raising or lowering of these standards followed a definite plan, for which Order 1042 furnished the basis.

That is the maximum that can be demanded of an orientation

plan. Naturally, the greatest significance was borne by the figures dealing with the first months, the first half year; the further figures had only theoretical significance. None of those who participated in the working out of the order thought at the time that its execution would last exactly four and a half years. When it proved possible to raise the norm, the theoretical period was reduced to three and a half years. The lack of materials caused the period to be prolonged again. But it remains nonetheless established that in the most critical period of the functioning of transportation (end of 1920, beginning of 1921) the order proved to be in conformity with reality, the repair of locomotives was effected according to a definite plan, was quadrupled, and the railroads averted the imminent catastrophe.

We do not know with what ideal plans our honorable critics compare Order 1042. It seems to us that it ought to be compared with the situation existing before its promulgation. In those days, locomotives were allocated to every factory that asked for them in order to provide itself with food products. It was a desperate measure that entailed the disorganization of transportation and a monstrous waste of the work needed for repairs. Order 1042 established unity and introduced into repair work the elements of rational organization of labor by assigning definite series of locomotives to definite plants, so that the repair of the stock no longer depended upon the diffused efforts of the working class as a whole but upon a more or less exact registration of the forces and resources of the transportation administration. Therein lies the importance in principle of Order 1042, regardless of the degree to which the figures of the plan coincide with the figures of its execution. But as we said above, in this respect too all went well.

Naturally, now that the facts are forgotten, anything that enters one's mind can be said about plan 1042 in the hope that nobody will think of checking up on it and that, come what may, something will stick. But in those days, the affair was perfectly clear and incontestable. Dozens of testimonials may be cited. We will choose three of them, from different authors, but each one characteristic of its type.

On June 3, *Pravda* evaluated the situation in transportation as follows: ". . . Now the functioning of transportation has, in certain respects, improved. Any observer, even a superficial one, can record that a certain, although elementary, order exists *now* but did not exist *before*. For the first time, *a precise production plan* was worked out, a definite task was assigned to the shops, the factories, and the roundhouses. This is the first time since the revolution that a complete and exact registration of all the production possibilities exists in reality and not merely on paper. In this respect, Order 1042, signed by Trotsky, represents a turn in our work in the field of transportation. . . ."

It may be objected that this testimony is only an anticipatory evaluation and that, being signed N.B., it was only the opinion of Bukharin. We do not contest that. Nevertheless, in this passage, *Pravda* recognized that a beginning had been made in introducing order into the repair of rolling stock.

But we shall report more authoritative testimony, based upon the experience of half a year. At the Eighth Congress of the Soviets, Lenin said: ". . . You have already seen in the theses of Emshanov and Trotsky, among others, that in this field [transport restoration] we have a genuine plan worked out for several years. Order 1042 covers five years; in five years we can restore our transportation and reduce the number of locomotives damaged; and—important fact—the ninth thesis points out that we have already cut down on the schedule.

"When big plans worked out for several years appear, skeptics frequently come forward to say: 'What good is making forecasts for years in advance? If we can fulfill our present tasks, we shall be doing well.' Comrades, we must learn to link the two things.

"You cannot work with any serious chance of success without having a plan set up for a prolonged period of time. What proves the necessity of such a plan is the incontestable improvement in the functioning of transportation. I wish to draw your attention to the ninth thesis where it says that the schedule for restoring transport would be four and a half years, but that has already been cut down because we are doing better than the scheduled norms; the schedule has already been set at three and a half years. That is how the work must be done in the other branches of economy. . . ."

Finally, one year after the publication of Order 1042, we read in the order of Dzerzhinsky, "Foundations of the Future Work of the Commissariat of Transport," dated May 27, 1921: "Whereas the reduction of the norms of Orders 1042 and 1157,* which were *the brilliant first experience in planned economy,* is temporary and produced by the fuel crisis we are undergoing . . . it is proper to

---

*Order 1157 did for car repairing what Order 1042 did for locomotives.— L.T.

take the necessary measures for the maintenance and restoration of the tool stock and the shops. . . ."

Thus, after an experience of a year and the forced reduction of the norms for repair work, the new director (after Emshanov) of the railroads recognized that Order 1042 was "the brilliant first experience in planned economy." I strongly doubt that it will now be possible to twist history long after the fact, even if only that history which relates to the repair of rolling stock. However, at the present moment, several persons are zealously engaged in precisely this type of "repair," trying to twist yesterday's history and adapt it to the "needs" of the hour. Nevertheless, I do not believe that this repair work (also carried out according to a "plan"!) has any social utility or that in the long run it will yield any tangible results.

Marx, it is true, called the revolution the locomotive of history. . . . But while it is possible to patch up the locomotives of the railroads, the same cannot be done to the locomotive of history, particularly not after the fact. In plain language, such attempts at repairing history are called falsifications.*

As we have seen, the Main Transportation Commission partially and gropingly realized a harmony of related branches of economy, a job which now represents, on a much bigger and more systematic scale, the task of the State Planning Commission (Gosplan). The example we adduced shows at the same time wherein consist the tasks and the difficulties of planned economy.

No branch of industry, big or small, nor any enterprise at all, can rationally distribute its resources and forces without having

---

*To muddle up the question you can, of course, ignore the facts and figures and speak of the Sectran (the merged Central Committees of the Railroad and Marine Transport Workers Unions, under Trotsky's direction, whose purpose was the reconstruction of transportation in Russia), or of orders for locomotives abroad. I therefore deem it necessary to point out that these questions have no relationship between them. Order 1042 continued to govern the repair work under Emshanov and then under Dzerzhinsky, whereas the composition of the Sectran was entirely changed. As to the ordering of locomotives abroad, I would note that **this whole operation was resolved and realized outside the Commissariat of Transport and independently of Order 1042 and its execution. Is there, by chance, anybody who will challenge this?**— L.T.

a plan of orientation before it. At the same time, all these partial plans are relative, depend upon each other, and condition each other. This reciprocal dependency must necessarily serve as the fundamental criterion in the working out of the plans and then in their realization, that is, in their periodic verification on the basis of results obtained.

It is cheap and easy to poke fun at plans set up for many years which subsequently prove to be soap bubbles. There have been many such plans, and it is not necessary to say that economic fantasies have no place in the economy. But in order to reach the point of setting up rational plans, it is unfortunately necessary to begin with primitive and rough plans, just as it was necessary to begin with the hatchet and the stone before getting to the steel knife.

It is worth noting that to this day many persons have puerile ideas on the question of planned economy: "We do not need," they say, "numerous [?!] plans; we have an electrification plan, let's carry it out!" Such reasoning denotes a complete lack of understanding of the very ABCs of the question. The orientation plan of electrification is entirely subordinate to the orientation plans of the fundamental branches of industry, transportation, finance, and finally agriculture. All these partial plans must first be harmonized with each other on the basis of the data we have at our disposal about our economic resources and possibilities.

It is such a concerted general plan, an annual plan for example (comprising the annual fractions of particular plans for three years, for five years, etc., and representing only working hypotheses), that can and should form the basis in practice on which the directing organ assures the realization of the plan, and that introduces into it the necessary modifications in the very course of this realization. Such leadership, employing all the necessary flexibility and freedom of movement, does not degenerate (that is, should not degenerate) into a series of improvisations, inasmuch as it will base itself upon a logical general conception of the whole course of the economic process and, while introducing the necessary modifications into it, will be imbued with the endeavor to perfect the economic plan and concretize it in conformity with material conditions and resources.

Such is the most general pattern of planning in state economy. But the existence of the *market* extraordinarily complicates its realization. In the peripheral regions, state economy allies itself or at least tries to ally itself with petty peasant economy. The direct organ of the *smychka* is the trade in products of light, and partly of medium, industry, and it is only indirectly, partially, or subsequently, that heavy industry, directly serving the state (army, transportation, state industry), comes into play. Peasant economy is not governed by a plan, it is conditioned by the market, which develops spontaneously. The state can and should act upon it, push it forward, but it is still absolutely incapable of channeling it according to a single plan. Many years will still be needed before that point is reached (probably thanks above all to electrification). For the next period, which is what interests us practically, we shall have a planned state economy, allying itself more and more with the peasant market and, as a result, adapting itself to the latter in the course of its growth. Although this market develops spontaneously, it does not follow at all that state industry should adapt itself to it spontaneously. On the contrary, our success in economic organization will depend in large part upon the degree to which we succeed, by means of an exact knowledge of market conditions and correct economic forecasts, in harmonizing state industry with agriculture according to a definite plan. A certain amount of competition between different state factories or between trusts changes nothing in the fact that the state is the owner of all nationalized industry and that as owner, administrator, and manager, it looks upon its property as a unit with relation to the peasant market.

Obviously, it is impossible to get an exact advance estimate of the peasant market, as it is of the world market with which our link will tighten principally through the export of grain and raw materials. Errors of evaluation are inevitable, if only because of the variability of the harvest, etc. These errors will manifest themselves through the market in the form of partial and even general scarcity of products, convulsions, and crises. Nevertheless, it is clear that these crises will be less acute and prolonged, the more seriously planned economy pervades all the branches of state economy, constantly uniting them among themselves. If the doctrine of the Brentanists (followers of the German economist Lujo Brentano) and the Bernsteinists, according to which the domination of the capitalist trusts "regulates" the market by making commercial-industrial crises impossible, was radically false, it is entirely correct when applied to the workers' state considered as a trust of trusts and bank of banks. Put differently, the extension or reduction of the scope of the crisis will be the clearest and most infallible barometer in our economy of the successes of state economy in comparison with the movement of private capital. In the struggle of state industry for the domination of the market, planned economy is our principal weapon. Without it, nationalization itself would become an obstacle to economic development, and private capital would inevitably undermine the foundations of socialism.

By state economy we mean of course transportation, foreign and domestic trade, and finance, in addition to industry. This whole "combine"—in its totality as well as in its parts—adapts itself to the peasant market and to the individual peasant as a taxpayer. But this adaptation has as its fundamental aim to raise, consolidate, and develop *state industry as the keystone of the dictatorship of the proletariat and the basis of socialism.* It is radically false to think that it is possible to develop and perfect certain parts of this "combine" in isolation: be it transportation or finances or anything else. Their progress and retrogression are in close interdependence. That is the source of the immense importance in principle of Gosplan, whose role it is so hard to make understood among us.

Gosplan must coordinate, i.e., systematically unite and direct, all the fundamental factors of the state economy and bring them into correct relationship with the national economy, that is, primarily with the peasant economy. Its principal concern must be the development of state (socialist) industry. It is precisely in this sense that I said that within the state combine, the "dictatorship" must be in the hands not of finance but of industry.[17] Naturally, the word "dictatorship"—as I have pointed out—has here a very restricted and very conditional character: it is counterposed to the "dictatorship" which was claimed by finance. In other words, not only foreign trade but also the restoration of a stable currency must be rigorously subordinated to the interests of state industry. It goes without saying that this is in no way directed against the *smychka,* that is, against correct relationships between the state combine as a whole and the peasant economy. On the contrary, it is only in this way that we will gradually succeed in transferring this *smychka* from the realm of mere rhetoric to the realm of economic reality. To say that by posing the question this way the peasantry is "neglected," or that a sweep is sought for state industry such as does not correspond to the condition of the national economy as a whole, is sheer absurdity and does not become more convincing with repetition.

The following words from my report to the Twelfth Congress

best show what upsurge was expected from industry in the next period and who were the ones that demanded such an upsurge:

"I said that we have been working at a loss. That is not only my personal assessment. It is shared by official economic administrators. I urge you to take the pamphlet by Khalatov, *On Wages,* which has just appeared for the congress. It contains a preface by Rykov which says: 'At the beginning of this third year of our New Economic Policy, it must be recognized that the successes obtained in the two preceding years are still insufficient, that we have not even succeeded in halting fully the decline in fixed capital and circulating capital, to say nothing of a transition to an accumulation and augmentation of the productive forces of the republic. During this third year, we must reach the point where the principal branches of our industry and transportation yield a profit.'

"Thus Rykov records that during this year our fixed capital and our circulating capital have continued to decline. 'This third year,' he says, 'we must reach the point where the principal branches of our industry and transportation yield a profit.' I readily associate myself with this desire of Rykov; but I do not share his optimistic hope in the results of our work during this third year. I do not believe that the fundamental branches of our industry can already bring in a profit during the third year and I consider that *it will be fine if we first of all figure our losses better during the third year of the NEP than we did during the second, and if we can prove that during the third year our losses in the most important branches of industry, transportation, fuel, and metallurgy will be lower than during the second.* What is important, above all, is to establish the tendency of development and to assist its unfolding. If our losses diminish and industry progresses, we shall have won the day, we shall reach victory, that is, profit. But the curve must develop in our favor."

Thus it is absurd to assert that the question boils down to the *tempo* of the development and is almost determined . . . by "temperament." In reality, it is a question of the *direction* of the development.

But it is very hard to discuss with people who bring every new, precise, concrete question back to a more general question that has already been resolved a long time ago. We must concretize the general formulas, and that is the point of a large part of our discussion: we must pass from the general formula of setting up the *smychka,* to the more concrete problem of the "scissors"

(Twelfth Congress), from the problem of the "scissors" to the effective planned regulation of the economic factors determining prices (Thirteenth Congress). There, to employ the Old Bolshevik terminology, is the struggle against economic "tail-endism." Without success in this ideological struggle, there can be no economic successes whatsoever.*

The repair of rolling stock was not, in 1920, a constituent part of a total economic plan, for at that time, despite the tower of Babel erected by bureaucratic "Centers," there was no question as yet of such a plan. The lever of planning was applied to transportation, that is, to the branch of economy which was then most imperiled and which threatened to collapse completely. That is precisely how we posed the question at the time. "In the conditions in which the entire Soviet economy now finds itself," we wrote in the theses for the Eighth Congress of Soviets, "when the working out and application of a single plan has not yet gone beyond empirical agreements of the most closely related *parts* of this future plan, it was absolutely impossible for the railroad administration to construct its plan of repair and management on the basis of data from a single economic plan which first had to be worked out." Improved, thanks to the repair plan, transportation ceased being a minus and in turn collided with other "minuses": metallurgy, grain, coal. By the same token, plan 1042 posed in its development the question of a general economic plan. The NEP modified the conditions in which this question was posed and consequently the methods of solving it. But the question itself remained in all its acuteness. That is attested to by the repeated decisions on the need of making Gosplan the general staff of the Soviet economy.

But we shall return to this in detail, for economic tasks demand an independent, concrete examination.

The historical facts I have just adduced show, I hope, that our critics raked up Order 1042 in vain. The fate of this order proves exactly the opposite of what they wanted to prove. Inasmuch as we already know their methods, we expect to hear them declaim aloud: What good does it do to bring up old questions and examine an order published four years ago! It is terribly hard to satisfy people who are determined at all costs to do a repair

---

*We once again advise all comrades seriously interested in this question to reread and, if possible, study attentively the discussions of the Twelfth Congress of the party on industry.—L.T.

job on yesterday's history. But we do not intend to satisfy them. We have confidence in the readers who are not interested in fixing up history but who endeavor to discover the truth, to turn it into an assimilated part of their experience, and, basing themselves upon it—to build further.

Appendix 1
The New Course
(A Letter to Party Meetings)

December 8, 1923

Dear Comrades:

I had confidently hoped to be recovered soon enough to be able to participate in the discussion of the internal situation and the new tasks of the party. But my illness came at a more inopportune time than ever before and proved to be of longer duration than the first forecasts of the doctors. There is nothing left but to expound my view to you in the present letter.

The resolution of the Political Bureau on party organization bears an exceptional significance. It indicates that the party has arrived at an important turning point in its historical road. At turning points, as has been rightly pointed out at many meetings, prudence is required; but firmness and resoluteness are required too. Hesitancy and amorphousness would be the worst forms of imprudence in this case.

Inclined to overestimate the role of the apparatus and to underestimate the initiative of the party, some conservative-minded comrades criticize the resolution of the Political Bureau. The Central Committee, they say, is assuming impossible obligations; the resolution will only engender illusions and produce negative results. It is clear that such an approach reveals a profound bureaucratic distrust of the party. The center of gravity, which was mistakenly placed in the apparatus by the "old course," has now been transferred by the "new course," proclaimed in the resolution of the Central Committee, to the activity, initiative, and critical spirit of all the party members, as the organized vanguard of the proletariat. The "new course" does not at all signify that the party apparatus is charged with decreeing, creating, or establishing a democratic regime at such and such a date. No. This regime will be realized by the party itself. To put it briefly: *the party must subordinate to itself its own apparatus* without for a moment ceasing to be a centralized organization.

In the debates and articles of recent times, it has been underlined that "pure," "complete," "ideal" democracy is not realizable and that in general for us it is not an end in itself. That is incontestable. But it can be stated with just as much reason that pure, absolute centralism is unrealizable and incompatible with the nature of a mass party, and that it can no more be an end in itself than can the party apparatus. Democracy and centralism are two faces of party organization. The question is to harmonize them in the most correct manner, that is, the manner best corresponding to the situation. During the last period there was no such equilibrium. The center of gravity wrongly lodged in the apparatus. The initiative of the party was reduced to the minimum. Thence the habits and procedures of leadership fundamentally contradicting the spirit of a revolutionary proletarian organization. The excessive centralization of the apparatus at the expense of initiative engendered a feeling of *uneasiness,* an uneasiness which, at the extremities of the party, assumed an exceedingly morbid form and was translated, among other ways, in the appearance of illegal groupings directed by elements undeniably hostile to communism. At the same time, the whole of the party disapproved more and more of apparatus methods of solving questions. The idea, or at the very least the feeling, that bureaucratism threatened to get the party into a blind alley, had become quite general. Voices were raised to point out the danger. The resolution on the "new course" is the first official expression of the change that has taken place in the party. It will be realized to the degree that the party, that is, its 400,000 members, want to realize it and succeed in doing so.

In a number of articles, efforts are being made to demonstrate that in order to give life to the party, it is necessary to begin by raising the level of its members, after which everything else, that is, workers' democracy, will come of its own accord. It is incontestable that we must raise the ideological level of our party in order to enable it to accomplish the gigantic tasks devolving upon it. But precisely because of this, such a purely *pedagogical,* professorial way of putting the question is insufficient and hence erroneous. To persist in it cannot fail to aggravate the crisis.

The party cannot raise its level except by accomplishing its essential tasks, and by exercising the kind of collective leadership that displays the initiative of the working class and the proletarian state. The question must be approached not from the *pedagogical* but from the *political* point of view. The application of workers' democracy cannot be made dependent upon the degree of "preparation" of the party members for this democracy. A party is a party. We can make stringent demands upon those who want to enter and stay in it; but once they are members, they participate most actively, by that fact, in all the work of the party.

Bureaucratism kills initiative and thus prevents the elevation of the general level of the party. That is its cardinal defect. As the apparatus is made up inevitably of the most experienced and most meritorious comrades, it is upon the political training of the young communist generations that bureaucratism has its most grievous repercussions. Also, it is the youth, the most reliable barometer of the party, that reacts most vigorously against party bureaucratism.

Nevertheless, it should not be thought that our system of solving questions—they are settled almost exclusively by the party functionaries—has no influence on the older generation, which incarnates the political experience and the revolutionary traditions of the party. There too the danger is very great. It is not necessary to speak of the immense authority of the group of party veterans, not only in Russia but internationally; that is universally recognized. But it would be a crude mistake to regard it as *absolute. It is only by a constant active collaboration with the new generation, within the framework of democracy, that the Old Guard will preserve itself as a revolutionary factor.* Of course, it may ossify and become unwittingly the most consummate expression of bureaucratism.

History offers us more than one case of degeneration of the "Old Guard." Let us take the most recent and striking example: that of the leaders of the parties of the Second International. We know that Wilhelm Liebknecht, Bebel, Singer, Victor Adler, Kautsky, Bernstein, Lafargue, Guesde, and many others were the direct pupils of Marx and Engels.[18] Yet we know that in the atmosphere of parliamentarism and under the influence of the automatic development of the party and the trade union apparatus, all these leaders turned, in whole or in part, to opportunism. We saw that, on the eve of the war, the formidable apparatus of the social democracy, covered with the authority of the old generation, had become the most powerful brake upon revolutionary progress. And we, the "elders," ought to say to ourselves plainly that our generation, which naturally enjoys the leading role in the party, is not *absolutely* guaranteed against the gradual and imperceptible weakening of the revolutionary and proletarian spirit in its ranks if the party were to tolerate the further growth and stabilization of bureaucratic methods, which transform the youth into the passive material of education and inevitably create an estrangement between the apparatus and the mass, the old and the young. The party has no other means to employ against this indubitable danger than a serious, profound, radical change of course toward party democracy and an increasingly large flow into its midst of working class elements.

I shall not dwell here upon the juridical definitions of party democracy, nor upon the limits imposed on it by the party statutes. However important they may be, these questions are secondary. We shall examine them in the light of our experience and will introduce into them the necessary modifications. But what must be modified before anything else is the spirit that reigns in our organizations. Every unit of the party must return to collective initiative, to the right of free and comradely criticism—without fear and without turning back—and to the right of organizational self-determination. It is necessary to regenerate and renovate the party apparatus and to make it feel that it is nothing but the executive mechanism of the collective will.

The party press has recently presented not a few examples that characterize the already ossified bureaucratic degeneration of party morals and relations. The answer to the first word of criticism is: "Let's have your membership card!" Before the publication of the decision of the Central Committee on the "new course," merely pointing out the need to modify the internal party regime was regarded by bureaucratized apparatus functionaries as heresy, as factionalism, as an infraction of discipline. And now the bureaucrats are ready formally to "take note" of the "new course," that is, *to nullify it bureaucratically.* The renovation of the party apparatus—naturally within the clear-cut framework of the statutes—must aim at replacing the mummified bureaucrats with fresh elements closely linked with the life of the collectivity or capable of assuring such a link. And before anything else, the leading posts must be cleared of those who, at the first word of criticism, of objection, or of protest, brandish the thunderbolts of penalties before the critic. The "new course" must begin by making everyone feel that from now on nobody will dare terrorize the party.

It is entirely insufficient for our youth to repeat our formulas. They must conquer the revolutionary formulas, assimilate them, work out their own opinions, their own character; they must be capable of fighting for their views with the courage which arises out of the depths of cor ·iction and independence of character. Out of the party with passive obedience, with mechanical leveling by the authorities, with suppression of personality, with servility, with careerism! A Bolshevik is not merely a disciplined person; he is a person who in each case and on each question forges a firm opinion of his own and defends it courageously and independently, not only against his enemies, but inside his own party. Today, perhaps, he will be in the minority in his organization. He will submit, because it is his party. But this does not always signify that he is in the wrong. Perhaps he saw or understood before the others did a new task or the necessity of a turn. He will persistently raise the question a second, a third, a tenth time, if need be. Thereby he will render his party a service, helping it to meet the new task fully armed or to carry out the necessary turn without organic upheavals, without factional convulsions.

Yes, our party would be unable to discharge its historic mission if it were chopped up into factions. That should not and will not happen. It will not decompose in this way because, autonomous collectivity that it is, its organism resists it. But it will successfully combat the dangers of factionalism only by developing and consolidating the new course toward workers' democracy. *Bureaucratism of the apparatus is precisely one of the principal sources of factionalism.* It ruthlessly represses criticism and drives discontent back into the depths of the organization. It tends to put the label of factionalism upon any criticism, any warning. Mechanical centralism is necessarily complemented by factionalism, which is at once a malicious caricature of democracy and a potential political danger.

Conscious of the situation, the party will accomplish the necessary turn with the firmness and decisiveness demanded by the tasks devolving upon it. By the same token, it will raise its revolutionary unity to a higher level, as a pledge that it will be able to accomplish its immeasurably significant national and international tasks.

I am far from having exhausted the question. I deliberately

refrained from examining here several essential aspects, out of
fear of taking up too much of your time. But I hope that I shall
soon succeed in recovering from malaria which—to judge from
myself—is in clear opposition to the "new course." Then I hope to
be able to do orally what was not possible in this letter—more
fully to supplement and elaborate my views.

With comradely greetings,

L. Trotsky

P.S.—The publication of this letter in *Pravda* having been
postponed for two days, I take advantage of the delay to add a
few supplementary remarks.

I have learned from some comrades that during the reading of
my letter to the district meetings, certain comrades expressed the
fear that my considerations on the relationships between the
"Old Guard" and the young generation might be exploited to
counterpose (!) the youth to the old. Unquestionably, this appre-
hension could have assailed only those who, but two or three
months ago, rejected with horror the very idea of the necessity of
a change in orientation.

At any rate, to place apprehensions of this type in the fore-
ground *at the present moment* and *in the present situation* denotes a lack of understanding of the real dangers and of their
relative importance. The present mood of the youth, symptomatic
to the highest degree, is engendered precisely by the methods
employed to maintain "calm" which are formally condemned by
the resolution *unanimously* adopted by the Political Bureau. In
other words, "calm," as it was understood, threatened the leading
layer with increasing estrangement from the younger communists, that is, from the vast majority of the party.

A certain tendency of the apparatus to think and to decide for
the whole organization leads to seating the authority of the
leading circles *exclusively* upon tradition. Respect for tradition is
incontestably a necessary element of communist training and
party cohesion, but it can be a vital factor only if it is nurtured
and fortified constantly by an active verification of this tradition,
that is, by the collective elaboration of the party's policy for the
present moment. Otherwise, it may degenerate into a purely
official sentiment, and be nothing more than a *hollow form.* Such
a link between the generations is obviously insufficient and most
fragile. It may appear to be solid right up to the moment when it
is ready to break. That is precisely the danger of the policy of
"calm" in the party.

And, if the veterans who are not yet bureaucratized, who have still kept a revolutionary spirit alive (that is, we are convinced, the vast majority), become clearly aware of the danger pointed out above and help the party with all their strength to apply the resolution of the Political Bureau of the Central Committee, every reason for counterposing the generations in the party will disappear. It would then be relatively easy to calm the passions, the possible "excesses," of the youth. But what is necessary first of all is to act so that the tradition of the party is not concentrated in the leading apparatus, but lives and is constantly renewed in the daily experience of the organization as a whole. In this way, another danger will be parried: that of the division of the old generation into "functionaries," charged with maintaining "calm," and nonfunctionaries. No longer enclosed within itself, the party apparatus, that is, its organic skeleton, far from being weakened, will find itself growing stronger. And it is beyond dispute that we need in our party a powerful centralized apparatus.

It may perhaps be objected that the example of the degeneration of the social democracy which I cited in my letter is incorrect in view of the profound differences in epochs: yesterday's stagnant reformism and today's revolutionary epoch. Naturally, an example is only an example and not at all an identity. Nevertheless, this indiscriminate contrast of epochs does not in itself decide anything. Not for nothing do we point to the dangers of the NEP, which are closely linked with the *retardation* of the world revolution. Our daily practical state work, which is more and more detailed and specialized, conceals, as the resolution of the Central Committee points out, a danger of the narrowing down of our horizon, that is, of opportunistic degeneration. It is quite plain that these dangers become all the more serious the more bossing by "secretaries" tends to replace the genuine leadership of the party. We would be shabby revolutionists if we were to rely upon the "revolutionary character of the epoch" for the overcoming of our difficulties, and above all of our internal difficulties. This "epoch" must be assisted by the rational realization of the new orientation *unanimously* proclaimed by the Political Bureau.

To conclude, one more remark. Two or three months ago, when the questions that are the object of the present discussion had not yet appeared on the party's agenda, some responsible comrades from the provinces shrugged their shoulders indulgently and told themselves that these are Moscow inventions; in the provinces all goes well. Even now this tone is reflected in certain correspondence from the provinces. To contrast the tranquil and reasonable province to the turbulent and contaminated capital, is to display that same bureaucratic spirit we spoke about above. In reality, the Moscow organization is the largest, the strongest, the most vital of all our party organizations. Even at the dullest moments of so-called "calm" (the word is a very expressive one, and should not fail to enter our party history!), its activity has been more intense than anywhere else. If Moscow is distinguished now from other points in Russia, it is only in that it has taken the initiative in reexamining the course of our party. That's a merit and not a defect. The whole party will follow in its footsteps and will proceed to the necessary reassessment of certain values of the current period. The less the provincial party apparatus resists this movement, the more easily will the local organizations traverse this inevitable stage of fruitful criticism and self-criticism, whose results will be translated into a growth of the cohesion and an elevation of the ideological level of the party.

L. Trotsky

Appendix 2
Functionarism in the Army and Elsewhere

December 3, 1923

I.

In the course of the last year, the military workers and I have on many occasions exchanged opinions, orally and in writing, on the negative phenomena visible in the army stemming from moldy *functionarism*. I dealt with this question thoroughly enough at the last congress of political workers in the army and navy. But it is so serious that it seems to me opportune to speak of it in our general press, all the more so because the malady is in no sense confined to the army.

Functionarism is closely related to bureaucratism. It might

even be said that it is one of its manifestations. When, as a result
of being habituated to the same form, people cease to think things
through; when they smugly employ conventional phrases without
reflecting on what they mean; when they give the customary
orders without asking if they are rational; when they take fright
at every new word, every criticism, every initiative, every sign of
independence—that indicates that they have fallen into the toils
of the functionary spirit, dangerous to the highest degree.

At the conference of the military political workers, I cited as an
(at first sight) innocent example of functionary ideology some
historical sketches of our military units. The publication of these
works dealing with the history of our armies, our divisions, our
regiments, is a valuable acquisition. It attests that our military
units have been constituted in battle and in technical apprentice-
ship, not only from the standpoint of organization but also from
the spiritual standpoint, as living organisms; and it indicates the
interest shown in their past. But most of these historical
outlines—there is no reason to hide the sin—are written in a
pompous and bombastic tone.

Even more, certain of these works make you recall the old
historical sketches devoted to the guard regiments of the tsar.
This comparison will no doubt provoke gleeful snickers from the
White press. But we would be old washrags indeed if we renounced self-criticism out of fear of providing our enemies with a
trump. The advantages of a salutary self-criticism are incomparably superior to the harm that may result for us from the fact that
Dan or Chernov will repeat our criticism.[19] Yes, let it be known to
the pious (and impious!) old ladies who fall into panic (or create
panic around themselves) at the first sound of self-criticism.

To be sure, our regiments and our divisions, and with them the
country as a whole, have the right to be proud of their victories.
But it wasn't only victories that we had, and we did not attain
these victories directly but along very roundabout roads. During
the civil war we saw displays of unexampled heroism, all the
more worthy because it most often remained anonymous, collective; but we also had cases of weakness, of panic, of pusillanim-
ity, of incompetence, and even of treason. The history of every
one of our "old" regiments (four or five years is already old age in
times of revolution) is extremely interesting and instructive if told
truthfully and vibrantly, that is, the way it unfolded on the
battlefield and in the barracks. Instead of that, you often find a
heroic legend in the most banal functionary manner. To read it,

you would think there are only heroes in our ranks; that every soldier burns with the desire to fight; that the enemy is always superior in numbers; that all our orders are reasonable, appropriate for the occasion; that the execution is brilliant, etc.

To think that by such procedures a military unit can be enhanced in its own eyes, and a happy influence be exerted on the training of the youth, is to be imbued with the moldy spirit of the functionary. In the best of cases, this "history" will leave no impression at all; the Red soldier will read it or listen to it the way his father listened to *Lives of the Saints:* just as magnificent and uplifting, but not true to life. Those who are older, or who participated in the civil war, or who are simply more intelligent, will say to themselves: the military people too are throwing sand in our eyes; or simpler yet: they're giving us a lot of hokum. The more naïve, those who take everything for good coin, will think: How am I, a weak mortal, to raise myself to the level of those heroes? . . . And in this way, this "history," instead of raising their morale, will depress them.*

Historical truth does not have a purely historical interest for us. These historical sketches are needed by us in the first place as a means of *education.* And if, for example, a young commander accustoms himself to the conventional lie about the past, he will speedily reach the point of admitting it into his daily practical and even military activity. If, for example, he happens to commit a blunder, he will ask himself: Ought I report this truthfully? He must! But he has been raised in the functionary spirit; he does not want to derogate the heroes whose exploits he has read in the history of his regiment; or, quite simply, the feeling of responsibility has deadened in him. In that case he trims, that is, he distorts the facts, and deceives his superiors. And false reports of subordinates inevitably produce, in the long run, erroneous orders and dispositions from the superiors. Finally—and this is the worst thing—the commander is simply afraid to report the truth to his chiefs. Functionarism then assumes its most repulsive character: lying to please superiors.

---

*To be sure, not only in the military world but everywhere else, including the field of art, there are advocates of the conventional lie which "uplifts the soul." Criticism and self-criticism to them seem an "acid" that dissolves the will. The petty bourgeois, as is known, needs pseudoclassical consolation and cannot bear criticism. But the same cannot hold for us, revolutionary army and revolutionary party. The youth must relentlessly combat such a state of mind in their ranks.—L.T.

Supreme heroism, in the military art as in the revolution, is veracity and the feeling of responsibility. We speak of veracity not from the standpoint of an abstract morality that teaches that one must never lie or deceive one's neighbor. These idealistic principles are pure hypocrisy in a class society where antagonistic interests, struggles, and wars exist. The military art in particular necessarily includes ruse, dissimulation, surprise, deception. But it is one thing consciously and deliberately to deceive the enemy in the name of a cause for which life itself is given; and another thing to give out harmful and misleading information, assurances that "all goes well," out of false modesty or out of fawning or obsequiousness, or simply under the influence of bureaucratic functionarism.

II.

Why do we now deal with the question of functionarism? How was it posed in the first years of the revolution? We have the army in mind here too, but the reader will himself make the necessary analogies in all other fields of our work, for there is a certain parallel in the development of a class, its party, its state, and its army.

The new cadres of our army were supplemented by revolutionists, fighting militants, and partisans, who had made the October Revolution and who had already acquired a certain past and above all character. The characteristic of these commanders is not lack of initiative but rather excess of initiative or, more exactly, an inadequate understanding of the need for coordination in action and firm discipline ("partisanism"). The first period of military organization was filled with the struggle against all forms of military "independence." The aim then was the establishment of rational relationships and firm discipline. The years of civil war were a hard school in this respect. In the end, the balance necessary between personal independence and the feeling of discipline was successfully established among the best revolutionary commanders from the first levy.

The development of our young army cadres takes place quite differently during the years of truce. As a young man, the future commander enters military school. He has neither revolutionary past nor war experience. He is a neophyte. He does not build up the Red Army as the old generation did; he enters a ready-made organization with an internal regime and definite traditions. Here is a clear analogy with the relationships between the young communists and the Old Guard of the party. That is why the means by which the army's fighting tradition, or the party's revolutionary tradition, is transmitted to the young people is of vast importance. Without a continuous lineage, and consequently without a tradition, there cannot be stable progress. But tradition is not a rigid canon or an official manual; it cannot be learned by heart or accepted as gospel; not everything the old generation says can be believed merely "on its word of honor." On the contrary the tradition must, so to speak, be conquered by internal travail; it must be worked out by oneself in a critical manner, and in that way assimilated. Otherwise the whole structure will be built on sand.

I have already spoken of the representatives of the "Old Guard" (ordinarily of the second and third order) who inculcate tradition into the youth after the example of Famusov: "Learn by looking at the elders: us, for example, or our deceased uncle. . . ."[20] But neither from the uncle nor from his nephews is there anything worth learning.

It is incontestable that our old cadres, which have rendered immortal services to the revolution, enjoy very great authority in the eyes of the young military men. And that's excellent, for it assures the indissoluble bond between the higher and lower commands, and their link with the ranks of the soldiers. But on one condition: that the authority of the old does not exterminate the personality of the young, and most certainly that it does not terrorize them.

It is in the army that it is easiest and most tempting to establish this principle: Keep your mouth shut and don't think. But in the military field, this "principle" is just as disastrous as in any other. The main task consists not in preventing but in aiding the young commander to work out his own opinion, his own will, his personality, in which independence must join with the feeling of discipline. The commander and, as a rule, anyone trained merely to say: Yes, sir! is a nobody. Of such people, the old satirist Saltykov said: "They keep saying yes, yes, yes, till they get you in a mess." With such yes-men the military administrative apparatus, that is, the totality of military bureaus, may still function, not without some success, at least seemingly. But what an army, a mass fighting organizaton, needs is not sycophantic functionaries but men who are strongly tempered morally, permeated with a feeling of personal responsibility, who on every important question will make it their duty to work out conscientiously their personal opinion and will defend it courageously by every means that does not violate rationally (that is, not bureaucratically) understood discipline and unity of action.

The history of the Red Army, like that of its various units, is one of the most important means of establishing mutual understanding and continuity between the old and the new generation of military cadres. That is why bureaucratic obsequiousness, spurious docility, and all other manners of empty well-wishers who know what side their bread is buttered on, cannot be tolerated. What is needed is criticism, checking of facts, independence of thought, the personal elaboration of the present and the future, independence of character, the feeling of responsibility, truth toward oneself and toward one's work. However, those are things that find in functionarism their mortal enemy. Let us therefore sweep it out, smoke it out, and smoke it out of every corner!

Appendix 3
On the 'Smychka'
Between Town and Country
(More Precisely:
On the 'Smychka' and False Rumors)

December 6, 1923

Several times in these recent months, comrades have asked me just what was my point of view on the peasantry and what distinguished it from Lenin's. Others have put the question to me in a more precise and more concrete way: Is it true—they have asked—that you underestimated the role of the peasantry in our economic development and, by that token, do not assign sufficient importance to the economic and political alliance between proletariat and peasantry? Such questions have been put to me orally and in writing.

—But where did you get that? I asked, astonished. On what facts do you base your question?

—That's just it, they answer, we don't know; but there are rumors abroad. . . .

At the outset, I attached no great importance to these conversations. But a new letter I have just received on the subject has made me reflect. Where can these rumors come from? And quite by accident, I recalled that rumors of this sort were widespread in Russia four or five years ago.

At that time, it was simply said: Lenin is for the peasant, Trotsky against. . . . I then set out to look into the articles that appeared on this question: mine, in *Izvestia*, the paper of the All-Union Central Executive Committee, of February 7, 1919, and Lenin's, in *Pravda* of February 15. Lenin was replying directly to the letter of the peasant G. Gulov, who recounted—I quote Lenin—"the rumor is spreading that Lenin and Trotsky are not in agreement, that there are strong differences of opinion between them precisely on the subject of the middle peasant."

In my letter I explained the general character of our peasant policy, our attitude toward the kulaks, the middle peasants, and the poor peasants, and I concluded with this: There have not been and there are not any differences of opinion on this subject in the Soviet power. But the counterrevolutionists, whose business is going from bad to worse, have left as their only resource to fool the toiling masses and to make them believe that the Council of People's Commissars is torn by internal dissension.

In the article which he published a week after mine, Lenin said, among other things: "Comrade Trotsky says that rumours of differences between him and myself are the most monstrous and shameless lie, spread by the landowners and capitalists, or by their witting and unwitting accomplices. For my part, I entirely confirm Comrade Trotsky's statement" [*CW*, Vol. 36, "Reply to a Peasant's Question" (February 14, 1919), p. 500].

Nevertheless, these rumors, as is seen, are difficult to uproot. Remember the French proverb: "Slander, slander, something will always stick." Now, to be sure, it is not the landed proprietors and the capitalists whose game would be played by rumors of this sort, for the number of these honorable gentlemen has declined considerably since 1919. On the other hand, we now have the Nepman and, in the countryside, the merchant and the kulak. It is undeniable that it is in their interests to sow trouble and confusion as to the attitude of the Communist Party toward the peasantry.

It is precisely the kulak, the retailer, the new merchant, the urban broker, who seek a market link with the peasant producer of grain and buyer of industrial products, and endeavor to crowd the Soviet state out of this *smychka*. It is precisely on this field that the main battle is now developing. Here too, politics serves economic interests. Seeking to forge a link with the peasant and to gain his confidence, the private middleman obviously readily welcomes and spreads the old falsehoods of the landlords—only with a little more prudence, because since then the Soviet power has become stronger.

The well-known article of Lenin entitled "Better Fewer, but Better" gives a clear, simple, and at the same time conclusive picture of the economic interdependence of the proletariat and the peasantry, or of state industry and agriculture. It is not necessary to recall or to quote this article, which everyone well remembers. Its fundamental thought is the following: During the coming years, we must adapt the Soviet state to the needs and the strength of the peasantry, while preserving its character as a *workers'* state; we must adapt Soviet industry to the peasant market, on the one hand, and to the taxable capacity of the peasantry, on the other, while preserving its·character as *state,* that is, *socialist* industry. Only in this way shall we be able to avoid destroying the equilibrium in our Soviet state until the revolution will have destroyed the equilibrium in the capitalist states. It is not the repetition of the word *"smychka"* at every turn (although the word itself is a good one), but the *effective adaptation of industry to rural economy* that can really solve the cardinal question of our economy and our politics.

Here we get to the question of the "scissors." The adaptation of industry to the peasant market poses before us in the first place the task of lowering the cost price of industrial products in *every way.* The cost price, however, depends not only on the organization of the work in a given factory, but also on the organization of the whole of state industry, state transportation, state finances, and the state trade apparatus.

If there is a disproportion between the different sections of our industry, it is because the state has an enormous unrealizable capital that weighs upon all of industry and raises the price of every yard of calico and every box of matches. If the staves of a barrel are of different length, then you can fill it with water only up to the shortest stave; otherwise, no matter how much water you pour in, it pours out. If the different parts of our state industry (coal, metals, machinery, cotton, cloth, etc.) do not mesh with each other, or with transportation and credit, the costs of production will likewise include the expenditures of the most inflated branches of industry and the final result will be determined by the less developed branches. The present selling crisis is a harsh warning that the peasant market is giving us: Stop jabbering about the *smychka*; realize it!

In the capitalist regime, the crisis is the natural and, in the long run, the only way of regulating economy, that is, of realizing a harmony between the different branches of industry, and between total production and the capacity of the market. But in our Soviet economy—intermediate between capitalism and social-ism—commercial and industrial crises cannot be recognized as the normal or even inevitable way of harmonizing the different parts of the national economy. The crisis carries off, annihilates, or disperses a certain portion of the possessions of the state and a part of this falls into the hands of the middlemen, the retailers— in general, of private capital. Inasmuch as we have inherited an extremely disorganized industry, the different parts of which, before the war, served each other in entirely different proportions than we must now have, there is great difficulty in harmonizing the different parts of industry in such a manner that it can be adapted, through the medium of the market, to the peasant econ-omy. If we resign ourselves to just letting the effect of the crises achieve the necessary reorganization, we will give all the advan-tages to private capital, which already interposes itself between us and the countryside, that is, the peasant and the worker.*

Private trading capital is now realizing considerable profits. It is less and less content with operating as a middleman. It tries to organize the producer and to rent industrial enterprises from the state. In other words, it is recommencing the process of primitive accumulation, first in the commercial field and then in the indus-trial field. It is plain that every failure, every loss that we experi-ence, is a plus for private capital: first, because it weakens us, and then because a considerable part of this loss falls into the hands of the new capitalist.

What instrument do we have at our disposal to fight success-fully against private capital under these conditions? Is there such an instrument? There is—a consciously *planned* approach to the market and to economic tasks in general. The workers' state has

---

*Until the final establishment of a socialist economy, we shall still have many crises, it goes without saying. The problem is to reduce their number to the minimum and to make each crisis decreasingly painful.— L.T.

in its hands the fundamental productive forces of industry and the means of transportation and credit. We do not need to wait until a partial or general crisis discloses the lack of coordination of the different elements of our economy. We do not need to grope in the dark, because we have in our hands the principal playing cards of the market. We can—and this we must learn!—evaluate better and better the fundamental elements of the economy, foresee their future mutual relationships in the process of production and on the market, bring into harmony quantitatively and qualitatively all the branches of the economy, and adapt the whole of industry to rural economy. That is the real way to work for the realization of the *smychka*.

To educate the village is an excellent thing. But the foundation of the *smychka* is the cheap plow and nail, cheap calico, and cheap matches. The way to reduce the price of the products of industry is through correct (i.e., systematized, planned) organization of the latter in conformity with the development of agriculture.

To say: "Everything depends upon the *smychka* and not upon industrial *planning*," means not to understand the very essence of the question, for the *smychka* cannot be realized unless industry is rationally organized, managed according to a definite plan. There is no other way and there can be none.

The correct posing of the work of our State Planning Commission is the direct and rational way of approaching successfully the solution of the questions relating to the *smychka*—not by suppressing the market, but on the basis of the market.* This the peasant does not yet understand. But we ought to understand it; every communist, every advanced worker, ought to understand it. Sooner or later the peasant will feel the repercussions of the work of Gosplan upon his economy. This task, it goes without saying, is very complicated and extremely difficult. It demands time, a system of increasingly precise and decisive measures. We must emerge from the present crisis as wiser men.

The restoration of agriculture is of course no less important.

---

*To avoid erroneous interpretatations, I will emphasize that it is a question precisely of a correct **approach**, since it is obvious that the question is not exhausted merely by the existence of Gosplan. The factors and conditions upon which the course of industry and the entire economy depend number dozens. But it is only with a solid, competent, ceaselessly working Gosplan that it will be possible to assess these factors and conditions properly and consequently to regulate all of our activity.—L.T.

But it takes place in a much more spontaneous manner, and sometimes depends much less upon the action of the state than upon that of industry. The workers' state must come to the aid of the peasants (to the degree that its means will permit!) by the institution of agricultural credits and agronomical assistance, so as to lighten the task of exporting their products (grain, meat, butter, etc.) on the world market. Nevertheless, it is mainly through industry that we can act directly, if not indirectly, upon agriculture. It must furnish the countryside with agricultural implements and machines at accessible prices. It must give it artificial fertilizers and cheap domestic articles. In order to organize and develop agricultural credits, the state needs a substantial revolving fund. In order to procure it, its industry must yield profits, which is impossible unless its constituent parts are rationally harmonized among themselves. That is the genuinely practical way of working toward the realization of the *smychka* between the working class and the peasantry.

To prepare this alliance politically, and in particular to refute the false rumors and gossip that are spread through the medium of the intermediary trading apparatus, a genuine peasant journal is necessary. What does "genuine" mean in this instance? A journal that would get to the peasants, be comprehensible to them, and bring them closer to the working class. A journal circulating in fifty or a hundred thousand copies will be perhaps a journal in which the peasant is talked to, but not a peasant journal, for it will not get to the peasant; it will be intercepted on the way by our countless "apparatuses," which will each take a certain number of copies for their own use. We need a weekly peasant journal (a daily paper would be too expensive and our means of communication do not make regular delivery possible), with a circulation in the first year of about two million copies. This journal should not "instruct" the peasants or "launch appeals" at them, but tell them what is happening in Soviet Russia and abroad, principally what affects them and their economy directly. The postrevolution peasants will rapidly acquire a taste for reading it if we know how to give them a journal that suits them. This journal, whose circulation will grow from month to month, will assure for the first period weekly communication at the very least between the Soviet state and the vast rural mass. But the very question of the journal itself brings us back to that of industry. The technical side of the journal must be perfect. The peasant journal should be exemplary, not only from the editorial standpoint but also from the typographical point of view, for it would be a shame to send the peasants specimens of our urban negligence every week.

That is all I can say, at this moment, in reply to the questions that have been put to me on the subject of the peasantry. If these explanations do not satisfy the comrades who addressed themselves to me, I am ready to give them more concrete new ones, with precise data drawn from the experience of our whole last six years of Soviet work. For this question is of capital importance.

Appendix 4
Two Generations*

The leading circles of the Russian Communist Youth have intervened in the party discussion. In view of the fact that an article signed by nine comrades ("Two Generations," *Pravda*, No. 1) and an address to the Petrograd militants pose the questions wrongly and may do harm to the party if a wide discussion follows in the RCY, we deem it necessary to analyze their declarations and the reasons that prompt them.

The Petrograd address and the article by the nine say that the youth must not be flattered, that they are not the comptrollers of the party, that the new generation of the party cannot be counterposed to the old, that no degeneration threatens us, that Trotsky is guilty of all these mortal sins, and that the youth must be put on their guard. Let us see: Is that the situation?

In their article the nine say that Trotsky drags in the question of the youth by the hair (we shall return to this later on), that he adapts himself to the youth, that he flatters it. Let us hear what Lenin says on this score: "Soviet schools, workers' schools have been founded; hundreds of thousands of young people are learning there. This work will yield its fruit. If we work without too much precipitateness, in a few years we shall have a mass of young people *capable of radically modifying* our apparatus."

---

*We publish a document that has been sent us and that characterizes the baselessness and the deliberate malice in the assertions about our so-called desire to "counterpose" the youth to the old.—L.T.

Why did Lenin speak this way of the youth? What drove him to it? The desire to get in good with the youth, to flatter them, to obtain their applause? Or was it his real understanding of the situation? It is least of all necessary to speak of "flattery" on the part of Trotsky, and there is absolutely no reason to contrast him to other leaders of our party. The nine comrades say that Lenin taught us to have a critical attitude toward the youth, not to encourage their shortcomings. Did not Comrade Trotsky follow this good advice when he said at the Eleventh Congress of the party, as he says now: ". . . That does not mean, of course, that all the acts and moods of the youth express healthy tendencies," or elsewhere: "The youth of the schools, recruited from all the layers and strata of Soviet society, reflect in their disparate ranks all our sides, good and *defective.*" To judge from these quotations, Trotsky, far from flattering, criticizes.

The question of degeneration is likewise expounded erroneously. Trotsky speaks of the danger of degeneration both for the youth generation and for the old. To this, the editorial board of *Pravda* replies: "The theoretical danger of degeneration exists among us. Its sources lie in the possibility of a steady and gradual victory of capitalist economy over socialist economy and in the possibility of a progressive fusion of our administrative cadres with the new bourgeoisie. But there is nobody among us who does not see this danger."

Yet, what the nine comrades say in their article—"This danger of political degeneration cannot exist among us"—harmonizes in no way with this declaration. Consequently, the accusation and the defense are out of whack.

Let us pass to the most serious accusation: Trotsky counterposes the two generations, eggs them on against each other, "wants to undermine the influence of the tested Bolshevik general staff."

Here is what Trotsky writes: "It would be madness to think of discarding the old generation. What is needed is that precisely this old generation should change its orientation and, by doing so, assure in the future the preponderance of its influence in all the work of the party."

Where is this counterposing of the youth to the old, this desire to undermine the old cadres, which is at the foundation of the arguments of the two documents? It seems to us that if all the above-quoted declarations of Trotsky are quietly and seriously examined, it is impossible to see in them any egging on of the two sections, any intention of animosity. On the contrary, Trotsky understands the "new course" as the best way of consolidating and raising the influence of the Old Bolshevik cadres.

But if all these legends, arbitrary interpretations, and distortions are rejected, and if the essence of the question of how to educate the young communists in the Leninist spirit is studied, it appears clearly that Trotsky is entirely right.

And if the nine militants of the RCY who spoke up take the trouble to examine more closely the situation of the young communist, who is best known to them, they will record the fact that the young communists—party members—feel not that they are party members in the RCY but "communist youth in the party." That is a fact pointed out on many occasions by the most esteemed activists.

What is the deep-seated reason for this? It is that in the narrow party regime, the youth do not have the opportunity to partake in the riches accumulated through our party's long years of work. The best means of transmitting the revolutionary Bolshevik traditions, and all the qualities inherent in the fundamental cadre of the party, is the "new course" of democracy applied "consciously by the old generation in the interest of preserving its leading influence."

Thus, as to the essence of the question, it is not Trotsky who "dragged in by the hair" the question of the youth (which he connects with all the reasons prompting the "new course" of the party) but the authors of the letters who attribute to him a point of view he has never supported.

In actuality (although involuntarily) the nine comrades who brought the RCY into the discussion have reduced the latter to the question of two generations, without linking it to the totality of the discussion and to all the questions the party is posing at the present time. And when the question of the generations itself is posed wrongly, when it is distorted, all statements on it can only be regrettable; and if they lead to a discussion among the militants of the RCY, this discussion will unfold along a false line and will provoke the dissension Trotsky has spoken out against.

The Central Committee of the RCY has decided not to submit the questions raised in the party discussion to special consideration by the party members working in the RCY. We consider this decision entirely correct. In no case can it legitimize the abovementioned article. If the decision barring the introduction of the discussion into the RCY is correct and if militants of the Central

Committee have deemed it necessary to plunge into this discussion not in order to say anything new, except for a clumsy accusation against Trotsky's alleged bowing down before some "divine trinity" or other, how else is their action to be explained than as one prompted by the desire to have "the youth" strike a blow at Trotsky?

Nobody (and Trotsky less than anyone) has challenged the need of preserving the preponderant influence, the leadership, of the old cadre of the party. This need is more than obvious to all of us. It is not on this point that our discussion of the article of the nine revolves.

We are against attributing to leading comrades of our party thoughts they have not expressed; by that token, we are against an incorrect and distorted posing of the question, particularly before the young communists. *We are against concealing the necessity of creating in the party the kind of situation that will permit the training of genuine Leninists,* and not the kind of communists of whom Lenin said at our Third Communist Youth Congress: "If a Communist took it into his head to boast about his communism because of the cut-and-dried conclusions he had acquired, without putting in a great deal of serious and hard work and without understanding facts he should examine critically, he would be a deplorable Communist indeed" [*CW*, Vol. 31, "The Tasks of the Youth Leagues" (October 2, 1920), p. 288].

We are for unity, and for the genuinely Bolshevik leadership of the party. We are far from shutting our eyes to the dangers that threaten the youth. Precisely because we are conscious of these dangers, we do not want to see the question of the "new course" obliterated under the pretext of defending the historic rights of the Old Guard of the party against nonexistent assaults.

V. Dalin, member of the Central Committee of the youth
M. Fedorov, Central Committee of the youth
A. Shokhin, collaborator of the Central Committee
A. Bezymensky, one of the founders of the youth
N. Penkov, one of the founders of the youth, member of the Moscow Committee
F. Delyusin, former secretary of the Moscow Committee
B. Treivas, former secretary of the Moscow Committee
M. Dugachev, activist of the Moscow Committee, one of the founders of the youth

SPEECH TO THE
THIRTEENTH PARTY CONGRESS

May 26, 1924

NOTE: The Thirteenth Party Congress opened in Moscow in May 1924. Trotsky faced a hostile audience to make a generally conciliatory speech in answer to the report of the Politburo majority on the situation in the party; by this time the apparatus was strong enough to prevent the election of a single Opposition delegate.

Between the Thirteenth Conference in January 1924 and the Thirteenth Congress in May, Lenin had died, and the party had begun a policy of indiscriminate recruitment in his honor (the "Lenin levy"), signing up 240,000 new members. Trotsky alludes to the Lenin levy as evidence that "confidence of the proletarian masses in the party has increased." Twelve years later, in his book The Revolution Betrayed, *he wrote: "By freeing the bureaucracy from the control of the proletarian vanguard, the 'Leninist levy' dealt a death blow to the party of Lenin" (p. 98). At the time, presented with an accomplished fact, and in any case not fully aware of its implications for the party's future, he did not speak out against it.*

Trotsky's comments on the question of factions and groupings also do not represent his final thinking on the matter. The prohibition of factions, passed by the Tenth Party Congress in March 1921, had been regarded as an extraordinary measure for an extraordinary state of affairs, to be reversed as soon as an improvement in the political situation made it possible. As described earlier, it had not been intended to stifle the internal life of the party, and the congress had taken precautions to guarantee the survival of party democracy. Furthermore, the resolution of the Tenth Congress had distinguished between "factions" and "groupings." The Stalinists seized upon the prohibition of fac-

tions as a weapon in their struggle with the Opposition; when the Forty-six insisted that the time had come for the party collectively to lift the ban on factions, they were accused of factionalism. Trotsky evidently decided to try to prevent the question of factions—which was an organizational question—from obscuring the political matters that were at stake, and did not challenge the ban on factions except to reiterate the formulation of the New Course resolution, unanimously adopted in 1923.

Because he had been ill throughout most of the campaign against him, he took this opportunity to answer some of the allegations that had been made. Chief among them was a resolution of the Thirteenth Party Conference in January 1924 declaring that the Opposition was "not only an attempt at a revision of Bolshevism, not only a direct aberration from Leninism, but also a blatant petty-bourgeois deviation." This was an early example of the transformation of Marxist terms into epithets in the hands of the Stalinists. Trotsky demonstrated at some length in his speech why this label was misplaced.

A section of his speech is devoted to replying to Zinoviev's demand for a "recantation"—the first such formal demand ever to be made of dissidents in the Russian party. He refused to recant his ideas—party discipline required only that, once outvoted, he agree to abide by the decision of the majority in action, reserving the right to his ideas and the right to present them to the party in the future. At the same time he reiterated his confidence in the historic role of the Communist Party, probably to differentiate himself from others in opposition to the official line of the party who were proclaiming the bankruptcy o   he Communist Party and calling for the formation of another party. It was not until 1933 that Trotsky gave up the effort to reform the parties of the Comintern and called for the formation of new, revolutionary parties.

The Thirteenth Congress closed the "discussion" in the party and enjoined Trotsky from speaking in public about the disputed questions.

Trotsky's speech to the Thirteenth Congress was translated for this volume by Marilyn Vogt and Robert Cantrick from the Stenographic Minutes of the Thirteenth Congress of the Russian Communist Party (published 1963).—Ed.

Comrades, I will touch upon only a very limited number of the questions that were elaborated upon or raised in the Central

Committee's reports. Let me focus your attention (or at least try to) on the question that the congress (or a certain part of it, quite likely the whole congress) expects me to clarify; and I will set aside beforehand—I believe the congress will understand the motives that lead me to do this—everything that could in any way exacerbate the problem, introduce personal elements, or make it harder to eliminate the difficulties that confront the party—difficulties we all want to lead the party out of for the sake of its future work. If, as a result, I do not mention a number of controversial issues that have involved my name in the recent period, it is not because I want to avoid giving the congress the answers to any questions, but rather because I am trying to single out the fundamental essence of the problem, setting it apart from matters of a personal nature.

It has been said here, comrades, that it was a most exceptional event in the life of our party for a heated discussion to erupt between two party congresses, a discussion that, as was stated, had the objective either of changing the composition of the Central Committee or of changing its policies. There is no doubt that the discussion that flared up between the two congresses was very intense; but I think, comrades, that if we were to look back over the period in question and single out the most striking feature of the discussion within the party, we would have to say that it is the fact that at a certain point between the two congresses the Central Committee itself recognized that it was necessary to *change* internal party policy, and openly proclaimed that fact.

The Danger of Bureaucratization

Allow me, comrades, to remind you of the resolution [on the "new course"] that was unanimously adopted December 5 [see p. 404]. I have it here before me. In this resolution, the objective contradictions, the difficulties, and the negative tendencies in the development of the working class and our party are enumerated, with the first section of the resolution saying that among these negative tendencies is *"the bureaucratization that can be observed in the party apparatus and the resulting threat of the party becoming isolated from the masses."* We cannot simply ignore this fact.

In the interval between the two congresses, the Central Committee of the party considered it necessary to state in a unanimously adopted resolution that there is a noticeable bureaucratization of the party apparatus and that from this bureaucratization there arises the threat of the party becoming isolated from the masses.

This same resolution stated that confidence of the proletarian masses in the party has increased. Is there a contradiction here? No, there is not. The confidence that the proletarian masses have in the party has built up over the course of many years. The masses think more slowly than the party, and this is precisely why the party is the vanguard of the class. The masses add up and draw the balance sheet of the party's activities slowly, over a long period of time. And in the resolution we jointly stated that the party's policies on all fundamental questions in recent years—during which time the masses have severed their ties with the Social Revolutionaries and Menshevism—have increased the confidence of the working masses in the party. At that time, it is true, none of us thought we would make such a rapid leap in expanding the proletarian cadres of the party, i.e., that by the Thirteenth Congress we would have had the opportunity to enroll at least 200,000 new members in the party, and very likely even more.

But the very fact that the working masses, in the person of their most honest and active elements, have moved closer to the party was clear to all of us, and this was formulated in the resolution. However, at the same time, the resolution states that a discernible bureaucratization is proceeding apace in the party apparatus and that this process entails the danger that the party will become isolated from the masses. What does the second assertion mean? It means that if the negative processes that the Central Committee has here noted and described are allowed to develop further, this would in the future make it more difficult for the party to reap the harvest of the confidence of the working masses.

What circumstances and what factors impelled the Central Committee as a whole, together with the Central Control Commission, despite various internal disagreements and nuances, to adopt a resolution of such exceptional importance, of such weight? Comrades, here, too, I would like to cite a statement—one that is least likely to be viewed with suspicion. Let me read a quotation, a lengthy one, from a speech by Comrade Bukharin that was delivered at the beginning of the discussion at a meeting in the Krasnaya Presnya district. I am using the stenographic record of the speech and will quote only the part that describes the features of this bureaucratization as Comrade Bukharin understood and interpreted them at that time. I could read many other quotations but I am taking precisely this one for reasons that all of you will understand. These are Comrade Bukharin's actual words:

"Comrades, I believe I must draw a rather specific picture of what it is that is disturbing the rank and file of our party. Here we must not speak of a priori premises, differentiation, etc.; rather, we must clearly pose the problem: What is it that is troubling the rank and file of our party and causing discontent among the mass of nonparty people—a discontent that everyone must take into account, from the Central Committee all the way down to the party's cell bureaus? There is an endless number of shortcomings that have led to a certain semicritical situation inside our party, a situation that has been aggravated chiefly by the economic crisis our country is experiencing. There is an abundance of such shortcomings, but they can all be said to fall under definite headings.

"What is the real question here? Consider the life of a party cell, and above all, its executive apparatus, because every cell has an apparatus of its own. Our cell secretaries—I am judging by the Moscow organizations, first of all—are usually appointed by the district committees. Moreover, the district committees do not even try to have their candidates accepted by these cells but content themselves with simply appointing someone. As a rule, the voting takes place according to a definite pattern. They come into the meeting and ask: 'Is anyone opposed?' And since everyone is more or less afraid to voice dissent, the individual who was appointed becomes secretary of the cell bureau. If we were to conduct a survey and ask how often the voting takes place with the chairman asking 'All in favor?' and 'All opposed?' we would easily discover that in the majority of cases the elections in our party organizations have in fact been transformed into mockery of elections, because the voting takes place not only without preliminary discussion, but, again, according to the formula, 'Is anyone opposed?' And since it is considered bad form for anyone to speak against the 'leadership,' the matter is automatically settled. This is what elections are like in the local cells.

"Let us now speak of our party meetings," Comrade Bukharin goes on. "How are they conducted? I myself have taken the floor at numerous meetings in Moscow and I know how the so-called discussion takes place in our party organizations. Take for example the election of the meeting's presiding committee. One of the members of the district committee presents a slate and asks: 'Is anyone opposed?' Nobody is opposed, and the matter is considered settled. The presiding committee is elected and the same comrade then announces that the presiding committee was elected unanimously. After this comes the reading of the agenda; with the agenda, the same procedure applies. Over the past years I recall only isolated and extremely rare instances in which new points were added to the agenda at party meetings. Next, a resolution, which has been prepared in advance, is read and adopted routinely. The chairman asks once more: 'Is anyone opposed?' Nobody is opposed, and the resolution is unanimously adopted.

"This is the customary pattern of functioning in our party organizations. We ought to understand that the most active part of the membership quite naturally expresses a definite discontent over this; it is definitely dissatisfied with this state of affairs.

"A large number of our local organizations cling to these protective formulas: 'No discussion,' 'Is anyone opposed?' etc. *And this entire system eliminates the internal life of the party.* It goes without saying that this gives rise to an enormous wave of dissatisfaction. I have cited some examples from the life of our local cells. But the same thing can be observed in a slightly altered form at each successive level of our party hierarchy."

That is how one of the most prominent members of the Central Committee described those tendencies within our party organization that compelled—as is obviously the case—the Central Committee to pass a resolution addressing itself to the noticeable bureaucratization of the party apparatus and the resulting danger of becoming isolated from the masses. And it goes without saying that there can be no greater danger than this.

What was the Central Committee's practical conclusion after making this diagnosis? We read its practical conclusion in the same December 5 resolution: "The interests of the party, both for its successful struggle against influences generated by the NEP and to enhance its fighting capacity in all areas of work, demand a serious change in the party's course in the sense of an active and systematic implementation of the principles of workers' democracy."

Thus, the Central Committee of the party in the interval between the two congresses recognized the need for a serious change of the party's course as a consequence of the sudden surfacing of disorders and negative features in the party's life, which the Central Committee itself has analyzed and attested to.

Comrades, I do not think under any circumstances we can simply ignore this fact, and I believe that this is precisely the fundamental distinguishing feature of the period under review at this congress. Thus, the Central Committee established, first, the need for a serious change in the party's course; and second, the need to enlarge the party's proletarian core. And on both there was unanimity. "The efforts toward enlarging the proletarian core of the party," we read in the resolution, "must be seen as one of the most important tasks facing all party organizations in the months ahead."

When the Central Committee established the need for serious changes in the party's course in the interval between the two congresses, did this perhaps signify a break with the organizational and other principles of Bolshevism? I believe not. It meant only that the Central Committee was stating that there were obvious errors and deviations in the application of these principles to the present situation, which were expressed in the bureaucratization of the party apparatus and the ensuing danger that in the future the party might become isolated from the masses. Consequently, it was precisely to safeguard the organizational and all other principles of Bolshevism under the present conditions that the Central Committee recognized the need for a serious change in the party's course in the period between the last two congresses.

The Question of Generations

Why, however, has this question been complicated by the question of generations within the party and within the working class? Comrades, so as not to complicate my account, I will not try to introduce statements by a number of comrades who from the very beginning (quite correctly, in my opinion) have posed the question of the regime within the party from the point of view of the relations between the generations both in our party and in the working class. To put it bluntly: the very essence of the question of the party regime under the present concrete conditions reduces itself for us, above all, to the question of the relations between the generations in the party and in the working class.

What is involved here, of course, is providing, or rather, guaranteeing the young generation of the working class the opportunity to make their way to Bolshevism under the new conditions (whether they are working in the factories and plants of our socialist country or, by decisions of the party and trade unions, studying in the educational institutions of our socialist country). The young generation cannot, and fortunately does not have to, repeat the history of the older generation. The older generation made its way to the road on which it now stands by other paths and under other conditions—the conditions of a bourgeois, capitalist country with the heavy lid of tsarism clamped upon it. The older generation has secured for the younger generation the opportunity to go forward under new, qualitatively different, conditions. And the task is to provide, or rather to guarantee, the young generation the opportunity to enter onto the same broad road of Bolshevism, communism, and Leninism by way of new paths and new routes that correspond to the nature of the workers' state and to the new circumstances.

If we ask ourselves what kind of party regime we are talking about and what we mean by a regime of democracy within the party, then, comrades, I will say from the very outset—although I think that to do so at a congress of our party may be superfluous—that of the people in our party with any sort of general understanding about communism, Marxism, and Bolshevism, there could hardly be more than a dozen who would approach the question of democracy within the party from a purely formal point of view—from the point of view of how often elections are held, what percentage voted, took part in discussion, etc., i.e., from the point of view of the statistics of democracy and from the point of view of the formal principles of parliamentarism as applied to party life. We have experienced too much history, and in particular too great a struggle against political falsifications, against margarine democracy—which is Menshevik ideology on the one hand and on the other, imperialism's last screening device—to approach the question of democracy from a formal point of view.

From what point of view, then, should we approach democracy in relation to the party regime? From the point of view of safeguarding the party against such phenomena as the possibility of bureaucratization of its apparatus, as well as the attendant danger that the party might become isolated from the masses. This is the criterion! And if I were to attempt to offer a definition of party democracy as applied to the party's present situation, to the present epoch, and to this particular period, I would say: On the one hand, party democracy is a regime that assures the theoretical, political, and organizational leadership of the old generation of underground Bolsheviks, rich in experience, because if this leadership is not assured (and only a child could fail to understand this) the party will not be able to navigate the ship of state and the ship of the international workers' movement through difficulties, narrow channels, rocks, and reefs. But at the same time, party democracy is a regime that while assuring the leading position of the older generation, also assures the younger generation access to the high road of Bolshevism and Leninism— not by formal education (such methods cannot accomplish this), but rather by active, independent, practical participation in the political life of the party and the country.

The unity of these two tasks should be guaranteed by a regime of party democracy. The disruption of this necessary unity and balance threatens to bureaucratize the party apparatus and isolate the party from the masses. That, in my opinion, is the essence of the matter. And when we ask ourselves whether we have the necessary balance, again I believe I am justified in pointing out that the Central Committee itself, in the period between the two congresses, stated that this balance was not being maintained. I remind you again of the extensive quotation that I read from Comrade Bukharin's speech, which was given not within the Central Committee but at a big district meeting. There he described in a concrete and unforgettable manner how the balance in the party's internal regime was being upset, creating a state of affairs that is very much to the disadvantage of the less mature, less educated elements of our party, that is, the broad circles of its young members, and is at the same time dangerous for the party's old cadres.

Factions and Groupings

In the party discussion the question of generations was linked with the question of factions and groupings within the party. And here, too, comrades, I believe it is necessary to recall how the question was posed in the December 5 resolution. There it was explained that party democracy in no way implies freedom for factional groupings, which are extremely dangerous for the ruling party, since they always threaten to split or divide the government and the state apparatus as a whole. I believe this is undisputed and indisputable. And we unanimously agreed to cite the resolution of the Tenth Congress, where Vladimir Ilyich personally defined both factions and groupings, and explained the political danger they entail.

The report that I was in favor of allowing groupings is not true. Comrades, it is not true. It is true that I made the great mistake of falling ill at the crucial moment in the party discussion and was not able to come forward and refute this allegation, and many others, at the proper time. But never did I believe and nowhere did I state that it was possible to allow groupings although factions had to be suppressed. On the contrary, every chance I had to speak about this, I reiterated that it was impermissible to draw distinctions between factions and groupings. If formal documentation of this should be called for, I could produce it. I am not going to take up the congress' time on this point. I believe that from the political point of view it is sufficient—as far as a statement for the record is concerned—to say that I have never recognized freedom for groupings inside the party, nor do I now recognize it, because under the present historical conditions groupings are merely another name for factions. But, comrades, at the same time I must remind you of another part of the Central Committee's resolution on this same question of factions and groupings. It says: "Only a constant, vital ideological life can maintain the character of the party as it was before and during the revolution, with the constant scrutiny of its past, the correction of its mistakes, and the collective discussion of the most important problems. Only these methods of work can provide effective guarantees that episodic disagreements will not lead to the formation of factional groupings with all the above-indicated consequences." And further: "In order to avert this, the leading party bodies must heed the voices of the broad party masses and not consider every criticism a manifestation of factionalism and thereby cause conscientious and disciplined party members to withdraw into closed circles and fall into factionalism."

This is part and parcel of this same resolution of the Central Committee, and I believe that we have neither the right nor any reason to blot it either from our memory or from the history of our party.

And if we ask ourselves why the Central Committee found it necessary to say that banning factions and groupings—which is binding on everyone—by itself does not solve the problem; that such a ban presupposes a course for the party that protects it against bureaucratization of the party apparatus and from the resulting danger of the party becoming isolated from the masses—if we ask ourselves why the Central Committee found it necessary to adopt a statement of such vast importance and consequence, we will find the answer in all that I said earlier. In other words, it is precisely the bureaucratization of the party apparatus, noticeable as it is, that constitutes one of the factors that—as the resolution states—is responsible for transforming accidental, episodic, and temporary differences into groupings and then these groupings into factions.

Comrades, this is how I interpret the basic questions of internal party life as they have emerged with the development of the party over the past year and as they were expressed in the resolution of the Central Committee of December 5. And, having said that, if I now ask why, at a certain point on December 5, the Central Committee considered it necessary to say to the party: Beware! Symptoms of bureaucratization are discernible and they are fraught with the hazard that the party may become isolated from the masses; we do not tolerate factions but we will bear in mind that a full and genuine guarantee against factions and groupings means eliminating the negative phenomena that we have indicated above—if, as I say, you can conceive of this, if you can picture the life of the party organizations as Comrade Bukharin described it for us, then, comrades, is it not clear that if the party continues along this line, as Comrade Bukharin himself also stated in that speech, a wave of dissatisfaction, a wave of criticism, must inevitably arise? And then, when I ask myself whether this criticism and dissatisfaction can be indiscriminately characterized and stigmatized with a term like "petty-bourgeois deviation"—then, comrades, I am filled with grave doubts and the greatest misgivings. Grave doubts and the greatest misgivings.

The Question of a Plan

The discussion has revolved, on the one hand, around the situation within the party, and on the other, around the planned management of the economy. How the Central Committee reacted to problems in the first category in its December 5 resolution I have already related. Allow me to quote the main points of the conclusions the Central Committee came to on December 5 with respect to the economy. After describing the economic situation that has arisen, the December 5 resolution says: "The whole party must come to the conclusion that further economic revival . . . can serve the cause of *socialist* construction only to the extent that we actually learn to coordinate the sectors of the national economy in the course of their constant interaction with one another and with the market." And further: "From this arises the *exceptional importance* of Gosplan, the economic staff of the socialist state, and all the economic planning organizations at the local level. *It is necessary to guarantee to them in practice the role indicated in the resolution of the Twelfth Congress.*"

In other words, on December 5 the Central Committee did consider a struggle necessary, but not against fantastic, utopian, or otherwise exaggerated ideas about the possibilities for planned management of the economy. I am considered by some to be one of those who exaggerate these possibilities. I consider this charge incorrect; but I shall not take up your time with this right now. What is important and significant is not that someone exaggerated on this question, but rather that the Central Committee on December 5 told the party: It is impermissible to *underestimate* the importance of planned management, for otherwise development will not follow the route of socialist construction. That is what the Central Committee said on December 5. Consequently the danger, as the Central Committee saw it, was not that someone or other had exaggerated the potential of a planned economy, but that the party was underestimating the importance of the principle of planning and that the State Planning Commission had not been accorded the priority in the overall system of our economy that it should have received on the basis of the resolution of the Twelfth Congress.

During my absence from Moscow, while I was in Sukhum, I read in our newspapers the following words by Comrade Kamenev at the first session of the rejuvenated Council of Labor and Defense on February 8: "We can commit a host of errors," said Comrade Kamenev, "if we do not set as our goal the planned coordination of the national economy. This coordination was always supposed to be the task of the Council of Labor and Defense, but in reality its task has consisted more in smoothing over differences among the individual departments that have reached it.

"It seems to me that this *ought to be changed;* and that further integration of the various branches of the economy must not be the result of clashes between the different administrative departments, but must flow from an economic plan that is well thought out in advance, even if only outlined in rough form."

We see here too, comrades, an indication of the need to *change* our policy on one of the most essential problems, the problem of the planned coordination of all our work; and this was not before the discussion, but after it. Thus, what is involved here is not an abstract, universal plan, nor a particular plan for electrification, even though we have a long-term perspective for one conceived on a gigantic scale; rather, what is involved, as the Twelfth Congress resolution put it, is a day-to-day plan for maneuvering in such a way as to "pair" all the sectors making up our economy, to make them, both individually and as a whole, all the more properly, surely, and painlessly compatible with our market—i.e., mainly, with a peasant market.

It was on February 8, therefore, after the discussion, that the need for a change of policy in the major economic institutions was affirmed. And, comrades, again I wonder whether anyone can say that the voices demanding this change before February 8 were an expression of a petty-bourgeois deviation. I do not think so, comrades. What can such accusations or descriptions be based on, whether with respect to the economic question or with respect to internal party affairs? One could say that during the discussion there were many voices that exaggerated the importance of party democracy out of all proportion and construed it in an absolute sense.

We will admit that. Thus we will grant that there were exaggerations involved with respect to party democracy. With respect to a planned economy it could be said, admittedly, that there were exaggerations in assessing the role of a planned economy. We will grant this, although exaggerations regarding planning can in no way be described as a "petty-bourgeois deviation," because the petty bourgeoisie—fragmented as it is, and with its anarchistic way of thinking—is not at all disposed toward a comprehensive economic plan. But I will not dwell on these contradictions. Let us assume that these accusations are directed at exaggerations in the sphere of planned economic management. But if these exaggerations did exist, does not the Central Committee resolution give us the full right to say that they have resulted from certain other negative and unhealthy phenomena? If we speak of exaggerations regarding party democracy, are these not reactions against the exaggerations of party bureaucracy? The Central Committee resolution categorically attests to the existence of such exaggerations and draws from them the ominous prospect of the party's becoming isolated from the masses.

Exaggerations in the area of party democracy in the concrete historical situation can, of course, become a channel for the penetration of petty-bourgeois influences. There is no doubt that every exaggeration, every mistake in any area can become a channel for other class influences, since as a party we live not in a vacuum but under the pressure of other forces, both domestically and internationally. This is a truism for us. I repeat, every exaggeration of possibility, potential, or perspective provides a channel for alien class influences. But I ask whether, on the other hand, the bureaucratization of the party apparatus, which the Central Committee itself acknowledged, is a technical and not a social phenomenon. I maintain that the bureaucratization of the apparatus stems from deep social causes and that the fundamental source of bureaucratization is the state apparatus, in which we find the disputes between classes mixed together with the areas of agreement between classes, and in which the low level of culture of the broad masses of toilers is reflected (as well as that of the working class itself). And because our party is at the head of the state, the state apparatus is the most direct and immediate source of bureaucratic influences on the party.

But if that is so, then bureaucratization is not a problem of formal administrative technique, but a social question, just like exaggerations in the area of formal democracy. They are phenomena of the same order. And if we say that exaggerated demands, exaggerated appraisals, and a formal approach to the question of democracy are possible sources of petty-bourgeois influence, if we pose the question in this way (and this is correct theoretically and in terms of an overall perspective), then it is just as correct to say that the tendencies toward bureaucratization of the party apparatus are no less a channel for petty-bourgeois influences and, moreover, represent a more fundamental and immediate danger. It is precisely this fundamental and immediate danger that the party reacted to so sharply, and we cannot view this reaction as a petty-bourgeois deviation under any circumstances.

Comrades, the same thing applies to a still greater degree to the question of planning. Whether or not some of us are guilty of overestimating the planning principle—we can argue calmly over this in books, and very likely in the future we will have to devote many books to an analysis of our economic development—books of a tranquil, scholarly character. But I believe it to be firmly established that the Central Committee between the Twelfth and Thirteenth Congresses raised the problem that the party, in the form of its leading apparatus, did not approach the tasks of planned guidance of the economy with the necessary energy. For the present, I would like to put aside particular problems, such as an active balance of trade or goods intervention,[21] which were also evaluated from the point of view of "petty-bourgeois deviation." Comrades, let us hold these questions in abeyance for the time being. Perhaps we will discuss them when we come to the question of trade; that is a more appropriate place for them. Insofar as there are and will continue to be differences on these questions, nine-tenths of them are practical and empirical in nature. For the moment, we already have the results of a serious test. No one, of course, has said that we do not need an active balance of trade—in general, I have not heard such an opinion at all—but rather that in view of our poverty, an active balance is a luxury we cannot afford, which must be reduced to the barest minimum. However, we find that we have not reduced it to this minimum and that we have accumulated too much foreign currency and we have begun to correct this mistake. This is point one.

Secondly, with respect to goods intervention, we have become convinced that since it is our task to regulate domestic prices by means of the strategic distribution of goods in massive quantities, we cannot blockade ourselves but rather are compelled to resort to foreign products—in which case, of course, we have to bring this task into strict coordination with the interests of the corresponding branches of industry. We will say more about this during the discussion of economic questions; but in any case, I do not see here any basis whatsoever for the charge of a petty-bourgeois deviation.

On Mistakes

Comrades, an invitation was extended here for all who have committed errors to stand up and confess them. Nothing could be simpler or easier, morally and politically, than to admit before your own party that you have made this or that mistake. For that, I believe, no great moral heroism is required. But, comrades, I believe it is also our obligation and duty to recall—because it was not mentioned—that at a certain time the Central Committee as a whole acknowledged before the entire party certain mistakes which are still to be corrected. The December 5 resolution, which declared the necessity of struggling against bureaucratic deviation, was in and of itself a declaration of mistakes in the party's internal policies. Otherwise, comrades, if we do not think that these mistakes existed, then indeed, there would be no need for changes. People change what is incorrect, what is mistaken.

We are holding the Thirteenth Congress under new circumstances. And these new circumstances were provided by the Lenin levy, which is altering the social composition of the party in a proletarian direction. Does this change or eliminate the question of party democracy? No, it does not change it; it does not eliminate it. Undoubtedly the Lenin levy brought our party closer to being an elected party, as was correctly stated here. I spoke about this in Tiflis, I spoke about it in Baku, and in several meetings in Moscow. If we approach the question on the level of political democracy—and indeed political democracy in the parliamentary countries decides, first and foremost, the question of which party shall govern the country—if we approach the question on this level and compare what has happened in our country—the fact of the Lenin levy—with the elections that have taken place in recent months in a number of parliamentary countries, we will have every right to say—and I personally have already said this dozens of times—that the form of democracy that found its expression in our country, when the working class at a certain stage of its development has shown in a particularly impressive, mass way how it views the balance sheet of the party's work over many years and has raised on its shoulders two or three hundred thousand workers and presented them to the party—this form of democracy is infinitely, immeasurably superior to the kind of democracy in which once every five years the people of a country have to go through the formal motion of placing their votes in the ballot box under the dictatorship of the bourgeois press, and under the dictatorship of the bourgeois class. This is obvious and indisputable. But our advantage—the advantage of the proletarian dictatorship and of the Soviet regime—does not remove from the agenda the question of the party's internal course, its merits and deficiencies. If we are to assess the situation realistically, we must say that this colossal expansion of the party, this powerful leap forward, is a product of the party's work over a number of years, many years. But at the same time the Central Committee, while correctly stating that the confidence of the proletarian masses in the party has grown, has put itself and the entire party on the alert against processes at work in the party apparatus that can damage this growth in the party's influence among the masses and even threaten to isolate the party from the masses. That is why the existence of the Lenin levy does not eliminate the question of the party's internal course.

I believe, on the contrary, that it makes this question all the more important and urgent for us, because here again we come face to face with the question of the relations between the old, theoretically schooled and tempered party generation and the new legions of youth who are now joining the party. And we are now compelled to say with particular force and insistence that if the processes that the December 5 resolution pointed to are allowed to develop further, this would threaten both of these basic party groups, i.e., both the generation that is leading the party and the younger generation. Only when seen in such a light does the December 5 warning by the Central Committee make sense.

Comrades, none of us wants to be or can be right against the party. In the last analysis, the party is always right, because the party is the sole historical instrument that the working class possesses for the solution of its fundamental tasks. I have already said that nothing would be simpler than to say before the party that all these criticisms, all these declarations, warnings, and protests—all were mistaken from beginning to end. I cannot say so, however, comrades, because I do not think it. I know that no one can be right against the party. It is only possible to be right with the party and through it since history has not created any other way to determine the correct position.

The English have a proverb: My country right or wrong. We can say with much greater historical justification: Whether it is right or wrong in any particular, specific question at any particular moment, this is my party. And although some comrades may think I was wrong in raising this or that point; although some comrades may think I have incorrectly described this or that danger; I for my part believe that I am only fulfilling my duty as a party member who warns his party about what he considers to be a danger. If anyone had mounted this platform at the Twelfth Congress and introduced a resolution saying that there had to be a serious change in the party's internal policies or else the party would be threatened with isolation from the masses, I can say with virtual certainty, comrades, that this comrade would have gotten no votes and would not have won the support of the Twelfth Congress for this resolution. Nevertheless, in the interval between the Twelfth and Thirteenth Party Congresses, the Central Committee was obliged to unanimously adopt just such a resolution pointing to the need for a change in the party's course.

The greatest difficulties are still ahead of us, comrades, and I trust that in surmounting these difficulties we will march together as good, firmly united Bolshevik soldiers. It would be ludicrous, perhaps even inappropriate, to make any personal statements here; but I have confidence that if it should come to that, I will not be the least soldier on the least Bolshevik barricade! But I firmly believe that history will not subject us to such a test, that our fight will be victorious and that we shall take the barricades of our enemies. In any case, comrades, difficulties—grave difficulties—are still to come; and I consider my duty at the present time to be the duty of a party member who knows that the party, in the last analysis, is always right, but that party opinion is formed by taking into account also those voices that at a particular moment are at variance with the prevailing attitude in the party's leading circles. And I say that the December 5 resolution is no less important or valid now that we have admitted into our ranks 200,000 or more workers. On the contrary, it takes on particular importance; and if we were to push it to the back of our minds because of this exaggerated attack against "petty-bourgeois deviations," we would be making a mistake, fraught with new difficulties and new complications for the party. And we are all interested in reducing the difficulties and complications to a minimum. And although there were mistakes of one kind or another—and I personally, like everyone else, am prepared to admit them—then, comrades, no one has the right to interpret these mistakes as being directly or indirectly aimed at undermining the unity, solidarity, and discipline of our party. [*Applause*]

Not only an individual party member but even the party itself can make occasional mistakes; such mistakes, for instance, were represented by individual decisions of the last conference, certain parts of which I believe were incorrect and unjustified. But the party could not make any decision, no matter how incorrect and unjustified, that could shake by even one iota our total devotion to the cause of the party, and the readiness of every one of us to shoulder the responsibility of party discipline under all circumstances. And if the party passes a resolution that one or another of us considers unjust, that comrade will say: Right or wrong, this is my party, and I will take responsibility for its decision to the end. [*Applause*]

ON THE DEFEAT
OF THE GERMAN REVOLUTION

NOTE: The defeat of the German revolution in 1923 was a turning point in Trotsky's assessment of the tasks of the Left Opposition. Writing about it seven years later, he said, "The internal discussion in the Russian Communist Party did not lead to a system of groups until the events in Germany in the fall of 1923. The economic and political processes in the USSR were molecular in character and had a comparatively slow tempo. The events of 1923 in Germany gave the measure of the differences on the scale of that gigantic class struggle. It was then and on that basis that the Russian Opposition was formed" ("Greetings to La Verite," Writings of Leon Trotsky, 1930). In the months that followed the German events, he devoted a great deal of time to an analysis of what had gone wrong and used whatever channels were open to get a wide public hearing for his analysis. The thrust of his ideas was clear to politically educated readers and listeners, but he couched them in such a way that it was hard for the bureaucracy—at least in the spring of 1924—to prohibit them as "factionalism."

Below are excerpts from two speeches. "On the Road to the European Revolution" was delivered on April 11, 1924, to a special session of the Tiflis Soviet in the capital of the Georgian Soviet Republic, and is the first critical analysis of the German defeat. The translation is by George Saunders from a 1924 pamphlet entitled Zapad i Vostok *(East and West) and is reprinted from* Leon Trotsky Speaks *(Pathfinder Press, 1972). "Through What Stage Are We Passing?" is a speech delivered to the Fifth All-Union Congress of Medical and Veterinary Workers, June 21, 1924. The translation is by Brian Pearce from* Zapad i Vostok *and is reprinted from the Summer 1964* Fourth International.—Ed.

On the Road to the European Revolution

April 11, 1924

. . . We lived through the past year under the sign of impending revolution in Germany. During the second half of the year the German revolution grew closer day by day. We saw this as the key factor of world development. If the German revolution had been victorious, this would have radically changed the world relationship of forces. The Soviet Union, with its population of 130 million and its innumerable natural riches, on the one hand, and Germany, with its technology, its culture, and its working class, on the other—this bloc, this mighty alliance, would have cut directly across the line of development in Europe and the world. The building of socialism would have acquired an altogether different tempo.

However, contrary to our expectations, the revolution in Germany has not been victorious thus far. Why? It is necessary to think about this question because it can teach us something of use not only to Germany but to ourselves as well.

Under what conditions is a victorious proletarian revolution possible? A certain development of the productive forces is necessary. The proletariat and those intermediate classes of the population that support and follow it must constitute the majority of the population. The vanguard must clearly understand the tasks and methods of proletarian revolution and have the resoluteness to bring it about. And it must lead the majority of the laboring masses with it into decisive battle.

On the other hand, it is necessary that the ruling class, that is, the bourgeoisie, be disorganized and frightened by the whole international and internal situation, that its will be undermined and broken. These are the material, political, and psychological prerequisites for revolution. These are the conditions for the victory of the proletariat. And if we are to ask: Were these conditions present in Germany?—I think we would have to answer with absolute clarity and firmness, Yes, all but one.

You recall the period after the middle of last year, the lack of success and the collapse of the passive resistance of bourgeois

Germany to the occupation of the Ruhr. This period was characterized by the thorough shaking up of German society. The mark
plummeted downward at such a mad pace that our quiet Soviet
ruble might have been the object of envy. Prices of basic necessi-
ties rose wildly. The dissatisfaction of the working masses was
expressed in open clashes with the state. The German bourgeoisie
was discouraged and incapable of action.

Ministries rose and fell. French troops stood on the German
side of the Rhine. Stresemann, premier of the great coalition,
declared: "We are the last bourgeois parliamentary government.
After us come either the communists or the fascists." And the
fascists said: "Let the communists take over; our turn will be
next." All this signified the last stage of the crumbling of the
foundations of bourgeois society. The workers poured into the
Communist Party day after day. To be sure, fairly broad masses
were still marking time in the ranks of the Menshevik party. But
you remember, when we took power in Petrograd in October, we
found Mensheviks still at the head of the unions, because the
Petrograd workers, led by our party, had moved forward to the
conquest of power so rapidly that they never got around to shaking off the old dust in the trade unions.

Why then in Germany has there been no victory thus far? I
think there can be only one answer: because Germany did not
have a Bolshevik party, nor did it have a leader such as we had
in October. We have here for the first time a tremendous body of
historical experience for comparison. Of course, one may say that
in Germany, victory is more difficult. The German bourgeoisie is
stronger and more clever than ours. But the working class cannot
pick and choose its enemies. You comrades here in Georgia
fought the Menshevik government that fate had brought you. The
German working class is obliged to fight the German bourgeoisie.
And one can say with full assurance that history will hardly
create objective conditions any more favorable to the German
proletariat than those of the latter half of the past year. What
was lacking? A party with the tempering that our party has. [*A
voice: "Right!"*] This, comrades, is the central question, and all
the European parties must learn from this experience, and we
must learn to understand and value more clearly and profoundly
the character, nature, and significance of our own party, which
secured victory for the proletariat in October and a whole series
of victories since October.

Comrades, I would not want my remarks to be taken in some

sort of pessimistic vein—as though, for example, I considered the victory of the proletariat to have been postponed for many years. Not at all. The future favors us. But the past must be analyzed correctly. The turnabout this past year, in October-November, when German fascism and the big bourgeoisie came to the fore, was an enormous defeat. We must record it, evaluate it, and fix it in our memories that way, in order to learn from it. It is an enormous defeat. But from this defeat the German party will learn, become tempered, and grow. And the situation remains, as before, a revolutionary one. But I will return to that point.

On the world scale there have been three occasions when the proletarian revolution reached the point where it required a surgeon's knife. These were: October 1917 here; September 1919 in Italy; and the latter half of the past year (July-November) in Germany.

In our country we had a victorious proletarian revolution— *begun, carried through,* and *completed* for the first time in history. In Italy there was a *sabotaged* revolution. The proletariat hurled itself with all its weight against the bourgeoisie, seizing factories, mines, and mills, but the Socialist Party, frightened by the proletariat's pressure on the bourgeoisie, stabbed it in the back, disorganized it, paralyzed its efforts, and handed it over to fascism.

Finally, there is the experience of Germany, where there is a good Communist Party, devoted to the cause of revolution, but lacking as yet in the necessary qualities: a sense of proportion, resoluteness, tempering. And this party at a certain moment let the revolution *slip through its fingers.*

Our entire International and each individual worker should constantly keep these three models in mind, these three historical experiences—the October Revolution here, a revolution prepared by history, begun, carried through, and completed by us; the revolution in Italy, prepared by history, lifted up on their backs by the workers, but sabotaged, exploded, by the Socialist Party; and the revolution in Germany, a revolution prepared by history, which the working class was ready to lift onto its back, but which an honest Communist Party, lacking the necessary tempering and leadership, could not master.

History does not work in such a way that, first, the foundation is laid, then the productive forces grow, the necessary relations between class forces develop, the proletariat becomes revolutionary, then all this is kept in an icebox and preserved while the training of a Communist party proceeds so that it can get itself ready while "conditions" wait and wait; then when it's ready, it can roll up its sleeves and start fighting. No, history doesn't work that way. For a revolution the *coinciding* of necessary conditions is required.

The fact is that if in Germany in the second half of last year our Bolshevik Party had been on the scene, with the will that it has now, had before, and will continue to have, with a will that shows itself in action, with a tactical skill that the working class senses, so that it says to itself, "We can trust our fate to this party"; if such a party had been on the scene, it would have carried with it in action and through action the overwhelming majority of the working class. . . .

Through What Stage Are We Passing?

June 21, 1924

. . . The whole problem now is whether the Communist Party will prove able to utilize these upheavals so as to take power and solve thereafter all the contradictions of capitalist society. If it be asked: Have we, as an International, become stronger in this period, then the answer must be that on the whole we have undoubtedly become stronger. Nearly all the sections have become bigger and more influential than they were. Does this mean that their strength is growing and will continue to grow continuously, in a single upward line? No, it does not mean that. This strength grows in zigzags, waves, convulsions—here also the dialectic of development prevails; the Comintern is not exempt from it.

Thus, in the second half of last year, the Communist Party of Germany was, politically, incomparably stronger than it is today. At that time it was marching directly toward the conquest of power, and the upheaval in the entire social life of Germany was so great that not only the most backward masses of the workers but also broad strata of the peasantry, the petty bourgeoisie, and the intelligentsia were all confident that the communists were soon about to come to power and reorganize society. Moods like this are in themselves among the most reliable symptoms of the maturity of a revolutionary situation. But it turned out that the communists were not yet able to take power. Not because the objective situation rendered this impossible—no, one could not imagine better prepared and more mature conditions for the seizure of power. If these conditions were to be exactly described, they could take their place as a classical example in the textbooks of proletarian revolution. But the party was not able to make use of them. We must stop and dwell upon this.

The first period in the history of the International ran from October 1917 to the revolutionary upheavals in Germany in March 1921. Everything was determined by the war and its immediate consequences. We expected an uprising of the European proletariat and its conquest of power in the near future. What mistake did we make? We underestimated the role of the party.

After the Third World Congress [1921] a new period began. The slogan "To the masses" meant in essence: "Build the party." This policy was carried out more fully and successfully in Germany than anywhere else. But in Germany also it happened that it came into contradiction with the situation brought into being in 1923 as a result of the occupation of the Ruhr, which at one blow upset the fictitious equilibrium of Europe.

At the end of 1923 we suffered in Germany a very great defeat, no less serious than our defeat in 1905. What, however, was the difference? In 1905 we lacked sufficient forces, as became apparent during the struggle. In other words, the cause of the defeat lay in the objective relationship of forces. In 1923 in Germany we suffered defeat without matters ever getting to the stage of a clash of forces, without forces being mobilized and used.

Thus the immediate cause of the defeat in this case was to be found in the leadership of the party. True, one may say that even if the party had followed a correct policy it still would not have been able to mobilize adequate forces and would have been beaten. This opinion is, however, to say the least, conjectural. As regards the objective situation, the relationship of class forces, the self-confidence of the ruling class and the masses of the people, that is, as regards all the prerequisites for revolution, we had a most favorable situation, as you can picture for yourselves: a crisis of existence for the nation and the state, brought to a climax by the occupation; a crisis of the economy and especially of the country's finances; a parliamentary crisis; an utter collapse in the ruling class' confidence in itself; disintegration of social democracy and the trade unions; a spontaneous increase in the influence of the Communist Party; a turn by petty-bourgeois elements toward communism; a sharp decline in the morale of the fascists.

Such were the political preconditions. What was the situation in the military sphere? A very small standing army, consisting of a hundred to two hundred thousand men, that is, a police force organized on army lines. The forces of the fascists were monstrously exaggerated and to a considerable degree existed only on paper. In any case, after July-August the fascists were severely demoralized.

Did the communists have the majority of the working masses behind them? This is a question which cannot be answered with statistics. It is a question which is decided by the dynamic of revolution. The masses were moving steadily toward the communists, and the opponents of the communists were weakening just as steadily. The masses who remained with social democracy showed no disposition to actively oppose the communists, as they had done in March 1921. On the contrary, the majority of the social democratic workers awaited revolution in a spirit of hope. This also is a requirement of revolution.

Were the masses in a fighting mood? The entire history of the year 1923 leaves no doubt at all on this score. True, toward the end of the year this mood had become more reserved, more concentrated, had lost its spontaneity, that is, its readiness for constant elemental outbreaks. But how could that be otherwise? By the second half of the year the masses had become a great deal more experienced, and felt or understood that matters were moving full speed ahead toward a decisive showdown.

Under such conditions the masses could go forward only if a firm, self-confident leadership existed and the masses had confidence in it. Discussions about whether the masses were in a fighting mood or not are very subjective in character and essentially express a lack of confidence among the leaders of the party itself. Assertions that no aggressive fighting mood was to be observed among the masses were made more than once here, too, on the eve of October. Lenin answered such assertions somewhat like this: Even if we were to admit that these assertions are true, that would only show that we have missed the most favorable moment. But that would not mean at all that the conquest of power is impossible at the present moment. After all, nobody will dare to affirm that the majority or even a substantial minority of the mass of the workers will *oppose* revolution. The most that the moderates want to claim is that the majority will not take an active part in the revolution. But it is sufficient if an active minority takes part, with a benevolent, expectant, or even passive mood prevailing among the majority.

That was Lenin's argument. Subsequent events showed that the fighting minority drew behind it the overwhelming majority of the working people. There can be no doubt that events would have followed the same pattern in Germany.

Finally, from the international standpoint as well, the situation of the German revolution cannot be said to have been hopeless. True, imperialist France lay next door to revolutionary Germany. But on the other hand, Soviet Russia also exists in the world, and communism had become stronger in all countries, including France.

What was the fundamental cause of the defeat of the German Communist Party?

This: that it did not appreciate in good time the onset of a revolutionary crisis from the moment of the occupation of the Ruhr, and especially from the moment of the termination of passive resistance (January-June 1923). It missed the crucial moment. . . .

It is very difficult for a revolutionary party to make the transition from a period of agitation and propaganda, prolonged over many years, to the direct struggle for power through the organization of armed insurrection. This turn inevitably gives rise to a crisis within the party. Every responsible communist must be prepared for this. One of the ways of being prepared is to make a thorough study of the entire factual history of the October Revolution. Up to now extremely little has been done in this connection, and the experience of October was most inadequately utilized by the German party. . . . It continued even after the onset of the Ruhr crisis to carry on its agitational and propagandist work on the basis of the united front formula—at the same tempo and in the same forms as before the crisis. Meanwhile, this tactic had already become radically insufficient. A growth in the party's political influence was taking place automatically. A sharp tactical turn was needed. It was necessary to show the masses, and above all the party itself, that this time it was a matter of immediate preparation for the seizure of power. It was necessary to consolidate the party's growing influence organizationally and to establish bases of support for a direct assault on the state. It was necessary to shift the whole party organization onto the basis of factory cells. It was necessary to form cells on the railways. It was necessary to raise sharply the question of work in the army. It was necessary, especially necessary, to adapt the united front tactic fully and completely to these tasks, to give it a firmer and more decided tempo and a more revolutionary character. On the basis of this, work of a military-technical nature should have been carried on.

The question of setting a date for the uprising can have significance only in this connection and with this perspective. Insurrection is an art. An art presumes a clear aim, a precise plan, and consequently a schedule.

The most important thing, however, was this: to ensure *in good time* the decisive tactical turn toward the seizure of power. And this was not done. This was the chief and fatal omission. From this followed the basic contradiction. On the one hand, the party expected a revolution, while on the other hand, because it had burned its fingers in the March events, it avoided, until the last months of 1923, the very idea of organizing a revolution, i.e., preparing an insurrection. The party's political activity was carried on at a peacetime tempo at a time when the denouement was approaching. The time for the uprising was fixed when, in essentials, the enemy had already made use of the time lost by the party and strengthened his position. The party's military-technical preparation, begun at feverish speed, was divorced from the party's political activity, which was carried on at the previous peacetime tempo. The masses did not understand the party and did not keep step with it. The party at once felt its severance from the masses, and proved to be paralyzed. From this resulted the sudden withdrawal from first-class positions without a fight—the bitterest of all possible defeats.

It cannot be thought that history mechanically creates the conditions for revolution and presents them thereafter, at the party's request, at any moment, on a plate: Here you are, sign the receipt, please. That does not happen.

A class must, in the course of prolonged struggle, forge a vanguard which will be able to find its way in a situation, which will recognize revolution when it knocks at the door, which at the necessary moment will be able to grasp the problem of insurrection as an art, to work out a plan, distribute roles, and deal a merciless blow to the bourgeoisie. Well, the German Communist

Party did not find in itself at the decisive moment this ability, this skill, this tempering, and this energy. In order to understand what is involved more clearly, let us imagine for a moment that in October 1917 we had begun to vacillate, to take up a waiting position, that we had drawn aside and said: Let us wait a bit; the situation is still not clear enough. At first sight it appears that the revolution is not a bear, it doesn't run off into the forest—if you haven't made it in October you can make it two or three months later. But such an idea is radically mistaken. It does not take into account the mobile relationship between all those factors which make up a revolution.

The most immediate and intimate condition for revolution is the readiness of the masses to carry out a revolution. But this readiness cannot be preserved. It has to be used at that very moment when it reveals itself. Before October the workers, soldiers, and peasants were marching behind the Bolsheviks. But this, of course, did not at all mean that they themselves were Bolsheviks, that is, that they were capable of following the party *under all conditions and in all circumstances.* They had suffered acute disappointment with the Mensheviks and SRs and that was why they were following the Bolshevik Party. Their disappointment with the conciliationist parties aroused in them hope that the Bolsheviks would be tougher, that they would prove to be made of different stuff from the others and that there would be no gulf between their words and their deeds. If in these circumstances the Bolsheviks had displayed vacillation and taken up a waiting position, then they too would in a short time have been equated in the minds of the masses with the Mensheviks and the SRs: the masses would have turned away from us as rapidly as they had come towards us. In this very way a fundamental change would have taken place in the relationship of forces.

For what is this "relationship of forces," in fact? It is a very complex conception and is made up of many different elements. Among these there are some which are very stable, such as technology and economics, which determine class structure; insofar as the relationship of forces is determined by the numbers of the proletariat, the peasantry, and other classes, we are concerned here with fairly stable factors. But with a given numerical size of a class, the strength of this class depends on the degree of organization and activity of its party, the interrelations between the party and the masses, the mood of the masses, and so on. These factors are much less stable, especially in a revolutionary period, and it is about them, precisely, that we are talking. If the extreme revolutionary party, which the logic of events has placed in the center of attention of the working masses, misses the crucial moment, then the relationship of forces changes fundamentally, for the hopes of the masses, aroused by the party, are replaced by disappointment or passivity and deep despair, and the party retains around itself only those elements which it has lastingly and conclusively won, i.e., a minority.

This is what happened last year in Germany. Everybody, including the social democratic workers, expected the Communist Party to lead the country out of the blind alley it was in; the party was unable to transform this universal expectation into decisive revolutionary actions and lead the proletariat to victory. That is why, after October-November, there began an ebbing of the revolutionary mood. That also provided the basis for the temporary strengthening of bourgeois reaction, for no other, deeper changes (in the class composition of society, in the economy) had been able, certainly, to bring this about up to that time.

In the last parliamentary elections [May 4, 1924] the Communist Party polled 3,700,000 votes. That, of course, is a very, very fine nucleus of the proletariat. But this figure has to be evaluated dynamically. There can be no doubt that in August-October of last year the Communist Party, all other things being equal, could have polled an incomparably larger number of votes. On the other hand, there is much to suggest that if the elections had taken place two or three months later, the Communist Party's vote would have been smaller. This means, in other words, that the party's influence is now on the decline. It would be absurd to shut one's eyes to this: revolutionary politics are not the politics of the ostrich. It is necessary, however, to have a clear understanding of the meaning of this fact.

I have already said that Communist parties are not exempt from the power of the laws of the dialectic, and that their development takes place in contradictions, through booms and crises. In a period of political flood tide the party's influence on the masses grows rapidly; in a period of ebb it is weakened, and the process of internal selection is intensified in the parties. All accidental and unreliable elements depart; the nucleus of the party is welded and tempered. Thereby it is prepared for a fresh revolutionary flood tide. A correct estimate of the situation and a sound view of the future preserve one from mistakes and disappointments. We have already seen the truth of this in relation to the question of industrial booms and crises in the postwar period. We see this again in relation to the question of Europe's entry into a neoreformist phase. Now we need to understand with all possible clarity the stage through which Germany is passing; otherwise we shall not know what the morrow will bring us.

After the defeat of 1905 we needed seven years before the movement, stimulated by the Lena events, began once again to turn upward, and we needed twelve years before the second revolution gave power to the proletariat. The German proletariat suffered last year a very big defeat. It will need a definite and considerable interval of time in order to digest this defeat, master its lessons, and recover from it, gathering its strength once more; and the Communist Party will be able to ensure the victory of the proletariat only if it, too, fully and completely masters the lessons of last year's experience. How much time will be needed for these processes? Five years? Twelve years? No precise answer can be given to this question. One can only express this general idea that the rate of development, in the sense of radical change in the political situation, has become much more rapid and feverish since the war than it was before the war. In economics we see that the productive forces grow very slowly, and, at the same time, downturns and improvements in the conjuncture succeed each other more frequently than before the war. A similar phenomenon is observed in politics too: fascism and Menshevism succeed one another very rapidly; yesterday's situation was profoundly revolutionary and today the bourgeoisie seems to be triumphing all along the line. In this consists also the profoundly revolutionary character of our epoch, and this character of the epoch compels us to draw the conclusion that the triumph of counterrevolution in Germany cannot be longlasting. But at the present moment what we observe are phenomena of ebbtide and not of flood tide, and our tactics should, of course, conform to this situation.

PROBLEMS OF CIVIL WAR

July 29, 1924

NOTE: Looking back in 1928 to summarize the differences that had unfolded after Lenin's death, Trotsky noted that one of them concerned military-revolutionary strategy and the bureaucratic attitude to it. "In 1924," he wrote in The Third International After Lenin,*"a collective work on the elaboration of the directives of civil war, that is, a Marxist guide to the questions of open clashes of the classes and the armed struggle for the dictatorship, was begun by a large circle of individuals grouped around the Military Science Society. But this work soon encountered opposition on the part of the Comintern—this opposition was a part of the general system of the struggle against so-called Trotskyism; and the work was later liquidated altogether. A more lightminded and criminal step can hardly be imagined. . . . Had such regulations been incorporated in a number of books, the serious study of which is as much the duty of every communist as the knowledge of the basic ideas of Marx, Engels, and Lenin, we might well have avoided such defeats as were suffered during recent years, and which were by no means inevitable. . . ."*

The issues involved in the 1924 dispute were analyzed by Trotsky in a speech entitled "Problems of Civil War," delivered to the Military Science Society on July 29, 1924, and reprinted below. Trotsky's remark that the work begun in 1924 "was later liquidated altogether" requires some amendment. Although the Stalinists clamped down on the project, they later revived it themselves—in their own way—in the form of a book published by the Comintern in German in 1928 and in French in 1931; it was translated into English and published by a bourgeois publisher (St. Martin's Press) in London in 1970 as Armed Insurrec-

tion, *by A. Neuberg. In it both theory and fact were subordinated to the interests of the Stalinist faction.*

This translation, from Vol. 12 of Trotsky's Sochineniya *(Collected Works), is by A.L. Preston, and was first published in* International Socialist Review, *March-April 1970. Trotsky and the Russian editor refer to it as a speech to the Military Science Society, but it is clearly a series of remarks with intervals between them for group discussion.—Ed.*

Permit me to make a short introduction to this discussion. Actually, comrades, I have already talked about this in my spring report to the academy. It is a fact that, as yet, no one has taken the trouble to sum up the experience of civil war, either ours or those of other countries. Yet, on practical and ideological counts, there is a very great need for such a work.

Throughout the history of mankind, civil war has played an exceptionally important role. From 1871 to 1914, it seemed (to the reformists) that this role was played out for *Western* Europe. But the imperialist war once more placed civil war on the order of the day. We know this and we understand this. We have included it in our program.

However, we lack almost completely a scientific approach to civil war, its stages, aspects, and methods. Even in regard to the mere description of what has taken place in this sphere over the past decade, we discover monstrous backwardness. I had occasion recently to point out that we devote much time and energy to the study of the Paris Commune of 1871 yet neglect altogether the struggle of the German proletariat, which is already rich in the experience of civil wars, and we hardly concern ourselves at all with the lessons of the Bulgarian insurrection of last September.[22] But what is most surprising is that it seems to be accepted that the experience of the October Revolution should long since have been relegated to the archives.

Yet, comrades, in the October Revolution there is much to be learned by military tacticians, since there is no doubt that to a degree infinitely greater than hitherto, future wars will be combined with various forms of civil war. The preparation for and experience of the Bulgarian insurrection of September last year are likewise of considerable military-revolutionary interest. Since many of the Bulgarian comrades who took part in that insurrection now live in Russia, we have at hand the necessary means for devoting ourselves to a serious study of those events. It is easy, moreover, to get a comprehensive view of them. The country which was the theater of that insurrection is no bigger than a Russian province. And the organization of the forces involved, the political groupings, etc., assumed the character of a government. Furthermore, for those countries (and they are many, notably all of the Eastern countries), where the peasant population predominates, the experience of the Bulgarian insurrection is of colossal importance.

Now, what is our task? To draw up a universal handbook, or guidebook, or textbook, or manual, or book of statutes on the problems of civil war, and consequently, and especially, on armed uprising as the highest stage of a revolution. It will be necessary to collect and coordinate data from civil wars, analyze the conditions under which they took place, study the mistakes, highlight the most successful operations, and draw the necessary conclusions from them. In doing this, what shall we enrich—science, that is, knowledge of the laws of historical evolution, or art, as the totality of rules of action drawn from experience? Both, it seems to me. In any case, our aim is strictly practical: to enrich the military-revolutionary art.

Such a manual will necessarily have a very complex structure. First of all, it will be necessary to characterize the conditions essential for the seizure of power by the proletariat. We remain, therewith, in the sphere of revolutionary politics, for, after all, isn't insurrection the continuation of politics by other means?

Analyses of the conditions essential for insurrection will have to be made for different types of countries. On one hand are those countries where the proletariat is the majority of the population, and on the other are those where the proletariat is a tiny minority among a peasant population. Between these two poles are countries of an intermediate type. That being so, we shall have to base our studies on at least three types of country: industrial, agrarian, and intermediate. The introduction (on the preconditions and conditions for revolution) must characterize each of these types from the standpoint of civil war.

We shall consider insurrection in two ways: first, as a definite stage of a historical process, as a definite refraction of the objective laws of the class struggle; then, from an objective and practical standpoint, how to prepare and carry through an insurrection in order to ensure its success effectively. In this matter war offers us a striking analogy because it, too, is the product of specific historic conditions, the result of a clash of interests. At the same time, warfare is an art. The theory of warfare is the study of the forces and means at one's disposal, their concentration and use, to ensure victory. Likewise, insurrection is an art. In a strictly practical way, in making something like a military manual, we can and should elaborate a theory of insurrection.

At the outset, of course, we shall come up against all kinds of bewilderment and objection from people who say that the idea of writing a manual of insurrection, still more, of civil war, is sheer bureaucratic utopianism: that we want to militarize history; that the revolutionary process is not subject to regulation; that in every country, revolution has its own peculiar features, its uniqueness; that in times of revolution the situation is modified every minute; and that it is chimerical to want to manufacture a series of outlines for the conduct of revolutions, or to draw up—after the fashion of the Austrian high command—a mass of unbreakable regulations and impose strict observance of them.

Now, if anyone were claiming to construct something of this kind, he would really be ridiculous. But basically the same thing can be said against our military manuals. Every war unfolds in a situation and under conditions that no one can foresee. However, without the help of manuals which collect the data of military experience, it would be unthinkable to expect to lead an army in time of peace, let alone of war. The old saying, "Don't cling to the manual like a blind man to a wall," in no way lessens its importance, any more than dialectics lessens the importance of formal logic or the laws of arithmetic.

Undoubtedly in civil war the elements necessary for drawing up plans, for organization, for dispositions, are infinitely more scarce than they are in wars between "national" armies. In civil war, politics participates more closely and more intimately in military actions than it does in "national" wars. Thus, it would be impermissible to mechanically transpose the same methods from one sphere to the other. But it does not at all follow that it is impermissible to base oneself on acquired experience in order to extract from it methods, procedures, indications, directives, and suggestions which show patterns, and to translate them into general rules which might find a place in a manual of civil war.

It is fully agreed that among the rules, mention will be made of the absolute need to subordinate purely military actions to the general political line, to take rigorously into account the overall situation and the mood of the masses.

In any case, before being frightened at the utopianism of such a work, and frightening others with it, it is necessary to decide after profound examination whether there do exist general rules which condition or facilitate victory, and what they are. Only in the course of such an examination will it be possible to define where precise, useful indications, which control the work to be done, stop, and where bureaucratic fantasy begins.

Let us try to deal with a revolution from this point of view: that the highest phase of a revolution is the insurrection, which decides the question of power. The insurrection is always preceded by a period of organization and preparation on the basis of a definite political campaign. As a general rule, the moment of insurrection is brief but decisive in the course of the revolution. If victory is achieved, it is followed by a period which includes the consolidation of the revolution by means of crushing the last enemy forces, and the organization of the new power and the revolutionary forces responsible for the defense of revolution.

That being so, the manual of civil war—we will for the moment arbitrarily give our work this name—will have to consist of three parts at least: the preparation for insurrection, the insurrection, and finally the consolidation of the victory. Thus, besides the basic introduction discussed above, characterizing (in the abridged form of general rules or directives) the prerequisites and conditions for revolution, our manual of civil war should include at least three parts covering the three principal stages of civil war in the order in which they occur. That will be the *strategic* architecture of the whole work.

It is precisely the strategic problem we have to resolve here: how to combine in a logical way all the various forces and resources so as to achieve the main goal, the seizure and defense of power. Each part of the strategy of civil war raises a series of specific, tactical problems, such as the formation of factory units, the organization of revolutionary command posts on the railways and in the towns, and the preparation in detail of the method of seizing vital points in towns. Similar tactical problems will be dealt with in our manual for the period of the crushing of the defeated enemy and the consolidation of the victor's power.

If we adopt such a plan for the work, it will be possible to deal with the many aspects at one and the same time. Thus, we can make one group of comrades responsible for certain tactical questions relating to civil war. Other groups will establish the general strategic plan, the basic introduction, and so on. At the same time, it will be necessary to examine from the angle of civil war the historical material available, for it is clear that it is not our intention to fashion a manual simply out of our heads, but a manual inspired by experience, enlightened and enriched on the one hand by Marxist theories and on the other by the facts of military science.

I am saying nothing for the moment about the system of exposition. It would be premature here to lay things down in advance. We know that military manuals contain only "schemes, but no times or occasions," that is, they give only general directives without the support of precise examples or detailed explanations. Can we adopt the same method of exposition to make the manual of civil war clear? I am not sure. Very possibly we shall have to cite, by way of example, in the manual itself or in an appendix, a certain number of illustrative historical facts, or at least refer to them. That would perhaps be an excellent way of avoiding an excess of schematism. But, I repeat, to lay down the literary construction now is, to say the least, premature.

The Insurrection and Its Timing

Which is it to be—a manual of civil war or a manual of insurrection? I think if we use the word "manual," it should be a manual of civil war.

It is said that some comrades have raised objections to this and have given the impression that they confuse civil war with the class struggle, and insurrection with civil war. Civil war is a definite stage of the class struggle when, breaking through the framework of legality, it brings the opposing forces onto the plane of confrontation, publicly and, to some extent, physically.

Considered in this way, civil war combines a spontaneous uprising determined by local causes, bloody intervention by counterrevolutionary hordes, a revolutionary general strike, an insurrection for the seizure of power, and a period of liquidating attempted counterrevolutionary uprisings. This all comes within the framework of the notion of civil war, which is more than insurrection and yet is very much less than the notion of the class struggle which runs all through history.

If we speak of an insurrection as a task to be carried out, we have to know what we are talking about, and not distort it, as is currently being done, by confusing it with revolution and thus reducing it to nothing. We have to free others from this confusion and begin by ridding ourselves of it.

Insurrection, everywhere and at all times, poses a precise task to be carried out. To this end, we distribute roles; entrust to each his mission (connected, of course, with the movement of the masses); distribute arms; choose the moment; deliver our blows, and seize power—if we are not crushed beforehand. Insurrection should be made according to a plan conceived in advance. It is a definite stage of revolution. The seizure of power does not end a civil war; it only changes its character. Our manual must include this stage, too. So, it is indeed a manual of civil war that is required and not simply of insurrection, although, of course, it is possible to highlight this task as the central one.

We have already referred to the dangers of schematism. Let us look, in the light of an example, at what it can consist of. I have had occasion to point out frequently one of the most dangerous manifestations of schematism in the way that our young staff officers deal with the military problems of the revolution. If we take the three stages we distinguished in civil war, we see that the military work of the leading revolutionary party has, in each of the three periods, a specific character. In the period of preparing for revolution, we clearly are still up against the forces (police, army) of the ruling class. Nine-tenths of the military work of the revolutionary party consists at this time of breaking up the enemy army, dislocating it internally, and one-tenth only of gathering and preparing forces for the revolution. It goes without saying that the mathematical proportions I give are arbitrary; but all the same they give some idea of what the clandestine military work of the revolutionary party should really be.

The nearer the time of insurrection approaches, the more must the work of forming combat organizations be intensified. That is when one can fear certain dangers of academic schematism. It is clear that the combat forces with whose help the revolutionary party is preparing to carry through the insurrection cannot have a regular character, even less the character of higher-level military units, such as brigades, divisions, and army corps. Of course, the leading organ of the uprising must strive to introduce as much planning as possible into it. However, the plan of insurrection is not built on centralized control of revolutionary troops but on the greatest initiative of each detachment which has been assigned in advance, with the maximum precision, the task it has to carry out.

As a general rule, insurgents fight according to "guerrilla" methods, that is, as detachments of a partisan or semipartisan type, bound together much more by political discipline and by the clear consciousness of the single goal to be reached than by some kind of regular, centralized hierarchy of control.

After the seizure of power the situation is changed completely. The struggle of the victorious revolution for self-preservation and development changes immediately into a struggle for the organization of a centralized state apparatus. The partisan attitudes which are not only inevitable, but even profoundly progressive in the period of the struggle for power can, after the conquest of power, become a cause of great danger, liable to rock the revolutionary state which is taking shape. It is here that the period of the organization of a regular Red Army begins. All these factors must be reflected appropriately in the manual of civil war.

The timing of a revolution is closely related to these measures. It goes without saying that it is not a matter of naming arbitrarily, outside of events, a fixed and irrevocable date for the insurrection. Nor is it a defiant, open proclamation of some time or other, in the spirit of an old chronicle: on such and such a date "I'll get you." That would be to have too simplistic an idea of the character of a revolution and its development.

As Marxists, we must know and understand that wanting an insurrection is not sufficient for carrying it out. When the objective conditions for an insurrection present themselves, it won't just happen—it has to be made. And for that, the revolutionary general staff must first have a plan for the insurrection before unleashing it.

The plan of insurrection will give an orientation as to time and place. In the most detailed way, account will be taken of all the factors and elements of the insurrection. An eye will be kept on them to determine accurately their dynamism, to define the distance the vanguard must keep between itself and the working class so as not to be isolated from it while at the same time making the decisive leap.

The timing of the insurrection is one of the necessary elements in this orientation. It will be fixed in advance, as soon as the symptoms of insurrection show themselves clearly. The date will certainly not be divulged to any and everybody. Quite the reverse: it will be concealed as much as possible from the enemy without, however, leading one's own party, and the masses who follow it, into error. The party's work in all spheres will be subordinated to the time set for the insurrection and everything should be ready for the appointed day. If a mistake has been made in the calculations, the date of the insurrection can be altered, although this may be accompanied at the same time by serious inconveniences and many dangers.

It must be recognized that the question of the timing of the insurrection in many cases has the character of litmus paper with which to test the revolutionary consciousness of very many Western European communists, who have still not rid themselves of their fatalistic and passive manner of dealing with the principal problems of revolution. Rosa Luxemburg remains the most profound and talented example. Psychologically, this is fully understandable. She was formed, so to speak, in the struggle against the bureaucratic apparatus of the German social democracy and trade unions. Untiringly, she showed that this apparatus was stifling the initiative of the masses and she saw no alternative but that a spontaneous uprising of the masses would sweep away all the barriers and defenses built by the social democratic bureaucracy. The revolutionary general strike, overflowing all the dikes of bourgeois society, became for Rosa Luxemburg synonymous with the proletarian revolution.

However, whatever its power and mass character, the general strike does not settle the problem of power; it only poses it. To seize power, it is necessary to organize an armed insurrection on the basis of the general strike. The whole of Rosa Luxemburg's evolution, of course, was going in that direction. But when she was snatched from the struggle, she had not yet spoken her last word, nor even the penultimate one.

However, there has been till very recently in the German Communist Party a very strong current of revolutionary fatalism. The revolution is coming, it was said; it will bring the insurrection and power. As for the party, its role at this time is to make revolutionary agitation and await its outcome. Under such conditions, squarely posing the question of the timing of the insurrection means snatching the party from passivity and fatalism and bringing it face to face with the principal problem of revolution, namely, the conscious organization of the insurrection in order to drive the enemy from power.

The question of the timing of the insurrection as outlined above must be dealt with in a manual of civil war. In this way we will facilitate the preparation of the party for insurrection or at least the preparation of its cadres.

It must be borne in mind that the most difficult thing for a Communist party will be passing from the work of preparing for revolution—of necessity long—to the direct struggle for power. This passage will not be made without provoking crises, and serious crises. The only way to reduce their extent and to facilitate the grouping of the most resolute in the leading elements is to lead the party cadres to think about and probe more deeply in advance the questions of the revolutionary insurrection, and this the more concretely the nearer events come.

In this context, a study of the October Revolution is of unique importance for all the European Communist parties. Unfortunately, this study is not being made and will not be as long as the means for it are not made available. We ourselves have neither studied nor coordinated the teachings of the October Revolution and especially the military-revolutionary teachings which emerge from it. It is necessary to follow step by step all the stages of the preparation of the revolution, extending from March to October; the way in which the October insurrection unfolded in some of the most critical points; then the struggle for the consolidation of power.

For whom do we propose this manual of civil war? For the workers, answer certain comrades, so that each of them knows how to handle himself. Obviously, it would be very good if "every" worker knew what he had to do. But that is to pose the question on too large a scale, and thus is utopian. In any case, it is not from this end that we should begin. Our manual should be meant in the first place for the party cadres, for the leaders of the revolution. Naturally, in some chapters, certain questions meant for larger circles of workers will be given a popular turn of phrase; but primarily, it will be addressed to the leaders.

As a preliminary step, we must collect for ourselves our own experiences and ideas, formulate them as clearly as possible, verify them in detail and, as far as is possible, systematize them. Before the imperialist war, some military writers complained that wars had become too scarce for the good instruction of officers. With no less reason, we can say that the scarcity of revolutions hampers the education of revolutionaries. But in this connection, our own generation has no cause for complaint. We who belonged to it had the good fortune to be mature enough to make the revolution of 1905 and to live long enough to take a leading part in the revolution of 1917.

But, needless to say, day-to-day revolutionary experiences are rapidly dissipated. How many new, practical, continuing, particular and pressing problems we now have in their place! Aren't we compelled today to discuss questions like the manufacture of cloth, the building of the Volkhov electrical factory, the production of aluminum, rather than how to make an insurrection? But this last question is far from being obsolete. More than once, history will demand an answer to it.

When to Begin

The German catastrophe of last year has placed before the Communist International the problem of how to organize a revolution and, in particular, a revolutionary insurrection. In this context, the problem of the timing of the revolution is of major importance, because it has emerged clearly and beyond evasion that here all questions relating to the organization of revolution become acute. The social democracy has adopted toward revolution the attitude that liberalism had toward the bourgeoisie's struggle for power against feudalism and the monarchy. Bourgeois liberalism speculates on revolution without assuming responsibility for it. At the propitious moment in the struggle of the masses, it throws into the balance its wealth, knowledge, and other means of class influence in order to lay its hands on the power. In November 1918, the German social democracy played just such a role. Basically, it constituted the apparatus which transmitted to the bourgeoisie the political power that had fallen from the hands of the Hohenzollerns. Such a policy of passive speculation is absolutely incompatible with communism, which sets itself the goal of seizing power in the name and interests of the proletariat.

Proletarian revolution is a revolution of huge and mostly unorganized masses. The blind upsurge of the masses plays a considerable part in the movement. Victory can be achieved only by a Communist party which is centralized; which sets itself as a precise objective the seizure of power; which carefully thinks out this aim, refines it, prepares it and fulfills it, relying on the insurrection of the masses. By its centralization, decisiveness, and planned approach to armed insurrection, the Communist party brings to the proletariat in the struggle for power the same advantages the bourgeoisie has from its economic position. In this context, the timing of the insurrection is not just some technical detail; it expresses in the clearest and most precise way the insurrection as an art.

Clearly, when it is a question of the timing of an insurrection, calculations cannot be based on purely military experiences. Having at its disposal adequate armed forces, a state can, generally speaking, unleash war at any moment. Then, during the war, the supreme command decides on the offensive—not, of course, arbitrarily, but after having weighed all the facts of the situation. However, it is still easier to analyze a purely military situation than a revolutionary-political one.

The military command has to deal with organized forces and relations which have been carefully studied and prepared, thanks to which the command has its armies, so to speak, in its hands. Clearly it cannot be the same in a revolution. Here the combat units are not separated from the masses of the workers; they can intensify the violence of their blows only when linked with the offensive movement of the masses. That being so, it is up to the revolutionary command to grasp the rhythm of the movement in order to decide, with sure judgment, on the time when the offensive is to take place. As we see, the timing of an insurrection poses a difficult problem.

It can happen, of course, that the situation is so clear that the party leadership has no further doubts about the timeliness for action: the hour has struck—it is necessary to go into action. But if such an evaluation of the situation is made twenty-four hours before the decisive moment, the call to action may arrive too late. The party, taken unawares, is consequently placed in the impossible position of leading a movement which, in this case, can end up in defeat. Hence the need to foresee as far in advance as possible the coming of the decisive moment or, in other words, to fix the timing of the insurrection well ahead on the basis of the general progress of the movement and the overall situation in the country.

If, for example, the time is fixed a month or two in advance, the Central Committee or the leading organ of the party takes advantage of the interval. It gives the party the necessary momentum through decisive agitation, which poses all fundamental questions point-blank and, through corresponding organizational preparations, the selection and appointment of the most combative elements, etc.

It goes without saying that a date fixed two or three—or, still more, four—months ahead cannot be irrevocable; but the tactic should be to verify throughout the determined interval whether the chosen date was correct. Let us look at an example.

The political preconditions for the success of an armed insurrection lie in the support which the majority of workers in the principal centers and regions of a country give to the militant vanguard, and the corresponding shattering of the governmental apparatus. Let us suppose that things have not yet reached the critical point but are near it. The forces of the revolutionary party are growing rapidly, but the party still finds it difficult to say whether it has the necessary majority behind it. Meanwhile, the situation is becoming increasingly serious. The question of insurrection is posed practically. What should the party Central Committee do? It can, for instance, reason this way:

1. Since, judging by the tempo of the last weeks, the influence of the party is growing rapidly, it is permissible to believe that in

such and such main centers of the country the majority of workers are on the point of following us. Under these conditions, let us concentrate the best forces of the party on the decisive points, and let us assume that we shall need about a month to win the majority.

2. Once most of the principal centers are with us, we can call on the workers to set up soviets of workers' deputies, on the condition—it is well understood—that the further shattering of the governmental apparatus will continue. Let us assume that setting up soviets in the main centers and regions of the country requires another two weeks.

3. Once the soviets are organizationally under the leadership of the party in the main centers and regions of the country, it follows naturally that the summoning of a national congress of soviets is called for. This requires a further three or four weeks.

Now, it is perfectly evident that in such a situation, the congress of soviets will simply crown the seizure of power; otherwise the congress will be an empty show and will be dispersed—in other words, by the time of the congress, the real apparatus of power will be in the hands of the proletariat. So the insurrection is indicated for two to two and a half months ahead: two and a half months is set as the interval for the preparation of the insurrection.

This time gap, flowing from the general analysis already made of the political situation and its later development, defines the character and tempo that must be given to the military-revolutionary work. Its aim will be the disorganization of the bourgeois army, the seizure of the railway networks, the formation and arming of worker detachments, and so on. We allot to the clandestine commander of the city to be conquered well-defined tasks: the taking of such and such measures during the first four weeks, the checking of all dispositions, and the intensification of preparations during the following two weeks so that in the subsequent two weeks everything will be ready for the action. In this way, by carrying out limited but clearly defined tasks, the military-revolutionary work is completed within the set interval.

We avoid falling into disorder and passivity, which can be fatal, and we get on the contrary the necessary fusion of effort flowing from the strengthened resolution of all the leaders of the movement. At the same time, political work will continue undiminished. The revolution follows its own logical course. After a month we will be in a position to check whether the party has really succeeded in winning the majority of workers in the princi-

pal centers of the country. This checkup can be made through
some kind of referendum, or trade union action, or by street
demonstrations; best of all, by a combination of all of them.

If we are convinced that the first stage we outlined to ourselves
has been passed as we expected, the date fixed for the insurrection is reinforced in an exceptional way. On the contrary, if it is
shown that whatever may have been the growth of our influence
during the past month, we still do not have the majority of
workers behind us, it would be prudent to postpone the date of
insurrection. During this period we shall have many opportunities for checking how far the ruling class has lost its head and to
what extent the army has become demoralized and the apparatus
of repression weakened. From these observations we shall be able
to assess the nature of any weaknesses that may have shown up
in our clandestine work of revolutionary preparation.

The organization of soviets will then become a future means of
verifying the relationship of forces and thereby establishing
whether the conditions are right for unleashing the insurrection.
Clearly, it will not always be possible at all times and in all
places to set up soviets before an insurrection. One must even
expect that soviets can be organized only during the action. But,
in all cases where, under the leadership of the Communist party,
it is possible to organize soviets before the overthrow of the
bourgeois regime, they will emerge as the prelude to the coming
insurrection. And the date will be only the easier to fix for this.

The party Central Committee will check up on the work of its
military organization. It will assess the results obtained in each
branch and, to the extent that the political situation requires it,
will give the necessary extra drive to that work. We must expect
that the military organization, which bases itself not on the
general analysis of the situation and the relationship of existing
forces, but on its appreciation of the results it has obtained in its
preparatory activity, will always consider itself insufficiently
prepared. But it goes without saying that what is decisive at this
time is the assessment made of the situation and the relationship
of the respective forces, the enemy's shock troops and ours. Thus
a date set two, three, or four months ahead can have an un-
equalled effect on the organization of the insurrection, even if we
are compelled by later developments to advance or postpone it a
few days.

It is clear that the preceding example is purely hypothetical,
but it is an excellent illustration of the ideas that should prevail
on the preparation of an insurrection. It is not a matter of playing

blindly with dates but of fixing the date for the insurrection, basing oneself on the progress of events themselves, checking the correctness of the date during the successive stages of the movement, and then setting the final date to which all other preparatory revolutionary work will be subordinated.

I repeat that in this context a most attentive study should be made of the lessons of the October Revolution, the only revolution to date which the proletariat has carried through successfully. From the strategic and tactical standpoints, we should compile a calendar of October. We should demonstrate how events developed, wave after wave, what the repercussions were in the party, in the soviets, inside the Central Committee, and in the party's military organizations. What was the meaning of the hesitation that showed itself in the party? How heavily did it weigh in the sum total of events? What was the role of the military organization? This is a work of incalculable value. To postpone it is to commit an unpardonable crime.

The Calm before the Storm

There is a further matter of considerable value for the understanding of civil war which, in one way or another, our future "manual" should deal with. Whoever kept in touch with the discussions following the German events of 1923 must certainly have noted the explanation given for the defeat: "The main reason was that the German proletariat was totally lacking in fighting spirit at the decisive moment; the masses did not want to fight—the best proof of which is that they did not react at all to the fascist offensive; so, faced with this attitude of the masses, what could the party do?" and so on, and so on, in the same strain.

That is what we heard from Comrades Brandler, Thalheimer, and the others. At first glance, the argument seems irrefutable: The masses did not want to fight; so what could the party do? However, where did the "decisive moment" come from? It was the result of a whole preceding period of struggles which kept increasing and growing sharper.

The year 1923 was marked from beginning to end by battles which the German proletariat was compelled to fight. So how did it happen that on the eve of its own October the German working class suddenly gave up its combative mood? This is incomprehensible. The question follows naturally: Is there any true indication that the workers did not want to fight? This question leads us back to our experience in the events of our October.

If we reread the newspapers (even only the party's) of the time preceding the October Revolution, we see comrades opposing the idea of an insurrection, arguing specifically about the unwillingness of the Russian workers to fight. Today, it scarcely seems credible, yet that was the main argument they brought forward. So we find ourselves in an analogous position: all through 1917 the Russian proletariat had been in action; yet, when the question of the seizure of power was posed, voices were raised saying that the masses of workers did not want to fight.

In fact, on the eve of October, the movement did slow down a little. Was that the effect of chance? Or rather, should we not see here some historical "law"? To formulate this law would, perhaps, be premature. But without a doubt, such a phenomenon must have some general cause. In nature, the phenomenon is called the calm before the storm. I am inclined to believe that in a revolutionary period this phenomenon has no other meaning.

During a given period the combativeness of the proletariat grows; it takes different forms: strikes, demonstrations, street confrontations. For the first time the masses begin to grow conscious of their strength. The growing dimensions of the movement are now sufficient for political satisfaction. Yesterday hundreds and thousands took part in the movement, today millions. A whole series of economic and political positions are adopted through elemental pressure; therefore the masses readily join in every new strike.

But this period inevitably exhausts itself. As the experience of the masses becomes greater, their organization develops. In the opposing camp, the enemy shows that it has decided not to yield without a fight. The result is that the revolutionary mood of the masses becomes more critical, more profound, more uneasy. The masses are looking—especially if they have made mistakes and suffered defeats—for a reliable leadership; they want to be convinced that we will and can lead them and that in the decisive battle they can count on victory.

Now, it is this turn from quasi-blind optimism to a clearer consciousness of the difficulties, that causes this revolutionary pause, corresponding, to some extent, to a crisis in the mood of the masses. If the rest of the situation lends itself to it, this crisis can be overcome but only by a political party, and above all by the impression this party gives of being genuinely decided on leading an insurrection.

Meanwhile, the historic grandeur of the goal to be attained (the seizure of power) inevitably raises hesitation right inside the party, especially in its leading circles on whom will soon be concentrated the responsibility for the movement. So the retreat of the masses before the battle and the hesitation of the leaders are two phenomena which, without being equivalent, are nonetheless simultaneous. That is why we hear warning voices saying: The masses don't want to fight; on the contrary, their mood is passive; under these conditions it would be adventurism to drive them to insurrection. It goes without saying that when such a mood prevails the revolution can only be defeated. And after the defeat, provoked by the party itself, there is nothing to stop the party telling all and sundry that the insurrection was an impossibility because the masses did not want it.

This question must be examined in full. Basing oneself on acquired experience, one must learn to recognize the preinsurrectionary moment when the proletariat says to itself: Nothing more is to be gained from strikes, demonstrations, and other protests. Now we must fight. I am ready because there is no other way out; but it must be a fight to the finish, that is, with all our strength and under a reliable leadership.

At such a time the situation is extremely critical. There is the most complete disequilibrium: a ball on the tip of a cone. The slightest shock can make it fall one way or another. In our case, thanks to the firmness and resolution of the party leadership, the ball followed the line which led to victory. In Germany, the party policy sent the ball on the line to defeat.

Politics and Military Affairs

How shall we characterize our "manual"—as political or military? We begin at the point where politics changes into military action, and therefore look at politics from the point of view of military action. At first glance this might appear contradictory because it is not politics which serves insurrection but insurrection which serves politics. In reality there is no contradiction here. Clearly, insurrection entirely serves the basic aims of proletarian politics. But when the insurrection is unleashed, the politics of the period must be entirely subordinate to it.

The turn from politics to military action and the conjunction of these two alternatives generally create great difficulties. We all know that the point of junction is always the weakest. Also it is easy to stumble at the point of the junction of politics and its military continuation. We have considered this a little here.

Comrade X has shown by negative example how difficult it is to combine politics and military action correctly. Comrade Y followed and aggravated the previous speaker's error. If we are to believe Comrade X, Lenin, in 1918, denied the importance of the Red Army, on the ground that our security depended on the struggle which had pitted the rival imperialisms against each other. According to Comrade Y we played "the role of third robber."

Comrade Lenin never did nor could he have used this kind of language. Both comrades have made here an incorrect transition from politics to military affairs. It is absolutely certain that at the time of the October Revolution, if we had had to contend with a victorious Germany, with peace concluded in Europe, Germany would not have failed to crush us even if we had had one hundred thousand, five hundred thousand, or three million men in the field. Neither in 1918 nor in 1919 would we have been able to find the strength to stand up against the triumphant German armies. Consequently, the struggle between the two imperialist camps was our chief line of defense.

But within the framework of that struggle we would have met death a hundred times if, in 1918, we had not had our small and weak Red Army. Was it because England and France had paralyzed Germany that the Kazan problem was solved?[23] Had our half-partisan, half-regular divisions not defended Kazan, making the Whites move on to Nizhny and Moscow, they would have cut our throats like chickens, and they would have been right to do so. At that time it would have been a sorry game to make a show of being "the third robber"—with our throats cut.

When Comrade Lenin said, "Dear friends, militant workers, do not exaggerate your importance; you represent one factor in the complex of forces, but you are neither the only nor the main one; in reality, we are maintaining ourselves thanks to the European war which is paralyzing the two rival imperialisms," he was taking a political point of view. But it does not follow that he was denying "the importance of the Red Army." Were we to apply this method of argumentation to the internal problems of a revolution, for example, to armed insurrection, we would end up with some very curious conclusions.

For instance, let us take the question of the organization of combat units. A Communist party whose existence is more or less illegal charges its clandestine military organization with the formation of fighting units, What, basically, do a few dozen units set up in this way represent in relation to the problem of the seizure of power? From the social and historical point of view, the question of power is decided by the composition of the society, by the role of the proletariat in production, by its political maturity, by the degree of disorganization in the bourgeois state, and so on. In reality, all these factors play their parts, but only in the long run, whereas the outcome of the struggle can depend directly on the existence of these few dozen units.

The requisite social and political conditions for the seizure of power are the preconditions of success (and the introduction to the manual should deal with them); but they do not automatically guarantee victory. They allow us to go forward to the point where politics gives way to insurrection—where we say: Now let's do some work with bayonets.

Once more, civil war is only the sharpened continuation of the class struggle. As for insurrection, it is the continuation of politics by other methods. That is why it can be understood only from the angle of its special methods. It is not possible to measure politics on the scale of war any more than it is possible to measure war on the scale of politics, if only for the matter of time. This is a special problem which merits serious treatment in our future manual of civil war. In the period of revolutionary preparation, we measure time on the political scale, that is, in years, months, and weeks. In the period of insurrection we measure time in days and hours.

It is not for nothing that we say that in time of war a month, sometimes even a single day, counts for a whole year. In April 1917 Comrade Lenin said, "Patiently, tirelessly, explain to the workers . . ." At the end of October there was no time to give explanations to those who had not yet understood; it was necessary to go over to the offensive, leading those who had already grasped what was what. In October, the loss of a single day could have brought to nought all the work of several months, even years, of revolutionary preparation.

This reminds me of a theme for maneuvers we gave some time ago to our Military Academy. There was some disagreement concerning the decision whether to immediately evacuate the Byelostok region, where the position was untenable, or whether to hold on in the hope that Byelostok, a workers' center, would rise in insurrection. It goes without saying that this kind of problem cannot be settled seriously except on the basis of precise and real data. A military maneuver does not have these data since everything about it is conventional. However, in practice, the controversy turned on two time scales: one purely military, the other revolutionary-political. Now all things being equal, which scale will give success in war?

The military one. In other words, it was doubtful whether Byelostok could rise in the space of a few days, and even granting that it could, it still remained to be learned what the insurgent proletariat could do, without arms and without any military preparation. And at the same time, it was very possible that in those two or three days, two or three divisions would be decimated while holding on in an untenable position, hoping for an insurrection which, even if it did take place, could not very well radically modify the military situation.

Brest-Litovsk gives us a classic example of an incorrect application of political and military time scales. As is known, the majority of the Central Committee of the Russian Communist Party, myself among them, decided, against the minority headed by Lenin, not to sign the peace, although we ran the risk of seeing the Germans go over to the offensive. What was the meaning of that decision? Some comrades were hoping in a utopian way for a revolutionary war. Others, including myself, thought it necessary to try out the German workers in order to learn whether they would oppose the Kaiser should he attack the revolution.

What was the error we committed? In the excessive risk we ran. To stir up the German workers would have required weeks, even months, whereas at that time the German armies needed only a few days to advance as far as Dvinsk, Minsk, and Moscow. The time scale of revolutionary politics is long; the time scale of war is short. And—this must be done with personal experience—whoever does not reach a clear conclusion, which has to be thought out and generalized, runs the risk of creating a source of new errors at the point where revolutionary politics and military action are conjoined, that is, in the field which gives us superiority over the enemy.

The Need for Utmost Clarity

Comrade P has brought us back to the question of what kind of manual we are to write, a manual of insurrection or of civil war. We should not, our comrade tells us, aim too high; otherwise, in a general way, our task will duplicate the tasks of the Communist International. Nothing of the kind! Whoever uses this kind of language shows that he is confusing civil war, using the term correctly, with class struggle.

If we take Germany as the subject for study, for example, we can, with great profit, begin by studying the events of March 1921. Then follows a long period of the regroupment of forces under the slogan of the united front. It is evident that no manual of civil war is suitable for this period. In January 1923, with the occupation of the Ruhr, again there is a revolutionary situation, which is sharply aggravated in June 1923 when the policy of passive resistance played by the German bourgeoisie collapses and the apparatus of the bourgeois state cracks at all its seams. This is the period we ought to study in detail, because it gives us on the one hand a classic example of how a revolutionary situation develops and ripens and, on the other hand, a no less classic example of a revolution that was missed.

Last year Germany had its civil war, but the armed insurrection that should have crowned and settled it did not come. The result was a truly exceptional revolutionary situation which was irremediably compromised, leading to a new consolidation of the bourgeoisie. Why? Because at the right moment politics was not continued by the other necessary means, that is, by the means of arms.

It is clear that the bourgeois regime which has been restored in Germany, following the abortion of the proletarian revolution, is of dubious stability. We can be sure we shall have again in Germany, in due course, sooner or later, a fresh revolutionary situation. It is clear that August 1924 will be very different from August 1923. But if we close our eyes to the experience of these events, if we do not use this experience to educate ourselves, if we continue passively to make mistakes like those already made, we can expect to see the German catastrophe of 1923 repeated, and the consequent dangers for the revolutionary movement will be immense.

That is why, on this question more than any other, we cannot tolerate any distortion of our fundamental ideas. We have heard here incoherent, skeptical objections on the subject of the timing of the insurrection. They only show the inability to pose in a Marxist way the question of insurrection as an art.

The argument that in the confusion of an extremely complex and variable situation, it is impermissible to tie one's hands in advance by some decision or other, was invoked as something new and instructive. But if we want to carry such commonplaces to their logical conclusion, we shall have to renounce plans and dates in military operations too, because in war it also happens that the situation changes sharply and unexpectedly. No military operation is ever fulfilled 100 percent; we must even count ourselves lucky if it is fullfilled 25 percent, in other words, if it only undergoes a 75 percent change while being executed. But any military leader who relied on this to deny the usefulness of a plan of campaign in general would quite simply deserve to be put in a straitjacket.

In any case, I recommend sticking closely to this method as the most correct and most logical one: first formulate the general rules, general norms; then see what can be omitted or held back. But if we begin by omitting and reserving, deviating, doubting, and hesitating, we shall never come to any conclusion.

One comrade participating in this discussion has challenged a remark I made on the evolution of the party's military organization in the period of revolutionary preparation, during the insurrection, and after the seizure of power. According to this comrade, the existence of partisan detachments should not be permitted because only regular military formations are necessary. Partisan detachments, he tells us, are chaotic organizations. . . .

Hearing these words, I was near to despair. What kind of impossible, doctrinaire, and academic arrogance is this? If partisan detachments are chaotic, then, from this purely formal point of view, we must recognize that revolution, too, is chaotic.

Now, in the first period of a revolution we are completely compelled to rely on such detachments. Objection is made to us that the detachments should be built along regular lines. If that means that in partisan warfare we must not neglect any element of order and method suited to this kind of warfare, we are in full agreement. But if someone is dreaming of some kind of hierarchical military organization, centralized and constituted before the insurrection has taken place, that would be utopianism which, when you put it in practice, would threaten to prove fatal.

If, with the help of a clandestine military organization, I have to seize a town (a partial goal in the overall plan for seizing power in a country), I divide my work into separate objectives: occupation of government buildings, railway stations, post offices, telegraph offices, printing works. And I allot the execution of each of these missions to heads of small detachments who are enlightened beforehand about the goals they have been assigned to. Each detachment must be self-reliant; it must have its own commissary, otherwise it can happen that after seizing the post office, for example, it will be totally lacking in food supplies. Any attempt to centralize and hierarchize these detachments would inevitably lead to bureaucratism, which in time of war is doubly reprehensible: first, because it would make the heads of detachments falsely believe that someone else will pass them orders whereas, on the contrary, they must be fully convinced that they can exercise the greatest freedom of movement and maximum initiative; second, because bureaucratism, tied to a hierarchical system, would transfer the best elements from the detachments to the needs of all kinds of general staffs. From the first moment of the insurrection, these general staffs for the most part will be suspended between heaven and earth, while the detachments, waiting for orders from above, will find themselves suffering inaction and loss of time. This will ensure that the insurrection will fail. For these reasons, the contempt of professional soldiers for "chaotic" partisan organizations must be condemned as unrealistic, unscientific, and non-Marxist.

Similarly, after the seizure of power in the principal centers of a country, the partisan detachments can play an extremely effective role in the periphery of the country. Do we have to remind ourselves of the help the partisan detachments brought to the Red Army and the revolution by operating behind the German troops in the Ukraine and behind Kolchak's troops in Siberia?

Nevertheless, we must formulate this incontrovertible rule: the revolutionary power works to incorporate the best partisan detachments and their most reliable elements into the system of a regular military organization. Otherwise these partisan detachments could undoubtedly become factors of disorder, capable of degenerating into armed bands in the service of petty-bourgeois anarchistic elements for use against the proletarian state. We have not a few examples of this.

It is true that among the partisans rebelling against the idea of a regular military organization there have also been heroes. The names of Sivers and Kikvidze have been cited. I could name many more. Sivers and Kikvidze fought and died as heroes. And today, in the light of their immense merits for the revolution, this and that negative side of their partisan actions fade to nothingness. Yet, at the time, it was absolutely necessary to fight against everything that was negative in them. Only through fighting against partisanism did we succeed in organizing the Red Army and achieve decisive victories.

Once again, I warn against confusion in terminology, because most often it masks confusion in ideas. Similarly, I warn against mistakes that can be made by refusing to pose the question of insurrection in a clear and courageous way on the pretext that situations vary and are constantly being modified.

Superficially, in a strange sort of way, this is called dialectics; in any case, it is willingly accepted as such. But in reality it is nothing of the kind. Dialectical thought is like a spring, and springs are made of tempered steel. Doubt and reservations teach nothing at all. When the essential idea is brought into high relief, reservations and limitations can be arranged around it in a logical way. If we stay only with the reservations, the result will be confusion in theory and chaos in practice. But confusion and chaos have nothing in common with dialectics. In reality, pseudo-dialectics of this kind most often hides social democratic or stupid sentiments about revolution, as though it were something made outside ourselves. Were it so, there would be no question of conceiving of insurrection as an art. And yet it is precisely the theory of this art we wish to study.

All the questions we have raised should be thought out, worked over, and formulated. They should be an integral part of our military instruction and education, at least for the high command.

The relation of these questions to the problems of the defense of the Soviet Union are indisputable. Our enemies continue to charge that the Red Army has what they call the task of artificially provoking revolutionary movements in other countries: they do this in order to stop these movements by force of bayonets. Needless to say, this caricature has nothing in common with the policy we pursue. We are above all interested in the maintenance of peace; we have proved this by our attitude, by the concessions we have made in treaties, and by the progressive reduction of our armed forces.

But we are sufficiently imbued with revolutionary realism to take clearly into account that our enemies will attempt to test us with their arms. And, if we are far from the idea of forcing, by artificial military measures, the development of revolution, we are on the other hand convinced that a war by capitalist states against the Soviet Union will be followed by violent social upheavals, the preconditions of civil war, in the lands of our enemies. We must be ready for this.

We must know how to combine the defensive war that will be imposed on our Red Army with civil war in the enemy camp. To this end, the manual of civil war should become one of the necessary elements in a superior type of military-revolutionary instruction.

THE LESSONS OF OCTOBER

September 15, 1924

NOTE: Unable to directly express most of his views in public, Trotsky turned to the historical record for vindication. In the autumn of 1924 the State Publishing House issued a volume of his speeches and writings from 1917. He prefaced it with a long article entitled "Lessons of October." Written under the influence of the recent defeat in Germany, the essay reexamines the crucial turning points of the Russian revolution and relates the German events to the failure to grasp and generalize the lessons of the Russian experience, and to the lack of understanding of the dynamics of a revolutionary period. In his review of the history of the Russian party during the October Revolution, Trotsky concentrates on the roles played by Zinoviev and Kamenev, instead of Stalin. This was because Zinoviev and Kamenev played more prominent roles in 1917 than Stalin, and also because Trotsky considered them more serious opponents in 1924.

"Lessons of October" was first published in English in Inprecorr, February 26, 1925. It was printed in book format in 1937 by Pioneer Publishers, in a translation by John G. Wright. Except for a few corrections and changes for stylistic consistency, that version has been used here.—Ed.

Chapter 1
We Must Study the October Revolution

We met with success in the October Revolution, but the October Revolution has met with little success in our press. Up to the present time we lack a single work which gives a comprehensive picture of the October upheaval and puts the proper stress upon its most important political and organizational aspects. Worse yet, even the available firsthand material—including the most important documents—directly pertaining to the various particulars of the preparation for the revolution, or the revolution itself, remains unpublished as yet. Numerous documents and considerable material have been issued bearing on the pre-October history of the revolution and the pre-October history of the party; we have also issued much material and many documents relating to the post-October period. But October itself has received far less attention. Having achieved the revolution, we seem to have concluded that we should never have to repeat it. It is as if we thought that no immediate and direct benefit for the unpostponable tasks of future constructive work could be derived from the study of October; the actual conditions of the direct preparation for it; the actual accomplishment of it; and the work of consolidating it during the first few weeks.

Such an approach—though it may be subconscious—is, however, profoundly erroneous, and is, moreover, narrow and nationalistic. We ourselves may never have to repeat the experience of the October Revolution, but this does not at all imply that we have nothing to learn from that experience. We are a part of the International, and the workers in all other countries are still faced with the solution of the problem of their own "October." Last year we had ample proof that the most advanced Communist parties of the West had not only failed to assimilate our October experience but were virtually ignorant of the actual facts.

To be sure, the objection may be raised that it is impossible to study October or even to publish documents relating to October without the risk of stirring up old disagreements. But such an approach to the question would be altogether petty. The disagreements of 1917 were indeed very profound, and they were not by any means accidental. But nothing could be more paltry than an attempt to turn them now, after a lapse of several years, into weapons of attack against those who were at that time mistaken. It would be, however, even more inadmissible to remain silent as regards the most important problems of the October Revolution, which are of international significance, on account of trifling personal considerations.

Last year we met with two crushing defeats in Bulgaria. First, the party let slip an exceptionally favorable moment for revolutionary action on account of fatalistic and doctrinaire considerations. (That moment was the rising of the peasants after the June coup of Tsankov.) Then the party, striving to make good its mistake, plunged into the September insurrection without having made the necessary political or organizational preparations. The Bulgarian revolution ought to have been a prelude to the German revolution. Unfortunately, the bad Bulgarian prelude led to an even worse sequel in Germany itself. In the latter part of last year, we witnessed in Germany a classic demonstration of how it is possible to miss a perfectly exceptional revolutionary situation of world-historic importance. Once more, however, neither the Bulgarian nor even the German experiences of last year have received an adequate or sufficiently concrete appraisal. The author of these lines drew a general outline of the development of events in Germany last year. Everything that transpired since then has borne out this outline in part and as a whole. No one else has even attempted to advance any other explanation. But we need more than an outline. It is indispensable for us to have a concrete account, full of factual data, of last year's developments in Germany. What we need is such an account as would provide a concrete explanation of the causes of this most cruel historic defeat.

It is difficult, however, to speak of an analysis of the events in Bulgaria and Germany when we have not, up to the present, given a politically and tactically elaborated account of the October Revolution. We have never made clear to ourselves what we accomplished and how we accomplished it. After October, in the flush of victory, it seemed as if the events of Europe would develop of their own accord and, moreover, within so brief a period as would leave no time for any theoretical assimilation of the lessons of October.

But the events have proved that without a party capable of directing the proletarian revolution, the revolution itself is rendered impossible. The proletariat cannot seize power by a spontaneous uprising. Even in highly industrialized and highly cultured Germany the spontaneous uprising of the toilers—in November 1918—only succeeded in transferring power to the hands of the bourgeoisie. One propertied class is able to seize the power that has been wrested from another propertied class because it is able to base itself upon its riches, its cultural level, and its innumerable connections with the old state apparatus. But there is nothing else that can serve the proletariat as a substitute for its own party.

It was only by the middle of 1921 that the fully rounded-out work of building the Communist parties really began (under the slogan "Win the masses," "United front," etc.). The problems of October receded and, simultaneously, the study of October was also relegated to the background. Last year we found ourselves once again face to face with the problems of the proletarian revolution. It is high time we collected all documents, printed all available material, and applied ourselves to their study!

We are well aware, of course, that every nation, every class, and even every party learns primarily from the harsh blows of its own experience. But that does not in the least imply that the experience of other countries and classes and parties is of minor importance. Had we failed to study the Great French Revolution, the revolution of 1848, and the Paris Commune, we should never have been able to achieve the October Revolution, even though we passed through the experience of the year 1905. And after all, we went through this "national" experience of ours basing ourselves on deductions from previous revolutions, and extending their historical line. Afterwards, the entire period of the counterrevolution was taken up with the study of the lessons to be learned and the deductions to be drawn from the year 1905.

Yet no such work has been done with regard to the victorious revolution of 1917—no, not even a tenth part of it. Of course we are not now living through the years of reaction, nor are we in exile. On the other hand, the forces and resources at our command now are in no way comparable to what we had during those years of hardship. All that we need do is to pose clearly and plainly the task of studying the October Revolution, both on the party scale and on the scale of the International as a whole. It is indispensable for the entire party, and especially its younger generations, to study and assimilate step by step the experience of October, which provided the supreme, incontestable, and irrevocable test of the past and opened wide the gates to the future. The German lesson of last year is not only a serious reminder but also a dire warning.

An objection will no doubt be raised that even the most thorough knowledge of the course of the October Revolution would by no means have guaranteed victory to our German party. But this kind of wholesale and essentially philistine rationalizing will get us nowhere. To be sure, mere study of the October Revolution is not sufficient to secure victory in other countries; but circumstances may arise where all the prerequisites for revolution exist, with the exception of a farseeing and resolute party leadership grounded in the understanding of the laws and methods of the revolution. This was exactly the situation last year in Germany. Similar situations may recur in other countries. But for the study of the laws and methods of proletarian revolution there is, up to the present time, no more important and profound a source than our October experience. Leaders of European Communist parties who fail to assimilate the history of October by means of a critical and closely detailed study would resemble a commander in chief preparing new wars under modern conditions, who fails to study the strategic, tactical, and technical experience of the last imperialist war. Such a commander in chief would inevitably doom his armies to defeat in the future.

The fundamental instrument of proletarian revolution is the party. On the basis of our experience—even taking only one year, from February 1917 to February 1918—and on the basis of the supplementary experience in Finland, Hungary, Italy, Bulgaria, and Germany, we can posit as almost an unalterable law that a party crisis is inevitable in the transition from preparatory revolutionary activity to the immediate struggle for power. Generally speaking, crises arise in the party at every serious turn in the party's course, either as a prelude to the turn or as a consequence of it. The explanation for this lies in the fact that every period in the development of the party has special features of its own and calls for specific habits and methods of work. A tactical turn implies a greater or lesser break in these habits and methods. Herein lies the direct and most immediate root of internal party frictions and crises. "Too often has it happened," wrote Lenin in July 1917, "that, when history has taken a sharp turn, even progressive parties have for some time been unable to adapt themselves to the new situation and have repeated slogans which had formerly been correct but had now lost all meaning—lost it as 'suddenly' as the sharp turn in history was 'sudden' "[*CW*, Vol. 25, "On Slogans" (mid-July 1917), p. 183]. Hence the danger arises that if the turn is too abrupt or too sudden, and if in the preceding period too many elements of inertia and conservatism have accumulated in the leading organs of the party, then the party will prove itself unable to fulfill its leadership at that supreme and critical moment for which it has been preparing itself in the course of years or decades. The party is ravaged by a crisis, and the movement passes the party by—and heads toward defeat.

A revolutionary party is subjected to the pressure of other political forces. At every given stage of its development the party elaborates its own methods of counteracting and resisting this pressure. During a tactical turn and the resulting internal regroupments and frictions, the party's power of resistance becomes weakened. From this the possibility always arises that the internal groupings in the party, which originate from the necessity of a turn in tactics, may develop far beyond the original controversial points of departure and serve as a support for various class tendencies. To put the case more plainly: the party that does not keep step with the historical tasks of its own class becomes, or runs the risk of becoming, the indirect tool of other classes.

If what we said above is true of every serious turn in tactics, it is all the more true of great turns in strategy. By tactics in politics we understand, using the analogy of military science, the art of conducting isolated operations. By strategy, we understand the art of conquest, i.e., the seizure of power. Prior to the war we did not, as a rule, make this distinction. In the epoch of the Second International we confined ourselves solely to the conception of social democratic tactics. Nor was this accidental. The social democracy applied parliamentary tactics, trade union tactics, municipal tactics, cooperative tactics, and so on. But the question of combining all forces and resources—all sorts of troops—to obtain victory over the enemy was really never raised in the epoch of the Second International, insofar as the practical task of the struggle for power was not raised. It was only the 1905 revolution that first posed, after a long interval, the fundamental or strategical questions of proletarian struggle. By reason of this it secured immense advantages to the revolutionary Russian social democrats, i.e., the Bolsheviks. The great epoch of revolutionary strategy began in 1917, first for Russia and afterwards for the rest of Europe. Strategy, of course, does not do away with tactics. The questions of the trade union movement, of parliamentary activity, and so on, do not disappear, but they now become invested with a new meaning as subordinate methods of a combined struggle for power. Tactics are subordinated to strategy.

If tactical turns usually lead to internal friction in the party, how much deeper and fiercer must be the friction resulting from strategical turns! And the most abrupt of all turns is the turn of the proletarian party from the work of preparation and propaganda, or organization and agitation, to the immediate struggle for power, to an armed insurrection against the bourgeoisie. Whatever remains in the party that is irresolute, skeptical, conciliationist, capitulatory—in short, Menshevik—all this rises to the surface in opposition to the insurrection, seeks theoretical formulas to justify its opposition, and finds them ready-made in the arsenal of the opportunist opponents of yesterday. We shall have occasion to observe this phenomenon more than once in the future.

The final review and selection of party weapons on the eve of the decisive struggle took place during the interval from February to October [1917] on the basis of the widest possible agitational and organizational work among the masses. During and after October these weapons were tested in the fire of colossal historic actions. To undertake at the present time, several years after October, an appraisal of the different viewpoints concerning revolution in general, and the Russian revolution in particular, and in so doing to evade the experience of 1917, is to busy oneself with barren scholasticism. That would certainly not be a Marxist political analysis. It would be analogous to wrangling over the advantages of various systems of swimming while we stubbornly refused to turn our eyes to the river where swimmers were putting these systems into practice. No better test of viewpoints concerning revolution exists than the verification of how they worked out during the revolution itself, just as a system of swimming is best tested when a swimmer jumps into the water.

Chapter 2
'The Democratic Dictatorship of the Proletariat and Peasantry'— in February and October

The course and the outcome of the October Revolution dealt a relentless blow to the scholastic parody of Marxism which was very widespread among the Russian social democrats, beginning in part with the Emancipation of Labor Group[24] and finding its most finished expression among the Mensheviks. The essence of this pseudo-Marxism consisted in perverting Marx's conditional and limited conception that "the country that is more developed industrially only shows, to the less developed, the image of its own future" into an absolute and (to use Marx's own expression) suprahistorical law; and then, in seeking to establish upon the basis of that law the tactics of the proletarian party. Such a formulation naturally excluded even the mention of any struggle on the part of the Russian proletariat for the seizure of power until the more highly developed countries had set a "precedent."

There is, of course, no disputing that every backward country finds *some* traits of its own future in the history of advanced countries, but there cannot be any talk of a repetition of the development as a whole. On the contrary, the more capitalist economy acquired a world character, all the more strikingly original became the development of the backward countries, which had to necessarily combine elements of their backwardness with the latest achievements of capitalist development. In his preface to *The Peasant War in Germany* [New York: International Publishers, 1966], Engels wrote: "At a certain point, which must not necessarily appear simultaneously and on the same stage of development everywhere, [the bourgeoisie] begins to note that this, its second self [the proletariat] has outgrown it" [p. 16].

The course of historical development constrained the Russian bourgeoisie to make this observation much earlier and more completely than the bourgeoisie of all other countries. Lenin, even prior to 1905, gave expression to the peculiar character of the Russian revolution in the formula "the democratic dictatorship of the proletariat and the peasantry." This formula, in itself, as future development showed, could acquire meaning only as a stage toward the socialist dictatorship of the proletariat supported by the peasantry. Lenin's formulation of the problem, revolutionary and dynamic through and through, was completely and irreconcilably counterposed to the Menshevik pattern, according to which Russia could pretend only to a repetition of the history of the advanced nations, with the bourgeoisie in power and the social democrats in opposition. Some circles of our party, however, laid the stress not upon the *dictatorship* of the proletariat and the peasantry in Lenin's formula, but upon its *democratic* character as opposed to its socialist character. And, again, this could only mean that in Russia, a backward country, only a democratic revolution was conceivable. The socialist revolution was to begin in the West; and we could take to the road of socialism only in the wake of England, France, and Germany. But such a formulation of the question slipped inevitably into

Menshevism, and this was fully revealed in 1917 when the tasks of the revolution were posed before us, not for prognosis but for decisive action.

Under the actual conditions of revolution, to hold a position of supporting democracy, pushed to its logical conclusion—*opposing* socialism as *"being premature"*—meant, in politics, to shift from a proletarian to a petty-bourgeois position. It meant going over to the position of the left wing of national revolution.

The February revolution, if considered by itself, was a bourgeois revolution. But as a bourgeois revolution it came too late and was devoid of any stability. Torn asunder by contradictions which immediately found their expression in dual power,[25] it had to either change into a direct prelude to the proletarian revolution—which is what actually did happen—or throw Russia back into a semicolonial existence, under some sort of bourgeois-oligarchic regime. Consequently, the period following the February revolution could be regarded from two points of view: either as a period of consolidating, developing, or consummating the "democratic" revolution, or as a period of preparation for the proletarian revolution. The first point of view was held not only by the Mensheviks and the Social Revolutionaries but also by a certain section of our own party leadership, with this difference: that the latter really tried to push democratic revolution as far as possible to the left. But the method was essentially one and the same—to "exert pressure" on the ruling bourgeoisie, a "pressure" so calculated as to remain within the framework of the bourgeois democratic regime. If that policy had prevailed, the development of the revolution would have passed over the head of our party, and in the end the insurrection of the worker and peasant masses would have taken place without party leadership; in other words, we would have had a repetition of the July days[26] on a colossal scale, i.e., this time not as an episode but as a catastrophe.

It is perfectly obvious that the immediate consequence of such a catastrophe would have been the physical destruction of our party. This provides us with a measuring stick of how deep our differences of opinion were.

The influence of the Mensheviks and the SRs in the first period of the revolution was not, of course, accidental. It reflected the preponderance of petty-bourgeois masses—mainly peasants—in the population, and the immaturity of the revolution itself. It was precisely that immaturity, amidst the extremely exceptional circumstances arising from the war, which placed in the hands of the petty-bourgeois revolutionists the leadership, or at least the semblance of leadership, which came to this: that they defended the historical rights of the bourgeoisie to power. But this does not in the least mean that the Russian revolution could have taken no course other than the one it did from February to October 1917. The latter course flowed not only from the relations between the classes but also from the temporary circumstances created by the war. Because of the war, the peasantry was organized and armed in an army of many millions. Before the proletariat succeeded in organizing itself under its own banner and taking the leadership of the rural masses, the petty-bourgeois revolutionists found a natural support in the peasant army, which was rebelling against the war. By the ponderous weight of this multimillioned army upon which, after all, everything directly depended, the petty-bourgeois revolutionists brought pressure to bear on the workers and carried them along in the first period. That the revolution might have taken a different course on the same class foundations is best of all demonstrated by the events immediately preceding the war. In July 1914 Petrograd was convulsed by revolutionary strikes. Matters had gone so far as open fighting in the streets. The absolute leadership of that movement was in the hands of the underground organization and the legal press of our party. Bolshevism was increasing its influence in a direct struggle against liquidationism and the petty-bourgeois parties generally. The further growth of the movement would have meant above all the growth of the Bolshevik Party. The soviets of workers' deputies in 1914—if developments had reached the stage of soviets—would probably have been Bolshevik from the outset. The awakening of the villages would have proceeded under the direct or indirect leadership of the city soviets, led by the Bolsheviks. This does not necessarily mean that the SRs would have immediately disappeared from the villages. No. In all probability the first stage of the peasant revolution would have occurred under the banner of the Narodniks [populists]. But with a development of events such as we have sketched, the Narodniks themselves would have been compelled to push their left wing to the fore, in order to seek an alliance with the Bolshevik soviets in the cities. Of course, the immediate outcome of the insurrection would have depended, even in such a case, in the first instance upon the mood and conduct of the army, which was bound up with the peasantry. It is impossible and even superfluous to guess now whether the movement of 1914-15 would have led to victory had not the outbreak of the war forged a new and gigantic link in the chain of developments. Considerable evidence, however, may be adduced that had the victorious revolution unfolded along the course which began with the events in July 1914, the overthrow of the tsarist monarchy would, in all likelihood, have meant the immediate assumption of power by the revolutionary workers' soviets, and the latter, through the medium of the left Narodniks, would (from the very outset!) have drawn the peasant masses within their orbit.

The war interrupted the unfolding revolutionary movement. It acted at first to retard but afterwards to accelerate it enormously. Through the medium of the multimillioned army, the war created an absolutely exceptional base, both socially and organizationally, for the petty-bourgeois parties. For the peculiarity of the peasantry consists precisely in the fact that despite their great numbers it is difficult to form the peasants into an organized base, even when they are imbued with a revolutionary spirit. Hoisting themselves on the shoulders of a ready-made organization, that is, the army, the petty-bourgeois parties overawed the proletariat and befogged it with *defensism*.[27] That is why Lenin at once came out furiously against the old slogan of "the democratic dictatorship of the proletariat and the peasantry," which under the new circumstances meant the transformation of the Bolshevik Party into the left wing of the defensist bloc. For Lenin the main task was to lead the proletarian vanguard from the swamp of defensism out into the clear. Only on that condition could the proletariat at the next stage become the axis around which the toiling masses of the village would group themselves. But in that case what should our attitude be toward the democratic revolution, or rather toward the democratic dictatorship of the proletariat and the peasantry? Lenin was ruthless in refuting the "Old Bolsheviks" who "more than once already have played so regrettable a role in the history of our Party by reiterating formulas senselessly *learned by rote* instead of *studying* the specific features of the new and living reality. . . . But one must measure up not to old formulas but to the new reality. Is this reality covered by Comrade Kamenev's Old Bolshevik formula, which says that 'the bourgeois democratic revolution is not completed'?

"It is not," Lenin answers. "The formula is obsolete. It is no good at all. It is dead. And it is no use trying to revive it" [*CW*, Vol. 24, "Letters on Tactics" (April 8–13, 1917), pp. 44–50].

To be sure, Lenin occasionally remarked that the soviets of workers', soldiers', and peasants' deputies in the first period of the February revolution did, *to a certain degree,* embody the revolutionary democratic dictatorship of the proletariat and the peasantry. And this was true insofar as these soviets embodied power in general. But, as Lenin time and again explained, the soviets of the February period embodied only demi-power. They supported the power of the bourgeoisie while exercising semioppositionist "pressure" upon it. And it was precisely this intermediate position that did not permit them to transcend the framework of the democratic coalition of workers, peasants, and soldiers. In its form of rule, this coalition tended toward dictatorship to the extent that it did not rely upon regulated governmental relations but upon armed force and direct revolutionary supervision. However, it fell far short of an actual dictatorship. The instability of the conciliationist soviets lay precisely in this democratic amorphousness of a demi-power coalition of workers, peasants, and soldiers. The soviets had to either disappear entirely or take real power into their hands. But they could take power not in the capacity of a democratic coalition of workers and peasants represented by different parties, but only as the dictatorship of the proletariat directed by a single party and drawing after it the peasant masses, beginning with their semiproletarian sections. In other words, a democratic workers' and peasants' coalition could only take shape as an immature form of power incapable of attaining real power—it could take shape only as a tendency and not as a concrete fact. Any further movement toward the attainment of power inevitably had to explode the democratic shell, confront the majority of the peasantry with the necessity of following the workers, provide the proletariat with an opportunity to realize a class dictatorship, and thereby place on the agenda—along with a complete and ruthlessly radical democratization of social relations—a purely socialist invasion of the workers' state into the sphere of capitalist property rights. Under such circumstances, whoever continued to cling to the formula of a "democratic dictatorship" in effect renounced power and led the revolution into a blind alley.

The fundamental controversial question around which everything else centered was this: whether or not we should struggle for power; whether or not we should assume power. This alone is ample proof that we were not then dealing with a mere episodic difference of opinion but with two tendencies of the utmost principled significance. The first and principal tendency was proletarian and led to the road of world revolution. The other was "democratic," i.e., petty bourgeois, and led, in the last analysis, to the subordination of proletarian policies to the requirements of bourgeois society in the process of reform. These two tendencies came into hostile conflict over every essential question that arose throughout the year 1917. It is precisely the revolutionary epoch—i.e., the epoch when the accumulated capital of the party is put in direct circulation—that must inevitably broach in action and reveal divergences of such a nature. These two tendencies, in greater or lesser degree, with more or less modification, will more than once manifest themselves during the revolutionary period in every country. If by Bolshevism—and we are stressing here its essential aspect—we understand such training, tempering, and organization of the proletarian vanguard as enables the latter to seize power, arms in hand; and if by social democracy we are to understand the acceptance of reformist oppositional activity within the framework of bourgeois society and an adaptation to its legality—i.e., the actual training of the masses to become imbued with the inviolability of the bourgeois state; then, indeed, it is absolutely clear that even within the Communist Party itself, which does not emerge full-fledged from the crucible of history, the struggle between social democratic tendencies and Bolshevism is bound to reveal itself in its most clear, open, and uncamouflaged form during the immediate revolutionary period when the question of power is posed point-blank.

The problem of the conquest of power was put before the party only after April 4, that is, after the arrival of Lenin in Petrograd. But even after that moment, the political line of the party did not by any means acquire a unified and indivisible character, challenged by none. Despite the decisions of the April Conference in 1917,[28] the opposition to the revolutionary course—sometimes hidden, sometimes open—pervaded the entire period of preparation.

The study of the trend of the disagreements between February and the consolidation of the October Revolution is not only of extraordinary theoretical importance, but of the utmost practical importance. In 1910 Lenin spoke of the disagreements at the Second Party Congress in 1903 as "anticipatory," i.e., a forewarning. It is very important to trace these disagreements to their source, i.e., 1903, or even at an earlier time, say beginning with "Economism."[29] But such a study acquires meaning only if it is carried to its logical conclusion and if it covers the period in which these disagreements were submitted to the decisive test, that is to say, the October period.

We cannot, within the limits of this preface, undertake to deal exhaustively with all the stages of this struggle. But we consider it indispensable at least partially to fill up the deplorable gap in our literature with regard to the most important period in the development of our party.

As has already been said, the disagreements centered around the question of power. Generally speaking, this is the touchstone whereby the character of the revolutionary party (and of other parties as well) is determined.

There is an intimate connection between the question of power and the question of war which was posed and decided in this period. We propose to consider these questions in chronological order, taking the outstanding landmarks: the position of the party and of the party press in the first period after the overthrow of tsarism and prior to the arrival of Lenin; the struggle around Lenin's theses; the April Conference; the aftermath of the July days; the Kornilov period; the Democratic Conference and the Pre-Parliament; the question of the armed insurrection and seizure of power (September to October); and the question of a "homogeneous" socialist government.

The study of these disagreements will, we believe, enable us to draw deductions of considerable importance to other parties in the Communist International.

Chapter 3
The Struggle Against War and Defensism

The overthrow of tsarism in February 1917 signaled, of course, a gigantic leap forward. But if we take February within the limits of February alone, i.e., if we take it not as a step towards October, then it meant no more than this: that Russia was approximating a bourgeois republic like, for example, France. The petty-bourgeois revolutionary parties, as is their wont, considered the February revolution to be neither bourgeois nor a step toward a socialist revolution, but as some sort of self-sufficing "democratic" entity. And upon this they constructed the ideology of revolutionary defensism. They were defending, if you please, not the rule of any one class but "revolution" and "democracy." But even in our own party the revolutionary impetus of February engendered at first an extreme confusion of political perspectives. As a matter of fact, during the March days, *Pravda* held a position much closer to revolutionary defensism than to the position of Lenin.

"When one army stands opposed to another army," we read in one of its editorial articles, "no policy could be more absurd than the policy of proposing that one of them should lay down arms and go home. Such a policy would not be a policy of peace, but a policy of enslavement, a policy to be scornfully rejected by a free people. No. The people will remain intrepidly at their post, answering bullet with bullet and shell with shell. This is beyond dispute. We must not allow any disorganization of the armed forces of the revolution" (*Pravda*, No. 9, March 15, 1917, in the article "No Secret Diplomacy"). We find here no mention of classes, of the oppressors and the oppressed; there is, instead, talk of a "free people"; there are no classes struggling for power but, instead, a free people are "remaining at their post." The ideas as well as the formulas are defensist through and through! And further in the same article: "Our slogan is not the empty cry 'Down with war!' which means the disorganization of the revolutionary army and of the army that is becoming ever more revolutionary. Our slogan is bring pressure [!] to bear on the Provisional Government so as to compel it to make, without fail, openly and before the eyes of world democracy [!], an attempt [!] to induce [!] all the warring countries to initiate immediate negotiations to end the world war. Till then let everyone [!] remain at his post [!]." The program of exerting pressure on an imperialist government so as to "induce" it to pursue a pious course was the program of Kautsky and Ledebour in Germany, Jean Longuet in France, MacDonald in England; but it was never the program of Bolshevism. In conclusion, the article not only extends the "warmest greetings" to the notorious manifesto of the Petrograd Soviet addressed "To the Peoples of the World" (a manifesto permeated from beginning to end with the spirit of revolutionary defensism), but underscores "with pleasure" the solidarity of the editorial board with the openly defensist resolutions adopted at two meetings in Petrograd. Of these resolutions it is enough to say that one runs as follows: "If the democratic forces in Germany and Austria pay no heed to our voice [i.e., the "voice" of the Provisional Government and of the conciliationist soviet—L.T.], then we shall defend our fatherland to the last drop of our blood" (*Pravda*, No. 9, March 15, 1917).

The above-quoted article is not an exception. On the contrary it quite accurately expresses the position of *Pravda*—prior to Lenin's return to Russia. Thus, in the next issue of the paper, in an article "On the War," although it contains some criticism of the "Manifesto to the Peoples of the World," the following occurs: "It is impossible not to hail yesterday's proclamation of the Petrograd Soviet of Workers' and Soldiers' Deputies to the peoples of the world, summoning them to force their governments to bring the slaughter to an end" (*Pravda*, No. 10, March 16, 1917). And where should a way out of war be sought? The article gives the following answer: "The way out is the path of bringing pressure to bear on the Provisional Government with the demand that the government proclaim its readiness to begin immediate negotiations for peace."

We could adduce many similar quotations, covertly defensist and conciliationist in character. During this same period, and even weeks earlier, Lenin, who had not yet freed himself from his Zurich cage, was thundering in his "Letters from Afar" (most of these letters never reached *Pravda*) against the faintest hint of any concessions to defensism and conciliationism. "It is absolutely impermissible," he wrote on March 9, discerning the image of revolutionary events in the distorted mirror of capitalist dispatches, "it is absolutely impermissible to conceal from ourselves and from the people that this government wants to continue the imperialist war, that it is an agent of British capital, that it wants to restore the monarchy and strengthen the rule of the landlords and capitalists." And later, on March 12, he said: "To urge that government to conclude a democratic peace is like preaching virtue to brothel keepers." At the time when *Pravda* was advocating "exerting pressure" on the Provisional Government in order to induce it to intervene in favor of peace "before the eyes of world democracy," Lenin was writing: "To urge the Guchkov-Milyukov government to conclude a speedy, honest, democratic and good-neighbourly peace is like the good village priest urging the landlords and the merchants to 'walk in the way of God', to love their neighbours and to turn the other cheek" [*CW*, Vol. 23, "Letters from Afar" (March 9 and 12, 1917), pp. 315-36].

On April 4, the day after his arrival at Petrograd, Lenin came out decisively against the position of *Pravda* on the question of war and peace. He wrote: "No support for the Provisional Government; the utter falsity of all its promises should be made clear, particularly of those relating to the renunciation of annexations.

Exposure in place of the impermissible, illusion-breeding 'demand' that *this* government, a government of capitalists, should *cease* to be an imperialist government" [*CW,* Vol. 24, "The Tasks of the Proletariat in the Present Revolution" (April 4, 1917), p. 22]. It goes without saying that the proclamation issued by the conciliators on March 14, which had met with so many compliments from *Pravda,* was characterized by Lenin only as "notorious" and "muddled." It is the height of hypocrisy to summon other nations to break with their bankers while simultaneously forming a coalition government with the bankers of one's own country. " 'The Centre' all vow and declare that they are Marxists and internationalists, that they are for peace, for bringing every kind of 'pressure' to bear upon the governments, for 'demanding' in every way that their own government should 'ascertain the will of the people for peace' " [*CW,* Vol. 24, "Tasks of the Proletariat in Our Revolution—a Draft Platform for the Proletarian Party" (May 28, 1917), p. 76].

But here someone may at first glance raise an objection: Ought a revolutionary party to refuse to "exercise pressure" on the bourgeoisie and its government? Certainly not. The exercise of pressure on a bourgeois government is the road of reform. A revolutionary Marxist party does not reject reforms. But the road of reform serves a useful purpose in subsidiary and not in fundamental questions. State power cannot be obtained by reforms. "Pressure" can never induce the bourgeoisie to change its policy on a question that involves its whole fate. The war created a revolutionary situation precisely by reason of the fact that it left no room for any reformist "pressure." The only alternative was either to go the whole way with the bourgeoisie, or to rouse the masses against it so as to wrest the power from its hands. In the first case it might have been possible to secure from the bourgeoisie some kind of sop with regard to home policy, on the condition of unqualified support of their foreign imperialist policy. For this very reason social reformism transformed itself openly, at the outset of the war, into social imperialism. For the same reason the genuinely revolutionary elements were forced to initiate the creation of this new International.

The point of view of *Pravda* was not proletarian and revolutionary but democratic-defensist, even though vacillating in its defensism. We had overthrown tsarism, we should now exercise pressure on our own democratic government. The latter must propose peace to the peoples of the world. If the German democracy proves incapable of exerting due pressure on its own government, then we shall defend our "fatherland" to the last drop of blood. The prospect of peace is not posed as an independent task of the working class which the workers are called upon to achieve over the head of the Provisional Government, because the conquest of power by the proletariat is not posed as a practical revolutionary task. Yet these two tasks are inextricably bound together.

Chapter 4
The April Conference

The speech which Lenin delivered at the Finland railway station on the socialist character of the Russian revolution was a bombshell to many leaders of the party. The polemic between Lenin and the partisans of "completing the democratic revolution" began from the very first day.

A sharp conflict took place over the armed April demonstration, which raised the slogan: "Down with the Provisional Government!" This incident supplied some representatives of the right wing with a pretext for accusing Lenin of Blanquism.[30] The overthrow of the Provisional Government, which was supported at that time by the soviet majority, could be accomplished, if you please, only by disregarding the majority of the toilers.

From a formal standpoint, such an accusation might seem rather plausible, but in point of fact there was not the slightest shade of Blanquism in Lenin's April policy. For Lenin the whole question hinged on the extent to which the soviets continued to reflect the real mood of the masses, and whether or not the party was mistaken in guiding itself by the soviet majority. The April demonstration, which went further "to the left" than was warranted, was a kind of reconnoitering sortie to test the temper of the masses and the reciprocal relationship between them and the soviet majority. This reconnoitering operation led to the conclusion that a lengthy preparatory period was necessary. And we observe that Lenin in the beginning of May sharply curbed the men from Kronstadt, who had gone too far and had declared against the recognition of the Provisional Government. . . .

The opponents of the struggle for power had an entirely different approach to this question. At the April Party Conference,

Comrade Kamenev made the following complaint: "In No. 19 of *Pravda,* a resolution was first proposed by comrades [the reference here is obviously to Lenin—L.T.] to the effect that we should overthrow the Provisional Government. It appeared in print prior to the last crisis, and this slogan was later rejected as tending to disorganization; and it was recognized as adventuristic. This implies that our comrades learned something during this crisis. The resolution which is now proposed [by Lenin—L.T.] repeats that mistake. . . ."

This manner of formulating the question is most highly significant. Lenin, after the experience of the reconnoiter, withdrew the slogan of the immediate overthrow of the Provisional Government. But he did not withdraw it for any set period of time—for so many weeks or months—but strictly in dependence upon how quickly the revolt of the masses against the conciliationists would grow. The opposition, on the contrary, considered the slogan itself to be a blunder. In the temporary retreat of Lenin there was not even a hint of a change in the political line. He did not proceed from the fact that the democratic revolution was still uncompleted. He based himself exclusively on the idea that the masses were not at the moment capable of overthrowing the Provisional Government and that, therefore, everything possible had to be done to enable the working class to overthrow the Provisional Government on the morrow.

The whole of the April Party Conference was devoted to the following fundamental question: Are we heading toward the conquest of power in the name of the socialist revolution or are we helping (anybody and everybody) to complete the democratic revolution? Unfortunately, the report of the April Conference remains unpublished to this very day, though there is scarcely another congress in the history of our party that had such an exceptional and immediate bearing on the destiny of our revolution as the conference of April 1917.

Lenin's position was this: an irreconcilable struggle against defensism and its supporters; the capture of the soviet majority; the overthrow of the Provisional Government; the seizure of power through the soviets; a revolutionary peace policy and a program of socialist·revolution at home and of international revolution abroad. In distinction to this, as we already know, the opposition held the view that it was necessary to complete the democratic revolution by exerting pressure on the Provisional Government, and in this process the soviets would remain the organs of "control" over the power of the bourgeoisie. Hence flows quite another and incomparably more conciliatory attitude to defensism.

One of the opponents of Lenin's position argued in the following manner at the April Conference: "We speak of the soviets of workers' and soldiers' deputies as if they were the organizing centers of our own forces and of state power. . . . Their very name shows that they constitute a bloc of petty-bourgeois and proletarian forces which are still confronted with uncompleted bourgeois democratic tasks. Had the bourgeois democratic revolution been completed, this bloc would no longer exist . . . and the proletariat would be waging a revolutionary struggle against the bloc. . . . And, nevertheless, we recognize these soviets as centers for the organization of forces. . . . Consequently, the bourgeois revolution is not yet completed, it has not yet outlived itself; and I believe that all of us ought to recognize that with the complete accomplishment of this revolution, the power would actually have passed into the hands of the proletariat" (from the speech of Comrade Kamenev).

The hopeless schematism of this argument is obvious enough. For the crux of the matter lies precisely in the fact that the "complete accomplishment of this revolution" could never take place without changing the bearers of power. The above speech ignores the class axis of the revolution; it deduces the task of the party not from the actual grouping of class forces but from a formal definition of the revolution as bourgeois, or as bourgeois-democratic. We are to participate in a bloc with the petty bourgeoisie and exercise control over the bourgeois power until the bourgeois revolution has been completely accomplished. The pattern is obviously Menshevik. Limiting in a doctrinaire fashion the tasks of the revolution by its nomenclature (a "bourgeois" revolution), one could not fail to arrive at the policy of exercising control over the Provisional Government and demanding that the Provisional Government should bring forward a policy of peace without annexations, and so on. By the completion of the democratic revolution was understood a series of reforms to be effected through the Constituent Assembly! Moreover, the Bolshevik Party was assigned the role of a left wing in the Constituent Assembly. Such an outlook deprived the slogan "All power to the soviets!" of any actual meaning. This was best and most consistently and most thoroughly expressed at the April Conference by the late Nogin, who also belonged to the opposition: "In the process of development the most important functions of the soviets will fall away. A whole series of administrative functions will be transferred to the municipal, district, and other institutions. If we examine the future development of the structure of the state, we cannot deny that the Constituent Assembly will be convoked and after that the Parliament. . . . Thus, it follows that the most important functions of the soviets will gradually wither away. That, however, does not mean to say that the soviets will end their existence in ignominy. They will only transfer their functions. Under these same soviets we shall not achieve the commune-republic in our country."

Finally, a third opponent dealt with the question from the standpoint that Russia was not ready for socialism. "Can we count on the support of the masses if we raise the slogan of proletarian revolution? Russia is the most petty-bourgeois country in Europe. To count on the sympathy of the masses for a socialist revolution is impossible; and, consequently, the more the party holds to the standpoint of a socialist revolution the further it will be reduced to the role of a propaganda circle. The impetus to a socialist revolution must come from the West." And further on: "Where will the sun of the socialist revolution rise? I believe that, in view of all the circumstances and our general cultural level, it is not for us to initiate the socialist revolution. We lack the necessary forces; the objective conditions for it do not exist in our country. But for the West this question is posed much in the same manner as the question of overthrowing tsarism in our country."

Not all the opponents of Lenin's point of view at the April Conference drew the same conclusions as Nogin—but all of them were logically forced to accept these conclusions several months later, on the eve of October. Either we must assume leadership of the proletarian revolution or we must accept the role of an opposition in a bourgeois parliament—that is how the question was posed within our party. It is perfectly obvious that the latter position was essentially a Menshevik position, or rather the position which the Mensheviks found themselves compelled to occupy after the February revolution. As a matter of fact, the Mensheviks had for many years tapped away like so many woodpeckers at the idea that the coming revolution must be bourgeois; that the government of a bourgeois revolution could only perform bourgeois tasks; that the social democracy could not take upon itself the tasks of bourgeois democracy and must remain an opposition while "pushing the bourgeoisie to the left." This theme was developed with a particularly boring profundity by Martynov. With the inception of the bourgeois revolution in 1917, the Mensheviks soon found themselves on the staff of the government. Out of their entire "principled" position there remained only one political conclusion, namely, that the proletariat dare not seize power. But it is plain enough that those Bolsheviks who indicted Menshevik ministerialism and who at the same time were opposed to the seizure of power by the proletariat were, in point of fact, shifting to the prerevolutionary positions of the Mensheviks.

The revolution caused political shifts to take place in two directions: the reactionaries became Cadets[31] and the Cadets became republicans against their own wishes—a purely formal shift to the left; the Social Revolutionaries and the Mensheviks became the ruling bourgeois party—a shift to the right. These are the means whereby bourgeois society seeks to create for itself a new backbone for state power, stability, and order. But at the same time, while the Mensheviks were passing from a formal socialist position to a vulgar democratic one, the right wing of the Bolsheviks was shifting to a formal socialist position, i.e., the Menshevik position of yesterday.

The same regroupment of forces took place on the question of war. The bourgeoisie, except for a few doctrinaires, kept wearily droning the same tune: no annexations, no indemnities—all the more so because the hopes for annexation were already very slim. The Zimmerwaldian Mensheviks and the SRs, who had criticized the French socialists because they defended their bourgeois republican fatherland, themselves immediately became defensists the moment they felt themselves part of a bourgeois republic. From a passive internationalist position, they shifted to an active patriotic one. At the same time, the right wing of the Bolsheviks went over to a passive internationalist position, (exerting "pressure" on the Provisional Government for the sake of a democratic peace, "without annexations and without indemnities"). Thus at the April Conference the formula of the democratic dictatorship of the proletariat and the peasantry was driven asunder both theoretically and politically, and from it emerged two antagonistic points of view: a democratic point of view, camouflaged by formal socialist reservations, and a revolutionary socialist point of view, the genuinely Bolshevik and Leninist point of view.

Chapter 5
The July Days; the Kornilov Episode;
the Democratic Conference
and the Pre-Parliament

The decisions of the April Conference gave the party a correct principled orientation but they did not liquidate the disagreements among the party leaders. On the contrary, with the march of events, these disagreements assume more concrete forms, and reach their sharpest expression during the most decisive moment of the revolution—in the October days.

The attempt to organize a demonstration on June 10 (on Lenin's initiative) was denounced as an adventure by the very same comrades who had been dissatisfied with the character of the April demonstration. The demonstration of June 10 did not take place because it was proscribed by the Congress of Soviets. But on June 18 the party avenged itself. The general demonstration at Petrograd, which the conciliators had rather imprudently initiated, took place almost wholly under Bolshevik slogans. Nevertheless, the government sought to have its own way. It lightmindedly ordered the idiotic offensive at the front. The moment was decisive. Lenin kept warning the party against imprudent steps. On June 21, he wrote in *Pravda:* "Comrades, a demonstrative act at this juncture would be inexpedient. We are now compelled to live through an entirely new stage in our revolution." But the July days impended—an important landmark on the road of revolution, as well as on the road of the internal party disagreements.

In the July movement, the decisive moment came with the spontaneous onslaught by the Petrograd masses. It is indubitable that in July Lenin was weighing in his mind questions like these: Has the time come? Has the mood of the masses outgrown the soviet superstructure? Are we running the risk of becoming hypnotized by soviet legality, and of lagging behind the mood of the masses, and of being severed from them? It is very probable that isolated and purely military operations during the July days were initiated by comrades who honestly believed that they were not diverging from Lenin's estimate of the situation. Lenin afterwards said: "We did a great many foolish things in July." But the gist of the July days was that we made another, a new and much more extensive reconnoiter on a new and higher stage of the movement. We had to make a retreat, under onerous conditions. The party, to the extent that it was preparing for the insurrection and the seizure of power, considered—as did Lenin—that the July demonstration was only an episode in which we had to pay dearly for an exploration of our own strength and the enemy's, but which could not alter the main line of our activity. On the other hand, the comrades who were opposed to the policy aimed at the seizure of power were bound to see a pernicious adventure in the July episode. The mobilization of the right-wing elements in the party became increasingly intensive; their criticism became more outspoken. There was also a corresponding change in the tone of rebuttal. Lenin wrote: "All this whining, all these arguments to the effect that we 'should not have' participated (in the attempt to lend a 'peaceable and organised' character to the perfectly legitimate popular discontent and indignation!!), are either sheer apostasy, if coming from Bolsheviks, or the usual expression of the usual cowed and confused state of the petty bourgeoisie" [*CW,* Vol. 25, "Constitutional Illusions" (July 26, 1917), p. 204]. The use of the word "apostasy" at such a time sheds a tragic light upon the disagreements. As the events unfolded, this ominous word appeared more and more often.

The opportunist attitude toward the question of power and the question of war determined, of course, a corresponding attitude toward the International. The rights made an attempt to draw the party into the Stockholm Conference[32] of the social patriots. Lenin wrote on August 16: "The speech made by Comrade Kamenev on August 6 in the Central Executive Committee on the Stockholm Conference cannot but meet with reproof from all Bolsheviks who are faithful to their Party and principles." And further on, in reference to certain statements alleging that a great revolutionary banner was being unfurled over Stockholm, Lenin said: "This is a meaningless declamation in the spirit of Chernov and Tseretelli. It is a blatant untruth. In actual fact, it is not the revolutionary banner that is beginning to wave over Stockholm, but the banner of deals, agreements, amnesty for the social imperialists, and negotiations among bankers for dividing up annexed territory" [*CW,* Vol. 25, "Kamenev's Speech in the Central Executive Committee on the Stockholm Conference" (August 16, 1917), pp. 240-41].

The road to Stockholm was, in effect, the road to the Second

International, just as taking part in the Pre-Parliament was the road to the bourgeois republic. Lenin was *for* the boycott of the Stockholm Conference, just as later he was *for* the boycott of the Pre-Parliament. In the very heat of the struggle he did not for a single moment forget the tasks of creating a new Communist International.

As early as April 10, Lenin came forward with a proposal to change the name of the party. All objections against the new name he characterized as follows: "It is an argument of routinism, an argument of inertia, an argument of stagnation. . . . It is time to cast off the soiled shirt and to put on clean linen" [*CW*, Vol. 24, "Tasks of the Proletariat in Our Revolution—a Draft Program for the Proletarian Party" (April 10, 1917), p. 88]. Nevertheless, the opposition of the party leaders was so strong that a whole year had to pass by—in the course of which all of Russia cast off the filthy garments of bourgeois domination—before the party could make up its mind to take a new name, returning to the tradition of Marx and Engels. This incident of renaming the party serves as a symbolic expression of Lenin's role throughout the whole of 1917: during the sharpest turning point in history, he was all the while waging an intense struggle within the party against the day that had passed in the name of the day to come. And the opposition, belonging to the day that had passed, marching under the banner of "tradition," became at times aggravated to the extreme.

The Kornilov events,[33] which created an abrupt shift in the situation in our favor, acted to soften the differences temporarily; they were softened but not eliminated. In the right wing, a tendency manifested itself during those days to draw closer to the soviet majority on the basis of defending the revolution and, in part, the fatherland. Lenin's reaction to this was expressed in his letter to the Central Committee at the beginning of September. "It is my conviction that those who become unprincipled are people who . . .* slide into defencism or (like other Bolsheviks) into a *bloc* with the S.R.s, into *supporting* the Provisional Government. Their attitude is absolutely wrong and unprincipled. We shall become defencists *only after* the transfer of power to the proletar-

---

*From the construction of the latter part of the sentence, it is clear that a reference to certain names has been omitted here.—L.T. [The 1966 edition of Lenin's **Collected Works** says "(like Volodarsky)."]

iat. . . . Even now we must not support Kerensky's government. This is unprincipled. We may be asked: aren't we going to fight against Kornilov? Of course we must! But this is not the same thing; there is a dividing line here, which is being stepped over by some Bolsheviks who fall into compromise and allow themselves to be *carried away* by the course of events" [*CW,* Vol. 25, "To the Central Committee of the R.S.D.L.P." (August 30, 1917), pp. 285-86].

The next stage in the evolution of divergent views was the Democratic Conference (September 14-22) and the Pre-Parliament that followed it (October 7).[34] The task of the Mensheviks and the SRs consisted in entangling the Bolsheviks in soviet legality and afterwards painlessly transforming the latter into bourgeois parliamentary legality. The rights were ready to welcome this. We are already acquainted with their manner of portraying the future development of the revolution: the soviets would gradually surrender their functions to corresponding institutions—to the Dumas, the Zemstvos, the trade unions, and finally to the Constitutent Assembly—and would automatically vanish from the scene. Through the channel of the Pre-Parliament, the political awareness of the masses was to be directed away from the soviets as "temporary" and dying institutions, to the Constituent Assembly as the crowning work of the democratic revolution. Meanwhile, the Bolsheviks were already in the majority in the Petrograd and Moscow soviets; our influence in the army grew, not from day to day, but from hour to hour. It was no longer a question of prognosis or perspective; it was literally a question of how we were to act the next day.

The conduct of the completely drained conciliationist parties at the Democratic Conference was the incarnation of petty vileness. Yet the proposal which we introduced to abandon the Democratic Conference demonstratively, leaving it to its doom, met with decisive opposition on the part of the right elements of the fraction who were still influential at the top. The clash on this question was a prelude to the struggle over the question of boycotting the Pre-Parliament. On September 24, i.e., after the Democratic Conference, Lenin wrote: "The Bolsheviks should have walked out of the meeting in protest and not allowed themselves to be caught by the conference trap set to divert the people's attention from serious questions" [*CW,* Vol. 26, "Heroes of Fraud and the Mistakes of the Bolsheviks" (September 22, 1917), p. 48].

The discussion in the Bolshevik fraction at the Democratic

Conference over the question of boycotting the Pre-Parliament had an exceptional importance despite the comparatively narrow scope of the issue itself. As a matter of fact, it was the most extensive and, on the surface, most successful attempt on the part of the rights to turn the party onto the path of "completing the democratic revolution." Apparently no minutes of these discussions were taken; in any case, no record has remained; to my knowledge even the secretary's notes have not been located as yet. The editors of this volume found a few scanty documents among my own papers. Comrade Kamenev expounded a line of argument which, later on, was developed in a sharper and more defined form and embodied in the well-known letter of Kamenev and Zinoviev (dated October 11) to the party organizations.[35] The most principled formulation of the question was made by Nogin: the boycott of the Pre-Parliament is a summons to an insurrection, i.e., to a repetition of the July days. Other comrades based themselves on general considerations of social democratic parliamentary tactics. No one would dare—so they said in substance— to propose that we boycott the Parliament; nevertheless, a proposal is made that we boycott an identical institution merely because it is called a *Pre-Parliament*.

The basic conception of the rights was as follows: the revolution must inevitably lead from the soviets to the establishment of bourgeois parliamentarism; the "Pre-Parliament" forms a natural link in this process; therefore, it is folly to refuse to take part in the Pre-Parliament in view of our readiness to occupy the left benches in the Parliament itself. It was necessary to complete the democratic revolution and "prepare" for the socialist revolution. How were we to prepare? By passing through the school of bourgeois parliamentarism; because, you see, the advanced country shows the backward country the image of its own future. The downfall of the tsarist monarchy is viewed as revolutionary—and so it was—but the conquest of power by the proletariat is conceived in a parliamentary way, on the basis of a completely accomplished democracy. Many long years of a democratic regime must elapse in the interval between the bourgeois revolution and the proletarian revolution. The struggle for our participation in the Pre-Parliament was the struggle for the "Europeanization" of the working class movement, for directing it as quickly as possible into the channel of a democratic "struggle for power," i.e., into the channel of social democracy. Our fraction in the Democratic Conference, numbering over a hundred individuals, did not differ greatly, especially during those days, from a party congress. The majority of the fraction expressed itself in favor of participating in the Pre-Parliament. This fact was itself sufficient cause for alarm; and from that moment Lenin did sound the alarm unceasingly.

While the Democratic Conference was in session, Lenin wrote: "It would be a big mistake, sheer parliamentary cretinism on our part, if we were to regard the Democratic Conference as a parliament; for even *if it were* to proclaim itself a permanent and sovereign parliament of the revolution, it would nevertheless *decide nothing*. The power of decision lies *outside it* in the working-class quarters of Petrograd and Moscow" [*CW,* Vol. 26, "Marxism and Insurrection—a Letter to the Central Committee of the R.S.D.L.P." (September 13 and 14, 1917), p. 25]. Lenin's appraisal of the importance of participation or nonparticipation in the Pre-Parliament can be gathered from many of his declarations and particularly from his letter of September 29 to the Central Committee, in which he speaks of "such glaring errors on the part of the Bolsheviks as the shameful decision to participate in the Pre-Parliament" [*CW,* Vol. 26, "The Crisis Has Matured" (September 29, 1917), p. 84]. For him this decision was an expression of the same democratic illusions and petty-bourgeois vacillations against which he had fought, developing and perfecting in the course of that struggle his conception of the proletarian revolution. It is not true that many years must elapse between the bourgeois and proletarian revolutions. It is not true that the school of parliamentarism is the one and only, or the main, or the compulsory training school for the conquest of power. It is not true that the road to power runs necessarily through bourgeois democracy. These are all naked abstractions, doctrinaire patterns, and they play only one political role, namely, to bind the proletarian vanguard hand and foot, and by means of the "democratic" state machinery turn it into an oppositionist political shadow of the bourgeoisie, bearing the name of social democracy. The policy of the proletariat must not be guided by schoolboy patterns but in accordance with the real flux of the class struggle. Our task is not to go to the Pre-Parliament but to organize the insurrection and seize power. The rest will follow. Lenin even proposed to call an emergency party congress, advancing as a platform the boycott of the Pre-Parliament. Henceforth all his letters and articles hammer at a single point: we must go, not into the Pre-Parliament to act as a "revolutionary" tail of the conciliators, but out into the streets—to struggle for power!

Chapter 6
On the Eve of the October Revolution;
the Aftermath—

An emergency congress proved unnecessary. The pressure exerted by Lenin secured the requisite shift of forces to the left, both within the Central Committee and in our fraction in the Pre-Parliament. The Bolsheviks withdrew from it on October 10. In Petrograd the soviet clashed with the government over the order transferring to the front the part of the garrison which sympathized with the Bolsheviks. On October 16, the Revolutionary Military Committee was created, the legal soviet organ of insurrection. The right wing of the party sought to retard the development of events. The struggle of tendencies within the party, as well as the class struggle in the country, entered its decisive phase. The position of the rights is best and most completely illumined in its principled aspects by a letter signed by Zinoviev and Kamenev and entitled "On the Current Situation." The letter was written on October 11, that is, two weeks before the insurrection, and it was sent to the most important party organizations. The letter comes out in decisive opposition to the resolution for an armed insurrection adopted by the Central Committee. Cautioning against underestimating the enemy, while in reality monstrously underestimating the forces of revolution and even denying that the masses are in a mood for battle (two weeks before October 25!), the letter states: "We are deeply convinced that to call at present for an armed uprising means to stake on one card not only the fate of our party but also the fate of the Russian and international revolution." But if the insurrection and the seizure of power are out of the question, what then? The answer in the letter is also quite plain and precise: "Through the army, through the workers, we hold a revolver at the temple of the bourgeoisie," and because of this revolver the bourgeoisie will be unable to quash the Constituent Assembly. "The chances of our party in the elections to the Constituent Assembly are excellent. . . . The influence of the Bolsheviks is increasing. . . . With correct tactics we can get a third and even more of the seats in the Constituent Assembly."

Thus, this letter openly steers a course towards our playing the role of an "influential" opposition in a bourgeois Constituent

Assembly. This purely social democratic course is superficially camouflaged by the following consideration: "The soviets, which have become rooted in life, cannot be destroyed. The Constituent Assembly will be able to find support for its revolutionary work only in the soviets. The Constituent Assembly plus the soviets— that is that combined type of state institution towards which we are going." It is of extraordinary interest with regard to characterizing the entire line of the rights that the theory of "combined" state forms, the correlation of the Constituent Assembly with the soviets, was reiterated in Germany a year and a half or two years later by Rudolf Hilferding, who also waged a struggle against the seizure of power by the proletariat. The Austro-German opportunist was unaware that he was plagiarizing.

The letter "On the Current Situation" refutes the assertion that the majority of the people in Russia were already supporting us, on the basis of a purely parliamentary estimate of this majority. "In Russia a majority of the workers," the letter states, "and a substantial part of the soldiers are with us. But all the rest is dubious. We are all convinced, for instance, that if elections to the Constituent Assembly were to take place now, a majority of the peasants would vote for the SRs. What is this, an accident?"

The above formulation of the question contains the principal and fundamental error, flowing from a failure to understand that the peasants might have strong revolutionary interests and an intense urge to realize them, but cannot have an independent political position. They might either vote for the bourgeoisie, by voting for its SR agency, or join in action with the proletariat. Which one of these two possibilities would materialize hinged precisely upon the policy we pursued. Had we gone to the Pre-Parliament in order to constitute an influential opposition ("a third and even more of the seats") in the Constituent Assembly, then we would have almost automatically placed the peasantry in such a position as would have compelled it to seek the satisfaction of its interests through the Constituent Assembly; and, consequently, they would have looked not to the opposition but to the majority. On the other hand, the seizure of power by the proletariat immediately created the revolutionary framework for the struggle of the peasantry against the landlords and the officials. To use the expressions so current among us on this question, this letter expresses simultaneously both an *underestimation* and an *overestimation* of the peasantry. It underestimates the revolutionary potential of the peasants (under a proletarian leadership!)

and it overestimates their political independence. This twofold error of overestimating and at the same time underestimating the peasantry flows, in its turn, from an underestimation of our own class and its party—that is, from a social democratic approach to the proletariat. And this is not at all surprising. All shades of opportunism are, in the last analysis, reducible to an incorrect evaluation of the revolutionary forces and potential of the proletariat.

Objecting to the seizure of power, the letter tries to scare the party with the prospect of a revolutionary war. "The masses of the soldiers support us not because of the slogan of war, but because of the slogan of peace. . . . If, having taken power at present by ourselves, we should come to the conclusion (in view of the whole world situation) that it is necessary to wage a revolutionary war, the masses of soldiers will rush away from us. The best part of the army youth will, of course, remain with us, but the masses of the soldiers will turn away." This line of reasoning is most highly instructive. We have here the basic arguments in favor of signing the Brest-Litovsk peace; in the present instance, however, they are being directed against the seizure of power. It is plain enough that the position expressed in the letter "On the Current Situation" later facilitated in the highest degree the acceptance of the Brest-Litovsk peace by those who supported the views expressed in the above letter. It remains for us to repeat here what we said in another place, namely, that the political genius of Lenin is characterized not by taking the temporary Brest-Litovsk capitulation as an isolated fact but only by considering Brest-Litovsk in combination with October. This must always be kept in mind.

The working class struggles and matures in the never-failing consciousness of the fact that the preponderance of forces lies on the side of the enemy. This preponderance manifests itself in daily life, at every step. The enemy possesses wealth and state power, all the means of exerting ideological pressure and all the instruments of repression. We become habituated to the idea that the preponderance of forces is on the enemy's side; and this habitual thought enters as an integral part into the entire life and activity of the revolutionary party during the preparatory epoch. The consequences entailed by this or that careless or premature act serve each time as most cruel reminders of the enemy's strength.

But a moment comes when this habit of regarding the enemy

as stronger becomes the main obstacle on the road to victory. Today's weakness of the bourgeoisie seems to be cloaked by the shadow of its strength of yesterday. "You underestimate the strength of the enemy!" This cry serves as the axis for the grouping of all elements opposed to the armed insurrection. "But everyone who does not want merely to talk about uprising," wrote the opponents of insurrection in our own country, two weeks before our victory, "must carefully weigh its chances. And here we consider it our duty to say that at the present moment it would be most harmful to underestimate the forces of our opponent and overestimate our own forces. The forces of the opponent are greater than they appear. Petrograd is decisive, and in Petrograd the enemies of the proletarian party have accumulated substantial forces: 5,000 military cadets, *excellently* armed, *organized, anxious* (because of their class position) and able to fight; also the staff, shock troops, Cossacks, a substantial part of the garrison, and very considerable artillery, which has taken up a position in fan-like formation around Petrograd. Then our adversaries will undoubtedly attempt, with the aid of the All-Russian Central Executive Committee of the Soviets, to bring troops from the front" ["On the Current Situation"].

In a civil war, to the extent that it is not a question of merely counting battalions beforehand but of drawing a rough balance of their state of consciousness, such an estimate can, of course, never prove completely satisfactory or adequate. Even Lenin estimated that the enemy had strong forces in Petrograd; and he proposed that the insurrection begin in Moscow where, as he thought, it might be carried out almost without bloodshed. Such partial mistakes of forecast are absolutely unavoidable even under the most favorable circumstances and it is always more correct to make plans in accordance with the less favorable conditions. But of interest to us in the given case is the fact that the enemy forces were monstrously overestimated and that all proportions were completely distorted at a time when the enemy was actually deprived of any armed force.

This question—as the experience of Germany proved—is of paramount importance. So long as the slogan of insurrection was approached by the leaders of the German Communist Party mainly, if not solely, from an agitational standpoint, they simply ignored the question of the armed forces at the disposal of the enemy (Reichswehr, fascist detachments, police, etc.). It seemed to them that the constantly rising revolutionary flood tide would

automatically solve the military question. But when the task
stared them in the face, the very same comrades who had previously treated the armed forces of the enemy as if they were
nonexistent, went immediately to the other extreme. They placed
implicit faith in all the statistics of the armed strength of the
bourgeoisie, meticulously added to the latter the forces of the
Reichswehr and the police; then they reduced the whole to a
round number (half a million and more) and so obtained a com-
pact mass force armed to the teeth and absolutely sufficient to
paralyze their own efforts.

No doubt the forces of the German counterrevolution were
much stronger numerically and, at any rate, better organized and
prepared than our own Kornilovites and semi-Kornilovites. But so
were the effective forces of the German revolution. The proletariat
composes the overwhelming majority of the population in Germany. In our country, the question—at least during the initial
stage—was decided by Petrograd and Moscow. In Germany, the
insurrection would have immediately blazed in scores of mighty
proletarian centers. On this arena, the armed forces of the enemy
would not have seemed nearly as terrible as they did in statistical
computations, expressed in round figures. In any case, we must
categorically reject the tendentious calculations which were
made, and which are still being made, after the debacle of the
German October, in order to justify the policy that led to the
debacle. Our Russian example is of great significance in this
connection. Two weeks prior to our bloodless victory in
Petrograd—and we could have gained it even two weeks earlier—
experienced party politicians saw arrayed against us the military
cadets, anxious and able to fight, the shock troops, the Cossacks,
a substantial part of the garrison, the artillery, in fan-like formation, and the troops arriving from the front. But in reality all this
came to nothing: in round figures, zero. Now, let us imagine for a
moment that the opponents of the insurrection had carried the
day in our party and in the Central Committee. The part that
leadership plays in a civil war is all too clear: in such a case the
revolution would have been doomed beforehand—unless Lenin
had appealed to the party against the Central Committee, which
he was preparing to do, and in which he would undoubtedly have
been successful. But, under similar conditions, not every party
will have its Lenin. . . .

It is not difficult to imagine how history would have been
written, had the line of evading the battle carried in the Central

Committee. The official historians would, of course, have explained that an insurrection in October 1917 would have been sheer madness; and they would have furnished the reader with awe-inspiring statistical charts of the military cadets and Cossacks and shock troops and artillery, in fan-like formation, and army corps arriving from the front. Never tested in the fire of insurrection, these forces would have seemed immeasurably more terrible than they proved in action. Here is the lesson which must be burned into the consciousness of every revolutionist!

The persistent, tireless, and incessant pressure which Lenin exerted on the Central Committee throughout September and October arose from his constant fear lest we allow the propitious moment to slip away. All this is nonsense, replied the rights, our influence will continue to grow. Who was right? And what does it mean to lose the propitious moment? This question directly involves an issue on which the Bolshevik estimate of the ways and means of revolution comes into sharpest and clearest conflict with the social democratic, Menshevik estimate: the former being active, strategic, and practical through and through, while the latter is utterly permeated with fatalism.

What does it mean to lose the propitious moment? The most favorable conditions for an insurrection exist, obviously, when the maximum shift in our favor has occurred in the relationship of forces. We are, of course, referring to the relationship of forces in the domain of consciousness, i.e., in the domain of the political superstructure, and not in the domain of the economic foundation, which may be assumed to remain more or less unchanged throughout the entire revolutionary epoch. On one and the same economic foundation, with one and the same class division of society, the relationship of forces changes depending upon the mood of the proletarian masses, the extent to which their illusions are shattered and their political experience has grown, the extent to which the confidence of intermediate classes and groups in the state power is shattered, and finally the extent to which the latter loses confidence in itself. During revolution all these processes take place with lightning speed. The whole tactical art consists in this: that we seize the moment when the combination of circumstances is most favorable to us. The Kornilov uprising completely prepared such a combination. The masses, having lost confidence in the parties of the soviet majority, saw with their own eyes the danger of counterrevolution. They came to the conclusion that it was now up to the Bolsheviks to find a way out of the situation. Neither the elemental disintegration of the state power nor the elemental influx of the impatient and exacting confidence of the masses in the Bolsheviks could endure for a protracted period of time. The crisis had to be resolved one way or another. It is now or never! Lenin kept repeating.

The rights said in refutation: "It would be a serious historical untruth to formulate the question of the transfer of power into the hands of the proletarian party in the terms: either now or never. No. The party of the proletariat will grow. Its program will become known to broader and broader masses. . . . And there is only one way in which the proletarian party can interrupt its successes, and that is if under present conditions it takes upon itself to initiate an uprising. . . . Against this perilous policy we raise our voice in warning" ["On the Current Situation"].

This fatalistic optimism deserves most careful study. There is nothing national and certainly nothing individual about it. Only last year we witnessed the very same tendency in Germany. This passive fatalism is really only a cover for irresolution and even incapacity for action, but it camouflages itself with the consoling prognosis that we are, you know, growing more and more influential; as time goes on, our forces will continually increase. What a gross delusion! The strength of a revolutionary party increases only up to a certain moment, after which the process can turn into the very opposite. The hopes of the masses change into disillusionment as the result of the party's passivity, while the enemy recovers from his panic and takes advantage of this disillusionment. We witnessed such a decisive turning point in Germany in October 1923. We were not so very far removed from a similar turn of events in Russia in the fall of 1917. For that, a delay of a few more weeks would perhaps have been enough. Lenin was right. It was *now* or *never!*

"But the decisive question"—and here the opponents of the insurrection brought forward their last and strongest argument—"is, is the sentiment among the workers and soldiers of the capital really such that they see salvation only in street fighting, that they are impatient to go into the streets? No. There is no such sentiment. . . . If among the great masses of the poor of the capital there were a militant sentiment burning to go into the streets, it might have served as a guarantee that an uprising initiated by them would draw in the biggest organizations (railroad unions, unions of postal and telegraph workers, etc.), where the influence of our party is weak. But since there is no such sentiment even in the factories and barracks, it would be a self-deception to build any plans on it" ["On the Current Situation"].

These lines written on October 11 acquire an exceptional and most timely significance when we recall that the leading comrades in the German party, in their attempt to explain away their retreat last year without striking a blow, especially emphasized the reluctance of the masses to fight. But the very crux of the matter lies in the fact that a victorious insurrection becomes, generally speaking, most assured when the masses have had sufficient experience not to plunge headlong into the struggle but to wait and demand a resolute and capable fighting leadership. In October 1917, the working class masses, or at least their leading section, had already come to the firm conviction—on the basis of the experience of the April demonstration, the July days, and the Kornilov events—that neither isolated elemental protests nor reconnoitering operations were any longer on the agenda—but a decisive insurrection for the seizure of power. The mood of the masses correspondingly became more concentrated, more critical, and more profound. The transition from an illusory, exuberant, elemental mood to a more critical and conscious frame of mind necessarily implies a pause in revolutionary continuity. Such a progressive crisis in the mood of the masses can be overcome only by a proper party policy, that is to say, above all by the genuine readiness and ability of the party to lead the insurrection of the proletariat. On the other hand, a party which carries on a protracted revolutionary agitation, tearing the masses away from the influence of the conciliationists, and then, after the confidence of the masses has been raised to the utmost, begins to vacillate, to split hairs, to hedge, and to temporize—such a party paralyzes the activity of the masses, sows disillusion and disintegration among them, and brings ruin to the revolution; but in return it provides itself with the ready excuse—after the debacle—that the masses were insufficiently active. This was precisely the course steered by the letter "On the Current Situation." Luckily, our party under the leadership of Lenin was decisively able to liquidate such moods among the leaders. Because of this alone it was able to guide a victorious revolution.

We have characterized the nature of the political questions bound up with the preparation for the October Revolution, and we have attempted to clarify the gist of the differences that arose;

and now it remains for us to trace briefly the most important moments of the internal party struggle during the last decisive weeks.

The resolution for an armed insurrection was adopted by the Central Committee on October 10. On October 11 the letter "On the Current Situation," analyzed above, was sent out to the most important party organizations. On October 18, that is, a week before the revolution, *Novaya Zhizn* [New Life] published the letter of Kamenev. "Not only Comrade Zinoviev and I, " we read in this letter, "but also a number of practical comrades think that to assume the initiative of an armed insurrection at the present moment, with the given correlation of forces, independently of and several days before the Congress of Soviets, is an inadmissible step ruinous to the proletariat and to the revolution" [*Novaya Zhizn*, No. 156, October 18, 1917]. On October 25 power was seized in Petrograd and the Soviet government was created. On November 4, a number of responsible party members resigned from the Central Committee of the party and from the Council of People's Commissars, and issued an ultimatum demanding the formation of a coalition government composed of all soviet parties. "Otherwise," they wrote, "the only course that remains is to maintain a purely Bolshevik government by means of political terror." And, in another document, issued at the same time: "We cannot assume any responsibility for this ruinous policy of the Central Committee which has been adopted contrary to the will of the great majority of the proletariat and the soldiers who are longing for the quickest possible cessation of bloodshed between the different sections of democracy. For this reason we resign from our posts in the Central Committee in order to avail ourselves of the right to express our candid opinions to the masses of workers and soldiers and summon them to support our cry: 'Long live the government of all soviet parties!' Immediate conciliation on this basis!" ["The October Revolution," *Archives of the Revolution, 1917*, pp. 407-10]. Thus, those who had opposed the armed insurrection and the seizure of power as an adventure were demanding, after the victorious conclusion of the insurrection, that the power be restored to those parties against whom the proletariat had to struggle in order to conquer power. And why, indeed, was the victorious Bolshevik Party obliged to restore power to the Mensheviks and the SRs? (And it was precisely the restoration of power that was in question here!) To this the opposition replied: "We consider that the creation of such a government is necessary for the sake of preventing further bloodshed, an imminent famine, the crushing of the revolution by Kaledin and his cohorts; and in order to insure the convocation of the Constituent Assembly and the actual carrying through of the program of peace adopted by the All-Russian Congress of Soviets of Soldiers' and Workers' Deputies" [Ibid., pp. 407-10]. In other words, it was a question of clearing a path for bourgeois parliamentarianism through the portals of the soviets. The revolution had refused to pass through the Pre-Parliament, and had had to cut a channel for itself through October; therefore the task, as formulated by the opposition, consisted in saving the revolution from the dictatorship, with the help of the Mensheviks and the SRs, by diverting it into the channel of a bourgeois regime. What was in question here was the liquidation of October—no more, no less. Naturally, there could be no talk whatever of conciliation under such conditions.

On the next day, November 5, still another letter, along the same lines, was published. "I cannot, in the name of party discipline, remain silent when in the face of common sense and the elemental movement of the masses, Marxists refuse to take into consideration objective conditions which imperiously dictate to us, under the threat of a catastrophe, conciliation with all the socialist parties. . . . I cannot, in the name of party discipline, submit to the cult of personal worship, and stake political conciliation with all socialist parties who agree to our basic demands, upon the inclusion of this or that individual in the ministry, nor am I willing for that reason to prolong the bloodshed even for a single minute" [*Rabochaya Gazeta* (Workers' Journal), No. 204, Nov. 5, 1917]. The author of this letter (Lozovsky) ends by declaring it urgent to fight for an emergency party congress which would decide the question "whether the Russian Social Democratic Labor Party (Bolsheviks) will remain a Marxist working class party or whether it will finally adopt a course which has nothing in common with revolutionary Marxism" [Ibid.].

The situation seemed perfectly hopeless. Not only the bourgeoisie and the landlords, not only the so-called "revolutionary democracy" who still retained the control of the leading bodies of many organizations (the All-Russian Central Executive Committee of Railwaymen [*Vikzhel*], the army committees, the government employees, and so on) but also some of the most influential members of our own party, members of the Central Committee and the Council of People's Commissars, were loud in their public condemnation of the party's attempt to remain in power in order to carry out its program. The situation might have seemed hopeless, we repeat, if one looked only at the surface of events. What then remained? To acquiesce to the demands of the opposition meant to liquidate October. In that case, we should not have achieved it in the first place. Only one course was left: to march ahead, relying upon the revolutionary will of the masses. On November 7, *Pravda* carried the decisive declaration of the Central Committee of our party, written by Lenin, and permeated with real revolutionary fervor, expressed in clear, simple, and unmistakable formulations addressed to the rank and file of the party. This proclamation put an end to any doubt as to the future policy of the party and its Central Committee: "Shame on all the faint-hearted, all the waverers and doubters, on all those who allowed themselves to be intimidated by the bourgeoisie or who have succumbed to the outcries of their direct and indirect supporters! *There is not the slightest* hesitation among the *mass* of the workers and soldiers of Petrograd, Moscow, and other places. Our party stands solidly and firmly, as one man, in defence of Soviet power, in defence of the interests of all the working people, and first and foremost of the workers and poor peasants" [*CW,* Vol. 26, "From the Central Committee of the R.S.D.L.P. (B.) to All Party Members and to All the Working Classes of Russia" (November 5-6, 1917), pp. 305-06].

The extremely acute party crisis was overcome. However, the internal party struggle did not yet cease. The main lines of the struggle still remained the same. But its political importance faded. We find most interesting evidence of this in a report made by Uritsky at a session of the Petrograd Committee of our party on December 12, on the subject of convening the Constituent Assembly. "The disagreements within our party are not new. We have here the same tendency which manifested itself previously on the question of the insurrection. Some comrades are now of the opinion that the Constituent Assembly is the crowning work of the revolution. They base their position on the book of etiquette. They say we must not act tactlessly, and so on. They object to the Bolsheviks, as members of the Constituent Assembly, deciding the date to convoke it, the relationship of forces in it, and so on. They look at things from a purely formal standpoint, leaving entirely out of consideration the fact that the exercise of this control is only a reflection of the events taking place outside the

Constituent Assembly, and that with this consideration in mind we are able to outline our attitude toward the Constituent Assembly. . . . At the present time our point of view is that we are fighting for the interests of the proletariat and the poor peasantry, while a handful of comrades consider that we are making a bourgeois revolution which must be crowned by the Constituent Assembly."

The dissolution of the Constituent Assembly may be considered as marking the close not only of a great chapter in the history of Russia, but of an equally important chapter in the history of our party. By overcoming the internal friction, the party of the proletariat not only conquered power but was able to maintain it.

Chapter 7
The October Insurrection
and Soviet 'Legality'

In September, while the Democratic Conference was in session, Lenin demanded that we immediately proceed with the insurrection. "In order to treat insurrection in a Marxist way, i.e., as an art, we must at the same time, without losing a single moment, organise a *headquarters* of the insurgent detachments, distribute our forces, move the reliable regiments to the most important points, surround the Alexandrinsky Theatre, occupy the Peter and Paul Fortress, arrest the General Staff and the government, and move against the officer cadets and the Savage Division those detachments which would rather die than allow the enemy to approach the strategic points of the city. We must mobilise the armed workers and call them to fight the last desperate fight, occupy the telegraph and telephone exchange at once, move *our* insurrection headquarters to the central telephone exchange and connect it by telephone with all the factories, all the regiments, all the points of armed fighting, etc. Of course, this is all by way of example, only to *illustrate* the fact that at the present moment it is impossible to remain loyal to Marxism, to remain loyal to the revolution *unless insurrection is treated as an art*" [*CW,* Vol. 26, "Marxism and Insurrection" (September 13-14, 1917), p. 27].

The above formulation of the question presupposed that the

preparation and completion of the insurrection were to be carried out through party channels and in the name of the party, and afterwards the seal of approval was to be placed on the victory by the Congress of Soviets. The Central Committee did not adopt this proposal. The insurrection was led into soviet channels and was linked in our agitation with the Second Soviet Congress. A detailed explanation of this difference of opinion will make it clear that this question pertains not to principle but rather to a technical issue of great practical importance.

We have already pointed out with what intense anxiety Lenin regarded the postponement of the insurrection. In view of the vacillation among the party leaders, an agitation formally linking the impending insurrection with the impending Soviet Congress seemed to him an impermissible delay, a concession to the irresolute, a loss of time through vacillation, and an outright crime. Lenin kept reiterating this idea from the end of September onward.

"There is a tendency, or an opinion, in our Central Committee and among the leaders of our Party," he wrote on September 29, "which favours *waiting* for the Congress of Soviets, and is *opposed* to taking power immediately, is *opposed* to an immediate insurrection. That tendency, or opinion, must be *overcome*" [*CW*, Vol. 26, "The Crisis Has Matured" (September 29, 1917), p. 82].

At the beginning of October, Lenin wrote: "Delay is criminal. To wait for the Congress of Soviets would be a childish game of formalities, a disgraceful game of formalities, and a betrayal of the revolution" [*CW*, Vol. 26, "Letter to the Central Committee, the Moscow and Petrograd Committees and the Bolshevik Members of the Petrograd and Moscow Soviets" (October 1, 1917), p. 141].

In his theses for the Petrograd Conference of October 8, Lenin said: "It is necessary to fight against constitutional illusions and hopes placed in the Congress of Soviets, to discard the preconceived idea that we absolutely must 'wait' for it" [*CW*, Vol. 26, "Theses for a Report at the October 8 Conference of the Petrograd Organisation, also for a Resolution and Instructions to Those Elected to the Party Congress" (September 29-October 4, 1917), p. 144].

Finally, on October 24, Lenin wrote: "It is now absolutely clear that to delay the uprising would be fatal. . . . History will not forgive revolutionaries for procrastinating when they could be victorious today (and they certainly will be victorious today), while they risk losing much tomorrow, in fact, they risk losing everything" [*CW*, Vol. 26, "Letter to Central Committee Members" (October 24, 1917), pp. 234-35].

All these letters, every sentence of which was forged on the anvil of revolution, are of exceptional value in that they serve both to characterize Lenin and to provide an estimate of the situation at the time. The basic and all-pervasive thought expressed in them is—anger, protest, and indignation against a fatalistic, temporizing, social democratic, Menshevik attitude to revolution, as if the latter were an endless film. If time is, generally speaking, a prime factor in politics, then the importance of time increases a hundredfold in war and in revolution. It is not at all possible to accomplish on the morrow everything that can be done today. To rise in arms, to overwhelm the enemy, to seize power, may be possible today, but tomorrow may be impossible. But to seize power is to change the course of history. Is it really true that such a historic event can hinge upon an interval of twenty-four hours? Yes, it can. When things have reached the point of armed insurrection, events are to be measured not by the long yardstick of politics, but by the short yardstick of war. To lose several weeks, several days, and sometimes even a single day, is tantamount under certain conditions to the surrender of the revolution, to capitulation. Had Lenin not sounded the alarm, had there not been all this pressure and criticism on his part, had it not been for his intense and passionate revolutionary mistrust, the party would probably have failed to align its front at the decisive moment, for the opposition among the party leaders was very strong, and the staff plays a major role in all wars, including civil wars.

At the same time, however, it is quite clear that to prepare the insurrection and to carry it out under cover of preparing for the Second Soviet Congress and under the slogan of defending it, was of inestimable advantage to us. From the moment when we, as the Petrograd Soviet, invalidated Kerensky's order transferring two-thirds of the garrison to the front, we had actually entered a state of armed insurrection. Lenin, who was not in Petrograd, could not appraise the full significance of this fact. So far as I remember, there is not a mention of it in all his letters during this period. Yet the outcome of the insurrection of October 25 was at least three-quarters settled, if not more, the moment that we opposed the transfer of the Petrograd garrison; created the Revolutionary Military Committee (October 16); appointed our own commissars in all army divisions and institutions; and thereby completely isolated not only the general staff of the Petrograd zone, but also the government. As a matter of fact, we had here an armed insurrection—an armed though bloodless insurrection of the Petrograd regiments against the Provisional Government—under the leadership of the Revolutionary Military Committee and under the slogan of preparing the defense of the Second Soviet Congress, which would decide the ultimate fate of the state power. Lenin's counsel to begin the insurrection in Moscow, where, on his assumptions, we could gain a bloodless victory, flowed precisely from the fact that in his underground refuge he had no opportunity to assess the radical turn that took place not only in mood but also in organizational ties among the military rank and file as well as the army hierarchy after the "peaceful" insurrection of the garrison of the capital in the middle of October. The moment that the regiments, upon the instructions of the Revolutionary Military Committee, refused to depart from the city, we had a victorious insurrection in the capital, only slightly screened at the top by the remnants of the bourgeois democratic state forms. The insurrection of October 25 was only supplementary in character. This is precisely why it was painless. In Moscow, on the other hand, the struggle was much longer and bloodier, despite the fact that in Petrograd the power of the Council of People's Commissars had already been established. It is plain enough that had the insurrection begun in Moscow, prior to the overturn in Petrograd, it would have dragged on even longer, with the outcome very much in doubt. Failure in Moscow would have had grave effects on Petrograd. Of course, a victory along these lines was not at all excluded. But the way that events actually occurred proved much more economical, much more favorable, and much more successful.

We were more or less able to synchronize the seizure of power with the opening of the Second Soviet Congress only because the peaceful, almost "legal" armed insurrection—at least in Petrograd—was already three-quarters, if not nine-tenths achieved. Our reference to this insurrection as "legal" is in the sense that it was an outgrowth of the "normal" conditions of dual power. Even when the conciliationists dominated the Petrograd Soviet it frequently happened that the soviet revised or amended the decisions of the government. This was, so to speak, part of the constitution under the regime that has been inscribed in the annals of history as the "Kerensky period." When we Bolsheviks assumed power in the Petrograd Soviet, we only continued and deepened the methods of dual power. We took it upon ourselves to revise the order transferring the troops to the front. By this very act we covered up the actual insurrection of the Petrograd garrison with the traditions and methods of legal dual power. Nor was that all. While formally adapting our agitation on the question of power to the opening of the Second Soviet Congress, we developed and deepened the already existing traditions of dual power, and prepared the framework of soviet legality for the Bolshevik insurrection on an All-Russian scale.

We did not lull the masses with any soviet constitutional illusions, for under the slogan of a struggle for the Second Soviet Congress we won over to our side the bayonets of the revolutionary army and consolidated our gains organizationally. And, in addition, we succeeded, far more than we expected, in luring our enemies, the conciliationists, into the trap of soviet legality. Resorting to trickery in politics, all the more so in revolution, is always dangerous. You will most likely fail to dupe the enemy, but the masses who follow you may be duped instead. Our "trickery" proved 100 percent successful—not because it was an artful scheme devised by wily strategists seeking to avoid a civil war, but because it derived naturally from the disintegration of the conciliationist regime with its glaring contradictions. The Provisional Government wanted to get rid of the garrison. The soldiers did not want to go to the front. We invested this natural unwillingness with a political expression; we gave it a revolutionary goal and a "legal" cover. Thereby we secured unprecedented unanimity within the garrison, and bound it up closely with the Petrograd workers. Our opponents, on the contrary, because of their hopeless position and their muddleheadedness, were inclined to accept the soviet cover at its face value. They yearned to be deceived and we provided them with ample opportunity to gratify their desire.

Between the conciliationists and ourselves, there was a struggle for soviet legality. In the minds of the masses, the soviets were the source of all power. Out of the soviets came Kerensky, Tseretelli, and Skobelev. But we ourselves were closely bound up with the soviets through our basic slogan, *"All power to the soviets!"* The bourgeoisie derived their succession to power from the state Duma. The conciliationists derived their succession from the soviets; and so did we. But the conciliationists sought to reduce the soviets to nothing; while we were striving to transfer power to the soviets. The conciliationists could not break as yet with the soviet heritage, and were in haste to create a bridge from the latter to parliamentarism. With this in mind they convened the Democratic Conference and created the Pre-Parliament. The participation of the soviets in the Pre-Parliament gave a semblance of sanction to this procedure. The conciliationists sought to catch the revolution with the bait of soviet legality and, after hooking it, to drag it into the channel of bourgeois parliamentarism.

But we were also interested in making use of soviet legality. At the conclusion of the Democratic Conference we extracted from the conciliationists a promise to convene the Second Soviet Congress. This congress placed them in an extremely embarrassing position. On the one hand, they could not oppose convening it without breaking with soviet legality; on the other hand, they could not help seeing that the congress—because of its composition—boded them little good. In consequence, all the more insistently did we appeal to the Second Congress as the real master of the country; and all the more did we adapt our entire preparatory work to the support and defense of the Congress of Soviets against the inevitable attacks of the counterrevolution. If the conciliationists attempted to hook us with soviet legality through the Pre-Parliament emanating from the soviets, then we, on our part, lured them with the same soviet legality—through the Second Congress. It is one thing to prepare an armed insurrection under the naked slogan of the seizure of power by the party, and quite another thing to prepare and then carry out an insurrection under the slogan of defending the rights of the Congress of Soviets. Thus, the adaptation of the question of the seizure of power to the Second Soviet Congress did not involve any naive hopes that the congress itself could settle the question of power. Such fetishism of the soviet form was entirely alien to us. All the necessary work for the conquest of power, not only the political but also the organizational and military-technical work for the seizure of power, went on at full speed. But the legal cover for all this work was always provided by an invariable reference to the coming congress, which would settle the question of power. Waging an offensive all along the line, we kept up the appearance of being on the defensive. On the other hand, the Provisional Government—if it had been able to make up its mind to defend itself seriously—would have had to attack the Congress of Soviets, prohibit its convocation, and thereby provide the opposing side with a motive—most damaging to the government—for an armed insurrection. Moreover, we not only placed the Provisional Government in an unfavorable political position; we also lulled their already sufficiently lazy and unwieldy minds. These people seriously believed that we were only concerned with soviet parliamentarism, and with a new congress which would adopt a new resolution on power—in the style of the resolutions adopted by the Petrograd and Moscow soviets—and that the government would then ignore it, using the Pre-Parliament and the coming Constituent Assembly as a pretext, and thus put us in a ridiculous position. We have the irrefutable testimony of Kerensky to the effect that the minds of the sagest middle-class wiseacres were bent precisely in this direction. In his memoirs, Kerensky relates how, in his study, at midnight on October 25, stormy disputes raged between himself, Dan, and the others over the armed insurrection, which was then in full swing. Kerensky says, "Dan declared, first of all, that they were better informed than I was, and that I was exaggerating the events, under the influence 'of reports from my 'reactionary staff.' He then informed me that the resolution adopted by the majority of the soviets of the republic, which had so offended 'the self-esteem of the government,' was of extreme value, and essential for bringing about the 'shift in the mood of the masses'; that its effect was already 'making itself felt,' and that now the influence of Bolshevik propaganda would 'decline rapidly.' On the other hand, according to Dan's own words, the Bolsheviks themselves had declared, in negotiations with the leaders of the soviet majority, their readiness to 'submit to the will of the soviet majority'; and that they were ready 'tomorrow' to use all measures to quell the insurrection which flared up against their own wishes and without their sanction! In conclusion, after mentioning that the Bolsheviks would disband their military staff 'tomorrow' (always tomorrow!) Dan declared that all the measures I had taken to crush the insurrection had only 'irritated the masses' and that by my meddling I was generally 'hindering the representatives of the soviet majority from successfully concluding their negotiations with the Bolsheviks for the liquidation of the insurrection. . . . To complete the picture, I ought to add that at the very moment Dan was imparting to me this remarkable information, the armed detachments of 'Red Guards' were occupying government buildings, one after another. And almost immediately after the departure of Dan and his comrades from the Winter Palace, Minister Kartashev, on his way home from a session of the Provisional

Government, was arrested on Milliony street and taken directly to Smolny, whither Dan was returning to resume his peaceful conversations with the Bolsheviks. I must confess that the Bolsheviks deported themselves at that time with great energy and no less skill. At the moment when the insurrection was in full blast, and while the 'red troops' were operating all over the city, several Bolshevik leaders especially designated for the purpose sought, not unsuccessfully, to make the representatives of 'revolutionary democracy' see but remain blind, hear but remain deaf. All night long these wily men engaged in endless squabbles over various formulas which were supposed to serve as the basis for reconciliation and for the liquidation of the insurrection. By this method of 'negotiating' the Bolsheviks gained a great deal of time. But the fighting forces of the SRs and the Mensheviks were not mobilized in time. But, of course, this is *Q.E.D.*!" (A. Kerensky, "From Afar," pages 197-98).

Well put! *Q.E.D.!* The conciliationists, as we gather from the above account, were completely hooked with the bait of soviet legality. Kerensky's assumption that certain Bolsheviks were specially disguised in order to deceive the Mensheviks and the SRs about the pending liquidation of the insurrection is in fact not true. As a matter of fact, the Bolsheviks most actively participating in the negotiations were those who really desired the liquidation of the insurrection, and who believed in the formula of a socialist government, formed by the conciliation of all parties. Objectively, however, these parliamentarians doubtless proved of some service to the insurrection—feeding, with their own illusions, the illusions of the enemy. But they were able to render this service to the revolution only because the party, in spite of all their counsels and all their warnings, pressed on with the insurrection with unabating energy and carried it through to the end.

A combination of altogether exceptional circumstances—great and small—was needed to insure the success of this extensive and enveloping maneuver. Above all, an army was needed which was unwilling to fight any longer. The entire course of the revolution—particularly during the initial stages—from February to October, inclusive, would have been, as we have already said, altogether different if at the moment of revolution there had not existed in the country a broken and discontented peasant army of many millions. These conditions alone made it possible to bring to a successful conclusion the experiment with the Petrograd garrison, which predetermined the victorious outcome of October.

There cannot be the slightest talk of sanctifying into any sort of a law this peculiar combination of a "dry" and almost imperceptible insurrection together with the defense of soviet legality against Kornilov and his followers. On the contrary, we can state with certainty that this experience will never be repeated anywhere in such a form. But a careful study of it is most necessary. It will tend to broaden the horizon of every revolutionist, disclosing before him the multiplicity and variety of ways and means which can be set in motion, provided the goal is kept clearly in mind, the situation is correctly appraised, and there is a determination to carry the struggle through to the end.

In Moscow, the insurrection took much longer and entailed much greater sacrifices. The explanation for this lies partly in the fact that the Moscow garrison was not subjected to the same revolutionary preparation as the Petrograd garrison in connection with the transfer of regiments to the front. We have already said, and we repeat, that the armed insurrection in Petrograd was carried out in two installments: the first in the early part of October, when the Petrograd regiments, obeying the decision of the soviet, which harmonized completely with their own desires, refused to carry out the orders from headquarters—and did so with impunity—and the second on October 25, when only a minor and supplementary insurrection was required in order to sever the umbilical cord of the February state power. But in Moscow, the insurrection took place in a single stage, and that was probably the main reason that it was so protracted.

But there was also another reason: the leadership was not decisive enough. In Moscow we saw a swing from military action to negotiations only to be followed by another swing from negotiations to military action. If vacillations on the part of the leaders, which are transmitted to the followers, are generally harmful in politics, then they become a mortal danger under the conditions of an armed insurrection. The ruling class has already lost confidence in its own strength (otherwise there could, in general, be no hope for victory) but the apparatus still remains in its hands. The task of the revolutionary class is to conquer the state apparatus. To do so, it must have confidence in its own forces. Once the party has led the workers to insurrection, it has to draw from this all the necessary conclusions. *A la guerre comme à la guerre* ("War is war"). Under war conditions, vacillation and procrastination are less permissible than at any other time. The measuring stick of war is a short one. To mark time, even for a few hours, is to restore a measure of confidence to the ruling class while taking it away from the insurgents. But this is precisely what determines the relationship of forces, which, in turn, determines the outcome of the insurrection. From this point of view it is necessary to study, step by step, the course of military operations in Moscow in their connection with the political leadership.

It would be of great significance to indicate several other instances where the civil war took place under special conditions, being complicated, for instance, by the intrusion of a national element. Such a study, based upon carefully digested factual data, would greatly enrich our knowledge of the mechanics of civil war and thereby facilitate the elaboration of certain methods, rules, and devices of a sufficiently general character to serve as a sort of "manual" of civil war. But in anticipation of the partial conclusions of such a study, it may be said that the course of the civil war in the provinces was largely determined by the outcome in Petrograd, even despite the delay in Moscow. The February revolution cracked the old apparatus. The Provisional Government inherited it, and was unable either to renew it or to strengthen it. In consequence, its state apparatus functioned between February and October only as a relic of bureaucratic inertia. The provincial bureaucracy had become accustomed to do what Petrograd did; it did this in February, and repeated it in October. It was an enormous advantage to us that we were preparing to overthrow a regime which had not yet had time to consolidate itself. The extreme instability and want of assurance of the February state apparatus facilitated our work in the extreme by instilling the revolutionary masses and the party itself with self-assurance.

A similar situation existed in Germany and Austria after November 9, 1918. There, however, the social democracy filled in the cracks of the state apparatus and helped to establish a bourgeois republican regime; and though this regime cannot be considered a pattern of stability, it has nevertheless already survived six years. So far as other capitalist countries are concerned, they will not have this advantage, i.e., the proximity of a bourgeois and a proletarian revolution. Their February is already long past. To be sure, in England there are a good many relics of feudalism, but there are absolutely no grounds for speaking of an independent bourgeois revolution in England. Purging the country of the monarchy, and the Lords, and the rest, will be achieved by the first sweep of the broom of the English proletariat when they come into power. The proletarian revolution in the West will have to deal with a completely established bourgeois state. But this does not mean that it will have to deal with a stable state apparatus; for the very possibility of proletarian insurrection implies an extremely advanced process of the disintegration of the capitalist state. If in our country the October Revolution unfolded in the struggle with a state apparatus which did not succeed in stabilizing itself after February, then in other countries the insurrection will be confronted with a state apparatus in a state of progressive disintegration.

It may be assumed as a general rule—we pointed this out as far back as the Fourth World Congress of the Comintern—that the force of the pre-October resistance of the bourgeoisie in old capitalist countries will generally be much greater than in our country; it will be more difficult for the proletariat to gain victory; but, on the other hand, the conquest of power will immediately secure for them a much more stable and firm position than we attained on the day after October. In our country, the civil war took on real scope only after the proletariat had conquered power in the chief cities and industrial centers, and it lasted for the first three years of soviet rule. There is every indication that in the countries of Central and Western Europe it will be much more difficult for the proletariat to conquer power, but that after the seizure of power they will have a much freer hand. Naturally, these considerations concerning prospects are only hypothetical. A good deal will depend on the order in which revolutions take place in the different countries of Europe, the possibilities of military intervention, the economic and military strength of the Soviet Union at the time, and so on. But in any case, our basic and, we believe, incontestable postulate—that the actual process of the conquest of power will encounter in Europe and America a much more serious, obstinate, and prepared resistance from the ruling classes than was the case with us—makes it all the more incumbent upon us to view the armed insurrection in particular and civil war in general as an art.

Chapter 8
Again, on the Soviets and the Party
in a Proletarian Revolution

In our country, both in 1905 and in 1917, the soviets of workers' deputies grew out of the movement itself as its natural organizational form at a certain stage of the struggle. But the young European parties, who have more or less accepted soviets as a "doctrine" and "principle," always run the danger of treating soviets as a fetish, as some self-sufficing factor in a revolution. Yet, in spite of the enormous advantages of soviets as the organs of struggle for power, there may well be cases where the insurrection may unfold on the basis of other forms of organization (factory committees, trade unions, etc.) and soviets may spring up only during the insurrection itself, or even after it has achieved victory, as organs of state power.

Most highly instructive from this standpoint is the struggle which Lenin launched after the July days against the fetishism of the organizational form of soviets. In proportion as the SR-Menshevik soviets became, in July, organizations openly driving the soldiers into an offensive and crushing the Bolsheviks, to that extent the revolutionary movement of the proletarian masses was obliged and compelled to seek new paths and channels. Lenin indicated the factory committees as the organizations of the struggle for power. (See, for instance, the reminiscences of Comrade Ordzhonikidze.) It is very likely that the movement would have proceeded on those lines if it had not been for the Kornilov uprising, which forced the conciliationist soviets to defend themselves and made it possible for the Bolsheviks to imbue them with a new revolutionary vigor, binding them closely to the masses through the left, i.e., Bolshevik wing.

This question is of enormous international importance, as was shown by the recent German experience. It was in Germany that soviets were several times created as organs of insurrection—without an insurrection taking place—and as organs of state power—without any power. This led to the following: in 1923, the movement of broad proletarian and semiproletarian masses began to crystallize around the factory committees, which *in the main* fulfilled all the functions assumed by our own soviets in the period preceding the direct struggle for power. Yet, during August

and September 1923, several comrades advanced the proposal
that we should proceed to the immediate creation of soviets in
Germany. After a long and heated discussion this proposal was
rejected, and rightly so. In view of the fact that the factory
committees had already become in action the rallying centers of
the revolutionary masses, soviets would only have been a parallel
form of organization, without any real content, during the preparatory stage. They could have only distracted attention from the
material targets of the insurrection (army, police, armed bands,
railways, etc.) by fixing it on a self-contained organizational
form. And, on the other hand, the creation of soviets as such,
prior to the insurrection and apart from the immediate tasks of
the insurrection, would have meant an open proclamation, "We
mean to attack you!" The government, compelled to "tolerate" the
factory committees insofar as the latter had become the rallying
centers of great masses, would have struck at the very first soviet
as an official organ of an "attempt" to seize power. The communists would have had to come out in defense of the soviets as
purely organizational entities. The decisive struggle would have
broken out not in order to seize or defend any material positions,
nor at a moment chosen by us—a moment when the insurrection
would flow from the conditions of the mass movement; no, the
struggle would have flared up over the soviet "banner," at a
moment chosen by the enemy and forced upon us. In the meantime, it is quite clear that the entire preparatory work for the
insurrection could have been carried out successfully under the
authority of the factory and shop committees, which were already
established as mass organizations and which were constantly
growing in numbers and strength; and that this would have
allowed the party to maneuver freely with regard to fixing the
date for the insurrection. Soviets, of course, would have had to
arise at a certain stage. It is doubtful whether, under the above-
mentioned conditions, they would have arisen as the direct organs of insurrection, in the very fire of the conflict, because of the
risk of creating two revolutionary centers at the most critical
moment. An English proverb says that you must not swap horses
while crossing a stream. It is possible that soviets would have
been formed after the victory at all the decisive places in the
country. In any case, a triumphant insurrection would inevitably
have led to the creation of soviets as organs of state power.

It must not be forgotten that in our country the soviets grew up
in the "democratic" stage of the revolution, becoming legalized,

as it were, at that stage, and subsequently being inherited and utilized by us. This will not be repeated in the proletarian revolutions of the West. There, in most cases, the soviets will be created in response to the call of the communists; and they will consequently be created as the direct organs of proletarian insurrection. To be sure, it is not at all excluded that the disintegration of the bourgeois state apparatus will have become quite acute before the proletariat is able to seize power; this would create the conditions for the formation of soviets *as the open organs of preparing the insurrection.* But this is not likely to be the general rule. Most likely, it will be possible to create soviets only in the very last days, as the direct organs of the insurgent masses. Finally, it is quite probable that such circumstances will arise as will make the soviets emerge either after the insurrection has passed its critical stage, or even in its closing stages as organs of the new state power. All these variants must be kept in mind so as to safeguard us from falling into organizational fetishism, and so as not to transform the soviets from what they ought to be—a flexible and living form of struggle—into an organizational "principle" imposed upon the movement from the outside, disrupting its normal development.

There has been some talk lately in our press to the effect that we are not, mind you, in a position to tell through what channels the proletarian revolution will come in England. Will it come through the channel of the Communist Party or through the trade unions? Such a formulation of the question makes a show of a fictitiously broad historical outlook; it is radically false and dangerous because it obliterates the chief lesson of the last few years. If the triumphant revolution did not come at the end of the war, it was because a party was lacking. This conclusion applies to Europe as a whole. It may be traced concretely in the fate of the revolutionary movement in various countries.

With respect to Germany, the case is quite a clear one. The German revolution might have been triumphant both in 1918 and in 1919, had a proper party leadership been secured. We had an instance of this same thing in 1917 in the case of Finland. There, the revolutionary movement developed under exceptionally favorable circumstances, under the wing of revolutionary Russia and with its direct military assistance. But the majority of the leaders in the Finnish party proved to be social democrats, and they ruined the revolution. The same lesson flows just as plainly from the Hungarian experience. There the communists, along with the left social democrats, did not conquer power, but were handed it by the frightened bourgeoisie. The Hungarian revolution— triumphant without a battle and without a victory—was left from the very outset without a fighting leadership. The Communist Party fused with the social democratic party, showed thereby that it itself was not a Communist Party; and, in consequence, in spite of the fighting spirit of the Hungarian workers, it proved incapable of keeping the power it had obtained so easily.

Without a party, apart from a party, over the head of a party, or with a substitute for a party, the proletarian revolution cannot conquer. That is the principal lesson of the past decade. It is true that the English trade unions may become a mighty lever of the proletarian revolution; they may, for instance, even take the place of workers' soviets under certain conditions and for a certain period of time. They can fill such a role, however, not apart from a Communist party, and certainly not *against* the party, but only on the condition that communist influence becomes the decisive influence in the trade unions. We have paid far too dearly for this conclusion—with regard to the role and importance of a party in a proletarian revolution—to renounce it so lightly or even to minimize its significance.

Consciousness, premeditation, and planning played a far smaller part in bourgeois revolutions than they are destined to play, and already do play, in proletarian revolutions. In the former instance the motive force of the revolution was also fur- nished by the masses, but the latter were much less organized and much less conscious than at the present time. The leadership remained in the hands of different sections of the bourgeoisie, and the latter had at its disposal wealth, education, and all the organizational advantages connected with them (the cities, the universities, the press, etc.). The bureaucratic monarchy defended itself in a hand-to-mouth manner, probing in the dark and then acting. The bourgeoisie would bide its time to seize a favorable moment when it could profit from the movement of the lower classes, throw its whole social weight into the scale, and so seize the state power. The proletarian revolution is precisely distinguished by the fact that the proletariat—in the person of its vanguard—acts in it not only as the main offensive force but also as the guiding force. The part played in bourgeois revolutions by the economic power of the bourgeoisie, by its education, by its municipalities and universities, is a part which can be filled in a proletarian revolution only by the party of the proletariat.

The role of the party has become all the more important in view of the fact that the enemy has also become far more conscious. The bourgeoisie, in the course of centuries of rule, has perfected a political schooling far superior to the schooling of the old bureaucratic monarchy. If parliamentarism served the proletariat to a certain extent as a training school for revolution, then it also served the bourgeoisie to a far greater extent as the school of counterrevolutionary strategy. Suffice it to say that by means of parliamentarism the bourgeoisie was able so to train the social democracy that it is today the main prop of private property. The epoch of the social revolution in Europe, as has been shown by its very first steps, will be an epoch not only of strenuous and ruthless struggle but also of planned and calculated battles—far more planned than with us in 1917.

That is why we require an approach entirely different from the prevailing one to the questions of civil war in general and of armed insurrection in particular. Following Lenin, all of us keep repeating time and again Marx's words that insurrection is an art. But this idea is transformed into a hollow phrase, to the extent that Marx's formula is not supplemented with a study of the fundamental elements of the art of civil war, on the basis of the vast accumulated experience of recent years. It is necessary to say candidly that a superficial attitude to questions of armed insurrection is a token that the power of the social democratic tradition has not yet been overcome. A party which pays superficial attention to the question of civil war, in the hope that everything will somehow settle itself at the crucial moment, is certain to be shipwrecked. We must analyze in a collective manner the experience of the proletarian struggles beginning with 1917.

The above-sketched history of the party groupings in 1917 also constitutes an integral part of the experience of civil war and is, we believe, of immediate importance to the policies of the Communist International as a whole. We have already said, and we repeat, that the study of disagreements cannot, and ought not in any case, be regarded as an attack against those comrades who pursued a false policy. But on the other hand it is absolutely impermissible to blot out the greatest chapter in the history of our party merely because some party members failed to keep step with the proletarian revolution. The party should and must know the *whole* of the past, so as to be able to estimate it correctly and assign each event to its proper place. The tradition of a revolutionary party is built not on evasions but on critical clarity.

History secured for our party revolutionary advantages that

are truly inestimable. The traditions of the heroic struggle against the tsarist monarchy; the habituation to revolutionary self-sacrifice bound up with the conditions of underground activity; the broad theoretical study and assimilation of the revolutionary experience of humanity; the struggle against Menshevism, against the Narodniks, and against conciliationism; the supreme experience of the 1905 revolution; the theoretical study and assimilation of this experience during the years of counterrevolution; the examination of the problems of the international labor movement in the light of the revolutionary lessons of 1905—these were the things which in their totality gave our party an exceptional revolutionary temper, supreme theoretical penetration, and unparalleled revolutionary sweep. Nevertheless, even within this party, among its leaders, on the eve of decisive action there was formed a group of experienced revolutionists, Old Bolsheviks, who were in sharp opposition to the proletarian revolution and who, in the course of the most critical period of the revolution from February 1917 to approximately February 1918, adopted on all fundamental questions an essentially social democratic position. It required Lenin, and Lenin's exceptional influence in the party, unprecedented even at that time, to safeguard the party and the revolution against the supreme confusion following from such a stituation. This must never be forgotten if we wish other Communist parties to learn anything from us.

The question of selecting the leading staff is of exceptional importance to the parties of Western Europe. The experience of the abortive German October is shocking proof of this. But this selection must proceed in the light of *revolutionary action.* During these recent years, Germany has provided ample opportunities for the testing of the leading party members in moments of direct struggle. Failing this criterion, the rest is worthless. France, during these years, was much poorer in revolutionary upheavals—even partial ones. But even in the political life of France we have had flashes of civil war, times when the Central Committee of the party and the trade union leadership had to react in action to unpostponable and acute questions (such as the sanguinary meeting of January 11, 1924). A careful study of such acute episodes provides irreplaceable material for the evaluation of a party leadership, the conduct of various party organs, and individual leading members. To ignore these lessons—not to draw the necessary conclusions from them as to the choice of personalities—is to invite inevitable defeats; for without a penetrating, resolute, and courageous party leadership, the victory of the proletarian revolution is impossible.

Each party, even the most revolutionary party, must inevitably produce its own organizational conservatism; for otherwise it would lack the necessary stability. This is wholly a question of degree. In a revolutionary party the vitally necessary dose of conservatism must be combined with a complete freedom from routine, with initiative in orientation and daring in action. These qualities are put to the severest test during turning points in history. We have already quoted the words of Lenin to the effect that even the most revolutionary parties, when an abrupt change occurs in a situation and when new tasks arise as a consequence, frequently pursue the political line of yesterday and thereby become, or threaten to become, a brake upon the revolutionary process. Both conservatism and revolutionary initiative find their most concentrated expression in the leading organs of the party. In the meantime, the European Communist parties have still to face their sharpest "turning point"—the turn from preparatory work to the actual seizure of power. This turn is the most exacting, the most unpostponable, the most responsible, and the most formidable. To miss the moment for the turn is to incur the greatest defeat that a party can possibly suffer.

The experience of the European struggles, and above all the struggles in Germany, when looked at in the light of our own experience, tells us that there are two types of leaders who incline to drag the party back at the very moment when it must take a stupendous leap forward. Some among them generally tend to see mainly the difficulties and obstacles in the way of revolution, and to estimate each situation with a preconceived, though not always conscious, intention of avoiding any action. Marxism in their hands is turned into a method for establishing the impossibility of revolutionary action. The purest specimens of this type are the Russian Mensheviks. But this type as such is not confined to Menshevism, and at the most criticial moment it suddenly manifests itself in responsible posts in the most revolutionary party.

The representatives of the second variety are distinguished by their superficial and agitational approach. They never see any obstacles or difficulties until they come into a head-on collision with them. The capacity for surmounting real obstacles by means of bombastic phrases, the tendency to evince lofty optimism on all questions ("the ocean is only knee deep"), is inevitably transformed into its polar opposite when the hour for decisive action strikes. To the first type of revolutionist, who makes mountains out of molehills, the problems of seizing power lie in heaping up and multiplying to the nth degree all the difficulties he has become accustomed to see in his way. To the second type, the superficial optimist, the difficulties of revolutionary action always come as a surprise. In the preparatory period the behavior of the two is different: the former is a skeptic upon whom one cannot rely too much, that is, in a revolutionary sense; the latter, on the contrary, may seem a fanatic revolutionist. But at the decisive moment, the two march hand in hand; they both oppose the insurrection. Meanwhile, the entire preparatory work is of value only to the extent that it renders the party and above all its leading organs capable of determining the moment for an insurrection, and of assuming the leadership of it. For the task of the Communist Party is the conquest of power for the purpose of reconstructing society.

Much has been spoken and written lately on the necessity of "Bolshevizing" the Comintern. This is a task that cannot be disputed or delayed; it is made particularly urgent after the cruel lessons of Bulgaria and Germany a year ago. Bolshevism is not a doctrine (i.e., not merely a doctrine) but a system of revolutionary training for the proletarian uprising. What is the Bolshevization of Communist parties? It is giving them such a training, and effecting such a selection of the leading staff, as would prevent them from drifting when the hour for their October strikes. "That is the whole of Hegel, and the wisdom of books, and the meaning of all philosophy. . . ."

A Brief Comment on This Book

The initial phase of the "democratic" revolution extends from the February revolution to the crisis in April, and its solution on May 6 by the formation of a coalition government with the participation of the Mensheviks and the Narodniks. Throughout this initial phase, the writer did not participate directly, arriving in Petrograd only on May 5, on the very eve of the formation of the coalition government. The first stage of the revolution and the revolutionary prospects were dealt with by me in articles written in America. In my opinion, on all fundamental points these articles are in complete harmony with the analysis of the revolution given by Lenin in his "Letters from Afar."

From the very first day of my arrival in Petrograd my work was carried on in complete coordination with the Central Committee of the Bolsheviks. Lenin's course toward the conquest of power by the proletariat I naturally supported in whole and in part. So far as the peasantry was concerned, there was not even a shade of disagreement between Lenin and myself. Lenin at that time was completing the first stage of his struggle against the right Bolsheviks and their slogan, "Democratic dictatorship of the proletariat and the peasantry." Prior to my formal entry into the party, I participated in drafting a number of resolutions and documents issued in the name of the party. The sole consideration which delayed my formal entry into the party for three months was the desire to expedite the fusion of the best elements of the Mezhrayontsi organization,[36] and of revolutionary internationalists in general, with the Bolsheviks. This policy was likewise carried out by me in complete agreement with Lenin.

The editors of this volume have drawn my attention to the fact that in one of the articles I wrote at that time in favor of unification, there is a reference to the organizational "clannishness" of the Bolsheviks. Some profound pundit like Comrade Sorin will, of course, lose no time in deducing this phrase directly and posthaste from the original differences on paragraph one of the party statutes. I see no necessity to engage in any discussion on this score, particularly in view of the fact that I have admitted both verbally and in action my real and major organizational errors. A somewhat less perverse reader will find, however, a much more simple and immediate explanation for the above-quoted phrase. It is to be accounted for by the concrete conditions at that time. Among the Mezhrayontsi workers there still survived a very strong distrust of the organizational policies of the Petrograd Committee. Arguments based on "clannishness"—bolstered as is always the case in such circumstances by references to all sorts of "injustice"—were current among the Mezhrayontsi. I refuted these arguments as follows: clannishness, as a heritage from the past, does exist, but if it is to diminish, the Mezhrayontsi must terminate their own separate existence.

My purely polemical "proposal" to the First Soviet Congress that it constitute a government of twelve Peshekhonovs has been interpreted by some people—by Sukhanov, I believe—to indicate either that I was personally inclined toward Peshekhonov, or that I was advancing a special political line, distinct from that of

Lenin. This is, of course, sheer nonsense. When our party demanded that the soviets, led by the Mensheviks and the SRs, should assume power, it thereby "demanded" a ministry composed of Peshekhonovs. In the last analysis, there was no principled difference at all between Peshekhonov, Chernov, and Dan. They were all equally useful for facilitating the transfer of power from the bourgeoisie to the proletariat. It may be that Peshekhonov was better acquainted with statistics, and made a slightly better impression as a practical man than Tseretelli or Chernov. A dozen Peshekhonovs meant a government composed of a dozen stalwart representatives of petty-bourgeois democracy instead of a coalition. When the Petersburg masses, led by our party, raised the slogan: "Down with the ten capitalist ministers!" they thereby demanded that the posts of these ministers be filled by Mensheviks and Narodniks. "Messrs. bourgeois democrats, kick the Cadets out! Take power into your own hands! Put in the government twelve (or as many as you have) Peshekhonovs, and we promise you, so far as it is possible, to remove you 'peacefully' from your posts when the hour will strike—which should be very soon!" There was no special political line here—it was the same line that Lenin formulated time and again.

I consider it necessary to underscore emphatically the warning voiced by Comrade Lentsner, the editor of this volume. As he points out, the bulk of the speeches contained in this volume were reprinted not from stenographic notes, even defective ones, but from accounts made by reporters of the conciliationist press, half ignorant and half malicious. A cursory inspection of several documents of this sort caused me to reject offhand the original plan of correcting and supplementing them to a certain extent. Let them remain as they are. They, too, in their own fashion, are documents of the epoch, although emanating "from the other side."

The present volume would not have appeared in print had it not been for the careful and competent work of Comrade Lentsner—who is also responsible for compiling the notes—and of his assistants, Comrades Heller, Kryzhanovsky, Rovensky, and I. Rumer. I take the opportunity to express my comradely gratitude to them. I should like to take particular notice of the enormous work done in preparing this volume as well as my other books by my closest collaborator, M.S. Glazman.[37] I conclude these lines with feelings of profoundest sorrow over the extremely tragic death of this splendid comrade, worker, and man.

OUR DIFFERENCES

November 30, 1924

NOTE: "Lessons of October" evoked a new anti-Trotsky campaign surpassing the one of the previous spring, and in November 1924 Trotsky wrote a lengthy point-by-point rejoinder to his critics. He did not publish it, however, either because he was prevented or because he thought it would only provoke a further escalation of the triumvirate's attacks. Once again suffering from the illness that had plagued him for two years, he remained silent. "Our Differences" remained the most complete contemporary exposition of the issues at stake that he would write.

Throughout this essay Trotsky's references to the preface of his book 1917 are to "Lessons of October."

The translation for this volume is by George Saunders from the copy in the open section of the Trotsky archives, by permission of the Harvard College Library. The pages of the typed manuscript, which bore the note "Only copy—never printed," were numbered 1-34 and 43-54. Whether this was an error in the pagination, or whether Trotsky deleted pages 35-42, or whether they were later lost, is not known. The eight missing pages, if that is what they were, would have followed what is now the end of Chapter 6. Perhaps the eventual opening of the Kremlin's large file on Trotsky will clear up the problem.—Ed.

Chapter 1
The Purpose of This Explanation

In the discussion now under way about my book on 1917 (in which the book has served only as a pretext—this is clear from the course of the discussion), a great many issues have been raised, of a factual, theoretical, and personal nature. I wish here to make some clarifications on those questions which, to my understanding, affect the interests of the party most of all.

1. Is it true that I am carrying out a revision of Leninism under the secret banner of "Trotskyism"?

2. Is it true that I wrote the preface to my book *1917* ["Lessons of October"] from a special "Trotskyist" point of view and even treated a number of questions falsely, with the aim of belittling Leninism?

3. Is it true that my preface is a "platform" and that in general I see my task as the organization of a "right wing" in the party?

Of course it is not only what I *wished* to say that is at issue here, but also how what I said has been *understood*. The question can certainly be approached as follows: Trotsky is not consciously trying to replace Leninism with Trotskyism; to accuse him of that would be far too unreasonable. But Trotsky does not understand Leninism, or at least certain important aspects of it. Thus without meaning to or trying to, Trotsky has distorted Leninism in practice and has created an ideological platform for a grouping incompatible with Leninism.

On the other hand, it could be admitted or supposed that the conditions of the past, the difficult situation that has developed since Lenin's death, and, in addition, one or another personal circumstance have created a certain predisposition that makes people see "Trotskyism" where there is none, or where, at most, there are certain inevitable shades of difference within the overall framework of Bolshevism.

What purpose, then, can or should the party see in my explanation?

It seems to me necessary, first, to clarify what it was I wished to say; and second, to remove incorrect interpretations where they have arisen, if only on the most important questions. In this way false differences based on misunderstanding or on a biased interpretation may at least be cleared away and disposed of. That alone would be a big advantage, because it would help to show whether there is a real, serious basis for the central and crucial accusation that I, consciously or unconsciously, am attempting to counterpose a special line of Trotskyism to Leninism. If it turned out, even after the elimination of misunderstandings, partial errors, biased interpretations, and so forth, that two different lines nevertheless did exist, there could of course be no question of any glossing over of such an important circumstance. The party is obliged, through whatever efforts and strict measures are required, to assure the unity of its revolutionary method, its political line, its traditions—the unity of Leninism. In such a case it would be incorrect to disavow the use of "repression," as some comrades have done (while at the same time accusing me of pursuing a special, non-Bolshevik line).

However, I do not believe for one moment that matters will come to that—despite the fact that the discussion has gone quite far and despite the fact that a certain interpretation of my book and my views has already been presented to the party.

My task in this explanation is to try to show that there are no grounds for bringing up the specter of "Trotskyism" as a party danger. Obviously I cannot take up all of the great multiplicity of arguments, references, quotations, and allusions made by the comrades who have written about "Trotskyism" and against "Trotskyism" in the recent period. It would be pointless to take this approach, and simply impossible to carry it out. I think it would be more helpful to the reader, and more useful for getting at the heart of the matter, if I begin with a clarification of those conclusions, drawn by my preface, which have been declared the most striking or obvious manifestations of "Trotskyism" and which for that very reason have served as the point of departure for the entire current campaign. I hope to show, by way of the most disputed questions, that in my interpretation of October, not only have I been guided by the method of Leninism but I have also remained fully in accord with Lenin's absolutely precise and specific analyses and conclusions on these same questions.

But I cannot limit myself solely to such clarifications. The fact is that the accusation of "Trotskyism," if it were based only on my statements, speeches, and articles of recent years, would by itself prove all too unconvincing. In order to give the accusation weight and significance, my political *past* is dragged in—that is, my revolutionary activity prior to the time of my joining the Bolshevik Party. I consider it necessary to provide clarifications in this area as well.

Such is the basic content of the present article.

If I thought that my explanations might add fuel to the fire of the discussion, or if the comrades on whom the printing of this essay depends were to tell me so openly and directly, I would not publish it, however burdensome it may be to remain under the charge of liquidating Leninism. I would tell myself that my only recourse was to wait until a calmer flow of party life allowed the opportunity, if only a belated one, to refute the untrue accusation.

But it seems to me that an open explanation—that is, a reply to the main charge brought against me—at this time is likely not so much to heighten the atmosphere of tension in the party as to relieve it by reducing the issue to its real proportions.

If, in fact, it proved true that a line of Trotskyism was being carried out against the line of Leninism, it would mean that we were dealing with an incipient struggle of different class tendencies. In that case, no explanations would help. The proletarian party preserves itself by purging itself. But if in reality there is no Trotskyism; if the *specter* of Trotskyism is a reflection, on the one hand, of the prerevolutionary past, and, on the other, of the rise of mistrust in the aftermath of Lenin's death; if the specter of Trotskyism cannot be conjured up except by dragging Trotsky's letter to Chkheidze out of the archives, etc.—in *that* case an open explanation may help. It may clear away the accumulation of old prejudices, disperse all apparitions, and clear the air inside the party.

That is precisely the purpose of the present explanation.

Chapter 2
The Past

I have already said that my preface to the book *1917* has been linked in the discussion with my entire previous activity in the revolutionary movement and portrayed as the expression of an attempt by "Trotskyism" to substitute itself for Leninism as the doctrine and the political method of the party.

Because the question was posed this way, it proved necessary to shift the party's attention largely away from the present and future and toward the past. Old documents, quotations from old polemics, etc., have been brought into currency in the party. Among these materials, in particular, a letter has been printed which I wrote to Chkheidze, who was then a social democratic (Menshevik) deputy in the Duma, on April 1, 1913, that is, almost twelve years ago. This letter could not help making the worst possible impression on all party members, but especially on those who never went through the experience of the prewar factional struggles under emigre conditions and to whom, therefore, the letter comes as a complete surprise.

The letter was written at a time of extremely sharp factional struggle. No purpose would be served by telling the reader all the details of how this letter came to be written. Suffice it to recall the principal causal factors that made it *possible* for such a letter to be written at all. The principal causes were that I, at that time, held an attitude toward Menshevism that differed fundamentally from Lenin's. I thought it was necessary to fight for the unification of the Bolsheviks and Mensheviks within a single party. Lenin thought it necessary to deepen the split with the Mensheviks in order to cleanse the party of the main source of bourgeois influence upon the proletariat. At a considerably later date I wrote that my basic political mistake had been that I did not understand in time the gulf between Bolshevism and Menshevism on matters of principle. For that very reason I did not understand the meaning of Lenin's organizational-political struggle, both against Menshevism and against the conciliationist line that I myself upheld.

The deep differences that divided me from Bolshevism for a whole number of years, and in many cases placed me in sharp and hostile opposition to Bolshevism were expressed most graphically in relation to the Menshevik faction. I began with the radically wrong perspective that the course of the revolution and the pressure of the proletarian masses would ultimately force both factions to follow the same road. Therefore I considered a split to be an unnecessary disruption of the revolutionary forces. But because the active role in the split lay with the Bolsheviks— since it was only by ruthless demarcation, not only ideological but organizational as well, that it was possible, in Lenin's opinion, to assure the revolutionary character of the proletarian party (and the entire subsequent history has fully confirmed the correctness of those policies)—my "conciliationism" led me at many sharp turns in the road into hostile clashes with Bolshevism. Lenin's struggle against Menshevism was inevitably supplemented by a struggle against "conciliationism," which was often given the name of "Trotskyism."

All the comrades who have read Lenin's works know this. It is ridiculous, then, to talk as though someone were trying to "hide something" here. It would never even enter my head now, long after the fact, to dispute the correctness in principle and the colossal historical farsightedness of Lenin's critique of Russian "conciliationism," which in its essential features was akin to the international current of centrism. I regard this, as I have for some time, as so obvious and indisputable for every member of the Bolshevik Party that the very idea of a discussion on this question would be simply absurd—after all that the party has done, has written, has absorbed, and has tested and confirmed in this area.

In fighting against a "general lining-up" and split in the social democratic movement, as I have said, I came into several harsh conflicts with the ideology and organizational methods by which Lenin was preparing, building, and training our party of today. The very word "Leninism" did not exist then in the Bolshevik faction. Lenin himself would not have permitted it. Only after his illness, and especially since his death, has the party taken the word "Leninism" into its current vocabulary—absorbing all of a sudden, as it were, the enormous creative work that was Lenin's life. This word is not counterposed to Marxism of course, but includes everything new with which the worldwide school of Marxism has been enriched theoretically and practically under Lenin's leadership. If we look at the prerevolutionary period, we find that the word "Leninism" was used only by the opponents of Bolshevism to characterize precisely what they considered most negative and destructive about Bolshevik politics. To a "conciliationist" such as I was, Bolshevism's most negative feature was its factionalism, its inclination toward splits, drawing of organizational lines, etc. It was precisely in that sense, at times when the polemics grew heated, that I used the term "Leninism" in those days.

It is possible now to make a big impression on an inexperienced or uninformed party member by asking, "Do you know what Trotsky says Leninism is?" and then reading some factional outburst against Leninism from old articles or letters. But this is hardly the right approach. It relies on lack of information. Today such quotations sound no less barbaric to my ears than to those of any party member. They can only be understood from a knowledge of past history, i.e., the history of the struggle between Bolshevism and conciliationism, a struggle in which both historical rightness and victory were entirely on the side of Bolshevism. Moreover, the entire history of Lenin's activity shows that he can only be understood—not just as a political figure but also as a human personality—by grasping his conception of history, his aims, and his techniques and methods of fighting. Lenin cannot be evaluated outside of the framework of Leninism. Lenin cannot be evaluated in halfway terms. His political character rules out any halfheartedness. Through his method of working he forced everyone either to march in step with him or to fight him. It is quite clear, then, that in the eyes of conciliationism, which signifies *halfheartedness in all fundamental questions of revolution,* the very figure of Lenin was strange and in many ways even incomprehensible. By fighting for what I then thought was correct—the unity of all social democratic factions for the sake of an imaginary "unity" of the labor movement—I found myself on a road that brought me more than once into conflict with Lenin as a political figure.

Until a revolutionist has arrived at the correct attitude toward the fundamental task of building a party and toward the methods by which a party functions, there can be no question of any correct, stable, or consistent participation by such a person in the labor movement. Without the proper mutual relations between doctrine, slogans, tactics, and the work of the party organization, there can be no revolutionary Marxist—Bolshevik—politics. It was precisely this thought that Lenin expressed in a sharply polemical way, declaring that my revolutionary ideas or proposals amounted to nothing but "phrases," since in my conciliationism I had come into conflict with Bolshevism, which was creating the primary nucleus of the proletarian movement. Was Lenin right? Absolutely.

Without the Bolshevik Party the October Revolution could not have been carried through or consolidated. Thus, the only truly revolutionary work was the work that helped this party take shape and grow stronger. In relation to this main road, all other revolutionary work remained off to the side, lacking any inner guarantee of success or dependability, and in many cases was directly detrimental to the main revolutionary work of that time. In this sense Lenin was right when he said that the conciliationist position, by giving protection and cover to Menshevism, often transformed revolutionary slogans, perspectives, etc., into mere phrases. This fundamentally Leninist assessment of centrism is absolutely indisputable. It would be monstrous to start up a discussion on that question within the Bolshevik Party. For my part, at least, I see no basis whatsoever for any discussion of that kind.

The changeover on this question began for me with the outbreak of the imperialist war. According to the general trend of my views, frequently presented after 1907, a war in Europe would have to create a revolutionary situation. But contrary to expectation, the revolutionary situation ended in total betrayal by the social democracy.

Gradually I reappraised my view of the relations between party and class and between revolutionary action and the proletarian organization. Under the impact of the social-patriotic treachery of international Menshevism, I came, step by step, to the conclusion that there was a need not only for ideological struggle against Menshevism (which I had earlier recognized—though to be sure with insufficient consistency) but also for an uncompromising organizational break with it. This reappraisal was not accomplished in one sitting. In my articles and speeches during the war one may find both inconsistency and backward steps. Lenin was absolutely right when he opposed any and every manifestation of centrism on my part, emphasizing them and even intentionally exaggerating them. But if the period of the war is taken as a whole, it becomes quite clear that the terrible humiliation of socialism at the beginning of the war was a turning point for me from centrism to Bolshevism—in all questions without exception. And as I worked out a more and more correct, i.e., Bolshevik, conception of the relations between class and party, between theory and politics, and between politics and organization, my general revolutionary point of view toward bourgeois society was naturally filled with a more vital and realistic content.

From the moment when I clearly saw that a struggle to the death against defensism was absolutely necessary, Lenin's position came through to me with full force. What had seemed to me to be "splitterism," "disruption," etc., now appeared as a salutary and incomparably farsighted struggle for the revolutionary independence of the proletarian party. Not only Lenin's political methods and organizational techniques, but also his entire political and human personality appeared to me in a new light, in the light of Bolshevism, that is, in a truly Leninist light. One can understand and recognize Lenin for what he is only after becoming a Bolshevik. Never again after that did the question of "Trotskyism" as a special tendency occur to me. Never did it enter my head to pose this or that question from the special angle of "Trotskyism."

It is untrue, and monstrously so, to assert that I joined the party with the idea of substituting Trotskyism for Leninism. I joined the Bolshevik Party as a Bolshevik. When Lenin, in a discussion about the unification of the Mezhrayontsi with the Bolsheviks, raised a question as to which of my cothinkers I thought should also go onto the Central Committee, I answered that for me the question did not exist politically, since I saw no differences that would separate me from Bolshevism.

Of course, I can be reproved for not arriving at the correct understanding of Menshevism earlier. This is to reproach me for not becoming a Bolshevik in 1903. But no one chooses a path of development arbitrarily. I came to Bolshevism by a long and complicated road. Along this road I had no interests other than those of the revolution and the proletariat. I fought against Leninism when I thought that it was wrongly dividing the working class. When I realized my mistake as a result of years of experience, I came over to Leninism. I of course take the political responsibility for the roundabout path of my development.

However, my entire past was thoroughly and completely known to the Central Committee of our party and to all its older members when in May 1917 I returned from America and placed myself at the disposal of the Bolshevik Party. In my past there were political mistakes, but there was nothing that placed the slightest stain on my revolutionary honor. If I came to Leninism later than many other comrades, nevertheless I came soon enough to take part as one of Lenin's closest co-workers in the July days, the October Revolution, the civil war, and the other work of the Soviet years. When I expressed the opinion once (this is bitterly held against me) that I considered the way I came to Bolshevism as no worse than other ways, I was referring of course to individuals and not to the collective proletarian road of the party. By this I only meant to say that insofar as it is given to people to make judgments about themselves, my way led me to Bolshevism solidly and for good.

Solely in order to clarify my point do I take the liberty of citing a historical example. Franz Mehring, the well-known German Marxist, came to Marx and Engels late in life and only after a great struggle. Moreover, Mehring first moved toward social democracy, then veered away from it, and only later joined it once and for all. One may find, in certain old archives, harsh statements by Mehring against Marx and Engels and devastating comments by Engels on Mehring. In the struggle within the party, Mehring was frequently reminded about this past of his. Nevertheless, Mehring came to Marxism firmly and remained solid to the end. He died a founder of the German Communist Party.

Comrade Kamenev has gathered together with great care all the quotations from Lenin that expose the error of my views. Kamenev turns the polemical blows dealt by Lenin over a number of years into the definitive characterization of my politics. But the reader is bound to get the impression that this characterization is incomplete. Thus the reader will find absolutely no answer here to the question of whether my revolutionary activity (before 1914 or before 1917) consisted only of mistakes, or whether there were features that linked me with Bolshevism, pointed toward it, and led me to it. Without an answer to that question, the character of my later role in party work remains totally inexplicable. Besides that, Kamenev's characterization unavoidably gives rise to questions of another order, ones of a purely factual nature. *Are what Kamenev compiled really the only things Lenin said or wrote on the subject? Aren't there other comments by Lenin as well, comments that are based on the experience of the revolutionary years? Is it really fair and honest now, in late 1924, to tell the party only about the comments of prerevolutionary years, and say nothing about the comments flowing from our joint work and struggle?* These are questions that must inevitably occur to every serious reader. Old quotations will not suffice. They will only encourage people to conclude that tendentiousness and bias are involved.

Chapter 3
The Role of the Party

In order to present this or that present-day view or article of mine as "Trotskyism" and to connect it, for that purpose, with my errors of the past, it is necessary to skip over a great deal, and above all the year 1917. But to do that, it must be shown, in retrospect, that I failed to understand the events of 1917, that my unconditional endorsement of Lenin's April Theses was the result of misunderstanding, that I did not truly grasp the role of the party in the revolutionary process, that I ignored the whole history of the party, and so on and so forth. This cannot be shown in any way on the basis of the events of 1917, because my part in those events never gave anyone, then or now, the slightest pretext for charging me with the pursuit of some separate, special line. Therefore the accusation of Trotskyism is geared not to those events or to my part in them, but to my article summarizing some of the lessons of those events. That is why the entire accusation of "Trotskyism" against me depends to a large extent, one may say to a decisive extent, on the question of whether it is true or not true that I distorted Leninism in discussing the events of

1917 and whether I have counterposed to Leninism a distinct, special, incompatible trend. The charge of "Trotskyism" against my "Lessons of October" thus becomes the central knot that ties together the whole structure of the "Trotskyist" danger in the party. Moreover—and this is the heart of the matter—the knot that holds this whole artificial structure together consists of a string of lies. Just approaching it seriously is enough to make it crumble to dust at one touch. Only extraordinary pickiness, combined with an even greater degree of prejudice, could bring someone to interpret my "Lessons of October" as a deviation from Leninism rather than as a conscientious and careful application of Leninism. That is what I now wish to show by taking up the main disputed questions.

It is especially surprising (because it is such an outrageous lie) to hear the assertion that in my account of the October overturn I have ignored the party. For the central idea of the preface and the purpose for which it was written arise from a recognition of the decisive role of the party in the proletarian revolution. "The fundamental instrument of proletarian revolution is the party" [see "Lessons of October," p. 203 above]. I illustrate this idea on the basis of the defeats experienced by the postwar revolutionary movement in a number of countries. Our error, I said and I repeat, inasmuch as we prematurely expected the victory of the European proletariat as a direct result of the war, was precisely that we still did not sufficiently appreciate the importance of the party for the proletarian revolution. The German workers were unable to win in 1918 or in 1919 because they did not have the main tool needed to win—a Bolshevik party. I doubly emphasized in my preface the fact that the bourgeoisie in seizing power enjoys a whole series of advantages as a class, while the proletariat can only make up for the lack of these advantages by having a revolutionary party.

If there is one idea that I have generally repeated, emphasized, and expanded upon with tenfold insistence since the defeat of the German revolution, it is precisely the idea that even the most favorable revolutionary conditions may not produce victory for the proletariat if it is not led by a genuinely revolutionary party capable of securing victory. This was the main theme of my report in Tiflis, "On the Road to the European Revolution" (April 11, 1924), of two other reports—"Perspectives and Tasks in the East" (April 21, 1924), "May Day in the East and West" (April 29, 1924)—the preface to my book *First Five Years of the Communist*

International, entitled "At a New Turning Point" (May 20, 1924), "Through What Stage Are We Passing?" (June 21, 1924), and so on.* In my Tiflis speech referred to above, in analyzing the causes of the defeat of the German revolution, I said: "Why then in Germany has there been no victory thus far? I think there can be only one answer: because Germany did not have a Bolshevik party, nor did it have a leader such as we had in October. . . . What was lacking? A party with the tempering that our party has. . . . This, comrades, is the central question, and we must learn to understand and value more clearly and profoundly the character, nature, and significance of our own party, which secured victory for the proletariat in October and a whole series of victories since October" [see "On the Road to the European Revolution," p. 165 above].

I repeat, this has been the central, guiding idea of all my reports and articles dealing with the problems of proletarian revolution, especially since last year's defeat in Germany. I could cite dozens of quotations to prove this. Is it reasonable to suppose that this central idea, this chief conclusion from the entire historical experience, especially our own experience, of the past decade, was suddenly forgotten by me or thrown out or distorted when I was working on "Lessons of October"? No, that is impossible and it did not happen. There isn't even the hint of such a thing. On the contrary, my entire preface is built around the guidelines that I laid out in my Tiflis report: "We must learn to understand and value more clearly and profoundly the character, nature, and significance of our party, which secured victory for the proletariat in October and a whole series of victories since October."

I am not of course going to prove this idea once again here, because I consider this "lesson" of October proved, tested, unquestionable, and irrefutable. But it was precisely the idea of the decisive role of the party and its leadership that constituted the central theme of my preface. All I need to do to prove this is to quote the entire work, underlining its central ideas in pencil. Unfortunately, that is impossible. I can only ask the interested reader instead to read or to reread the preface from this point of view, with pencil in hand, and to pay particular attention to

---

*See in particular L. Trotsky, **Zapad i Vostok** [West and East], Moscow, 1924.—L.T. [**Zapad i Vostok** contains the five articles listed above plus two others, entitled "The Amsterdam International and War" (June 7, 1924) and "We and the East" (June 10, 1924).]

pages 200-03, 231-33, 236-37 above, and the chapter "Again, on the Soviets and the Party in a Proletarian Revolution" [pp. 249-56]. Here I will limit myself to but one example.

In the concluding chapter of the preface I reject the idea that has sprung up in our press during the past year that in England the revolution might pass "not through the channel of the party but through the trade unions." In my preface I say on this point: "Without a party, apart from a party, over the head of a party, or with a substitute for a party, the proletarian revolution cannot conquer. That is the principal lesson of the last decade. It is true that the English trade unions may become a mighty lever of the proletarian revolution; they may, for instance, even take the place of the workers' soviets under certain conditions and for a certain period of time. They can fill such a role, however, not apart from a Communist party, and certainly not *against* the party, but only on the condition that communist influence becomes the decisive influence in the trade unions. *We have paid far too dearly for this conclusion—with regard to the role and importance of a party in a proletarian revolution—to renounce it so lightly or to minimize its significance"* [see pp. 251-52 above]. And now I am being accused of nothing less than renouncing it and minimizing its significance!

It is enough, after all that has been said here, to cite this one quotation to show that a tendency is being ascribed to me by the name "Trotskyism" which is the exact opposite not only of the spirit and letter of my preface but also of my entire conception of the proletarian revolution. From this point of view, the references to my allegedly forgetting or consciously failing to mention the role of the Petrograd Committee in the revolution appear to be altogether inappropriate quibbling. My preface is not a narrative dealing with the role of particular institutions or organizations in the party. It is not a general exposition of the events. It is an attempt to clarify the general role of the party in the course of the proletarian revolution. I am not recounting the facts; rather I assume that they are by and large well known. I proceed from the basic proposition of the leading role of the party—of course in the form of its living and functioning organizational units. I have not ignored or passed over something in silence if in the course of my presentation I assume it is understood. No sophistry and no stretching of the point can gainsay the fact that the central charge brought against me—minimizing the significance of the party—is a thoroughgoing lie and stands in crying contradiction to everything I actually said and demonstrated in my preface.

Equally inaccurate are the assertions that in my evaluation of the party I shift attention from the masses of the party to the "higher-ups," to the chiefs. On this theme some have even uttered nonsense about a theory of "heroes" and "the crowd." Nevertheless, the crucial point is that after specifying the general significance of the party in the process of proletarian revolution—and in such a categorical way that hardly anything could be added—*I have posed the particular, partial, but exceptionally important question of the role of the central leadership in a period of revolution.* Here the question of so-called "chiefs" of course enters in.

In characterizing the nature of Lenin's work in October, I twice pointed out that the strength of his opposition to every sign of wavering lay in the fact that he could always rely at the decisive moment on the "party rank and file." If I had reduced the entire problem of the revolution or even the problem of party leadership to the question of "chiefs," I would have fundamentally contradicted Marxism. But when, on the basis of a Marxist definition of the role of the party in the proletarian revolution, I raised the question of the relation between the leading center of the party, the party as a whole, and the mass of workers, as a special question but an exceptionally important one for the revolution, it was a completely valid way to pose the question, and after last year's defeat of the German revolution, more than ever an obligatory one. But we will discuss that further below.

I am told that the party is needed not only to seize power but to maintain it, to build socialism, to maneuver in international affairs. Am I really unaware of that? But the point is that the European parties still face the task of winning power in all its enormity. That is what they have to concentrate on and subordinate all their efforts to. After the seizure of power, new difficulties will present themselves. Here one may even say in advance, with confidence, that the transition from a victorious armed insurrection to "organic" work, with its necessarily gradual pace, will inevitably produce new crises in every or nearly every party—and cause a discontented *left* wing to differentiate itself out. In different countries this would of course occur in different ways. But this is a danger and difficulty of a later stage. Communism can cope with it; what is needed first is to take power.

Similar in kind—that is, obviously biased and painfully stretching the point—is the charge that my account of the lessons of October ignores our party's *past,* that is, its history before the war and revolution. But as has been said, my entire line of argument points to the conclusion that the proletariat cannot take advantage of even the most favorable revolutionary situation *if in the preceding, preparatory period the vanguard of the proletariat has not taken shape in a genuinely revolutionary, i.e., Bolshevik, party.* This is the central lesson of October. All others are subordinate to it.

The party cannot be improvised for the needs of the moment or thrown together for the purpose of armed insurrection: this has been shown all too irrefutably by the experience of the European proletariat since the war. By saying nothing more than this the importance of the entire pre-October history of our party was totally and completely clarified, even if I had not said a single word directly about this pre-October history. But in fact I spoke quite specifically and exactly about the conditions of the party's development which prepared it for its role in October and after October. Here is what I said on this point in my preface: "History secured for our party revolutionary advantages that are truly inestimable. The traditions of the heroic struggle against the tsarist monarchy; the habituation to revolutionary self-sacrifice bound up with the conditions of underground activity; the broad theoretical study and assimilation of the revolutionary experience of humanity; the struggle against Menshevism, against the Narodniks, and against conciliationism; the supreme experience of the 1905 revolution; the theoretical study and assimilation of this experience during the years of counterrevolution; the examination of the problems of the international labor movement in the light of the revolutionary lessons of 1905—these were the things which in their totality gave our party an exceptional revolutionary temper, supreme theoretical penetration, and unparalleled revolutionary sweep" [pp. 253–54 above].

Where is there any "ignoring" of the party, or of its pre-October history, here? It is not only the preface's overall trend of thought that is aimed at clarifying the decisive importance of preparing and tempering the party for proletarian revolution. There is a thoroughly precise, concrete, and—despite its brevity—virtually definitive characterization of the conditions of party development that made it what it is. Of couse I do not relate the full history of the party in the pages of the preface, because the theme of the book is the history not of the party, but of October, i.e., a particular period in its history. But I do not know what objections could be made to this characterization of the party's conditions of development which secured "revolutionary advantages that are truly inestimable."

But that is still not all. The charge that I "passed over in silence" the struggle of Bolshevism against the tendency that I personally stood for in the past can be refuted quite sufficiently in the present instance by the argument that once again it is not the preceding history, not the struggle against conciliationism before the revolution, but October that is under discussion. But there is no need for this argument either. For among the conditions I listed as giving the party its exceptional tempering, its supreme theoretical penetration, and unparalleled revolutionary sweep, I mentioned the struggle not only against Menshevism and Narodnikism but against conciliationism as well.

Nowhere do I even hint at the idea that Bolshevism, as it emerged from its prerevolutionary history, was in need of any change of nature through the medium of "Trotskyism." On the contrary, I say outright that an essential element in the formation of Bolshevism was the struggle against those tendencies which were known by the name of Trotskyism. In other words I said the exact opposite of what is being attributed to me. Without any belittling of the role of the party on my part, without any ignoring on my part of the meaning and importance of the unparalleled pre-October preparatory period, the whole structure of the revived danger of Trotskyism loses its central prop. But of such belittling and such ignoring there is not even a hint in my work. My main idea, around which all the rest turns like a wheel on its axis, has been indicated here, and I will now repeat it once again: "We must learn to understand and value more clearly and profoundly the character, nature, and significance of our own party, which secured victory for the proletariat in October and a whole series of victories since October." This is the central idea of Leninism. I am not trying to replace or dilute it. I advocate and defend it.

Chapter 4
'The Democratic Dictatorship
of the Proletariat and Peasantry'

We have seen how things stand with the "Trotskyist" conception of the role of the party. But my supposed criticism of Leninism is deduced in other ways as well, and ambiguous ones at that.

First, when I characterize the October position of Comrade Kamenev and others who opposed the insurrection, it is said that I am using the pretext of criticizing Lenin's opponents of that time to combat Lenin himself. My second line of criticism of Lenin consists in what is called my blunt account of Lenin's "errors" in October and of my alleged corrections of those errors. It is necessary to give careful consideration both to the first question and to the second.

What was the essence of the differences between Comrade Kamenev and Lenin in October? The fact that Comrade Kamenev advocated the completion of the bourgeois revolution under the slogan of the "democratic dictatorship of the proletariat and the peasantry," while Lenin, on the grounds that the bourgeois revolution had already unfolded, was preparing and calling for the socialist dictatorship of the proletariat, drawing the rural poor after it. Such were the two positions in October in their bare essentials. Lenin adamantly opposed Kamenev's position and rejected the "democratic dictatorship of the proletariat and the peasantry" as an outlived formula. "One must measure up," he said, "not to old formulas but to the new reality. Is this reality covered by Comrade Kamenev's Old Bolshevik formula, which says that 'the bourgeois-democratic revolution is not completed'?" Lenin asks. "It is not," he replies. "The formula is obsolete. It is no good at all. It is dead. And it is no use trying to revive it" [*CW*, Vol. 24, "Letters on Tactics" (April 8-13, 1917), p. 50].

Does this mean that Lenin was simply "renouncing" the formula? No, not at all. I have not tried in the slightest to impose such a renunciation on him. On the contrary, I say plainly [see p. 206 above] that Lenin—in opposition to the entire superficial Westernizing tradition in the Russian social democracy, starting with the Emancipation of Labor Group—gave expression to the particularity of Russian history and of the Russian revolution in the formula "democratic dictatorship of the proletariat and the peasantry." But to him this formula, like all other political and tactical formulas, was a totally dynamic, action-oriented, and consequently concretely determined one. It was not a dogma but a guide to action.

In my preface I ask whether the "democratic dictatorship of the proletariat and the peasantry" came into existence in the circumstances of the 1917 revolution, and I answer, basing myself solidly on Lenin, that it did so only in the form of the workers' and soldiers' soviets, which held only half the power and did not want to take full power. Lenin recognized his own formula in this highly modified and refracted reality. He discerned the fact that this old formula would go no further than that halfway realization in the existing historical situation. While the opponents of the seizure of power thought that we had to "complete" the democratic revolution, Lenin replied that everything that could be done along "February" lines had been done, had already become a reality; the old formula had already outlived itself. It was necessary to extract a new formula for action from the development of reality.

Lenin accused his opponents of not recognizing the "democratic dictatorship" in the form it took under the conditions of the February revolution. As early as the beginning of April Lenin tirelessly explained: "The person who *now* speaks only of a 'revolutionary democratic dictatorship of the proletariat and peasantry' is behind the times, consequently, he has in effect *gone over* to the petty bourgeoisie against the proletarian class struggle; that person should be consigned to the archive of 'Bolshevik' prerevolutionary antiques (it may be called the archive of 'Old Bolsheviks')" [*CW,* Vol. 24, "Letters on Tactics" (April 8-13, 1917), p. 45].

Lenin insistently repeated that his opponents who counterposed an outdated formula to the needs of the revolution were "surrendering helplessly to petty bourgeois revolutionism" [ibid., p. 50]. That is the Leninist way of posing the problem. That is precisely the way I too presented it. Why does my solidarity with Lenin and not with Comrade Kamenev on this cardinal question of the October Revolution turn out to be a revision of Leninism? Why is it that the concept of Leninism, in relation to October, encompasses Kamenev, who opposed Lenin in matters of principle, but excludes me, although I stood with Lenin? Hasn't the term *Leninism* become too flexible and accommodating in this case?

In order to build a semblance of a bridge to such a totally surprising and improbable distinction between Leninism and anti-Leninism in relation to October, it is necessary to make it seem as though I considered the mistake of Kamenev and others to lie in their *consistent adherence to Bolshevism,* as though I were saying, "See how these comrades actually followed the line of Lenin's formula through to the end and fell captive to petty-bourgeois revolutionism." But I never suggested that the mistakes of Lenin's opponents in October lay in their "consistent" application of Lenin's formula. No. Their mistake was that they approached the Leninist formula in a non-Leninist way; they did not recognize the peculiar and unique way in which this formula had come into existence in reality; they did not understand the transitional character of the 1905 formula, its application to a particular stage; they used Lenin's words to counterpose a formula learned by rote to the study of reality; in other words, *they did not understand Lenin's formula in a Leninist way.* Lenin said this himself and gave the definitive analysis of this error.

For the same purpose, i.e., to turn my (or more exactly, Lenin's) criticism of Kamenev and the others into an alleged criticism of Leninism, it was necessary to quote my article of 1909—not my 1924 preface but my article of 1909—where I said that there was a danger that the formula "democratic dictatorship of the proletariat" would reveal its antirevolutionary features at a certain stage of the revolution. Yes, I wrote this in 1909 in Rosa Luxemburg's magazine. This article became part of my book *1905*,[38] which has been reprinted more than once since 1917, both in Russian and in other languages, without any protests or objections from anyone, because everyone understood that this article had to be taken in the context of the time in which it was written. At any rate, one cannot take a sentence out of a polemical article of 1909 and paste it onto my preface of 1924.

In regard to this 1909 quotation it can be said with full justification that when I wrote it I did not allow for the fact that the formula I was arguing against had no self-sufficient value for Lenin, but was a preparatory formula applying to a particular stage. Such a charge would be correct and I would accept it. But after all it was precisely Comrade Kamenev and the others who tried—against Lenin—to turn this dynamic formula into a dogma and to counterpose it to the demands of the developing revolution. And it was precisely Lenin who explained to them that their position held back the necessary development of the revolution. I only repeated his view and his criticism in a very toned-down and summary form. How can one deduce from this any tendency toward revision of Leninism?

In view of the persistent attempt to drag in a "Trotskyism" that was long ago eliminated by history, one can only say the following: In his preface, Trotsky solidarizes himself with Lenin's position on the question of the transition from the democratic revolution to the socialist one; in so doing, however, Trotsky says nothing about rejecting his old formula of permanent revolution. One must conclude from this that on the basis of the experience of the 1917 revolution, Trotsky interprets his old formula in a Leninist sense. That is the only conclusion one can draw in this regard—and even this cannot be done on the basis of the preface, where the question of the permanent revolution is not even raised, since it has been resolved by history, but only by comparing the preface with my old articles, reflecting different political stages of development. And such a conclusion would to a certain extent be correct. What was basic to me in the formula of the so-called permanent revolution was the conviction that the revolution in Russia, beginning as a bourgeois revolution, would inevitably be carried through to completion by a socialist dictatorship. If, as I have indicated above, centrist tendencies with respect to tactics separated me from Bolshevism and placed me in opposition to it, still my basic political conviction—that the Russian revolution would transfer power to the proletariat—placed me in opposition to Menshevism and through all stages tended to draw me into the camp of Bolshevism. But this is all incidental to the question that concerns us. I reject in any case, as something completely laughable, the opinion attributed to me, that Lenin or the Bolshevik Party came over to "my" formula on the revolution after realizing the erroneousness of their own.

I must concede, however, that one may reach any conclusion one wishes concerning the smuggling in of Trotskyism to replace Leninism if one makes indiscriminate use of quotations dating from different periods over the course of two decades, arbitrarily throwing them together, and especially if one attributes to me things that I never even said. As is well known, more than anything else in this discussion we have had occasion to hear the formula "No tsar, but a workers' government."   I think that no less than a dozen authors (and how many orators!) have taken turns in attributing this incorrect political formula to me. I must say, however, that the popularized proclamation with this heading, "No tsar, but a workers' government," was written in the summer of 1905 by Parvus,[39] who was not in the country, whereas I was living illegally in Petrograd at the time and had no contact with him whatsoever. This proclamation was put out by a foreign publisher *with Parvus's personal signature on it,* and was not reprinted by anyone inside Russia. Never did I assume responsibility for this simplistic formula of Parvus's. In that very same period I wrote a number of proclamations, the most important of which were printed by the Bolsheviks' secret press at Baku (summer, 1905). One of these was specially addressed to the peasants. In none of these proclamations of mine, the majority of which have now been dug up, is there any "leaping over" of the democratic phase of the revolution. They all raise the demand for a Constituent Assembly and an agrarian revolution.

The articles directed against me contain errors of this nature without number. But there is no need to dwell upon this. The issue is not after all what formula I personally used at any of the various stages of my political development to define the tasks and perspectives of the revolution, but *whether I am correct— now, in 1924—in my analysis of the Leninist approach to the fundamental question of tactics in its inner connection with the course of the October Revolution.*

None of my critics has pointed to any error by me in this sphere. In my theoretical interpretation of the October Revolution I remain to the fullest extent on the ground of Leninism, just as in the practical work of carrying out the revolution I marched in step with Lenin.*

---

*One author has even come up with the assertion that I evaluate October—a la Sukhanov. Then, by way of contrast, he refers to Lenin's well-known article on Sukhanov's book. Obviously, Trotskyism is opposed to Leninism! Our worthy author has certainly gone wide of the mark. On February 5, 1923, that is, long before we heard Lenin's comments, I wrote a letter to the editors of **Pravda** in which among other things I gave the following characterization of Sukhanov's book: "In the last few days I have been looking through one of the recently published volumes of Sukhanov's **Memoirs of the Revolution.** It seems to me this book should be given a scathing review. A more thoroughgoing caricature of intellectual egocentrism would be hard to imagine. First he [Sukhanov] groveled at Kerensky's feet, then he squired Tseretelli and Dan around by their left elbows, urging upon them the noblest possible code of conduct, and then—he lectured the Bolsheviks on the truly revolutionary way to conduct themselves. Sukhanov was ever so greatly incensed, being so noble, when Lenin went into hiding after the July days. He, Sukhanov, would never have behaved in that way," etc., etc.

A review appeared in **Pravda,** written in the spirit of my letter and even including part of it. The reader will see from this how much I am inclined to view the revolution "a la Sukhanov."—L.T.

Chapter 5
Leninism and Blanquism

Now we must return to the charge that is at once the most monstrously conceived and the most absurdly insupportable. I have portrayed Lenin, don't you see, as a "Blanquist" (!!!)—and myself as little short of the savior of the revolution from Lenin's Blanquism. Only complete polemical blindness could prompt one to make such an accusation.

What was the pretext, though, for this absolutely unbelievable discussion about "Blanquism"?

In September, during the Democratic Conference, Lenin proposed to the Central Committee (from Finland, where he was in hiding) that the Aleksandrinka, where the conference was being held, be surrounded, its members arrested, the Peter-Paul fortress occupied, etc. In the name of the Petrograd Soviet, it was not yet possible in September to carry out this plan, for the soviet organization had not yet been sufficiently Bolshevized and was thus not suited to that task: the Revolutionary Military Committee did not yet exist. "The above formulation of the question," I say in my preface [see pp. 238-39 above] in regard to Lenin's September proposal, "presupposed that the preparation and completion of the insurrection were to be carried out through party channels and in the name of the party, and afterwards the seal of sanction was to be placed on the victory by the Congress of Soviets." For some reason, certain comrades have drawn the conclusion from this that I consider Lenin's September proposal to have been—Blanquism!!! I absolutely cannot understand what Blanquism has to do with it. What is really meant by Blanquism is the desire to seize power in the name of a revolutionary minority, without being based on the working class. But the entire crux of the situation in September-October 1917 was that *the majority of working people were following our party* and that majority was visibly growing. Consequently, the question was whether the Central Committee of the party that had the following of the majority should assume the task of organizing the armed insurrection, seize power, convene the Congress of Soviets, and thus sanction the accomplished fact of the revolution. To speak of Blanquism in relation to this proposal is to monstrously twist the meaning of fundamental political concepts.

Insurrection is an art: the problem of insurrection is open to various solutions, some of which may be more effective, others less so. Lenin's September proposal had the undoubted advantage that it provided for taking the enemy by surprise, denying him the chance to bring up reliable units and pass over to the counteroffensive. The awkwardness of the proposal lay in the fact that to a certain extent it might catch by surprise not only the enemy but a section of the workers and of the garrison as well. It might cause confusion in their ranks and thus weaken the force of our attack. It was an important question but a purely practical one, having nothing to do with the conflict in principle between Blanquism and Marxism.

The Central Committee, as everyone knows, did not accept Lenin's September proposal and I voted along with all the others on this question. What was involved was not a general definition of the entire course of development, and surely not a conflict between Blanquism (!!!) and Marxism, but a concrete, specific evaluation of the completely practical, and to a significant degree' technical, conditions of the insurrection, the political prerequisites for which were already at hand.

It was in this sense that I pointed out that Lenin had to judge the purely practical conditions of the Petrograd situation "from the underground." These words have called forth completely unexpected protests. And yet, here too, I am only repeating what Vladimir Ilyich himself said and wrote on this question. During the Third Comintern Congress he wrote "to console" certain Hungarian comrades whom he had dealt with harshly on the eve of the congress because of their extravagantly "left" position. "When I was an emigre myself . . . I took 'too Leftist' a stand several times (as I now realise). In August 1917, I was also an emigre and moved in our Party Central Committee a much too 'Leftist' proposal which, happily, was flatly rejected. It is quite natural for emigres frequently to adopt attitudes which are 'too Leftist' "* [*CW,* Vol. 45, "To the Participants in a Sitting of the Commission on Tactics of the Third Congress of the Comintern" (July 7, 1921), p. 203]. We can see that Vladimir Ilyich called his own plan too far to the left and explained his "leftism" by the fact that he was then condemned to the position of an emigre. Here too, then, I have only presented Lenin's own evaluation.

---

*There is a misprint in these lines: the plan referred to was written not in August but in September.—L.T.

Nevertheless, this plan, rejected by the CC, had a *positive* effect on the course of events. Lenin knew that there would be no lack of caution, circumspection, and of applying the brakes in general, and therefore he pressed with all his might, striving to force each responsible party worker and all of them as a whole to face up to the armed insurrection as an absolutely unpostponable practical task. Lenin's September letter, which had nothing in common with Blanquism (!!!), was part of that systematic application of pressure to the party and was useful and effective in that it forced people to come to grips with the problems of insurrection more concretely, firmly, and audaciously.

Another crucial episode of the October Revolution is closely linked with this, namely Kerensky's attempt to remove the Petrograd garrison.

I pause to go into this episode not because I have anything new to add to what has already been said on this point but exclusively for the reason that my account of this episode has given Comrade Kamenev the pretext to present matters as though I counterposed my "correct" policy to Lenin's "incorrect" (Blanquist) policy. I will not repeat here all the truly repulsive arguments and insinuations that have been made in this regard. I reread the relevant part of my preface, being sure ahead of time, of course, that there is not even a hint of what is attributed to me. But in my preface I found even more: there is a passage which quite precisely and sharply excludes any possibility of false interpretation whatsoever concerning any "special" strategic plan of mine in relation to the Petrograd garrison. This is what is said in the preface: "When we Bolsheviks assumed power in the Petrograd Soviet, we only continued and deepened the methods of dual power. We took it upon ourselves to revise the order transferring the troops to the front. By this very act we covered up the actual insurrection of the Petrograd garrison with the traditions and methods of legal dual power. Nor was that all. While formally adapting our agitation on the question of power to the opening of the Second Soviet Congress, we developed and deepened the already existing traditions of dual power, and prepared the framework of soviet legality for the Bolshevik insurrection on an All-Russian scale" [pp. 241-42 above].

Thus the account in the preface itself is given not in the name of any person but in the name of the party ("we Bolsheviks"). And subsequently the account of the struggle around the garrison is developed not from anyone's plan but from the regime of dual power inherited by us from the SRs and Mensheviks. Kerensky wanted to transfer the garrison to the front; this could not be done, according to tradition, without consulting the soldiers' section of the soviets. The general staff applied to the presidium of the soldiers' section, but the Bolsheviks were already firmly installed there. The conflict then arose which in its further development was full of consequences of such importance to the October Revolution. That, then, is how I described the episode of the garrison, fully in accordance with the actual course of events.

But even that is not yet all. As though deliberately to exclude the possibility of any false interpretations whatsoever, like those of Comrade Kamenev, I openly said, further on: "Our 'trickery' proved 100 percent successful—*not because it was an artful scheme devised by wily strategists* seeking to avoid a civil war, but because it *derived naturally from the disintegration of the conciliationist regime* with its glaring contradictions" [p. 242]. Thus the very word "trickery" is here placed in quotation marks to show that it was not a question of someone's subjective cleverness but the result of the objective development of relations growing out of dual power. The preface states outright that no "artful schemes devised by wily strategists" were involved. Thus not only is the presentation of events given in the name of the party, that is, its representatives in the soviet, but it is clearly and plainly stated that individual schemes or personal shrewdness or trickiness had no place here.

On what, then, is the assertion based that I have exalted my own policies at the expense of Lenin's? Decidedly on nothing. Of course, from Finland, Lenin could not see or know about this episode from the moment of its origin or follow it in all its stages of development. One may suppose that if Lenin had been informed in a timely way of all the details of the business with the Petrograd garrison, i.e., had based himself on direct personal observation, his anxiety over the fate of the revolution would perhaps not have been so great. But that surely would not have kept him from applying all the pressure that he did. He was undeniably right in demanding that power be seized before the convening of the Congress of Soviets and only because of his pressure was that accomplished.

Chapter 6
'The Combined Type of State'

Central to the October differences was the question of the armed insurrection for the seizure of power. Without thoroughly understanding Lenin's approach to this question, one obviously cannot understand the October differences themselves. In this connection, I now wish to show, by an example which has played a central role in the present discussion, that many comrades who accuse me of retreating from Leninism in fact do not know their Lenin very well and have not thought very carefully about Lenin's approach to the question of taking power.

In the preface, I referred in passing to the fact that the authors of the letter "On the Current Situation," in opposing the seizure of power, were forced to adopt approximately the same position that had been taken at a certain point in the German revolution of 1918-19 by Hilferding, then the head of the Independent Social Democratic Party in Germany—namely, proposing that the soviets be included in the democratic constitution.

This comparison of mine has been criticized with special severity. I am accused, first, of absolutely incorrectly and even "dishonestly" linking Comrade Kamenev's position with Hilferding's. At the same time they tell me that Lenin too made statements to the effect that the soviets could be combined with the Constituent Assembly and that, consequently, I am again revising Leninism. I am charged with failing to understand the transitional phase when the party was fighting for soviet power but at the same time had not yet abandoned the Constituent Assembly. Finally, I am denounced for the fact that I myself, in agitating for power to the soviets, spoke for the convening of a Constituent Assembly. The main accusation, however, as in all the other cases, is that I am supposedly likening Lenin's position to Hilferding's: thus a revision of Leninism, a belittling of Leninism. Let us see if this is so. Clarification of this highly important episode will throw a bright light on the question of the 1917 differences as well.

It is indeed true that the party was fighting at that time for power to the soviets and simultaneously for the convening of a Constituent Assembly. One of the most popular agitational slogans asserted that unless the soviets took power, the Constituent Assembly would not be convened, and that if it were convened, it would become an instrument of the counterrevolution. That was precisely how Lenin and the party presented the problem. The road to the Constituent Assembly lay not through the Provisional Government and Pre-Parliament but through the dictatorship of the proletariat and poor peasantry. Not a Constituent Assembly that would be an essential part of the workers' and peasants' state. That was the crux of the matter. To Lenin's path of insurrection, the opponents of the seizure of power replied with— hopes for a Constituent Assembly. They argued (see the letter "On the Current Situation") that the bourgeoisie "would not dare" to prevent the convening of the Constituent Assembly and would not be in a position to rig the elections to it. They argued that our party would be a powerful opposition in the Constituent Assembly, with approximately one-third of the votes. This led them to the following perspective: "The soviets, which have become rooted in life [?], cannot be destroyed. The Constituent Assembly will be able to find support for its revolutionary [?] work only in the soviets. The Constituent Assembly plus the soviets—that is that combined type of state institution toward which we are going."

Thus the combined type of state system means that the power, through the Provisional Government, the Pre-Parliament, and the Constituent Assembly convened by them, remains in the hands of the bourgeois classes. We play the role of the opposition in the Constituent Assembly and at the same time remain the leading party in the soviets. In other words, here we had the perspective of a continuation of dual power, which had been possible for a certain length of time under the professional class collaborators, the Mensheviks and SRs, but which became absolutely impossible in conditions where the Bolsheviks would have a majority in the soviets and a minority in the Constituent Assembly.

Naturally, Lenin's position had nothing in common with this. He said: *First* we will take power, *then* we will convene the Constituent Assembly and, if necessary, we will combine it with the soviets. In what way did Lenin's position differ from that of the oppositional authors of the letter "On the Current Situation"? In regard to the central question of revolution: *the question of power*. In Lenin's view both the Constituent Assembly and the soviets are organs of one and the same class, or of an alliance of the nonpropertied classes (the proletariat and the rural poor). The question of combining the Constituent Assembly with the soviets had a technical, organizational significance for Lenin. For his opponents, the soviets represented one class (the proletariat and the poor peasants) and the Constituent Assembly remained the organ of the propertied classes. To steer a course toward such a combined type of state would only be possible if one proceeded from phantasmagorical hopes that the powerless soviets would serve as "a revolver at the temple of the bourgeoisie" and that the bourgeoisie would "combine" its policies with the soviets.

It was precisely here that the similarity with Hilferding's position lay. At his most left-leaning moment, Hilferding came out against the dictatorship of the proletariat and proposed that the soviets be included in the constitution as a means of pressuring the propertied classes, i.e., as a revolver that would not shoot!

Or is all this still not clear? Then let us turn to the witness and interpreter who is the most authoritative for all of us: Lenin. If my critics had done this in a timely and attentive way, they would have spared their readers a great deal of confusion. We open Lenin's works and find there the "Letter to Comrades" of October 16-17, 1917, with the following truly remarkable lines: "There is no way for our sad pessimists to turn. A renunciation of the uprising is a renunciation of the transfer of power to the Soviets and implies a 'transfer' of all hopes and expectations to the kind bourgeoisie, which has 'promised' to convoke the Constituent Assembly.

"Is it so difficult to understand that once *power* is in the hands of the Soviets, the Constituent Assembly and its success are *guaranteed?* The Bolsheviks have said so thousands of times and *no one* has ever attempted to refute it [emphasis in original]. Everybody has recognized this 'combined type', *but to smuggle in a RENUNCIATION of the transfer of power to the Soviets under cover of the words 'combined type', to smuggle it in SECRETLY while FEARING to renounce our slogan openly is a matter for wonder. Is there any parliamentary term to describe it?* [Trotsky's emphasis].

"Someone has very pointedly retorted to our pessimist: 'Is it a revolver with no cartridges?' If so, it means going over directly to the Lieberdans,[40] who have declared the Soviets a 'revolver' thousands of times and have deceived the people thousands of times. For *while they were in control* the Soviets proved to be worthless.

"If, however, it is to be a revolver 'with cartridges', this cannot mean anything but *technical* preparation for an uprising; the cartridges have to be procured, the revolver has to be loaded—and cartridges alone will not be enough.

"Either go over to the side of the Lieberdans and *openly* renounce the slogan 'All Power to the Soviets', or start the uprising.

"There is no middle course" [*CW,* Vol. 26, "Letter to Comrades" (October 16-17, 1917), p. 200].

When you read these striking lines, it seems as though Lenin is simply adding his voice to the present discussion. Without waiting for further explanations from anyone, Lenin declares that the formula "combined type of state" is being used to "smuggle in" political ideas directly contrary to those that he, Lenin, supports. And when my preface repeated, in a very toned-down way, this characterization by Lenin of the "combined state" based on dual power, my critics declared that I was waving the banner of Leninism while *smuggling in*—"Trotskyism"! Is this not truly astonishing!? Does this not lay bare the entire mechanics by which the "Trotskyist" danger in the party has been contrived? If by "Trotskyism" (in the old prewar sense) is to be understood the attempt to reconcile essentially irreconcilable tendencies, then the "combined" type of state, without the seizure of power, would with unquestionable theoretical correctness be categorized as "Trotskyism" in that sense of the word. But I was not the one who advocated that "Trotskyism." And I am not the one who now defends it after the fact against Lenin.

I assume and I hope that the question is now clear. At any rate, making it any clearer is beyond my power. One cannot say something *for* Lenin any clearer then he has said it himself. And still they rebuke me with the claim that even Communist Youth members have grasped my error. Alas, following in the wake of certain older comrades, such Communist Youth members have only demonstrated how poorly they have read, or how poorly understood, Lenin on the fundamental question of the October Revolution: the question of power.

The quotation from Lenin which so thoroughly sums up and exhausts our dispute on the "combined type of state" dates from mid-October, that is, it was written by him ten days before the insurrection. However, he returned to the same question later on. With ruthless theoretical clarity Lenin formulated the revolutionary Marxist stand on this question on December 26, 1917, that is, two and a half months after the just-cited "Letter to Comrades." The October insurrection was already far behind us. Power was already in the hands of the soviets. Nevertheless, Lenin, who was not inclined to artificially revive differences that had been left behind if there was no pressing need to do so, felt that it was necessary on December 26, that is, before the convening of the Constituent Assembly, to return to this disputed question. Here is what we read on this question in his "Theses on the Constituent Assembly": "Every direct or indirect attempt to consider the question of the Constituent Assembly from a formal, legal point of view, within the framework of ordinary bourgeois democracy and disregarding the class struggle and civil war, would be a betrayal of the proletariat's cause, and the adoption of the bourgeois standpoint. The revolutionary Social-Democrats are duty bound to warn all and sundry against this error, into which a few Bolshevik leaders, who have been unable to appreciate the significance of the October uprising and the tasks of the dictatorship of the proletariat, have strayed" [*CW,* Vol. 26, "Theses on the Constituent Assembly" (December 26, 1917), pp. 382-83].

As we see, Lenin regarded himself as "duty bound" to warn "*all and sundry*" against the very error revealed in the dispute over the "combined" type of state. He considered it necessary to issue such a warning, in a very harsh tone, two months after the victorious insurrection. We have seen, however, that the point of this warning has been half forgotten and half misinterpreted by certain comrades. Nevertheless, on the international arena—and consequently for us as well—it retains all its force even today. After all, every Communist Party still faces the task of passing through the actual stage of overthrowing the democratic state. This is a task of enormous difficulty; in the lands where democracy has existed for a long time it will be a thousand times more difficult than it was for us. Formally all communists share the viewpoint of "denying" formal democracy. But that of course does not solve the problem at all. The most important thing still remains: the revolutionary overthrow of a democracy that has penetrated deeply into the national customs, its overthrow in practice.

The pressure of bourgeois-democratic public opinion offers the most powerful resistance along this path, and that must be understood and evaluated in advance. This resistance inevitably penetrates into the Communist parties themselves, creating groupings within them that correspond to that pressure. One may be sure in advance that without a doubt the most widespread, normal, typical form of "collaborationism" with bourgeois democracy will be precisely the idea of a "combined state"—to avoid an insurrection and the seizure of power. This flows naturally from the whole situation, from all the traditions, from the whole relationship between classes. That is why it is necessary to "warn all and sundry" against this inevitable danger, which could prove fatal to less well-tempered parties. That is why we must say to the European comrades: Look, here in Russia, even in our exceptional party, illusions about democracy, even though refracted in a unique way, took hold on the consciousness of outstanding revolutionaries at the crucial moment. This danger is immeasurably greater among you. Prepare for it. Study the experience of October. Think it through in all its revolutionary concreteness. Absorb it into your flesh and blood! To issue such warnings is not substituting for Leninism. No, it is serving Leninism loyally and truly.

Comrade Zinoviev asks whether the pre-October and October opposition to the seizure of power was a rightist grouping, or rightist tendency, or right wing. This question—which it would seem is not a question at all—Zinoviev answers in the negative. His answer is a purely formalist one: since the Bolshevik Party is monolithic, it could not have had a right wing within itself in October. But it is quite obvious that the Bolshevik Party is monolithic not in the sense that no right-wing tendencies ever *arose* in it, but in the sense that it always successfully *dealt with* such tendencies. Sometimes it expelled them, sometimes it absorbed them. That is how it was in the October period. There would seem to be nothing to argue about here: at the very moment when the revolution had matured, an opposition to it appeared within the party. Thus it was an opposition from the right and not the left. As Marxists we cannot after all limit ourselves to a purely psychological characterization of the opposition: "wavering, doubts, indecisiveness, etc." This vacillation was of a political kind, and no other. This vacillation placed itself in opposition to the proletariat's struggle for power. The opposition was given theoretical grounding and conducted with political slogans.

How can one refuse to give a political characterization to an opposition in the party which at the crucial moment comes out against the seizure of power by the proletariat? And why is it necessary to refrain from a political appraisal in this way? I absolutely refuse to try to understand this. One can of course present the problem in a psychological and personal way, for example: *Was it accidental or not* that this comrade or that ended up in the ranks of those opposed to the seizure of power? I did not take up this question at all, because it lies outside the sphere of evaluating the tendencies in the party's history and development. The fact that the opposition of some comrades was measured in months while that of others was measured in weeks can only have personal, biographical significance, but does not affect the actual political evaluation of their stand. Their position reflected the pressure of bourgeois public opinion on the party at a moment when mortal danger had gathered over the heads of bourgeois society. Lenin accused the representatives of the opposition of showing a "fatal" optimism in respect to the bourgeoisie and "pessimism" regarding the revolutionary forces and capacities of the proletariat. Anyone who simply reads over Lenin's letters, articles, and speeches of this period can easily see running through them like a red thread the repeated characterization of the opposition as a right wing that reflects the pressure of the bourgeoisie on the proletarian party on the eve of the conquest of power. And this characterization is not limited just to the immediate period of sharp struggle against the right opposition but is repeated by Lenin at a considerably later time. Thus at the end of February 1918, that is, four months after the October Revolution, during the "ferocious" struggle against the left communists, Lenin called the oppositionists of October the "October opportunists" [*CW*, Vol. 27, "The Revolutionary Phrase," pp. 26–27]. One may, of course, attack this evaluation too: Could there be opportunists in an opposition inside the Bolshevik Party? But that kind of formalistic argument has no effect when you are dealing with a political appraisal. And this was a political appraisal made by Lenin, substantiated by him, and generally taken for granted in the party. I do not know why a question mark is now placed over it.

Why is the correct political appraisal of the October opposition important? Because it has international significance; it will acquire its full significance only in the future. Here we come directly to one of the main lessons of October, and that lesson is now taking on gigantic new dimensions after the negative experience of the German October. We will encounter this lesson in every proletarian revolution.

Among the many difficulties of the proletarian revolution there is one that is absolutely definite, concrete, and specific: it results from the problem of a *revolutionary party leadership*. At a sharp turn of events even the most revolutionary party, as Lenin often said, runs the danger of being left behind and counterposing yesterday's slogans or methods of struggle to the new tasks and new requirements. And in general there can be no sharper turn of events than the one created by the need for armed insurrection by the proletariat. And this is where the danger arises of a disproportion between the party leadership, the policies of the party as a whole, and the behavior of the class. In "normal" conditions,

that is, when political life moves relatively slowly, such dispro-
portions can be straightened out without any catastrophe, even
though there may be some losses. But at times of severe revolutionary crises there is not enough *time* to eliminate dispropor-
tions and, so to speak, straighten out the front while under fire.
The months of greatest intensity in a revolutionary crisis, by
their very nature, pass most swiftly. Disparities between the
revolutionary leadership (wavering, vacillation, a wait-and-see
attitude) and the objective tasks of the revolution can sometimes,
in the course of a few weeks or even days, lead to catastrophe, to
the loss of what was prepared through years of work.

Of course, disparities between the leadership and the party (or
class, or entire situation) can also have the opposite character:
this is when the leadership *runs ahead* of the development of the
revolution, taking the fifth month of pregnancy for the ninth. The
most glaring example of that kind of disparity was in Germany
in March 1921. There we had in the party an extreme manifestation of the "infantile disorder of ultraleftism," and as a result,
putschism (revolutionary adventurism). This danger, too, is a
very real one for the future. The lessons of the Third Comintern
Congress retain their full validity for that reason.

But the German experience of last year showed us the opposite
danger in harsh and vivid detail. The situation was ripe but the
leadership lagged behind. While the leadership was catching up
with the situation, it changed: the masses retreated, and the
relationship of forces worsened abruptly.

In the German defeat of last year there were of course many
particular national features, but there were also some profoundly
typical features which represent a general danger. This can be
called the crisis of revolutionary leadership. The lower ranks of
the proletarian party are, relatively, much less responsive to the
pressure of bourgeois-democratic opinion. But certain elements in
the upper ranks and the middle layers of the party will inevitably, to a greater or lesser degree, be subject to the material and
ideological terror of the bourgeoisie at the decisive moment. One
cannot wave this danger away.

Of course there is no safety device for use on all occasions
against this danger. But the first step in a struggle against any
danger is to understand its source and nature. The appearance (or
growth) of a rightist grouping in a Communist party in an "October" period reflects, on the one hand, the enormous objective
difficulties and danger, and on the other, the frantic pressure of
bourgeois public opinion. This is the essential significance of a

rightist grouping. That is precisely why wavering and vacillation inevitably appear inside Communist parties at precisely the moment when they are the most dangerous. These vacillations and disputes in our case had a minimal character. That is what made it possible for us to bring about October. At the opposite extreme is the German Communist Party, where a revolutionary situation was missed, and the internal crisis in the party was so sharp that it led to the total replacement of the leading apparatus of the party. In all likelihood, all Communist parties will fall somewhere between these two extremes in their "October" periods. To reduce the inevitable crises of revolutionary leadership to the minimum is one of the most important tasks of each party and of the Comintern as a whole. This can be done simply by understanding our October experience and the political content of the October opposition in our party.

Chapter 7
Problems of the Present

In order to make the transition from the lessons and appraisals of the past to present problems, I will begin with a partial but extremely graphic and pointed accusation, which struck me by its unexpectedness.

One of the critics went so far as to say that in my memoirs of Lenin[41] I laid the "responsibility" (?!?) for the Red Terror on Lenin. What exactly could an idea like that mean? It apparently presupposes a certain need to *dissociate oneself from* the responsibility for the terror as an instrument of revolutionary struggle. But where could such a need come from? This I do not understand, either politically or psychologically.

It is true that bourgeois governments that come to power through revolutions, palace coups, conspiracies, etc., have always felt the need to throw the veil of forgetfulness over the conditions by which they came to power. Prettification and falsification of their "illegal" past, eradication from it of all recollection of the bloody use of force, become perennial features of the work of bourgeois governments that come to power through forceful means, once they have consolidated and fortified their position and developed the necessary conservative habits.

But how could such a need arise for proletarian revolutionists? We have existed as a state for more than seven years. We have diplomatic relations even with the arch-conservative government of Great Britain. We receive titled ambassadors. But we do not retreat one iota from the methods which brought our party to power and which through the October experience have been added to the powerful arsenal of the world revolutionary movement. Today we have no more reason to renounce the methods of revolutionary violence we used or to keep quiet about them than we did in the days when we were forced to resort to them to save the revolution.

Yes, we receive titled ambassadors, and we permit private capitalist trade, a foundation on which a body of opinion of the Sukharevka marketplace type has revived.[42] Of course, this is an All-Russian Sukharevka, which is forced to submit to Soviet power, which is full of hopes and dreams that the Soviet government, having come to power through the most "illegal" and "barbaric" means, will acquire some graces and eventually become a truly "civilized," "honorable," and democratic, that is, conservative bourgeois, power. Under these conditions not only our own underdeveloped bourgeoisie but also the world bourgeoisie would readily excuse Soviet power for its "illegal" origins if they felt sure that we ourselves would cease to remind people of them. But since we are not about to change our class nature even a little bit, and since we have kept our revolutionary disdain for bourgeois public opinion fully intact, there can be no need for us to renounce our past, to "throw off" responsibility for the Red Terror.

How completely unworthy is this very idea of wanting to throw the responsibility off onto—Lenin. Who could "throw this off" onto him? He already assumes full responsibility for it. For October, for the revolution, for the overthrow of the old order, for the Red Terror, for the civil war—he takes full responsibility for all this in the eyes of the working class and of history and will do so "throughout the ages."

Or perhaps what is referred to here are excesses, overreaction? But where and when was a revolution ever made without cases of "overdoing" things, committing excesses? How many times did Lenin explain this simple idea to the philistines who had collapsed in terror at the excesses of April, July, and October!

No power and no person can take away from Lenin the "responsibility" for the Red Terror. Not even certain overly accommodating "defenders." The Red Terror was a necessary weapon of the revolution. Without that it would have perished. More than once before now, revolutions have perished from soft-heartedness, indecisiveness, and the general good nature of the working people. Even our party, despite all its prior tempering, contained elements of this good-natured and easygoing "revolutionary" attitude. No one had thought through in advance all the unbelievable difficulties of the revolution, its internal and external dangers, so thoroughly as had Lenin. No one understood so clearly even before the overturn that without reprisals against the propertied classes, without measures amounting to the severest form of terror in history, the proletarian power would never be able to survive, hemmed in by enemies on every side. Drop by drop, Lenin imparted this understanding of his (and the intense concentration of will-power in readiness for battle which followed from it) to his closest co-workers, and through them, and with them, to the entire party and the masses of workers. That is exactly what I was talking about in my memoir on Lenin. I described the way Lenin, during the first days of the revolution, seeing negligence, carefree attitudes, and excessive self-confidence everywhere in the face of threatening dangers and disasters, taught his co-workers at every turn that the revolution could be saved only if it transformed its own character along more serious lines and armed itself with the sword of the Red Terror. That is what I was talking about in my memoir. About Lenin's great perspicacity, his great strength of character, and his revolutionary ruthlessness—which exist alongside his great personal humanity. To look for anything else in my words, to discover in them a desire to "place at Lenin's door" the responsibility for the terror, could only be done out of obtuseness on the political level and crass pettiness in psychology.

If I wished to throw poisonous suspicions around as lightly as some of the critics do, I would say that any search for NEPist tendencies should begin not with me but with those to whom the very idea of renouncing the Red Terror could occur. And if some of the Sukharevka scum should take these and similar accusations seriously and start building up their hopes on that basis, it would only mean that my accusers have created a specter of Trotskyism suitable for Sukharevka. It would not signify any connection whatsoever between the specter and myself.

Arguments deriving from the marketplace mentality of Sukharevka, whether emigre or internal, ought in general to be used with the greatest of caution. Of course our enemies of every stripe rejoice at any differences, any discussions, among us and try to widen every breach. But in order to draw this or that conclusion from their appraisals, one must examine, first, whether they know what they are talking about—for only a serious, business-like, and solidly grounded appraisal by an *intelligent* enemy can have symptomatic importance; and second, one must examine the question of whether they have specially fabricated their views in order to intensify our differences by adding fuel to the fire of our discussion. This applies especially to the emigre press, which has no immediate political goals to reach, because it has no mass readership, and which therefore speculates, for the most part, on whether it can elicit an echo of its opinions in the Soviet press.

I will cite only one example, but one that strikes me as indicative. Our press has reported that the Menshevik *Sotsialistichesky Vestnik* during last year's discussion placed great hopes upon the "opposition," or on certain elements within it. I have not verified this report but I fully admit the possibility that such penetrating realists as Dan and Company, who spent their lives hoping for the democratization of the bourgeoisie, are now filled with hopes for the Menshevization of the Bolshevik Party. However, I did happen to take a look at issue No. 7 of the right-wing Menshevik publication *Zarya* [Dawn] and found there quite by chance an article by one S. Ivanovich with the following criticism directed against the hopes of Dan and Company for an evolution of the Bolshevik Party: "Perhaps something is known to them [Dan and Company—L.T.] concerning this opposition that remains unknown to all others. But if they only know what all others do, it cannot be unknown to them that precisely among the oppositionists within the RCP are found the most utopian supporters of the dictatorship, the most rock-hard defenders of orthodoxy, whose influence has been felt in the recent outbreaks of left madness, in the anti-NEP policy line, etc. How precisely can these orthodox 'October people' produce, in the words of [Dan's] platform, 'elements able . . . , because of their position, to play a significant role in preparing the democratic liquidation of the dictatorship'? The platform finds that all this can be accomplished 'under the pressure of the workers' movement, which is developing and attaining class consciousness.' But this is a completely arbitrary hypothesis, and one that was refuted by life itself even before it found its way into the platform. It was precisely under the impact of a long wave of stormy strikes, sometimes even raising political demands, that the opposition in the RCP called for a strengthening of the dictatorship, for the blood of the bourgeoisie, and for a new course. Life has shown that the opposition puts forward the most inveterate demagogues of the dictatorship, but the platform looks for elements of democracy to come forward from this source. . . . How irrational life is to depart so much from the platform!" (*Zarya*, No. 7, p. 197)

This quotation from a White Menshevik scoundrel I reproduced here, in an essay dealing with the internal problems of the party, with natural feelings of repugnance. Far be it from me even to think of drawing political conclusions from this quotation—with this exception: Beware of the comments and opinions of the emigres! Beware of conveniently excerpted observations from the European bourgeois press!

It is always useful to consider the views of the enemy. But this must be done in a critical way and without ascribing to the enemy more penetration than he actually has. Let us not forget that the bourgeoisie judge blindly on those matters which, while completely incomprehensible to them, are the main content of our work. Let us not forget that the world capitalist press, more than once during the existence of the Soviet regime, declared that Lenin was trying to steer Russia back onto the national-conservative track but that "leftists" were preventing him—with Bukharin or Zinoviev or the present author figuring under that designation. Were those opinions really symptomatic of anything but the obtuseness of bourgeois thought vis-a-vis the tasks of the proletarian dictatorship? It is especially impermissible to act in such a way as to lead the bourgeois press astray with our own biased and artificial accusations, tormented with hopes and longings as it is, and then present its distorted reflection of our own words as a bourgeois appraisal worth considering. In this way we present as reality the shadow of a specter of our own creation!

In order to give some currency (or topicality) to the specter of "Trotskyism," built up out of a combination of old quotations, some critics, especially Comrade Zinoviev, have brought forward—true, in very general and indefinite form—questions of *current domestic politics*. I have not initiated any discussion on these questions. And Comrade Zinoviev refers to no specific clashes over these questions.

My preface provides no basis for a discussion of these questions. Nowhere have I disputed the decisions of the Thirteenth Congress, and I have carried them out to the letter in all my

work. Somehow or other, nevertheless, my preface has been interpreted not against the background of the defeat of the German
revolution, but against the background of last year's discussion.
In this connection, my preface has become a pretext for raising
the question of my "line" as a whole.

Comrade Zinoviev raises a whole series of points which in his
opinion characterize my line as one directed against that of the
party.

Supposedly, I am trying to weaken the leading role of the party
in the state. I cannot accept this charge, not in the least. In order
to approach this general question in an absolutely specific way, I
will only recall to mind that in a number of policy statements
recently the Central Committee expressed itself once again, and
quite categorically, against party bodies *substituting themselves*
for local agencies of Soviet power. Is this likely to weaken the role
of the party? No, the correct implementation of this line will only
strengthen and consolidate the party's role. Within this framework, naturally, there can be disagreements of a practical nature.
However, even in relation to such purely practical differences,
Comrade Zinoviev cites no new examples, because in our practical work there have been none.

Neither can I in any way accept the accusation that I am
trying to turn the party into an agglomeration of factions and
groupings—in the spirit of the British Labour Party. The caricatured nature of this assertion speaks for itself. Whether my
understanding of the lessons of October is correct or not, it is
absolutely impossible to regard my book on October as the tool of
a factional grouping. I did not set myself such a goal, nor could I
have. In general, it is absurd to think that in a ruling party with
a mass membership a "grouping" could be built on the basis of
historical interpretations.

I will not go into questions of "specialists," finances, the State
Planning Commission, and so on, because I see absolutely no
subject for "discussion" here, nor have I provided pretexts, in any
respect, for these questions to be raised again.

Finally, there remains the question of my underestimation of
the peasantry as the alleged basic source of my errors, real and
imagined. I will not discuss the past, for that would lead us into
impossible labyrinths. I will not dwell on the fact that my Brest-
Litovsk error stemmed not from "ignoring" the peasantry (I did
not count on it to fight a revolutionary war) but from hopes for a
more rapid development of the revolutionary movement in Ger-

many.* But with the present and future in mind, I feel obliged to take up this basic charge, so formless but so persistent.

First of all, it is necessary to reject the caricatured notion that to me the formula "permanent revolution" is some sort of fetish or symbol of faith from which I derive all my political conclusions and deductions, especially insofar as they relate to the peasantry. There is not a shadow of the truth in this version of things. After I wrote about the permanent revolution, with the aim of clarifying for myself the *future* course of revolutionary developments, many years went by. The revolution itself was made, and the extremely rich experience of the Soviet state transpired. Can anyone seriously believe that my present attitude toward the peasantry is determined, not by the collective experience of our party but by my personal experience and by theoretical recollections of how, in such and such a year, I expected the Russian revolution to develop?

We have gone through, and even learned something from, the

---

*I cannot help commenting at this point, however, on the totally barbaric distortions of the history of Brest-Litovsk made by Kuusinen. His version goes like this: I went to Brest-Litovsk with instructions from the party, in the event of an ultimatum, to sign the treaty. I violated these on my own initiative and refused to sign. This lie exceeds all bounds. I went to Brest-Litovsk with one assignment: to prolong the talks as much as possible and in the event of an ultimatum to bargain for an adjournment and return to Moscow to take part in the decision of the Central Committee. Only Comrade Zinoviev proposed that I be given instructions to sign the treaty immediately. But that was rejected by all the other votes, including Lenin's. Everyone agreed of course that prolonging the talks further would worsen the terms of the treaty. But they felt that this negative factor would be outweighed by the positive propaganda considerations.

That was how I proceeded at Brest-Litovsk. When things came to the point of an ultimatum, I reached an agreement for a recess in negotiations, returned to Moscow, and the question was discussed in the Central Committee. It was not I personally but the Central Committee majority, on my motion, that decided not to sign. This was also the decision of the majority at the All-Russian party conference. I went to Brest-Litovsk for the last time with the absolutely clear decision of the party—not to sign the treaty. All this can easily be verified from the minutes of the Central Committee. Kuusinen has crudely distorted the history of Brest-Litovsk. However, I leave open the possibility that what is involved here is not a case of ill will but simply lack of knowledge and failure to understand.—L.T.

period of the imperialist war, Kerensky's rule, the Land Committees, the peasant congresses, the fight against the Right SRs, and the days of nonstop meetings of soldiers' deputies at Smolny, when we fought for influence over the peasant-in-arms. There was the experience of the Brest-Litovsk peace, during which a significant section of the party, led by Old Bolsheviks having no connection with "permanent revolution," placed their hopes on revolutionary war and taught the party a great deal by the experience of their mistake. There was the formative period of the Red Army when, through a series of experiments and attempts, the party created a military alliance between worker and peasant. There was the period of grain requisitioning and the severe class conflicts on that ground, and so on. Then the party steered a course toward the middle peasant, and that gradually led to a substantial change in party orientation—again of course on the same foundations of principle. Thereafter the transition was made to the NEP and the free trade in grain, with all the consequences flowing from them.

Is it really possible to place on one side of the scales all this gigantic historical experience, from which we all draw nourishment, and on the other, my old formula of permanent revolution, which supposedly leads me always, everywhere, and regardless of conditions to the underestimation of the peasantry? This is unbelievable, and untrue. I emphatically reject any such theological attitude toward the formula of permanent revolution.

In itself this formula reflected a stage in our development that we have long since passed through. It is dragged out and blown up now only because it is difficult otherwise to find any grounds for today's alleged "underestimation of the peasantry" and to conjure up the specter of Trotskyism.

In his article on the Workers and Peasants Inspection (Rabkrin) Lenin wrote that the main political danger, which could under certain circumstances become the source of a split in the party, was the danger of a schism between the proletariat and the peasantry, the two fundamental classes whose collaboration is an absolute necessity for maintaining and developing the conquests of October [*CW,* Vol. 33, "How We Should Reorganize the Workers and Peasants Inspection" (January 23, 1923), pp. 481-86]. If we approach this danger from the angle of the interests of the two fundamental classes, we must say the following: Only by maintaining a *certain balance between the material interests of the workers and peasants* can we assure the political stability of the

Soviet state. This balance must be achieved by the ruling party under constantly changing circumstances, for the economic level of the country changes, the contribution to the common enterprise by each of the partners varies, the amount stolen from each of them by private capital varies, and the return that each of the partners receives from his mutual labors varies.

What, under these circumstances, could underestimation of the peasantry or lack of attention to it really mean? That the leading partner in the alliance, the proletariat, seeking through the party to guarantee its own base, i.e., industry, as quickly as possible, or to raise its cultural level as rapidly as possible, places too great a load on the peasant. This could lead to a political rupture, with the initiative in this case being taken by the peasantry. This kind of impatient and narrow tendency, to the extent that it has been manifested, we have more than once characterized as trade-unionist, concerned exclusively with conditions on the job, and not communist. The question of the proletariat's present-day share in the overall national economy—a question that is of course extremely important—cannot be placed *above* the question of preserving the dictatorship of the proletariat as the condition for building socialism. I should think that we are all agreed on that, and not just since yesterday, either.

But something else is also quite obvious to us all, and that is that the same historic danger of a rupture can face us from the opposite pole. If conditions develop in such a way that the proletariat is forced to bear too many sacrifices in order to preserve the alliance, if the working class came to the conclusion over a number of years that in the name of preserving its political dictatorship it had been forced to agree to excessive self-denial of its class interests, that would undermine the Soviet state from the other direction.

We are speaking about these two sides of one and the same historical danger of a split between the proletariat and peasantry not because we regard the danger itself as immediate and urgent. No, none of us thinks that. We consider such a danger from the historical perspective in order to orient ourselves in the politics of today more correctly. It is beyond all question that this can only be a politics of maneuverability, one which requires the greatest attention to the soundings of the channel bottom, with special attention to possible shoals, and careful steering to avoid both banks, right and left. It is equally beyond all question that at the *present* stage the balance of interests has been upset, primarily to the detriment of the village, and that this must be reckoned with seriously, both in economics and in politics.

The general considerations set forth above apply first and foremost to the question of developing industry and the rate at which to develop it.

If the Soviet state maintains itself on the basis of the alliance of workers and peasants, the socialist dictatorship of the proletariat is maintained through state industry and transport. The Soviet state without a socialist dictatorship would be a body without a "soul." It would be doomed to inevitable bourgeois degeneration. Industry, the basis of the socialist dictatorship, depends, however, on the peasant economy. But this relation is a reciprocal one. Peasant economy depends, in its turn, upon industry. Of these two component parts the more dynamic (driving, forward-thrusting) element is industry. The mightiest influence Soviet power can exert upon the village is that which passes through the channels of industry and transport. The other means of influencing it, quite important in themselves, still remain in second or third place. Without increasing the role of state industry properly, without strengthening its organizing influence on the village, all other measures are doomed ultimately to remain powerless.

The rate of industrial development, the acceleration of which is in the interest of both the city and the village, does not of course depend on our good will. There are objective limitations here: the level of peasant economy, the actual equipment of industry, the availability of working capital, the cultural level of the country, and so forth. Any attempt to leap over these limitations would surely take its own bitter revenge, striking the proletariat at one end and the peasantry at the other. But no less danger would arise if industry *lagged behind* the economic upturn of the rest of the country. That would give rise inevitably to the phenomena of a goods famine and high retail prices, which would inevitably lead in turn to the enrichment of private capital. The rate of socialist accumulation and industrial development cannot be unlimited, then, in another respect as well—that is, it is limited not only by a certain maximum but also by a certain minimum. This minimum is directly determined by the competition of private capital from within and the pressure of world capital from without.

The dangers deriving from our whole development have a *two-sided* character. Industry cannot rush ahead too far, for then it would not have the necessary economic foundation. But it is equally dangerous to lag behind. Every delay, every omission by state industry means the growth of its rival, private capital, the growth of the kulak in the village, and the growth of the economic and political influence of the kulak upon the village. A lag in industry means a shift in the relationship of forces from the city to the village and, within the village, from the poor peasants to the kulaks of the new Soviet type. This shift in the center of gravity, weakening the proletariat, must subsequently force it to make further economic and political concessions in the name of preserving the worker-peasant alliance. But it is quite obvious that along this road the dictatorship of the proletariat would be emptied of its socialist content.

Thus all the difficulties and dangers that grow out of the transitional period of our economic development, in which the proletariat engages in socialist construction upon a multimillioned foundation of petty commodity producers—all our difficulties taken together and each one considered separately, will always have, as we have said, a *two-sided, not a one-sided,* character. Trying to force too rapid a growth rate in industry is just as dangerous as too slow a rate of growth.

These considerations, I would hope, are completely indisputable. They can be attacked for being too general. But it is far more general and vague (not to mention extremely one-sided) to accuse me of underestimating the peasantry. The peasantry must be "estimated" not separately and apart, by itself, but within the framework of the shifting balance between classes. There is no previously given mathematical formula that would tell how far one may go and where one must stop in order to reconcile the interests of the proletariat and peasantry. No such formula exists in this world. One must orient oneself and feel one's way in the situation by means of constant, active maneuvering. This maneuvering, however, has never had and will never have an unprincipled, back-and-forth character (as the Mensheviks and Anarchists portray it). Our maneuvering, both economic and political, comes down to this—a series of measures, based on the alliance of workers and peasants, by which *the dictatorship of the proletariat, and consequently the possibility of further socialist construction, can be ensured.* That is our supreme criterion.

The persistent accusation of "underestimating the peasantry," so incorrect in its one-sidedness, is all the more harmful in that it unavoidably begets fears—surely quite unfounded ones—that the theoretical groundwork is being laid for a change of course from the socialist dictatorship toward a peasants'-and-workers' democracy. This, of course, is nonsense. Our party, while retaining full freedom to maneuver, is united from top to bottom by our program for the *socialist* reorganization of social relations. That is the chief legacy left us by Lenin, which we have all unanimously pledged to carry out to the end. And we shall do so!

LETTER TO THE PLENUM
OF THE CENTRAL COMMITTEE

January 15, 1925

NOTE: After mobilizing the party cells in the army against him, the triumvirate called a plenary session of the Central Committee to deal with the "Trotsky question." Trotsky did not attend the plenum, but instead addressed a letter to it explaining his silence and defending himself against the charges circulating about him.

The official text of Trotsky's letter and the resolution of the Central Committee removing him from the post of commissar of war were published in English in Inprecorr, *February 7, 1925. That translation, with minor editing for style, is used here.—Ed.*

Dear Comrades:

The first item on the agenda of the forthcoming plenum of the Central Committee is the question of the resolutions from local organizations on Trotsky's "conduct." Because of my state of health I will not be able to take part in the work of the plenum, but I think I can contribute to the elucidation of this question by making the following remarks:

1. I considered and still consider that I could, in the discussion, bring forward a sufficient number of principled and factual refutations of the charge brought against me, that I am aiming to "revise Leninism" or "belittle" the role of Lenin. I have refrained from doing so, however, not only because of the state of my health, but also because in the atmosphere of the present discussion, every statement made on this question, regardless of its content, character, and tone, would only serve as an impetus to intensify the controversy, to turn it from a one-sided to a two-sided controversy and give it a more acute character.

Even now, weighing the whole progress of the discussion and in spite of the fact that throughout it, many false and even monstrous charges have been brought forward against me, I think that my silence was correct from the standpoint of the general interests of the party.

2. However, under no circumstances can I admit the charge that I am advocating a special policy ("Trotskyism") and that I am striving to revise Leninism. The conviction that is ascribed to me—to the effect that I did not come to Bolshevism but Bolshevism came to me—is simply monstrous. In my "Lessons of October" I frankly stated [see p. 254 above] that Bolshevism prepared for its role in the revolution by an irreconcilable struggle not only against the Narodniks and the Mensheviks, but also against the "conciliators," i.e., the tendency to which I belonged. Never at any time during the past eight years has it entered my head to regard any question from the point of view of "Trotskyism," which I have considered and still consider to have been politically liquidated long ago. Quite apart from whether I was right or wrong concerning any other questions that came before our party, I always endeavored to solve them in accordance with the general theoretical and practical experiences of our party. Throughout all this time, no one ever told me that any of my thoughts or proposals indicated a special tendency, i.e., "Trotskyism." Quite unexpectedly for me this expression came out during the course of the discussion of my book *1917*.

3. In this connection, the question of the estimation of the peasantry is of the greatest political importance. I absolutely deny that the formula "permanent revolution," which applies wholly to the past, in any way caused me to adopt a careless attitude toward the peasantry in the conditions of the Soviet revolution. If at any time after October I had occasion, for private reasons, to revert to the formula "permanent revolution," it was only a reference to party history, i.e., to the past, and had no reference to the question of present-day political tasks. To my mind, the attempt to construct an irreconcilable contradiction in this matter is not justified either by the eight years' experience of the revolution, which we have gone through together, or by the tasks of the future.

Equally I reject the statements and references to my alleged "pessimistic" attitude toward the progress of our work of socialist construction in the face of the retarded progress of the revolution in the West. In spite of all the difficulties arising out of our capitalist encirclement, the economic and political resources of the Soviet dictatorship are very great. I have repeatedly developed and argued this idea on the instructions of the party, particularly at international congresses, and I consider that this idea preserves all its force for the present period of historical development.

4. I have not spoken once on the controversial questions settled by the Thirteenth Congress of the party, either in the Central Committee or in the Council of Labor and Defense, and I certainly have never made any proposal outside of leading party and Soviet institutions that would directly or indirectly raise questions that have already been decided. After the Thirteenth Congress new problems arose—or, to speak more clearly, defined themselves—of an economic, Soviet, and international character. The solution of these problems presented an exceptional problem. The attempt to put forward any kind of "platform," as against the work of the Central Committee in solving these questions, was absolutely alien to my thoughts; for the comrades who were present at the meetings of the Politburo, the plenum of the Central Committee, the Council of Labor and Defense, or the Revolutionary Military Committee of the USSR, this assertion requires no proof. The controversial questions settled at the Thirteenth Congress which were again raised in the course of the last discussion not only had no connection with my work, but as far as I can judge at the moment had no connection with the practical questions of party policy.

5. Insofar as my preface to my book *1917* has served as the formal ground for the recent discussion, I consider it necessary, first of all, to repudiate the charge that I published my book, as it were, behind the back of the Central Committee. As a matter of fact, my book was published (while I was undergoing treatment in the Caucasus) on exactly the same terms and conditions as all other books, whether mine or those of other members of the Central Committee or those of party members generally. Of course, it is the business of the Central Committee to establish some form of control over party publications, but I have not in any way or in the slightest degree violated the forms of control which have been established up till now, and of course I had no reason to violate them.

6. "Lessons of October" represents a further development of the ideas which I have frequently expressed in the past and particularly during the past year. Here I enumerate only the following

speeches and articles: "On the Road to the European Revolution" (Tiflis, April 11, 1924); "Perspectives and Tasks in the East" (April 21); "May Day in the East and West" (April 29); "At a New Turning Point" (the introduction to *The First Five Years of the Communist International*); "Through What Stage Are We Passing?" (June 21); "Problems of Civil War" (July 29).

All the speeches enumerated above were prompted by the defeat of the German revolution in the autumn of 1923, and were printed in *Pravda, Izvestia,* and other publications. Not a single member of the Central Committee or indeed of the Politburo ever pointed out to me anything wrong with these speeches, nor did the editor of *Pravda* make any comment on these speeches or make any attempt to point out to me anything in them with which he did not agree.

Of course, I never regarded my analysis of October in connection with the German events as a "platform" and never believed that anybody would regard it as a "platform," which it never was and never could be.

7. In view of the fact that the charges brought against me mention a number of my books, including many that have been published in several editions, I consider it necessary to state that not only did the Politburo as a whole never indicate that any of my articles or books could be interpreted as a "revision of Leninism," but neither did any single member of the Central Committee. Particularly does this apply to my *1905*, which was published during Comrade Lenin's lifetime, went through several editions, was warmly recommended by the party press, was translated by the Comintern into foreign languages, and is now being used as *the principal evidence in the charge of revising Leninism.*

8. The purpose I pursue in putting forward these views, as I stated in the beginning of this letter, is but one, namely, to assist the plenum to settle the question which stands as the first item on the agenda.

With regard to the statement, which has been repeated in the discussion, to the effect that I am aiming to secure "a special position" in the party, that I do not submit to discipline, that I refuse to perform work given me by the Central Committee, etc., I categorically declare, without entering into an investigation of the value of these statements, that I am ready to perform *any* work entrusted to me by the Central Committee in *any* post and, of course, under *any form* of party control.

There is no particular necessity, therefore, to point out that after the recent discussion, the interests of our cause demand my speedy release from the duties of chairman of the Revolutionary Military Committee.

In conclusion, I think it necessary to add that I will not leave Moscow prior to the plenum so that if necessary it will be possible for me to reply to any questions or give any explanation that may be required.

L. Trotsky

TWO STATEMENTS 'BY TROTSKY'

NOTE: Not only was Trotsky gagged and prevented from defending himself, but the only time the gag was lifted was to force him to lie about himself and the Opposition.

In May 1925 Max Eastman's book Since Lenin Died *was published, containing the first true account of the inner-party struggle and the first public report of Lenin's Testament. Two months later the book arrived in the USSR and created something of a scandal. Eastman, an American sympathizer of communism, had been won over to the Opposition in Moscow and had received information about the struggle in the party from Trotsky. Coming as it did in the context of the bitter campaign against the Opposition, and in light of the Opposition's reluctance to provoke a confrontation, the publication of Eastman's book produced an acute dilemma. The Opposition had been threatened with expulsion if it engaged in public controversy. The publication of this book, by a man known to be Trotsky's friend, had the appearance of an underhanded intervention in the controversy. To avoid that charge, Trotsky had either to acknowledge or to deny responsibility for the book; he could not remain silent. The other leaders of the Opposition did not want to be drawn into the fray over Eastman's book, and they urged Trotsky to disclaim all responsibility for it. But the Politburo insisted that he deny the story about Lenin's Testament, and it dictated the terms of that denial. Thus, in order to prevent a renewal of hostilities, Trotsky was compelled to deny what he knew to be true and to put himself in the service of the campaign of falsification and distortion directed against himself.*

From his exile in Alma-Ata, on September 11, 1928, Trotsky wrote about this incident in a letter to N.I. Muralov. After defending Eastman, he described what had led him to sign his name to the letter attacking him in 1925: "In the autumn of 1925 the majority in the Political Bureau foisted upon me a statement concocted by themselves containing a sharp condemnation of

Max Eastman. Insofar as the entire leading group of the Opposition considered it inadvisable at that time to initiate an open political struggle, and steered toward making a number of concessions, it naturally could not initiate and develop the struggle over the private question of Eastman, who had acted . . . on his own accord and at his own risk. That is why, upon the decision of the leading group of the Opposition, *I signed the statement on Max Eastman* foisted upon me by the majority in the Political Bureau *with the ultimatum: either sign the statement as written, or enter into an open struggle on this account"* (New International, *November 1934).*

In 1924 two of Trotsky's old comrades, Pierre Monatte and Alfred Rosmer, had been expelled from the French party for siding with the Opposition. When they began to write in support of the Russian Opposition in their journal, La Revolution prole-tarienne, *the Central Committee of the French party wrote to Trotsky asking his position on the public airing of the controversy. Seeking to avoid the charge that he was allying himself with nonparty elements to attack the party's policies, Trotsky was again put in the humiliating position of having to speak out against his cothinkers. His answer was printed both in* l'Humanité, *the French party's paper, and in* Revolution proletarienne.

"Letter on Eastman's Book" was originally published in Bolshevik *on September 1, 1925, and was subsequently translated into English in three different versions in* Inprecorr *and in the* Sunday Worker *(New York), where its title was "Trotsky Trounces Eastman." The version used here is based on the "final text" published in* Inprecorr, *September 3, 1925. "A Statement on Monatte and Rosmer" was translated for this volume by Russell Block from* Revolution proletarienne, *October 1925.—Ed.*

Letter on Eastman's Book

July 1, 1925

Soon after my return from Sukhum to Moscow, a telegraphic inquiry from Comrade Jackson, editor of the *Sunday Worker* in London, informed me of the publication of a book, *Since Lenin*

Died, which was used by the bourgeois press to attack our party and the Soviet government. Although my reply to Jackson was published by the press at the time, it will be appropriate to repeat the first part of it here: "Eastman's book to which you refer is unknown to me. The bourgeois newspapers that quoted it have not reached me. Of course, I deny in advance and most categorically any commentaries directed against the Russian Communist Party."

In the following part of the telegram I protested against the insinuations alleging that I was turning toward bourgeois democracy and free trade.

I afterwards received the book in question (*Since Lenin Died*) from Comrade Inkpin, secretary of the Communist Party of Great Britain, who at the same time sent me a letter to the same effect as Comrade Jackson's telegram. I had no intention of reading Eastman's book, much less of reacting to it, as I assumed that my telegram to Comrade Jackson, which was published everywhere by the British and foreign press, was entirely sufficient. But party comrades who had read the book expressed the opinion that since the author referred to conversations with me, my silence could be regarded as an indirect support of this book, which is directed entirely against our party. This placed me under the obligation to devote more attention to Eastman's book, and above all to read it carefully through. On the basis of certain episodes in the inner life of our party, the discussions on democracy in the party and the state regulation of our economy, Eastman arrives at conclusions directed entirely against our party, which are likely, if given credence, to discredit the party as well as the Soviet government.

We shall first deal with a question that is not only of historical importance, but of vital timeliness at the present moment: the Red Army. Eastman asserts that since changes have taken place among its leaders, the Red Army is divided, that it has lost its fighting capacity, etc. I do not know where Eastman got all this information. But its absurdity is obvious. At any rate, we would not advise the imperialist governments to base their calculations on Eastman's revelations. Besides, he fails to observe that in thus characterizing the Red Army he is reviving the Menshevik myth of the Bonapartist character of our army, its resemblance to a Praetorian guard. For it is plain that an army capable of "splitting" because its leader is changed is neither proletarian nor communist, but Bonapartist and Praetorian.

In the course of the book the writer quotes a large number of documents, and refers to episodes which he has heard second-hand or even more indirectly. This little book thus contains a considerable number of obviously erroneous and incorrect assertions. We shall only deal with the more important of these.

Eastman asserts in several places that the Central Committee has "concealed" from the party a large number of documents of extraordinary importance, written by Lenin during the last period of his life. (The documents in question are letters on the national question, the famous "Testament," etc.) This is pure slander against the Central Committee of our party. Eastman's words convey the impression that Lenin wrote these letters, which are of an advisory character and deal with the inner-party organization, with the intention of having them published. This is not at all in accordance with the facts.

During his illness, Lenin repeatedly addressed letters and proposals to the leading bodies and congresses of the party. It must be definitely stated that all these letters and suggestions were invariably delivered to their destination and they were all brought to the knowledge of the delegates to the Twelfth and Thirteenth Congresses, and have invariably exercised their influence on the decisions of the party. If all of these letters have not been published, it is because their author did not intend them to be published. Comrade Lenin has not left any "Testament"; the character of his relations to the party, and the character of the party itself, preclude the possibility of such a "Testament." The bourgeois and Menshevik press generally understand under the designation of "Testament" one of Comrade Lenin's letters (which is so much altered as to be almost unrecognizable) in which he gives the party some organizational advice. The Thirteenth Party Congress devoted the greatest attention to this and to the other letters, and drew the appropriate conclusions. All talk with regard to a concealed or mutilated "Testament" is nothing but a despicable lie, directed against the real will of Comrade Lenin and against the interests of the party created by him.

Eastman's assertion that the Central Committee was anxious to conceal (that is, not to publish) Comrade Lenin's article on the Workers and Peasants Inspection is equally untrue. The differences of opinion arising on this subject within the Central Committee—if it is possible to speak of "differences of opinion" at all in this case—were of a purely secondary significance, dealing solely with the question of whether or not the publication of Lenin's article should be accompanied by a statement from the

Central Committee pointing out that there was no occasion to fear a split.

But on this question too a unanimous decision was arrived at in the same session. All the members of the Political and Organization Bureaus of the Central Committee present at the meeting signed a letter addressed to the party organizations containing, among other things, the following passage: "Without entering, in this purely informational letter, into the criticism of the historically possible dangers made at the time by Comrade Lenin in his article, the members of the Political and Organization Bureaus consider it necessary, in order to avoid all possible misunderstandings, to declare unanimously that there is nothing in the inner activity of the Central Committee giving occasion to fear the danger of a split."

Not only is my signature affixed to this document along with the other signatures, but the text itself was drawn up by me (January 27, 1923).

In view of the fact that this letter, expressing the unanimous opinion of the Central Committee on Comrade Lenin's proposal with regard to the Workers and Peasants Inspection, also bears the signature of Comrade Kuibyshev, we have here a refutation of Eastman's assertion that Comrade Kuibyshev was placed at the head of the Workers and Peasants Inspection as an "opponent" of Lenin's plan of organization.

Eastman's quotation from the wording of the "Testament" is equally wrong. This was published in the *Sotsialistichesky Vestnik* and was stolen from the party archives, so to speak, by counterrevolutionists. In reality the wording as published in the *Vestnik* passed through many hands before its appearance in this paper. It was "freshened up" again and again, and distorted to such an extent that it is absolutely impossible to restore its original meaning. It is possible that the alterations were made by the editorial staff of this paper.

Eastman's assertions that the Central Committee confiscated my pamphlets and articles in 1923 or 1924, or at any other time or by any other means has prevented their publication, are untrue, and are based on fantastic rumors.

Eastman is again wrong in asserting that Comrade Lenin offered me the post of chairman of the Council of People's Commissars, and of the Council of Labor and Defense. I hear of this for the first time from Eastman's book.

An attentive perusal of Eastman's book would doubtless give me the opportunity of pointing out a number of other inaccuracies, errors, and misrepresentations. I do not, however, think that it would be of interest to go further.

The bourgeois press, especially the Menshevik press, makes use of Eastman's statements, quotes from his reminiscences, in order to emphasize his "close relations," his "friendship" with me (as my biographer) and by such indirect means attaching an importance to his conclusions which they do not and cannot have. I must therefore devote a few remarks to this matter.

The character of my real relations with Eastman is perhaps best shown by a business letter written by me at a time before there was any thought of Eastman's book *Since Lenin Died.*

During my stay in Sukhum I received from one of my Moscow friends, a publisher of my books, the manuscript of a book by . . . M. Eastman, entitled *Leon Trotsky: Portrait of a Youth.* My collaborator informed me in his accompanying letter that the manuscript, which had been sent to the State Publishing Office by the writer for the purpose of being published in the Russian language, had made a strange and unusual impression among us on account of the sentimentality permeating it.

I replied as follows in my letter of April 3, 1925: "Even without being familiar with the contents of Eastman's manuscript, I am perfectly in agreement with you that the publication of the book is inopportune. Although you have been kind enough to send me the manuscript, I cannot read it. I have absolutely no inclination to do so. I readily believe that it does not suit our taste, especially our Russian and communist taste.

"Eastman has been endeavoring for a long time to convince me that it is very difficult to interest the Americans in *communism,* but that it is possible to interest them in the *communists.* His arguments have been fairly convincing. For this reason I gave him a certain help, of a limited nature; the letter I sent him shows these limits.* I did not know that he had the intention of publishing this book in Russia, or I should probably have advised the State Publishing House at that time not to publish it. I cannot prevent Eastman from publishing this book abroad; he is a "free

---

*On May 22, 1925, I sent the following reply to Eastman's repeated requests: "I shall do my utmost to assist you by means of conscientious information. But I cannot agree to read your manuscript, for this would make me responsible not only for the facts, but for the characterizations and estimates as well. This, of course, is impossible. I am prepared to take responsibility—if only a limited one—for the factual information which I send you in reply to your request. For everything else you alone bear the responsibility."

writer"; for a time he lived in Russia and collected material; at present he is in France, if not in America. Shall I ask him as a personal favor not to publish this book? I am not sufficiently intimate with him to do this. And such a request would hardly be appropriate."

I repeat that the subject of this letter was a biographical sketch, the story of my youth up to about 1902. But the tone of my letter leaves no room for doubt on the nature of my relations with Eastman, relations which differ in no way from those maintained by me with other foreign communists or "sympathizers" who have turned to me for help in understanding the October Revolution, our party, and the Soviet state—there can be no question of anything more.

Eastman sneers with vulgar aplomb at my "Quixotism" in my relations with the comrades of the Central Committee, of whom I have spoken in friendly terms even in the midst of the most embittered discussion. Eastman seems to think himself called upon to correct my "error," and he characterizes the leading comrades of our party in a manner which cannot be designated as anything else but slanderous.

We see from the above that Eastman has attempted to erect his construction on completely rotten foundations. He seizes upon isolated incidents occurring within our party in the course of some discussion, in order, by distorting the meaning of the facts and exaggerating the relations in a ridiculous manner, to slander our party and undermine confidence in it.

It seems to me, however, that the attentive and thoughtful reader will not require an examination of the assertions made by Eastman and his documents (for which not everyone has the opportunity) but that it suffices to ask: If we assume that the malicious character of our leading party comrades alleged by Eastman is even partly correct, how is it possible that this party should have emerged from long years of illegal struggle? How could it stand at the head of millions of human beings, carry through the greatest revolution in history, and contribute to the formation of revolutionary parties in other countries?

There is no sincere worker who will believe in the picture painted by Eastman. It contains within itself its own refutation. Whatever Eastman's intentions may be, this botched piece of work is none the less objectively a tool of the counterrevolution, and can only serve the ends of the enemies incarnate of communism and of the revolution.

A Statement on Monatte and Rosmer

September 8, 1925

I knew Monatte and Rosmer in 1915. I met them in Paris while—like a man looking for a needle in a haystack—I was looking for the few revolutionaries who had not adopted the bourgeois position of social patriotism. During the following years, whenever we spoke about French revolutionaries loyal to the International, Monatte and Rosmer were the first to be mentioned. They were with the October Revolution and the Third International right from the beginning. Rosmer was one of the founders of the Third International. For a long time, Monatte refused to belong to the French Communist Party, pointing out that there were numerous parliamentarist and careerist elements in its leadership. After the Fourth Congress of the Comintern, when the French party was cleansed of the reformists with the help of the French left led by Rosmer, Monatte joined. What has just been said defines clearly enough my political as well as my personal attitudes toward Rosmer and Monatte.

The active role that I played in questions relating to the life of the French Communist Party ended around the winter of 1923-24. An internal struggle broke out in the French Communist Party, which was fundamentally a reflection of the discussion in the Russian party. This led to the expulsion of Rosmer and Monatte from the French party, which was subsequently confirmed by the Fifth Congress of the Comintern. If at that time I had participated in the discussion and decision on this question, I would certainly have come out strongly against their expulsion. But it was presented to me as an accomplished fact. Insofar as I did not speak out against their expulsion and in general did not raise this question—by this in itself I bore and still bear the responsibility for it.

After their expulsion, Monatte and Rosmer undertook the publication of the magazine *La Revolution proletarienne*. I learned of its appearance this spring on returning from the Caucasus, and I have become acquainted with it only in the last few days.

By its character and by its tone, this magazine justifies their expulsion. Despite the tragic blow that Monatte and Rosmer received—the hardest blow that could befall such loyal revolutionists—it was their duty, even though formally outside the party, to conduct themselves as soldiers of the party and thereby sooner or later to regain their place in the party. This is exactly the same advice that I gave to a French Communist who asked for my opinion in an analogous case. Having founded the magazine, they seem to have had the intention of explaining in articles in the first issue that the accusations of reformism, etc., raised against them were unfounded. But each succeeding issue carried them further along the road of struggle against the leadership of the French party and the Comintern. Anger is a bad counselor. The magazine—and this must be frankly stated—despite the name *La Revolution proletarienne,* was transformed into a weapon directed against the real proletarian revolution, the one that is embodied above all in the Soviet Union and the Russian Communist Party.

In Monatte and Rosmer's magazine a definite place is also set aside to defending me against various attacks and accusations. I firmly disavow this defense. This is not because I accept the criticisms raised against me in the magazine *Les Cahiers du bolchevisme;* to my regret, in this publication I often find interpretations of my views that have nothing in common with my actual positions. But the French Communist Party is *our* party. It is altogether criminal to defend one's point of view by methods that are suited to discrediting the party, undermining its authority and its influence. Our French party is an integral part of the International, and the fate of the world proletariat and the oppressed peoples is bound up with the development of the International.

In France, at this time, only the Communist Party is leading a vigorous struggle against militarist imperialism. Undermining its work with accusations that, politically speaking, are monstrously out of proportion means playing the game of the enemies of the working class—quite apart from how these accusations are intended. This is even more evident in the attitude of *La Revolution proletarienne* on Russian affairs.

The work of the Russian Communist Party is developing under extraordinarily difficult conditions, particularly at present, when all the forces of world reaction are again mobilizing against the Soviet Union. Our party is clearing a path for which there is no historical precedent. The faults and maladies in the development of the party, which flow from objective conditions, can only be combated by the party's own forces, and consequently by methods that the party can adopt, adapt, and put into practice. Any other course signifies a lack of faith in those forces that are *in the vanguard* of our world party. And, of course, those who distrust the party can play no further role in it.

As for the struggle against Eastman's methods, I have already said all that is necessary. There is nothing more to add there.

The road that *La Revolution proletarienne* has taken has its internal logic: it leads men, without their being aware of it, to the other side of the barricades. But I don't hold this to be inevitable. Rosmer and Monatte are enough the tempered old revolutionists that they may set aside considerations of false self-esteem. They can and they should call a halt. *Cease publication of the magazine immediately; while remaining outside the party, act like soldiers of the party; appeal to the Executive Committee of the Comintern to review the matter. There is no other way.*

TOWARD CAPITALISM OR SOCIALISM?

August 28, 1925

NOTE: In May 1925 Trotsky was appointed to serve on the Supreme Council of the National Economy, where he became chairman of three commissions: the Concessions Committee, the Board of Electrotechnical Development, and the Industrial-Technological Commission. He wrote "Toward Capitalism or Socialism?" in August 1925, in response to the appearance of control figures for the national economy issued by Gosplan (the State Planning Commission) for the year 1925-26. "Toward Capitalism or Socialism?" was a way Trotsky could get his views on planning published without incurring the charge of factionalism and the threat of expulsion.

"Toward Capitalism or Socialism?" was originally published in Pravda, *September 1, 2, 16, 17, 20, and 22, 1926. Under the title "Whither Russia?" two English translations appeared in 1926, published by Methuen in London and International Publishers in the United States. The version used here is based on the American edition, slightly edited for accuracy and current usage.—Ed.*

Introduction

The object of this little book is to outline the principal factors in our economic development. The difficulties of such an analysis are apparent when the reader considers the sharp turns that have taken place in the course of our development. When development proceeds along a straight line, two points are sufficient to determine its direction. But when, at a crucial moment, the course of affairs describes a complicated curve, it is difficult to judge the various sectors of this curve. And in a new social order eight years are but a short period.

Our opponents and enemies, however, have not hesitated to deliver themselves—on more than one occasion—of their "infallible" judgments on our economic development, nor have they waited until eight years elapsed after our October Revolution. These judgments are of two kinds. In the first place, we are told that we are ruining the country by our work of socialist construction; in the second place, we are told that our development of the productive forces is in reality carrying us toward capitalism.

Criticism of the first type is characteristic of the mode of thought of the bourgeoisie. The second style of criticism is rather that of social democracy, i.e., bourgeois thought in a socialist disguise. It would be hard to draw a sharp line between the two styles of criticism, and frequently the two exchange their arsenal of arguments in a neighborly manner, without noticing it themselves, intoxicated as they are with the sacred war against communist barbarism.

The present book, I hope, will prove to the unprejudiced reader that both camps are lying, not only the outright big bourgeoisie, but also the petty bourgeoisie who pretend to be socialist. They lie when they say that the Bolsheviks have ruined Russia. Indisputable facts prove that in Russia—disorganized by imperialist and civil wars—the productive forces in industry and agriculture are approaching the prewar level, which will be reached during the coming year. It is a falsehood to state that the evolution of the productive forces is proceeding in the direction of capitalism. In industry, transportation, communications, commerce, finance, and credit operations, the part played by the nationalized economy is not lessened with the growth of the productive forces; on the contrary, this role is assuming increasing importance in the total economy of the country. Facts and figures prove this beyond dispute.

The matter is much more complicated in the field of agriculture. No Marxist will be surprised by this; the transition from scattered single peasant establishments to a socialist system of land cultivation is inconceivable except after passing through a number of stages in technology, economics, and culture. The fundamental condition for this transition is the retention of power in the hands of the class whose object is to lead society to socialism (and which is becoming ever more able to influence the peasant population by means of the state industry), and by raising agricultural technology to a higher level and thus creating the prerequisites for a collectivization of agriculture.

It is hardly necessary to state that we have not yet solved this task; we are only beginning to create the prerequisites for a consistent gradual realization of it. Moreover, these achievements will themselves develop new contradictions, new dangers. What is the nature of these?

The state today furnishes four-fifths of the industrial production for our domestic market. About one-fifth is provided by private producers, particularly by the small establishments of home industry. Railway and marine transportation is 100 percent in the state's hands. Three-quarters of today's trade is accounted for by the state and the cooperatives. Ninety-five percent of all foreign trade is in the hands of the state.

The credit institutions are likewise a centralized state monopoly. But these mighty self-contained state trusts are confronted by 22 million peasant establishments. The uniting of state and peasant economies—the productive forces meanwhile increasing as a whole—thus constitutes the principal *social* problem of socialist construction in our country.

Unless the productive forces grow, there can be no question of socialism. On the economic and cultural level that we now occupy, the development of the productive forces can be attained only by involving the personal interest of the producers themselves in the system of the social economy. This is being done in the case of the industrial workers by making their wages depend on the productivity of their labor. Great successes have already been attained in this field. The peasant's personal interest is secured if only by the fact that he manages a private establishment and is working for the market. But this condition also involves difficulties. Wage differentials, great as they may be, do not introduce social differentiation among the proletariat: the workers remain workers for the state enterprises. With the peasantry the case is different. The work done for the market by the 22 million peasant establishments (of which the state farms, peasant collective establishments, and agricultural "communes" at present constitute but an insignificant minority) leads inevitably to the creation, at one pole of the peasant mass, of wealthy and even exploiting establishments, while at the other pole we have a transformation of a section of our present-day middle peasantry into poor peasants, and of poor peasants into farm laborers.

When the Soviet government, under the leadership of the Communist Party, introduced the New Economic Policy and then extended the field of its operations to the provinces, it had no illusions as to either the inevitable social consequences of the market system or the political dangers it brought with it. We do not regard these dangers, however, as fatal consequences, but as problems which must be studied with attention and solved in practice at every stage of our work.

The difficulty could hardly have been eliminated if the state had given up its direction of industry, commerce, and finance while the class differentiation in the village was advancing. For in that case, private capital would have strengthened its influence on the market, particularly on the peasant market, and thus accelerated the process of differentiation in the village and shunted our entire economic development onto the path of capitalism. Precisely for this reason, it is extremely important for us to determine in the first place the direction of the alignment of class forces in the fields of industry, communications, finance, and domestic and foreign trade. The increasing predominance of the *socialist* state in all the areas named (which has been presented in indisputable terms by Gosplan) has created an entirely new relationship between city and countryside. Our state is far too firmly at the helm to enable the growth of capitalist and semicapitalist tendencies in agriculture to get out of our control in the near future. And to gain time in this connection means everything.

Insofar as there is a struggle between capitalist and socialist tendencies in our economy (and the very essence of the NEP consists of both collaboration and competition between these tendencies), it may be said that the outcome of the struggle depends on the speed of development of each of these tendencies. In other words: if state industry develops more slowly than agriculture; if the latter should proceed to produce with increasing speed the two extreme poles mentioned above (capitalist farmers "above," proletarians "below"); this process would, of course, lead to a restoration of capitalism.

But just let our enemies try to prove the inevitability of this prospect. Even if they approach this task more intelligently than poor Kautsky (or MacDonald), they will burn their fingers. On the other hand, is such a possibility entirely precluded? Theoretically, it is not. If the dominant party were guilty of one mistake after another, in politics as well as in economics; if it were thus to retard the growth of industry, which is now developing so promisingly; if it were to relinquish its control over the political and economic processes in the village; then, of course, the cause of socialism would be lost in our country. But we are not at all obliged to make any such assumptions in our prognosis.

How power is lost, how the achievements of the proletariat may be surrendered, how one may work for capitalism—all this has been brilliantly demonstrated to the international proletariat by Kautsky and his friends, after November 9, 1918. Nothing needs to be added to this lesson.

Our tasks, our goals, our methods, are different. We want to show how power, once achieved, may be retained and consolidated, and how the form of the proletarian state may be filled with the economic content of socialism. We have every reason to count on our industry's overtaking and neutralizing the process of differentiation in the village, and thus creating the technical conditions and economic prerequisites for the gradual collectivization of agriculture.

In my present book, I do not provide statistical data about differentiation in the village, because no figures have been collected which would make a general estimate of this process possible. This absence must be explained not so much by the defects of our statistics as by the peculiarities of the social process itself, which embraces the "molecular" alterations of 22 million peasant establishments. Gosplan, on whose calculations the present work is based, has entered into a profound study of the economic differentiation of our peasantry. The conclusions which Gosplan has thus attained will be published at the proper time; they will be of great importance for national decisions in the arenas of taxes, rural credits, cooperatives, etc. But these data will in no way affect the basic outlines of the view expressed in this book.

It is clear that this general problem is closely linked to the destinies of the West and East, both economically and politically. Every step forward made by the world proletariat, every success attained by the suppressed colonial peoples, will consolidate our position materially and morally, and bring the hour of general victory so much the nearer.

Chapter 1
The Language of Figures

Gosplan has published a general table giving the economic "control" figures for the USSR for the year 1925-26.* The above sentence may have a very dry and even bureaucratic sound; but these dry statistical figures and the almost equally dry explanations of the figures are the accompaniment to the mighty historical music of the progress of socialism. Here are no mere conjectures, no assumptions, no mere empty hopes, no theoretical speculation—we have here the powerful language of figures, which cannot fail to convince even the New York Stock Exchange. We must dwell for a moment on the most important, most fundamental of these figures, for they deserve attention.

In the first place, the mere circumstance of the publication of this general table is—economically speaking—a cause of rejoicing for us. The day of its publication (August 20, 1925) is a red-letter day in the Soviet calendar. Agriculture and industry, domestic and foreign trade, the amount of money in circulation, prices of commodities, credit operations, and the state budget, have found in this table an expression of their development and their correlation. We have before us a clear, simple, and readable *comparative presentation* of all the basic data for 1913, for 1924-25, and the prospective figures for 1925-26. The explanatory text also supplies figures where necessary for the other years of the Soviet economy, so that we now possess a *complete picture* of the progress of our reconstruction and a bird's-eye view of our work for the next economic year. The mere possibility of such a comparative statement is a very important accomplishment.

Socialism means accounting. Under the NEP system, the forms of accounting are of course different from those which we attempted to apply in the period of war communism (1917-21), and from those which will find their full expression under completely developed socialism. Yet socialism means accounting, and at present, under the NEP, socialism probably requires more accounting than it will require in its completed form; for then our reckoning will have a purely economic content, while now it also involves the most intricate political problems. In the general

---

*See Table I, p. 377.

table of control figures, the socialist state for the first time gives an account of all the branches of its economy in their mutual relations and in their development. This is a tremendous achievement. The mere possibility of such a step is a splendid testimonial not only to the material achievements of our economy, but also to the success of the idea that governs this economy and dictates its guiding lines. This table may be regarded as a kind of diploma, and the reader must not forget that diplomas are not issued when maturity has been attained, but at the moment of transition from secondary to higher education. And the tasks which are imposed upon us by Gosplan's general table are precisely tasks of a higher order; this is the question which we shall now proceed to analyze.

A glance at the table at once raises the first question: To what extent is the table accurate? This provides a broad field for reservations, modifications, and even skepticism. Everyone knows that our statistics and our forms of accounting are not infrequently defective, not because they are poorer than the other phases of our economic and cultural activities, but because such statistics reflect all, or at least many, aspects of our backwardness. But this reflection by no means justifies a general vote of mistrust, accompanied by the hope that perhaps we may—after a lapse of a year and a half or two years—be able to ascertain the erroneousness of one figure or another and then play the sage after the fact! It is extremely probable that there are a number of errors. But such wisdom after the fact is the cheapest sort of wisdom. For the present moment the figures of Gosplan represent the highest possible approximation to the truth. There are three reasons for this: in the first place, they are based on the most complete material available, and therefore on material that has not been gathered at random but has been worked up day by day by the various sections of Gosplan; in the second place, this material has been prepared by the most capable and best qualified economists, statisticians, and technicians; and in the third place, this task has been carried out by an institution that is free from any government interference and can at any moment convince the economic authorities by means of direct confrontation.* To this we must add that Gosplan has no business secrets or any other kind of economic secrets. Any process of production and

---

*"The accounting reports of the operative economic bodies are worse than incomplete: they are biased," observes the commentary of Gosplan. This severe judgment is worthy of note. The operative economic bodies must be trained, with the cooperation of Gosplan and the press, to deliver objective business reports, in perfect accord with the facts.—L.T.

any commercial calculation may be verified, either directly or through the Workers and Peasants Inspection. All balance sheets as well as all official calculations are available to Gosplan even while still in rough-draft form. To be sure, certain figures may still be disputed. The objections, whether accepted or not, may be of great importance for certain practical matters (for instance, for the volume of exports and imports, for the size of items in the budget, for this economic need or that, and the like). But these adjustments will not involve any change in the fundamental data. Better, more carefully checked figures than those afforded by the table published by Gosplan cannot be found at the present time. One thing, furthermore, is certain. An inaccurate "control" figure—as our entire economic experience has shown—is of incomparably greater value than working at random. In the former case, corrections and additions may be made on the basis of experience; in the latter, we are merely "muddling along."

The table covers the period up to October 1, 1926. This means that after a lapse of about twelve months, when we shall have received the annual economic reports for 1925-26, we shall be able to compare our actual situation of tomorrow with our statistical assumptions of today. But however widely the two may differ, this mere comparison will alone be an indispensable lesson in planned economy.

Since we are speaking of a greater or lesser degree of accuracy in prediction, we must clearly understand the nature of the prediction in this case. The statisticians of the Harvard Economic Service, when they attempt to determine the tendencies and rates of growth of certain branches of the U.S. economy, are proceeding to a certain extent like astronomers; i.e., they attempt to grasp the dynamics of processes that are entirely independent of their control. The difference is merely in the fact that these statisticians by no means work with the accurate methods that are at the disposal of the astronomer. The Russian statisticians, however, are in an entirely different position: they work as members of institutions which are in charge of economic life. A preliminary plan in our case is not merely a product of passive prediction, but also a lever for active economic forethought. In this case, each figure is not only a photograph, but also a guideline. The table of control figures was elaborated by a state institution which controls—to an enormous extent—the dominant economic positions. For instance, when the table says that our exports in the year 1925-26 must advance to 1.2 billion rubles from the export figures of 462 million rubles in 1924-25, i.e., by 160 percent, this is not a mere forecast, but an objective to be realized! On the basis of what *is* we are told what *shall be*. When the table informs us that the investment of capital in industry (i.e., the outlay for the renewal and extension of basic capital) must amount to 900 million rubles, we have again not a passive arithmetical estimate, but a statistically motivated practical problem of the first importance. Such is the character of the table from beginning to end. It represents a dialectical combination of theoretical prediction and practical volition, i.e., a union of the calculated objective conditions and tendencies with the subjectively imposed tasks of the workers' and peasants' state. Herein lies the chief difference between Gosplan's general review table and all the statistical summaries, calculations, and approximations of any capitalist state. As we shall have occasion to see later, we are dealing here with the immense superiority of *our*, i.e., socialist, methods over those of capitalist states.

The view afforded by Gosplan's general table does not furnish, however, any estimate of the economic methods of socialism in general, but only of their application under certain conditions, i.e., in a specific stage of the so-called New Economic Policy. The elemental economic processes above all may be grasped objectively and statistically. On the one hand, the economic processes conducted by the state go "into the market" at a certain stage and are united by means of the market with the elemental—so to speak, uncontrollable—economic processes, particularly through the economic methods created by the "atomized" individual peasant economy that prevails in our country. Planned economic management today consists to a large degree precisely in uniting those economic processes that are under control and guidance with those that are as yet subject to the operation of their own market laws. In other words, in our economy, socialist tendencies (of various degrees of development) are combined and intertwined with capitalist tendencies, the latter also of varying degrees of maturity and immaturity. The control figures reflect the relationship of one set of processes with the other set and thus disclose the components of the forces of development. Herein lies the fundamental importance for socialism of the provisional plan.

We have always been fully aware of the fact—and have never concealed it—that the economic processes going on in our country have involved these contradictions because they constitute a struggle between two mutually exclusive systems—socialism and capitalism. On the contrary, it was precisely at the moment of transition to the NEP period that Lenin formulated the historic question in three words: "Who beats whom?" The Menshevik theoreticians, including in the first place Otto Bauer, condescendingly welcomed the NEP as a sober capitulation of the premature, violent, in short, "Bolshevik" methods of the socialist economy to a tried and trusty capitalism. The fears of some and the hopes of others have been subjected to a very serious examination, and the result has been expressed in the control figures of our economic budget. These figures are important also for the fact that it now becomes impossible to continue operating with commonplaces concerning the socialist and capitalist elements of our economy (concerning the plan "in general" and uncontrollable factors "in general"). Even though only in rough and provisional form, we are nevertheless aware of our condition. We have succeeded in setting up a quantitative estimate of the relation between socialism and capitalism in our economy, for today and for tomorrow. We have thus attained valuable data needed to answer the historic question, "Who beats whom?"

Chapter 2
The NEP and the Peasantry

All of the above serves merely to indicate the methodological significance of Gosplan's general table, i.e., we have pointed out the enormous importance of the fact that we have at last achieved the chance to estimate all the basic processes of our economy in their interconnections and in their development, and have thereby obtained a point of departure for incomparably more conscious and more foresightful planning (and this not only in the field of economics). But far more important for us is of course the direct *material* content of the general table, i.e., the actual figures by means of which the table characterizes our social development.

In order to answer properly the question of whether we are tending toward socialism or toward capitalism, we must first of all formulate this question properly. It may be divided logically into three sections: (1) Are the productive forces developing in our country? (2) What are the social forms in which this development is proceeding? (3) What is the rate of this development?

The first question is the simplest and also the most important.

Neither capitalism nor socialism is conceivable without the development of the productive forces. War communism, the outgrowth of cast-iron historical necessity, soon ran its course after it brought the development of the productive forces to a standstill. The most elementary and imperative principle of the NEP was the development of the productive forces as the basis of all social movement in general. The NEP was regarded by the bourgeoisie and the Mensheviks as the necessary (but of course "insufficient") step toward unchaining the productive forces. The Menshevik theoreticians approved of the NEP as the dawn of capitalist restoration in Russia. They added: Either the NEP will overthrow the Bolshevik dictatorship (the "desirable" outcome) or the Bolshevik dictatorship will ultimately overthrow the NEP (a "deplorable" event). The *Smena Vekh* group[43] owed its origin at first to the belief that the NEP would facilitate the development of the productive forces along capitalist lines. Now Gosplan's general table affords us the basic data for answering not only the question as to the development of the productive forces, but also the question as to the social form in which this development is taking place.

Of course, we are well aware that the social form of our economic development has a dual nature, since it is based on both the collaboration and the struggle between capitalist and socialist methods, forms, and ends. Such are the conditions in which our development has been placed by the New Economic Policy. Furthermore, the fundamental content of the New Economic Policy is involved in these conditions. However, such a general notion of the contradictory nature of our development is no longer sufficient for us. We now seek and demand extremely precise criteria for our economic contradictions, i.e., we require not only dynamic coefficients of our general development, but also comparative coefficients for the specific weight of this tendency or that. A great many things depend on the answer to this question; in fact, everything in our domestic and foreign policy depends on it.

In order to approach the question most clearly, we shall say: It is impossible to obtain a clear and fully dependable conception of the prospects and the possible dangers of our peasant policy without having answered the question as to the balance of power between the capitalist and socialist tendencies, the question as to the direction in which the relation of their specific weight is altering with the growth of the productive forces. As a matter of fact, if it should turn out that as the productive forces develop, the capitalist tendencies increase or expand at the expense of the socialist tendencies, this expansion of the volume of commodity capitalist relations in the village might be of cataclysmic importance and might shunt our course of development definitely onto the track of capitalism. And vice versa, if the specific weight of the state economy (i.e., in our case, the socialist economy) should increase in the total economic life of the country, a more or less extensive "liberation" of the commodity capitalist forces in the village would then enter into the definite alignment of forces, and the questions as to how, when, to what extent, will be determined in a purely objective way. In other words, if the productive forces in the hands of the socialist state, which assure to that state the possession of all the commanding positions in the economy, are not only rapidly growing in an absolute way, but also are growing more rapidly than the private capitalist productive forces in city and countryside; if this has been confirmed by the experience of the hardest period of reconstruction; then it is clear that by expanding to a certain extent the commodity capitalist tendencies growing out of the primitive roots of the peasantry, we are by no means incurring the danger of being exposed to any economic crises, to a sudden shifting from quantity to quality, i.e., to sudden transitions to capitalism.

In the third place, we must also answer this question: What is our *rate* of development when viewed from the standpoint of world economy? At first glance it might appear that this question—in spite of its importance—is nevertheless of a subsidiary nature; that while, to be sure, it is desirable to advance to socialism "as quickly as possible," the rate of this advance is not extremely important since the advance is assured by the victorious development of socialist tendencies under NEP conditions. But this would be incorrect. Such a conclusion would be justified (and then only in part) if we were dealing with a closed, self-sufficient economy. But this is not the case. Precisely because of our successes we have gone into the world market, i.e., we have entered the system of the universal division of labor. And at the same time we have remained encircled by capitalism. Under these conditions, the rate of our economic development will determine the strength of our resistance to the economic pressure of world capitalism and to the military-political pressure of world imperialism. These factors may not be left out of the account for the present.

If we now approach the general table and the commentary of Gosplan with our three "control" questions, we shall easily be convinced that the first two questions—(1) the development of the productive forces; and (2) the social forms of this development— are not only answered clearly and distinctly by the table, but also favorably. And as for the third question—the question of the rate of the process—we have only begun, in the course of our economic growth, to witness its unfolding on a world scale. But here also we shall find that the favorable answers to the first two questions also provide the necessary preliminaries for the solution of the third question. And it becomes the highest criterion, the surest touchstone of our economic development in the period that is now beginning.

Chapter 3
The Growth of the Productive Forces

The rapid recovery of our productive forces is now generally known and is excellently illustrated by the figures given in the general table. If we calculate production in prewar prices, the agricultural production of the year 1924-25 (in which falls the *poor* harvest of 1924) amounted to 71 percent of the production of the good crop year 1913. The coming fiscal year, that of 1925-26, which includes among its assets our present good crop, promises—according to the latest available data—to exceed the agricultural production of 1913 and almost to attain that of the year 1911. While in the last few years the total yield of grain has never reached 3 billion poods [one pood=36 lbs.], the crops this year are estimated at about 4.1 billion poods.*

This year (1924-25) our industry has attained 71 percent, as measured by the value of its products, of the production of the same "normal" year of 1913. In the next year it will attain not less than 95 percent of the production of 1913, i.e., it will practically have completed its recovery. If we recall that in 1920 our production had gone down to one-fifth or one-sixth of the normal capacity of our factories, we shall be in a position to fully appreciate the speed of this recovery process. The production of our large-scale industries has more than tripled since 1921. Our exports, which in that year were under half a billion rubles, prom-

---

*This is the estimate of August 28, 1925; of course, changes in either direction may be expected.—L.T.

ise to exceed considerably a billion rubles in the coming year. The same development is shown by our imports. The state budget promises to increase from 2.5 billion to more than 3.5 billion rubles. These are the basic control figures. The quality of our products is of course still quite imperfect, but has improved considerably when compared with the first two years of the NEP. We thus obtain, as our answer to the question as to how our productive forces are developing, the quite convincingly demonstrated result: *the "freeing" of the market has given the productive forces an immense impetus.*

But the very fact that the impulse came from the market— which is a factor of the capitalist economic order—afforded a malicious pleasure to the bourgeois theoreticians and politicians. It seemed as if the nationalization of industry (1917-19) and the methods of economic planning were compromised beyond repair by the mere transition to the NEP and by its undoubted economic successes. And therefore only the answer to the second question put by us—namely, the question as to the social *forms* of our economy—can provide a socialist assessment of our development. The productive forces are growing also, for instance, in Canada, which is stimulated by capital from the United States. They are growing also in India in spite of the bonds of colonial slavery. In fact, there has been a growth of the productive forces since 1924— in the form of a reconstruction process—even in Dawes-ized Germany.[44] But in all these cases we are dealing with capitalist development. Precisely in Germany, the nationalization and socialization plans which flourished so luxuriantly in 1919-20, at least in the massive tomes of the professorial socialists and Kautskyites, have now been cast aside as "old junk" and, under strict American supervision, the principle of private capitalist initiative is entering—though some of its teeth have fallen out and others have been knocked out—into its "second youth."

How do matters stand with us? What is the *social form* in which the development of the productive forces is taking place in our country? Are we proceeding toward capitalism or toward socialism?

The premise for a socialist economy is the nationalization of the means of production. How has this premise stood the test of the NEP? Has the market distribution of commodities led to a weakening or a strengthening of the nationalization? Gosplan's general table furnishes excellent material for judging the reciprocal effects of the struggle between the capitalist and socialist tendencies in our economy. We have altogether reliable "control"

figures, covering basic capital, production, commercial capital—
in short, all the most important economic processes of the country.

The most vulnerable figures are perhaps those indicating the
distribution of basic capital; yet this vulnerability applies to the
absolute figures rather than to their mutual relation, and we are
now concerned, of course, chiefly with the latter. According to the
statements of Gosplan, "the most conservative calculations" at
the beginning of the current economic year showed capital to the
extent of at least 11.7 billion gold rubles held by the state; 500
million gold rubles held by the cooperatives; and 7.5 billion gold
rubles held by the private—chiefly peasant—establishments. In
other words, more than 62 percent of the total means of production has been socialized, and this includes the technically best-
developed sections. About 38 percent remains not socialized.

As for agriculture, we find investigated here not so much the
effects of the nationalization of the land as those of liquidation of
feudal landholding. The results of this investigation are solid and
instructive. The liquidation of landlordism—as well as of almost
all holdings of land that exceed the proportions of the peasant
economy—led to an almost complete liquidation of the large-scale
agricultural estates, including also the model estates. This was
one of the causes—to be sure, not the decisive one—of the temporary decline in agriculture. But we have already seen that this
year's crops will attain the figures of the agricultural production
of the prewar period, and this without large-scale landholdings
and without capitalist "model" farms. And add to this the fact
that the development of agriculture, freed from the great landed
proprietors, has only begun! We therefore see that the "liquidation" of the feudal landholding class, together with all its strong-
holds, is proving itself to be economically sound. This is our first,
and by no means insignificant, conclusion.

As for the *nationalization* of the land, it has not yet been
possible to estimate its results, owing to the extreme smallness of
the divided peasant lands. The "populist" halo which inevitably
was associated with the socialization of the land in the first
period has just as inevitably disintegrated and dropped off. Simultaneously, however, the significance of nationalization as a
measure of essentially socialist character when applied under the
rule of the working class, has been made sufficiently clear to
prove its immense importance in the further development of
agriculture. Thanks to the nationalization of the land, we have
provided the state with unlimited possibilities in the domain of

land distribution. No walls erected by individual or collective private property can present any obstacle to us in our task of adapting the forms of land use to the demands of the production process. At this moment the agricultural means of production have only been socialized 4 percent. The remaining 96 percent are still the private property of the peasants. But we must bear in mind that the agricultural means of production, the peasant holdings as well as the state holdings, constitute only a little over one-third of the total means of production of the Soviet Union. It is hardly necessary to say that the significance of the nationalization of the land can only become completely evident as the final result of a high stage of development in agricultural technology and the resulting collectivization of agriculture, i.e., after a lapse of a number of years. But it is precisely in this direction that we are going.

Chapter 4
The Soundness of Socialized Industry

We Marxists were well aware, even before the revolution, that the socialist transformation of the economy must necessarily begin with industry and mechanized transport, and later involve the village. Therefore a statistical study of the activity of nationalized industry is the fundamental test of the socialist development of our transitional economy.

In the field of industry, the socialization of the means of production is 89 percent; together with railroad transportation, 97 percent; in heavy industry alone, 99 percent. These figures indicate that the system of ownership which resulted from nationalization has not suffered any change at the expense of the state. This mere fact is of the very greatest importance. We are chiefly interested, however, in another matter. What percentage of annual production comes from the socialized means of production? i.e., how efficiently is the state employing the means of production appropriated by it? Gosplan's general table affords the following information on this point. In 1923-24, nationalized and cooperative industries furnished 76.3 percent of the gross product; this year they have furnished 79.3 percent; the forecast figures of Gosplan for next year (1925-26) show that they will furnish 79.7

percent. As far as private industry is concerned, its share of production in 1923-24 was 23.7 percent; in 1924-25 it was 20.7 percent; and for next year (1925-26) its share will be 20.3 percent. However cautiously the preliminary figures for next year may have been arrived at, a comparison of the dynamics of nationalized and private production within the total sum of commodities in the country has an immense significance. We find that in the past year as well as this year, i.e., in the years of dramatic economic progress, the share of nationalized industry has decreased by the same figure. This percentage is the measure of the *gain* made by socialism over capitalism in this short period. The percentage may appear small but, as we shall see, its symptomatic importance is really very great.

What danger could there have been during the transition to the New Economic Policy and the first years of that policy? The danger was that the state—because of the complete exhaustion of the country—might have turned out to be incapable of lifting the great industrial enterprises onto its shoulders in a sufficiently short time. In view of the then quite insufficient activity of the large-scale enterprises (they were working at about 10 or 20 percent of capacity) the middle, smaller, and even domestic establishments might, by virtue of their adaptability, their "elasticity," have attained a considerable preponderance. The so-called "wastefulness" of the first period, representing a socialist tribute to capitalism in return for starting the operation of the factories confiscated from capitalism, threatened to hand over a great share of the national wealth to all sorts of traders, middlemen, and speculators. The first enterprises to breathe new life from the NEP atmosphere were the domestic industries and small workshops. The combination of private commercial capital with petty private industry, including home industry, might have led to a fairly rapid process of primitive capitalist accumulation, along the old beaten track. Under these circumstances, we were menaced with such a loss of speed as might tear the reins of economic leadership from the hands of the workers' state with elemental force. This does not necessarily mean that *every* passing or even lasting growth of the specific gravity of private industry within the framework of the general volume automatically involves catastrophic or even fatal consequences. Here also, quality depends on quantity. If the final figures should show that the specific weight, the share of capitalist production in the last two or three years, had increased by 1 or 2 or 3 percent, this would not be equivalent to a menacing situation. Nationalized production would still constitute fully three-quarters of the total quantity, and to make up for this lost speed would not be an insoluble task when we consider how much of their capacity the large-scale enterprises have reached. If it had turned out that the share of private capitalist production had increased 5 or 10 percent, the fact might be somewhat more serious, but even such a result in the first period—the period of reconstruction—would by no means signify that nationalization was economically unfavorable. The inference could only be that the most significant section of nationalized industry had not yet begun its necessary process of development. Far more importance must be assigned to the fact that—as a result of the first period of the NEP, which is concerned only with reconstruction and which is most difficult and dangerous for the state—nationalized industry not only lost none of its territory to capitalist industry, but on the contrary forced the latter back to the extent of an additional 3 percent. This is the immense symptomatic significance of this little figure!

Our inference becomes still clearer when we proceed to not only the data concerning production, but also those concerning trade. In the first half of 1923, private capital involved in domestic trade constituted about 50 percent of the total, in the second half of 1923 about 34 percent, while in 1924-25, it amounts to about 26 percent. In other words, the specific weight of private capital involved in domestic commerce has dropped more than 50 percent (from one-half to one-quarter). This condition was not attained by merely "choking trade," for in the same period the volume of state and cooperative trade increased more than 100 percent.

We are, therefore, witnessing a reduction in the social role not only of private industry, but also of private commerce. And this, in both cases, while the productive forces and the volume of trade are both increasing! As we have seen, the general table also provides for a further decrease—to be sure, a small one—in the specific weight of private industry and private trade. We may await with composure the realization of this prediction. The victory of nationalized industry over private industry should not be interpreted unconditionally as an unbroken ascending line. There may be periods in which the state, depending upon its economically protected forces, and desirous of accelerating the rate of development, will consciously permit a provisional increase of the "specific weight" of private enterprises: in agriculture, in the form of "strong," i.e., capitalist farm establishments; in industry, and again in agriculture, in the form of concessions. If we consider the extremely "atomized" dwarf-like character of the greater part of our private industry, it would be naive to suppose that any increase of the specific weight of private production beyond the present 20.7 percent would necessarily be equivalent to a menace to socialist construction. In fact, it would be erroneous to attempt to set any rigid limits in this field. The question will be determined not by a formal barrier, but by the general dynamics of development, and the study of these dynamics shows that in the most difficult period, when the large-scale enterprises showed their negative instead of their positive qualities, the state was able to resist the first attack of private capital. In the period of the most rapid progress, the last two years, the relationship of the economic forces brought about by the revolutionary insurrection has been systematically shifted in favor of the state! Now that the chief positions have been far more securely occupied—if only by reason of the fact that the large-scale enterprises are approaching 100 percent production—there is no reason to fear any surprises as far as the internal factors of our economy are concerned.

Chapter 5
Coordination of City and Countryside

In the matter of the coordination of the economic activities of city and countryside, the general table provides fundamental—and therefore very convincing—data.* As will be seen from the table, the peasantry throws less than one-third of its gross production on the market, and this mass of commodities constitutes more than one-third of the total goods in circulation.

The ratio between the totals for agricultural and industrial commodities fluctuates within very narrow limits about the figure 37:63. This means that if we measure commodities not by the piece, the pound, and the yard, but in rubles, we shall find that somewhat more than one-third of the commodities on the market

---

*I do not maintain here—nor in the other cases that may arise—that all the figures of the table are new; but they have been checked, supplemented, and systematized; they now embrace our entire economy. It is to this that they owe their extreme importance.—L.T.

are agricultural, and somewhat less than two-thirds urban, i.e., industrial commodities. This may be explained by the fact that the village satisfies its own requirements to an enormous extent without resorting to the market, while the city throws almost its entire production into the market. The consumption of the much-divided peasant economy is excluded from the market to the extent of more than two-thirds of its total economic consumption, and only the remaining third has a direct influence on the economy of the country. Industry, on the other hand, by its very nature participates in the total national turnover with all its products; for the "internal" turnover within industry, within the trusts and syndicates themselves, which reduces the commodity content of production by 11 percent, not only does not reduce the influence of industry on the total economic process, but on the contrary (due to the simplification of the turnover) strengthens this influence.

Though the mass of agricultural products consumed by the peasantry does not influence the market, this should not be taken to mean that it does not influence the economy. In the present economic situation, this mass represents the necessary natural foundation for that one-third of peasant production that goes on the market. This one-third is the value in exchange for which the village requires an equivalent value from the city. From this fact the enormous importance for the entire economy of village production in general (and of its one-third that goes to market in particular) becomes quite apparent. Realizing our crops, and particularly carrying out export operations, is one of the most important factors in our annual economic balance sheet. The mechanism of cooperation between city and countryside will become more and more complicated. We have long been unable to say that we are dealing merely with the problem of exchanging so many pounds of peasant grain for so many yards of calico. Our economy has entered the world arena, and has thus added new links to the chain uniting city and countryside. The peasants' grain is exchanged for foreign gold; the gold, in turn, is transformed into machinery, agricultural implements, and replacement inventory for city and countryside. Textile machinery obtained with the gold realized on exports of grain maintains the equipment of the textile industry and thus lowers the prices of textiles sent to the village. This process of circulation becomes quite complicated, but its basis remains a certain economic relationship between city and countryside.

But it must not be forgotten for a moment that this relationship is a dynamic one and that the *dominant principle* in these complicated dynamics is *industry*. In other words, if agricultural production, and more particularly the commodity portion of this production, sets certain definite limits for the development of industry, these limits are not altogether rigid and immovable. The development of industry cannot be limited only by the amount by which the harvest has increased, for the mutual interdependence is far more complicated. Industry, to be sure, rests on the village, particularly as far as finished goods are concerned; but the growth of the village is paralleled by the development of a larger and larger market for industrial goods within industry itself.

Now that agriculture and industry are approaching the completion of the process of recovery, industry is assuming the character of the stimulating element to an incomparably higher degree than hitherto. The problem of a socialist influence on the village by the city—not only through cheap commodities but also through better and better implements for agricultural production, which forces the introduction of a collective exploitation of the land—this problem now faces our industry in all its concreteness and immensity.

The socialist reconstruction of agriculture will of course be achieved not only by the cooperatives as a mere *form* of organization, but by means of cooperatives based on the mechanization of agriculture, on its electrification, on its general industrialization. This means that the technical and socialist progress of agriculture cannot be separated from an increasing predominance of industry in the total economy of the nation. And this, in turn, involves an at first slow—but later faster and faster—overtaking of the dynamic coefficient of agriculture by the dynamic coefficient of industry.

Chapter 6
Accomplishments of Socialism in Industry

The production of all our industries in 1924-25 exceeded the production of the preceding year by 48 percent. Next year an increase of 33 percent may be expected as compared with this year (ignoring the lowering of prices). But the various categories of our industrial enterprises are by no means developing uniformly.

In the current year, large-scale enterprises showed an increase in production of 64 percent. The second group, which we may provisionally designate the middle enterprises, showed an increase of 55 percent. The small enterprises increased their production by only 30 percent. In consequence, we have reached a position in which the advantages of the large-scale enterprises as compared with the small and middle enterprises are already quite evident. But we cannot yet assert that we have already fully and completely realized the possibilities inherent in a socialist economy. To the extent that we are concerned with the predominance in *production* of the large-scale enterprises over the middle and small enterprises, we are at present enjoying only those advantages of large-scale enterprises that exist even under capitalism. As for the standardization of products on a national scale, the rationalization of the processes of production, the specialization of establishments, the transformation of entire industrial plants into huge parts of one single manufacturing organization of the entire Soviet Union, the linking up of the productive processes of heavy industry and the finishing industries—these fundamental tasks of production under socialism are only beginning to receive our attention. Boundless prospects here open before us, affording possibilities that we shall far exceed our old standards. But this is a matter of the future and will receive attention in due time.

Up to now, the advantages afforded by state management of the economy have not been utilized in the field of production itself, i.e., the field of the organization and coordination of the material processes of production, but in that of distribution: the providing of substances, raw materials, equipment, etc., to individual branches of industry, or to use the language of the market, the investment of operating capital and partly of original capital. Freed from the fetters of private property, the state—by means of the state budget, the state bank, the industrial bank, etc.—could at any moment pump cash resources to the point where they were most needed for the preservation or the rebuilding or development of the economy. This advantage of socialist economic methods has saved us in the last few years. In spite of frequent crude mistakes and errors in the distribution of resources, we have nevertheless handled them far more economically and practically than would have been possible in an unrestricted capitalist process of reconstruction of the productive forces. It is only by this circumstance that we have been able to attain our present stage in so short a time without resorting to foreign loans.

But this does not exhaust the question. The economics and consequently the social feasibility of socialism are apparent also in the fact that socialism has liberated the reconstruction of the economy from all the superfluous outlay in favor of the parasitic classes. It remains a fact that we are approaching the production level of 1913, although the country is considerably poorer than before the war. This means that we are able to attain the same production results by means of *smaller* social overhead expenses. We no longer spend money on the monarchy, the nobility, the bourgeoisie, excessively privileged intellectual strata, or finally, for the insane frictions within the capitalist machinery itself.* Because we approached the task in a socialist way, we were able to mobilize directly for the purposes of production a far greater section of our as yet limited material resources, and thus to prepare for a more rapid rise of the material standard of living of the population at the next stage.

We are dealing, therefore, on our nationalized land, with a scattered peasant economy whose commodities production amounts to somewhat more than one-third of the values handled on the market. Of the capital employed in agriculture, barely 4 percent represents socialized capital.

We have an industry 89 percent of whose basic capital is socialized, and this socialized industry furnishes more than 79 percent of the gross raw production of industry. The 11 percent of

---

*Deposits and current accounts amounted in 1924-25 to not more than 11 percent, on the average, of the deposits in 1913. By the end of the next year, it is expected that this item will rise to about 36 percent of the 1913 level. This is one of the striking indications of the meagerness of our savings. But the very fact that although we have attained a deposit figure amounting to only 11 percent of the prewar figure, our economy has nevertheless been raised to about 75 percent of the prewar level, is the most striking proof of the fact that the workers' and peasants' state applies its social resources in a way that is incomparably more efficient, systematic, and practical than is the case in a bourgeois system.

The comparative slowness of the development of transportation efficiency, as compared with that of agriculture and industry, may be in part explained by the fact that in the prewar period the specific weight of imports and exports was considerably higher than now. This is a further indication pointing to our having attained the prewar level of industry in spite of our far more modest resources and social overhead expenses than obtained in 1913.—L.T.

nonsocialized means of production consequently yields more than 20 percent of gross production.* The share held by the state production is increasing.

Railway transportation has been socialized 100 percent. The use of transportation is increasing constantly. In 1921-22 it was about 25 percent of prewar efficiency; in 1922-23, 37 percent; in 1923-24, 44 percent; and in the year 1924-25, it will exceed 50 percent of the prewar figure. For next year, we expect to attain 75 percent of our freight transportation in the prewar period.

In the domain of trade, the socialized (i.e., state and cooperative) resources of production constituted 70 percent of the total capital involved in the turnover, and this percentage is constantly increasing. Foreign trade has been entirely socialized; the state monopoly of foreign trade remains an immutable principle of our economic policy. The total volume of foreign trade will rise to 2.2 billion gold rubles next year. The share of private capital in this turnover—even adding contraband goods, which should be included—can hardly be more than 5 percent of the total.

The banks and the entire credit system have been socialized almost 100 percent. And this tremendously increasing apparatus is now more and more capable of mobilizing cash resources to feed the process of production.

The state budget is rising to 3.7 billion gold rubles, now amounting to 13 percent of the gross national income (29 billion rubles) or 24 percent of its total commodities (15.2 billion rubles). The budget is becoming a powerful internal lever for the nation's economic and cultural advance. Such are the figures in the general table.

These figures are of world-historic importance. For the first time, the activity of socialists—now more than a century old—which began with the utopians and later developed into a scientific theory, has been put to a powerful economic "test," a test which is already entering its ninth year. All that has been

---

*This disparity between the instruments of production and production itself may be explained chiefly by the varying organic composition of capital: it is natural for the inventory of installations to be extremely small as compared with the living human force which is expended without being fully recorded. At the other extreme, we must also consider the fact that the efficiency of our greatest establishments, for instance our huge metallurgical establishments, is still very far from 100 percent of capacity.—L.T.

written on socialism and capitalism, freedom and tyranny, dictatorship and democracy, has been subjected to the acid test of the October Revolution and has acquired a new, incomparably more concrete form. The figures issued by Gosplan make up the first, though as yet imperfect, balance sheet of the first chapter of the great experiment of transforming bourgeois society into socialist society. And this balance sheet is entirely favorable to socialism.

War after war had reduced Soviet Russia to a stage of devastation and exhaustion such as had hardly ever been reached by any other country. All those capitalist countries that had suffered most in the war rehabilitated themselves chiefly with the aid of foreign capital. Only the land of the Soviets, once the most backward of all, and the most devastated and exhausted by wars and revolutionary convulsions, was able to rise out of absolute poverty through its own power alone; with the active hostile intervention of the entire capitalist world. It is only owing to the complete abolition of feudal landholding and bourgeois property, only owing to the nationalization of all the principal means of production, to state socialist methods, and to the mobilization and distribution of the necessary resources, that the Soviet Union has risen out of the dust and is now forcing its way into the system of world economy as a factor of increasing importance. Gosplan's general table is connected by unbroken threads all the way back to the *Communist Manifesto* of Marx and Engels, which appeared in 1847, and all the way out into the socialist future of mankind. The spirit of Lenin pervades these dry columns of figures.

Chapter 7
Russia and the Capitalist World

Given the present historical conditions, we shall have accomplished a huge task when we attain the prewar level, not only quantitatively but qualitatively. The preceding chapters have been devoted to this question. But only this attainment will bring us to the starting point from which our real economic race with world capital begins.

The final lines of the commentary by Gosplan formulate the

total task as follows: "To retain the conquered positions and to advance, at every point where such is permitted by the economic situation, consistently, year by year, toward socialism—*though it be only a step at a time.*" Taken too literally these lines might give rise to false conclusions. The words "though it be only a step at a time," each year, in the advance toward socialism, might be interpreted as implying that the rate of advance is more or less a matter of indifference; if only the diagonal of the parallelogram of forces tends toward socialism, we must ultimately attain the goal. Such an inference would be entirely wrong, and Gosplan never intended to say any such thing. For, as a matter of fact, the rate of advance is precisely the decisive element! It is only because state industry and state trade developed more rapidly than private enterprise that they were able to secure a "socialist" diagonal of the parallelogram of forces for the period we have covered. But far more important is the relation of the rate of our total development compared with the development of the world economy. This question is not touched on directly in the commentary issued by Gosplan. We therefore consider it all the more important to discuss the matter very fully, since this new criterion will serve to determine our successes and failures in the next effort, just as the criterion of the "prewar level" has served to measure the successes of our reconstruction period.

It is quite evident that as we become part of the world market, not only our prospects but also our dangers will increase. The source, as of so many other conditions, is here again the dispersed form of our peasant economy, our technological backwardness, and the present immense productive superiority of world capitalism as compared with us. This plain statement of the case by no means contradicts the fact that the socialist mode of production, in its methods, tendencies, and possibilities, is incomparably stronger than the capitalist mode of production. The lion is stronger than the dog; but an adult dog may be stronger than the lion's cub. The young lion's best chance of survival is to grow up to have strong teeth and claws, which is merely a matter of time.

What constitutes the most powerful point of superiority of adult capitalism over youthful socialism, at least for the present? Not the vaults full of gold, not the total mass of accumulated and appropriated wealth. The accumulated resources of the past are not without their importance, but they are not the decisive factor. A living society cannot live for long on its old stock; it must meet its needs with the products of living labor. In spite of its wealth, ancient Rome could not resist the advancing "barbarians" when they developed a labor productivity that was higher than that of the decaying slave economy. The bourgeois society of France, awakened by the Great Revolution, simply took away the riches that had been accumulated by the Italian city-states since the Middle Ages. If America's labor productivity should drop below the European level, America would find but little assistance in the 9 billion dollars in gold that she has stored in her bank vaults. The fundamental economic superiority of bourgeois states consists in the fact that capitalism *at present still* produces cheaper and better goods than socialism. In other words, the productivity of labor in the countries that are still living in accordance with the law of inertia of the old capitalist civilization is *for the present* still considerably higher than in that country which is beginning to apply socialist methods under conditions of inherited barbarism.

We are acquainted with the fundamental law of history: the victory *ultimately* falls to that system which provides human society with the higher economic plane.

The historical dispute will be decided—*and of course not at once*—by the comparative coefficients of labor productivity.

The whole question at present is this: In what direction, and at what speed, will the relationship between our economy and that of the capitalist world alter in the next few years?

Our economy may be compared with the capitalist economies in various ways. The capitalist economy itself is of course quite varied. Our comparison may be a static comparison, i.e., it may use as a point of departure the economic condition at the present moment; or, it may be a dynamic comparison, i.e., it may be based on a comparison of the rates of development. We may compare the national income of the capitalist countries with our national income; or we may compare the coefficients of the expansion of production. All such comparisons and contrasts have their point—some more, others less—so long as their relation and their mutual dependence are borne in mind. We shall take the liberty to give a number of examples below in order to illustrate our thought more fully.

In the United States of America, the capitalist process has reached a culminating point. The present material superiority of capitalism over socialism may be excellently assessed by studying this superiority at the point at which it is most marked.

The Council of American Industrial Committees recently published a table from which we take a few figures. The population of the United States amounts to about 6 percent of the total population of the earth and produces 21 percent of the cereals, 32 percent of other food plants, 52 percent of the cotton, 53 percent of the forestry products, 62 percent of the pig iron, 60 percent of the steel, 57 percent of the paper, 60 percent of the copper, 46 percent of the lead, and 72 percent of the petroleum of the entire world. The United States owns one-third of the world's wealth. It possesses 38 percent of the world's water power, 59 percent of its telegraph and telephone lines, 40 percent of the railroad mileage, and 90 percent of the automobiles.

The strength of the current produced by the public power stations of the Soviet Union will rise to 775,000 kilowatts next year. In the United States, the amount of current produced last year was 15 million kilowatts. As for the power stations of the factories, our census of the year 1920 shows their total current strength to be almost one million kilowatts. In the United States, about 10.5 million kilowatts were recorded in the same period.

A general expression of the productivity of labor is found in the national income, the calculation of which is, as is well known, a matter of great difficulty. According to the data of our Central Statistical Department, the national income of the Soviet Union in 1923-24 was about 100 rubles per capita; that of the United States, on the other hand, about 550 rubles per capita. Foreign statisticians, however, give the figure of the national income of the United States not as 550, but as 1,000 rubles per head. This shows that the average productivity of labor, conditioned by the available machinery, organization, working routine, etc., may be as high as ten times, and surely not less than six times, as great as in our country.

These figures, important though they may be, by no means make it certain that we shall be defeated in this historic struggle, not only because the capitalist world does not consist of America alone; not only because immense *political* forces are concerned in the historic struggle, which have been created by the entire preceding economic development; but particularly because the further course of the economic development of North America itself is a huge unknown quantity. The productive forces of the United States are by no means fully employed, and the lowering of the percentage of employment signifies simultaneously a lowering of the productive forces. The United States is by no means adequately supplied with sales markets. The problem of sales is daily becoming a more and more disturbing one. It is not at all impossible that in the near future the comparison coefficient of the productivity of labor may tend to adjust itself in two ways: by our figure going up, and by the American figure going down. This, of course, applies far more emphatically to Europe, whose productivity is already far below that of the United States.

One thing is evident: the superiority of the capitalist technology and economy is as yet a mighty one. A steep ascent confronts us; the tasks and difficulties are truly colossal. A safe path can be found only with the aid of the yardsticks of world economy.

Chapter 8
Comparison Coefficients
of the World Economy

The dynamic equilibrium of the Soviet economy should by no means be considered as the equilibrium of a closed and self-sufficient unit. On the contrary, as time goes on, our internal economic equilibrium will be maintained more and more by the accomplishments of our imports and exports. This circumstance deserves to be traced to its logical conclusion, with every inference drawn. The more we are drawn into the system of the international division of labor, the more openly and directly are such elements of our domestic economy as the price and quality of our goods made to depend on the corresponding elements in the world market.

Our industry has hitherto been developed with our eye on its prewar level. In order to compare or determine the values of production, we are making use of the catalog prices of 1913. But our first period, one of recovery, in which such comparisons—rather imperfect ones, we may add—were appropriate, is approaching its conclusion, and the whole question of a criterion for our economic development is being shifted to another plane. From now on, we shall need to know at every moment to what extent our production lags behind that of the European or world market in quantity, quality, and price. The end of our reconstruction period will permit us finally to cast aside our 1913 catalogs and to lay in a supply of catalogs of German, English, American, and other firms. We shall have to concentrate our attention on new index figures which, both in quality and in price, will present a comparison between our production and that of the world market. Only these new yardsticks, these comparison coefficients—no longer taken from our own country alone, but now having universal application—can serve in the future as a measure of the various stages of the process expressed in Lenin's formula, "Who beats whom?"

In the face of the contending forces in world economy and world politics, decisive importance must be assigned to the *speed* of our advance, i.e., the speed of the quantitative and qualitative growth of our labor performance.

At present, our backwardness and poverty are undoubted facts. We do not dispute them; on the contrary, we constantly emphasize them. Systematic parallels with the world economy can only serve as a statistical expression of this fact. Is there not a danger that precisely in the immediate future, which will not see a sufficient advance on our part, the world market may crush us by reason of its tremendous material superiority? If we put the question thus, no infallible answer, and certainly no statistical answer, can be given, just as it is impossible to give such an answer to the question of whether the farmer-capitalist tendencies (the kulak tendencies) do not involve a danger of absorbing the middle peasants, of crippling the influence of the proletariat on the village, and of providing *political* obstacles to socialist construction. Nor can we answer categorically the question whether capitalism—if its present extremely relative stabilization process should continue—will not succeed in mobilizing considerable armed forces against us and thus retard our economic advance by means of a new war.

Such questions cannot be answered by means of passive prognosis. We are dealing here with a *struggle,* in which the factors of creativity, maneuvering, energy, etc., play an important, sometimes even a decisive, role. The investigation of these questions is not the task of the present work, in which we are aiming to determine *the internal tendencies of economic development* and to exclude other factors as far as possible.

At any rate, we must make the following reply to the question as to whether the world market will succeed in crushing us by reason of its economic superiority alone. We do not stand defenseless before the world market; our economy is protected by specific state institutions, which are applying a versatile system of socialist protectionism. But how great is its effectiveness? The history of capitalist development may furnish an answer to this question. For long periods Germany and the United States were far behind England from the industrial standpoint; their backwardness may have appeared insurmountable. But the utilization of natural and historical circumstances later permitted these backward countries, with the support of a protective tariff, not only to catch up with their more successful rival, but to far outdistance her. National boundaries, state power, the tariff system, all these were powerful factors in the history of capitalist development, and they are far more effective in the case of a socialist country. A carefully planned, persistent, and yet flexible system of socialist protectionism is the more important for us, the more extensive and complicated our connection with the capitalist market may become.

But it is self-evident that protectionism, the highest expression of which is the monopoly of foreign trade, is by no means omnipotent. It may force back the flood of the capitalist mass of commodities and regulate it in accordance with our domestic production and consumption. In this way, protectionism may secure the necessary reprieves for socialist industry in evaluating its level of production. Our process of construction would be impossible without the foreign trade monopoly. On the other hand, only our real production successes permit us to retain our socialist protectionism; in the future, the foreign trade monopoly may, to be sure, protect our domestic industry against blows from without, but it cannot serve as a substitute for the development of industry itself. This development must from now on be measured against the coefficient of the world market.

Our present comparison with the prewar level is made entirely from the point of view of quantity and price. We are considering the product from the standpoint not of its composition but of its nomenclature, which is, of course, wrong. The comparative production coefficients must also include *quality;* otherwise they may become merely a source, or instrument, of self-delusion. We have had some experience in this matter in connection with prices that went down while quality also declined in certain cases. When the quality of one and the same commodity is the same both in our country and abroad, the comparison coefficient will vary with the cost of production. Cost being the same in both domains, the coefficient will vary according to quality. Costs being different, and quality also different, a combined estimate based on both criteria becomes necessary. The determination of cost is a portion of the arithmetic of production. But the quality of the product can for the most part be determined only with the aid of a number of criteria. A classical example is the electric light bulb: the quality of the bulb is measured according to the length of its life, the quantity of energy consumed per candlepower, the uniformity of its distribution of light, etc. The fixing of certain technical norms and standards of perfection, including also the "qualitative" standards, immensely facilitates the derivation of comparison coefficients. The relation between our standards and the standards of the world market will be a fixed quantity for each specific period. We need only to know whether our product is up to the accepted standard. As for comparisons of value, this question will be very simply solved when the qualitative relation has been fixed. The combined coefficient is obtained by a simple process of multiplication. For example, if a certain commodity is twice as poor as the foreign commodity and one and a half times as expensive, the comparison coefficient is *one-third*.

If it is objected that we do not know how high foreign production costs are, this objection may be correct, to be sure, but it is of subordinate importance from a practical standpoint. It is sufficient to know the price—it is indicated in the catalogs. The difference between cost and price is the profit. A lowering of our costs will permit us to meet the prices on the world market independently of the foreign costs of manufacture. We shall then have achieved, at least in outline, a basis for the next period. This period will be followed—perhaps not so soon—by the third period, which will face the task of defeating capitalist production on the world market with the products of the socialist economy.

The objection is sometimes raised that the number of commodities is altogether too great, and that the derivation of the comparison coefficient is a task "transcending human energy." Two different answers may be made to this objection. In the first place, all the available commodities are subject to arithmetical calculation and recorded in books and catalogs, and the great variety of commodities seems to involve no element transcending human power. In the second place, the student may for the time being content himself with a discussion of the most important articles of mass consumption, the so-called key commodities in each branch of production, and assume that the other commodities occupy an intermediate position in the system of comparative evaluations.

A further objection calls attention to the difficulties involved in the measurement or even in the mere definition of quality. In fact, what *is* the quality of calico? Its durability, its cotton content per square yard, the fastness of its color, or its attractiveness to the eye? There is no doubt that the determination of quality is very difficult in most commodities; but the task is nonetheless not unsolvable. It must not, however, be approached from the standpoint of fictitious or absolute criteria. In the case of calico intended for the peasant market or the workers' market, the durability of the material will stand first, the permanence of the color second. In evaluating these two factors—and this is quite possible if strictly objective methods are pursued—we may obtain a basic definition of quality numerically expressed. It is far easier to obtain a precise, i.e., numerical, comparison coefficient of our plow, our threshing machine, our tractor, as compared with the same machines of American manufacture. This question will play the same part in the agriculture of the next few years as the renewal of the basic capital did in industry. In the purchase of a horse or a cow, the peasant himself determines all the necessary "coefficients," and with astonishing precision, too. But he is almost helpless when about to purchase a machine; if he has been duped in the purchase of a poor transmission, he will infect his neighbor with his timidity to purchase more machinery. We must succeed in getting the peasant to know what machine he is buying. The Soviet threshing machines must become a commonplace commodity on which a comparison coefficient may be based. The peasant will know precisely what he is buying, and the state will know precisely what the relation is between our production and the production of the United States of America.*

The idea of comparison coefficients, which at first glance may appear an abstraction, a product of the specialist's study, is in reality deeply rooted in life and literally cries out from all economic relations and oozes from all the pores of daily life. Even our present comparison coefficients, based on the prewar standard, were not a result merely of a theoretical understanding of the matter, but also of the needs of daily life. The average consumer, who has no access to statistical tables and price curves, makes use of his consumer's memory, his own memory as well as his family's. The statistical table gives us a certain

---

*Our adducing a number of objections above should not be interpreted as equivalent to a statement on our part that the idea of comparison coefficients is encountering the resistance of interested parties. On the contrary, the specialists active in production, in state commerce, in the cooperative system, and in the technical-scientific institutes, are very sympathetic to this idea, arising, as it does, out of our own economic development. The necessary preliminary investigations have been begun, both in a "special conference for quality of production" and in the technical-scientific institutes.—L.T.

percentage of the prewar level, calculated almost exclusively from the point of view of quantity, but the consumer's memory adds: "In peacetime (i.e., before the imperialist war) boots cost so many rubles and could be worn so many months." Whenever he bought boots, the consumer always worked out a comparison coefficient for himself. And the same operation has always been performed by every purchaser: whether it was the leather trust buying machinery from the Voronezh or Kiev machine works, or the peasant woman buying three yards of calico at the weekly village market. The only difference has been that the trust made its comparisons on the basis of catalogs and office records, while the peasant woman worked from her memory. And we must admit that in these two cases, the comparison coefficients of the peasant woman, based as they were on actual experience, were far more real than the coefficients of the trust, which were compiled hastily and almost always without any regard to quality, and were sometimes even biased. However this may be, the statistical economic analysis and the daily work of the consumer's memory have been in agreement in that both sought a point of departure in the conditions of the prewar economy.

This peculiar national limitation, which seeks comparisons with the national past, is approaching its end. Our connection with the world market is already sufficiently voluminous to oblige us at every step to compare our wares with those of foreign origin. And as the old comparisons weaken and disappear (for the memory of prewar products is becoming weaker, particularly in the younger generation), the new comparisons become more and more illuminating, being based not on memory, but on the living facts of today. Our economic specialists bring us from abroad the offers of specific firms, with specific goods, many kinds of catalogs, and also their own consumers' experience. The questions which we had ceased asking in past years are now heard more and more, namely: What does this thing cost abroad? How does its quality differ abroad from the quality here? Assignments to foreign travel will become more frequent; we must acquaint the managers of our trusts, our factory directors, our best technical students, our foremen, mechanics, specialists, in one way or another with foreign industry—of course, not all of them at once, but in a certain reasonable rotation. The purpose of such foreign travel is to enable the shock troops of our production leadership to judge any unfavorable comparison coefficient from every possible angle, and to alter such a coefficient in a favorable manner with the greatest certainty. It would be evidence of bureaucratic narrow-mindedness to imagine that our orientation toward Western countries should include only the heads of our economy. On the contrary, this orientation to the West is of a profoundly general character and is "trickling down" in many ways.

Contraband plays a fairly considerable role in this connection, a role that should not be underestimated. Contraband, while not a laudable section of our economic life, is nevertheless an important section, and besides, it is still based absolutely on the comparison coefficients of the world market, for the contraband trader only imports such foreign products as are considerably better and cheaper than our own. By the way, for just this reason, the struggle for quality in production is the best mode of combating contraband trade, which at the present time is draining dozens and dozens of millions of rubles in actual money from the country. Contraband is active particularly in small articles, but it is just these small articles that enter into every phase of our daily life.*

There is another field in which a comparison with foreign countries has really never ceased to be made; namely, that of agricultural implements and machinery. The peasant was acquainted with the Austrian scythe and always compared it with our own. He knew the American McCormick, the Canadian Harris, the Austrian Heydt, etc. Now all these comparisons, as our industry advances toward a higher level, again become quite serious, and another even more important comparison arises: the comparison between the American Ford and our tractor. When a peasant who has bought a threshing machine operated by horsepower sees a defective cast-iron rod go to pieces before his very eyes after two or three hours of work, his comment on this incident is couched in terms that exceed all our literary talents.

As for the worker, we find him interested in comparison coefficients not so much in the case of the products produced by himself as in the case of those serving him as tools or as articles of consumption. He is very well acquainted with the quality of American and Russian lathes, tools, tempering processes, precision instruments, etc. It is hardly necessary to point out that the skilled worker is very sensitive to these differences and that one of the tasks of education in production in our country consists

---

*The study of contraband commodities is extremely important both from the specialized production standpoint as well as from the general economic standpoint.—L.T.

precisely in enhancing this delicacy of feeling toward the instruments of production.

What has been said should be sufficient to prove that the comparison coefficients of world production are not a mere figment of our imagination, but a matter of extreme practical importance, reflecting, as they do, the new tasks of our economic development.

Such a system of comparison coefficients furnishes us also with a cross-section of our present-day economy in the light of the level attained by the world economy. The properly weighted average coefficient for our total production will indicate the degree of our backwardness in production in a precise numerical figure. Measured at periodic intervals, the commodities figures and the above-mentioned weighted average coefficient together will afford us a picture of what we have attained and will indicate for us our rate of progress in individual branches of industry, as well as in industry as a whole.

A man driving a wagon estimates the distance he has covered by his eye and by his hearing; but the automobile has its automatic speedometer for this purpose. Our industry will, in the future, not be permitted to proceed in its onward course without the use of international measurements of velocity, and the data obtained by these measurements will give us a point of departure not only in our most important economic measures, but also in many of our political decisions.

If it is true that the victory of any order of society depends on the superiority of the productivity of labor inherent in it—and no Marxist will dispute this statement—we need a correct quantitative and qualitative mode of measuring the production of the Soviet economy, for our current market operations as well as for the judgment of the given stage in our world-historic course.

Chapter 9
Material Limits and Possibilities
of the Rate of Economic Development

In the years 1922-24, the general industrial advance in our country was due chiefly to the advance in light industry. In the current economic year (1924-25), the primacy is beginning to pass to the industrial branches producing instruments of production. But the latter will also, for the present, continue to be restored on the basis of the old basic capital. In the impending fiscal year, in which the fixed investment capital taken over from the bourgeoisie will be exploited 100 percent, we shall already begin to undertake a renewal of our basic capital. Altogether, Gosplan is providing for 880 million rubles in capital expenditures for industry (including electrification); 236 million rubles for transportation; 375 million rubles for the construction of housing and other buildings; 300 million rubles for agriculture; a total of almost 1.8 billion rubles, of which more than 900 million rubles represent new investments, i.e., those provided by new accumulations in the whole economy. This plan, as yet only outlined and by no means officially checked, constitutes a tremendous step forward in the distribution of the material resources of the country; hitherto we have been working with the available basic capital, occasionally supplemented and renewed by us. From now on, we shall have to create our basic capital anew. Herein lies the fundamental difference between the coming economic period and that which we are leaving behind.

From the point of view of an individual administrator (let us say, the head of a trust) it might appear that the rate of development depends on the credits he can receive from the bank. "Give me so and so many millions, and I shall put up a new roof, put in new engine-lathes, increase production tenfold, bring down manufacturing costs by one-half, and attain a European quality of production"—we often have occasion to hear these words. But the fact remains that financing is never and nowhere a primary factor. The rate of economic development is determined by the material conditions of the production process itself. The already-cited explanatory remarks by Gosplan are appropriate as a reminder of this fact. "The sole universal limitation upon the possible rate of economic development," we read here, "the limitation determining in turn all the individual limiting factors, is the volume of the total national accumulation in material form, i.e., the aggregate of all newly created commodities exceeding the demands of mere reproduction, and thus constituting the material basis for extended reproduction, for reconstruction."

Bank notes, shares of stock, bonds, bills of exchange, and other securities have as such no significance in determining the volume and rate of economic development; they are mere auxiliary devices to aid in the recording and distribution of material values. Of course, from a private capitalist—or any private economic—

point of view, these certificates have an independent significance: they guarantee to their holders a certain sum of material values. But from the national economic standpoint, which under our conditions coincides in practice with the national interest, paper securities as such can have no effect on the aggregate of material products serving for the expansion of production. We must therefore proceed from this real basis of the expansion of production as our point of departure. The application of many resources by way of the budget, by way of the banks, by way of the reconstruction loan, by way of the industry fund, etc., is merely a method of distributing certain material commodities among the various branches of our economy.

In the prewar years our industry grew, on an average, 6 or 7 percent per year. This coefficient may be considered rather high, but it is quite insignificant when compared with the coefficient of today, with industry increasing 40 to 50 percent annually. But it would be a crude mistake to put these two coefficients of increase in direct juxtaposition without further ado. Before the war, the expansion of industry was effected chiefly by the construction of new factories. At present, this expansion is being accomplished to a far greater extent by the exploitation of old factories, already available, and by the utilization of the old inventory. Hence this entirely extraordinary speed of expansion. It is consequently quite natural that the coefficient of expansion will of necessity decrease when the reconstruction period comes to an end. This circumstance is of extraordinary importance, for it determines in great measure our position within the capitalist world. The struggle for our socialist "place in the sun" will necessarily be, in one way or another, a struggle to attain as high a coefficient of production expansion as possible. But the basis and also the limit—the limiting value—of this expansion remains the available mass of material values.

If all this is true, if the process of reconstruction succeeds in reestablishing the old relations between agriculture and industry in our country, between domestic and foreign markets (exports of grain and raw materials, imports of machinery and manufactured articles), would this not be equivalent to a restoration of the prewar coefficient of economic expansion, and to our declining from our present pinnacle of a 40 to 50 percent expansion annually to the 6 percent prewar expansion, after a period of a year or two? Of course, it is impossible to give a precise answer to this question at this moment. Yet we may declare with certainty: given the existence of a socialist state, a nationalized industry, and a progressively consolidated regulation of the fundamental economic processes (including exports and imports), it will be possible for us to retain, even after reaching our prewar condition, a coefficient of expansion that far exceeds our own prewar coefficient as well as the average capitalist comparison figures.

What are our points of superiority? We have already suggested what they are:

1. In our country there are no—or practically no—parasitic classes. Accumulation before the war amounted not to 6 percent but to at least twice as much. But only half of the accumulated resources was applied in production. The other half was squandered and dissipated in parasitic practices. Therefore the elimination of the monarchy, the bureaucracy, the nobility, and the bourgeoisie, will assure us—assuming the realization of the other necessary conditions—an increase of the coefficient of expansion from 6 percent to 12 percent, or at least to 9 or 10 percent.

2. The elimination of the barriers of private property affords our state the opportunity to control the necessary resources for any branch of the economy at any moment. The unproductive expenses of economic parallelism, competition, and other overlapping activities, have been much decreased and will be decreased still more in the future. It is only owing to these circumstances that it was possible for us to advance so far in the last few years without foreign assistance. In our further course, the planned distribution of resources and forces will afford us the possibility of attaining a higher production result, as compared with capitalist society, to a far greater measure than has hitherto been the case, and making use of only the same volume of resources.

3. The introduction of the economic planning principle into production methods (standardization, specialization of enterprises, combination of enterprises in a single production organization) promises us for the near future a considerable, and furthermore a continually growing, production coefficient.

4. Capitalist society lives and develops in a periodic cycle of prosperity and crisis, a cycle which, during the postwar period, has assumed the form of sporadic convulsions. To be sure, our economy, too, has not been free from crises. We may even go so far as to say that the increase in our relations with the world market involves, as we shall see in the sequel, a possible source of crises in our own economy. But there is no doubt that the increase in the habit of planned economic production and regulation in our country will blunt the peaks of the crisis curves in our development and thus assure a considerable surplus accumulation.

These are our four points of advantage, our strong points, as they have been developed in the past few years. Their significance will not decrease but rather increase after the conclusion of the reconstruction period. Considered together, these four advantages, if rightly utilized, will enable us in the next few years to increase the coefficient of our industrial expansion not only to twice the figure of 6 percent attained in the prewar period, but to three times that figure, and perhaps to even more.

But this does not exhaust the question. The advantages that have just been enumerated on the part of the socialist economy will not only give evidence of their influence in the domestic economic processes, but will be immensely enhanced by the possibilities afforded by the world market. We have hitherto considered the latter chiefly from the standpoint of the economic dangers lurking within it. But the capitalist world market not only holds dangers for us; it also presents great prospects. It enables us to secure more and more access to the accomplishments of technology, to its most complex achievements. While the world market, when it adds a socialist economic system to its other units, conjures up certain dangers for this socialist system, it also affords the socialist state powerful antidotes for these dangers, provided that state properly regulates its economic intercourse. If we use the world market for our own ends in the right way we shall be able to considerably accelerate the process of altering the comparison coefficients in favor of socialism.

There is no doubt that we shall advance along our course by cautiously and conscientiously sounding every fathom of our channel, for this channel is being navigated for the first time by our socialist boat. But all our soundings so far give promise that the channel will become broader and deeper as we advance.

Chapter 10
Socialist Development
and the Resources of the World Market

From the standpoint of the nationalized economy, as opposed to private economy, paper values cannot in themselves encourage an advance in production, any more than a man's shadow can increase his stature. But in the world economic arena the matter is quite different. American bank notes cannot in themselves create a single tractor, but a sufficient number of such bank notes, held by the Soviet state, will enable us to import tractors from the United States. In the capitalist world economic system, the Soviet state is a—gigantic—private owner: it exports its goods, imports foreign goods, requires credits, purchases foreign technical equipment; finally, it attracts foreign capital in the form of mixed companies and concessions.

Our reconstruction process has also restored us our rights on the world market. We should not forget for a moment the intricate system of interrelations existing before the war between the economy of capitalist Russia and that of world capital. It should be sufficient to point out that almost two-thirds of the installment inventory of the factories was imported from abroad, and this condition remains practically unchanged. This means that it will hardly be of advantage to us, economically, to produce more than perhaps two-fifths or at most one-half of our machinery in our own country in the next few years. If we attempt to readapt our ways and means at a leap to the production of new machines, we would either disturb the necessary proportions between the various branches of economy and between the basic and regulating capital within the same branch of the economy, or—if we retained these proportions—we would greatly retard the rate of economic expansion. A retardation of this rate, however, is far more dangerous to us than the importation of foreign machines or of any necessary foreign commodities in general.

We are borrowing foreign technology, foreign production formulas. More and more of our engineers have gone to Europe and America and those among them who have eyes to see have been bringing back everything calculated to accelerate our economic progress. We are more and more acquiring foreign technical resources by direct purchase, by connecting our trusts with prominent foreign firms who undertake to develop the production of specific products in our country within a certain time.

The decisive importance of foreign trade for our agriculture is very evident. The industrialization and consequently the collectivization of agriculture will advance parallel with the growth of our exports. In exchange for the products of agriculture we shall obtain agricultural machinery or machinery to be used in the production of agricultural machinery.

But it is not only machinery we need. Every foreign product that can fill a gap in our economic system—whether it be a raw material, an intermediate product, or an article of consumption—

may under certain circumstances accelerate the rate of our reconstruction process and thus facilitate this process. Of course, the importation of articles of luxury, articles of consumption of the parasitic type, can only retard our development. On the other hand, importing certain articles of consumption at the right time—where such articles serve to restore the necessary equilibrium in the market and fill the gaps in the workers' or peasants' budget—can only accelerate our general economic progress. In foreign trade, as conducted by the state, which elastically supplements the work of national industry and domestic commerce, we possess a mighty tool for the acceleration of our economic defense. The benevolent influence of this foreign trade will of course be greater, the more extensive the credit opportunities acquired by it in the world market.

What is the significance of foreign credits in our economic dynamics? Capitalism furnishes us with an advance on an accumulation that does not yet exist, that we still have to create—in one or two or five years. The basis of our progress is thus advanced beyond the framework of the material resources that we have accumulated so far. If with the aid of a European technical formula we are enabled to accelerate our production process, we shall be able to do this even more with the aid of an American or European machine obtained on credit. The dialectics of historical evolution involve capitalism's assuming for a certain time the role of a creditor of socialism. Did not capitalism itself draw nourishment from the breasts of feudalism? The debts of history must be paid.

The concessions must also be considered in this connection. Concessions include the furnishing of foreign machinery and foreign production methods to us and the financing of our economy out of the accumulation of world capital. In certain branches of industry the concessions may—and must—acquire a larger significance. It is superfluous to say that our concessions policy must be subject to the same limitations as private capital in general: the state retains the commanding positions in its hands and is vigilantly on guard against any assignment of a decisive predominance in the national industry to the "concessionaires." But within these limits, the concessions policy still has a broad field in which to operate.

In this connection we must also consider the "crown" of the whole system, the possible national loans. Such loans are the purest form of advance on our future socialist accumulation. The gold granted as a loan, being the "universal equivalent," enables us to purchase abroad finished products, raw materials, machines, patents; and to attract to our country from Europe and America the best mechanics and technicians. From all the above it is apparent that it is necessary for us now, more than ever, to adapt ourselves in all economic questions correctly, i.e., systematically and scientifically. What machinery is to be imported, for what enterprises, and when? What other commodities and in what order? In what proportions is the fund of capital to be distributed among the various branches of industry? What specialists must be recruited? For what economic branches shall we attract concessions capital? To what extent? For what periods?

Obviously, these questions cannot be answered from day to day, by muddling along, by considering each incident as a new case. The brains of our economists at this moment are persistently and not unsuccessfully being directed to the problem of finding systematic methods for the solution of these and many other questions indissolubly connected with them, particularly in the matter of exports. The question is to maintain the dynamic proportion between the basic branches of industry and the entire economy by inserting in this equation at the proper time such elements of the world economy as may aid in accelerating the dynamics of the process as a whole.

In the solution of the various practical questions arising from this situation, as well as in the elaboration of comprehensive plans for the future—plans covering one year, five years, or even longer terms—the use of comparison coefficients will constitute an invaluable and indispensable aid. In important branches of industry, in which the comparison coefficient yields particularly unfavorable results, the necessity will thus become apparent to look abroad for aid: for the acquisition either of finished products, patents and formulas, new machinery, specialists, or concessions. Our foreign commercial policy and our concessions policy can have a truly stimulating and systematic effect only if they are based on a generously conceived system of comparison coefficients in industry.

The same methods will in the future become a basis for deciding on the *renewal of basic capital* and expansion of production. In what branches of production must machinery be chiefly renewed? What new establishments must be built? It hardly requires stating that our needs and the anticipation of our needs exceed all possibilities of filling them. What approach must therefore be used in deciding these questions?

Before everything else, we must attain clarity on what portion of our accumulation can be devoted to the renewal of the machinery in the existing enterprises and the creation of new enterprises. The most urgent and acute needs can be covered out of our own accumulation. If access to other sources should turn out to be closed, domestic accumulation will simply have to determine the extent of the expansion of production.

But, side by side with this, it is absolutely necessary to determine the priority of our needs from the point of view of the economic process as a whole. The comparison coefficients will here indicate directly those fields in our economy that require investments of capital in the first place.

Such, in its crude outline, is the nature of the transition to a planned solution of the questions connected with the renewal and expansion of basic capital in industry, from which quite a number of complicating factors have been intentionally omitted.

Chapter 11
Socialization of the Productive Process

A state that has in its hands a nationalized industry, a monopoly of foreign trade, and a monopoly in the receiving of foreign capital for one branch of its economy or another, by this fact alone already controls a rich arsenal of resources, which it can combine to accelerate its economic development. But all these devices, though they arise from the nature of the socialist state, do not as yet impinge directly on the production process itself. In other words, had we been able to retain all the factories to the present day in the condition in which they were working in 1913, their nationalization would afford us, even if they had remained in that condition, immense advantages, through a planned and efficient distribution of resources.

The economic advances of the reconstruction period have been attained, to a very great extent, thanks to socialist methods of organizing production, i.e., thanks to planned or semiplanned methods of securing the necessary means for the various branches of the national economy. We also consider the possibilities afforded by our relations with the world market chiefly from the point of view of resources of production and not yet from the point of view of the domestic organization of industry.

But we must not forget for a moment that the fundamental advantages of socialism lie precisely in the field of production itself. These advantages, hitherto utilized by us in our Soviet economy to but a slight degree, present the most generous prospects for accelerating the rate of our economic development. The first objective, in this connection, must be a true nationalization of scientific-technical knowledge and of all industrial inventions; the second, a centralized, planned solution to the energy requirements of industry as a whole and of each branch of the economy in particular; the third, the standardization of all products; and, finally, a consistent specialization of the factories themselves.

The intellectual labor of science and technology is no longer subject in our country to the confining barriers of private property. Every organizational or technical achievement of any specific enterprise, every improvement in chemical or other formulas, at once becomes the common property of all the factories concerned. The scientific-technical institutes in our country have an opportunity to test their conjectures and hypotheses in any state factory; conversely, any of these establishments may, with the aid of the institutes, make use of all the accumulated experience of the entire industry at any moment. Scientific-technical ingenuity has in principle been socialized in our country. But we have by no means entirely liberated ourselves in this respect from the conservative barriers, partly ideological, partly material, which we acquired as a heritage together with the nationalized property taken from the capitalists. We are engaged in the process of learning how to apply on a larger scale the possibilities arising from the nationalization of scientific-technical ingenuity and invention. In this way, innumerable advantages will be obtained in the next few years; in the aggregate, these advantages will lead to the one result that is invaluable for us: the acceleration of the rate of our development.

Another source of the greatest economic saving, and consequently of enhanced labor productivity, may be found in a proper power system. The need for power is felt in every branch of industry, in all the enterprises, in fact, in all the material activity of humanity, which means that power may be considered as a more or less common factor in all branches of industry. It is obvious what a tremendous saving would be attained if we could "depersonalize" the power sources, i.e., separate them from the individual enterprises with which only private property connected them, and not considerations of technical or economic expediency. Planned electrification is only a portion of the total program of the rationalization of heat and power. Unless this program is carried out, the nationalization of the instruments of production is deprived of its most important fruits. Private property, abolished in our country as a legal institution, is the organizational form of the enterprises themselves, which are technically constituted isolated microcosms of their own. Our present task is that of permitting the principle of nationalization to permeate the production process and its material-technical conditions. It is important to truly nationalize the power resources. This applies not only to the already existing power stations but, to a far greater extent, to those still to be created. The Dnieper Valley power station (conceived as a combination of a huge power station and a great number of consumers in the field of industry and transportation) has already been constructed, right from the beginning, on the principle of socialism. The future belongs to similar enterprises conceived with the same ends in view.

A further lever of industrial progress is the standardization of products. Such standardization is applicable not only to matches, bricks, and textiles, but also to the most intricate machines. We must put a stop to the arbitrary demands of the purchaser, which are an expression not of his needs but of his helplessness. Each purchaser today is forced to improvise and grope around instead of having access to the finished samples best representing his needs, the result of scientific investigation. Standardization must reduce the number of types of a product to a minimum, by adapting them only to the peculiarities of the specific branches of the economy or to the specific character of the needs in a certain branch of production.

Standardization means socialization applied to the technical side of production. We have seen the technology of the leading capitalist countries bursting the shell of private property in this field and entering upon a path which in its very essence is a denial of the principle of competition, of "free labor," and of everything connected with it.

The United States has made tremendous progress in lowering production costs by standardizing types and qualities and by working out scientific-technical norms of production. The Bureau of Standards (Division of Simplified Practice), together with the interested producers and consumers, has carried out investigations in fields involving many dozens of large and small objects. The result has been: 500 types of files instead of 2,300; 70 types of wire cables instead of 650; 3 types of bricks instead of 119; 76

types of plows instead of 312; 29 types of sewing machines instead of almost 800; and 45 types of penknives instead of 300.

Standardization receives the newborn babe with open arms: the simplification of the baby carriage means a saving of 1,700 tons of iron and 35 tons of lead. Standardization deserts not the patient on his bed of pain: where there were 40 types of hospital beds, now there is one. Even the undertaker's art has been standardized: copper, bronze, wool, and silk have been eliminated from the production of coffins. The savings on the dead, who are thus also subjected to standardization, amount annually to thousands of tons of metal and coal, and hundreds of thousands of feet of timber.

In spite of the conditions of capitalism, technology has led to standardization; socialism is crying aloud for standardization and offers far greater possibilities for it. As yet we have hardly approached this task. Now the advance in our production has created the necessary material prerequisites for standardization. All the processes of renewal of basic capital must tend in the direction of standardization. The number of types of our products must be reduced to much fewer than the number of American types.

Standardization not only permits a higher specialization in the enterprises, but even presupposes such higher specialization. We are moving away from factories in which *anything* is produced in some way or other to factories in which *something* is produced in absolute perfection.

But to our shame it must be admitted that even now, in the ninth year of our socialist economy, we quite frequently hear from the mouths of managers, even of engineers, complaints that specialization in production destroys the "spirit," clips the wings of creativity, makes labor in the enterprise monotonous, "boring," and the like.

This whining and out-and-out reactionary view reminds one emphatically of the old Tolstoyan-populist lucubrations on the advantages of home industry as opposed to factory industry. The task of transforming all of industry into a closed, automatically operating mechanism is the most imposing problem that any community can face. It opens up an unlimited field of labor to technical, organizational, and economic creative power. But this task may only be solved by pursuing an ever bolder and more persistent specialization in industry, automation of production, and an ever more complete combination of the specialized production giants into a single producing chain.

The present achievements of foreign laboratories, the capacity of foreign power stations, the spread of American activities in standardization, and the advances of American enterprises in specialization, are far superior in these respects to our mere beginnings. But the conditions presented by our nationalized property relations are far more favorable to this goal than the conditions in any of the capitalist countries, and this advantage will become more and more victoriously evident as we march on. The problem ultimately always amounts to an estimate of all possibilities and a utilization of all resources. The results will not fail to materialize, and then will be the time to record them.

Chapter 12
Crises and Other Dangers
of the World Market

When our relations with the world market were still insignificant, the fluctuating conditions of capitalism did not operate to influence us through the channels of commodities exchange so much as through politics, in some cases exacerbating our relations with the capitalist world, in other cases ameliorating them. Under these conditions, we have become accustomed to consider our economy almost entirely independent of the economic processes at work in the capitalist world. Even after the reestablishment of our market, and therefore of market fluctuations, sales crises, etc., we continued to judge these phenomena quite independently of capitalist dynamics in Europe or America. In this we were right insofar as our reconstruction process was going on within the framework of an almost isolated economy. But with the rapid increase of exports and imports this situation is changing completely. We are becoming a portion—to be sure an extremely peculiar portion, but a portion nevertheless—of the world market, and this means that all its general factors, whenever they change in one direction or another, must also have an effect on our economy. The present economic stage is expressed most clearly in the manner in which the market operates. We appear in the same world market as a buyer and as a seller. This fact alone subjects us, to a certain extent, to the effect of ebb and flow in the trade and industry of the world market.

The significance of this situation will be made clear if we make use of a comparison to characterize the new elements it involves. Every great economic upheaval has obliged public opinion in our country to occupy itself intensively with the question of whether and to what extent crises are inevitable with us, etc. In these questions, owing to the nature of our economic situation, we usually did not transcend the framework of a nearly isolated economy. We contrasted the principle of economic planning, whose economic basis is nationalized industry, and the elemental principle of the market, whose economic basis is the village. The combination of a definite plan with a force of nature is the more difficult for us, as the economic elemental force depends on a force of nature. The following prospect necessarily presented itself: the advance of the principle of economic planning will continue in the same measure as the advance of industry, the advance of its influence on agriculture, the advance of industrialization, the development of cooperatives in the provinces, etc. This process—however we may estimate its speed—was conceived as an ascending one. But here too the path follows a zigzag and we have come to a new *turn*. This is most apparent in grain exports.

We are here concerned not only with the crops but also with the realization of these crops, not only on our own market but also on the European market. Grain exports to Europe depend on Europe's purchasing power; the purchasing power of the industrial countries (of course it is the industrial countries which import grain) in turn depends on the economic situation. When there is a crisis in trade and industry, Europe will import much less grain from us, and far less timber, flax, furs, oil, etc., than in industrial boom periods. Our decline in exports will necessarily be followed by a decline in imports. If we cannot export a sufficient quantity of industrial raw material, we shall also not be able to import the necessary machines, cotton, etc. If, as a consequence of the incomplete realization of our export stocks, the purchasing power of the peasants should turn out to be lower than we have foreseen, this might lead to a crisis of overproduction; in the opposite case—where we suffer a commodities famine—we would be deprived, if our exports are reduced, of the possibility of remedying this lack by importing finished products, the necessary machines, and raw materials (for instance cotton, already mentioned). In other words, a commercial and industrial crisis in Europe, and still worse, a universal crisis of this kind, may produce a wave of crises in each country. On the other hand, in the event of a considerable boom in European trade and industry, the demand

for timber and flax, raw materials needed for industry, will necessarily increase; likewise the demand for grain, of which Europe's population can consume much larger quantities when its
economic conditions are favorable. In this manner a boom in
trade and industry in Europe will give the necessary stimulus to
our advance in trade, industry, and agriculture by facilitating our
turnover of export products. Our former independence of the
fluctuations of the world market is disappearing. All the fundamental processes of our economy are not only becoming connected with the corresponding processes dominant in the world
market, but are also becoming subject in some degree to the
operation of the laws dominant in capitalist development, including changes in economic conditions. There arises a situation in
which we, as a business entity, are interested within certain
limits in an improvement in the conditions in capitalist countries,
and in which, on the other hand, we may be made to suffer some
disadvantage as a result of a worsening of these conditions.

This circumstance, somewhat surprising at first glance, is
merely a more emphatic expression of the contradiction involved
in the very nature of the so-called NEP, already mentioned by us
in connection with the narrower limits of the isolated national
economy. Our present order is based not only on the struggle of
socialism against capitalism, but within certain limits on cooperation between socialism and capitalism. In the interest of developing our productive forces we not only permit trade of a private
capitalist type, but we even encourage such trade and—also
within certain limits!—foster it in the form of concessions and
leases of factories. We have a very great interest in the development of our peasant economy, although it now has an almost
exclusively private commodities character, and although its
growth affords advantages not only to the socialist but also to the
capitalist tendencies of our development. The danger involved in
this coexistence and cooperation between two economic systems—that of capitalism and that of socialism (the latter applying the methods of the former)—lies in the possibility that the
capitalist forces may get the better of us.

But this danger was already present within the limits of the
"isolated" economy,* although on a smaller scale. The significance of Gosplan's control figures consists precisely in the fact

---

*We hardly need to point out that our economy never was perfectly
isolated, and that we are merely contrasting pure economic types for
greater simplicity.—L.T.

that these figures, as we have shown in our first chapters, prove beyond dispute the predominance of the socialist tendencies over the capitalist tendencies, on the basis of the general advance of the productive forces. If it were our intention (or rather, if it were possible for us) to remain an economically isolated state forever, we might consider this question solved in principle. Danger would then threaten us only in the political field, or in the event of a military penetration of our isolation from outside. But now that we have entered the field of the universal division of labor, economically speaking, and have thus become subject to the operation of the laws controlling the world market, the cooperation and struggle between the capitalist and socialist tendencies in the economy acquire far greater proportions, which involves greater and greater hardships.

There exists therefore a profound and very natural analogy between the questions that faced us within our domestic economy when the NEP was first introduced, and those now arising from our closer relation with the world market system. But the analogy is not a perfect one. The cooperation and struggle between capitalist and socialist tendencies within Soviet territory proceed under the watchful eye of the proletarian state. While the state authority may not be omnipotent in economic questions, the economic power of the state is nonetheless tremendous when it is consciously supporting the progressive tendencies of historical development. While it grants the existence of capitalist tendencies, the workers' state can hold them in check to a certain extent by favoring and encouraging the socialist tendencies. The instruments that may be used in this connection are: the national budget system and measures of a general administrative character; domestic and foreign commerce; state encouragement of the consumers' cooperative movement; a concessions policy strictly adapted to national needs. In short: *a versatile system of socialist protectionism*. These measures presuppose a dictatorship of the proletariat, and the sphere of their activities is thus limited to the territory of the dictatorship. In the countries with which we are entering into wider and wider commercial relations, precisely the opposite system prevails: capitalist protectionism in the broadest sense of the word. Herein lies the difference. On Soviet territory the socialist economy is fighting the capitalist economy, but it has the workers' state on its side! On the territory of the world market, socialism must face capitalism, the latter protected by the imperialist state. Here not only does economy fight economy, but politics fights politics. The monopoly of foreign trade and the concessions policy are powerful tools of the economic policy of the workers' state. If, in consequence, the laws and methods of the socialist state may not be forced on the world market, the relation of the socialist economy to the world market nevertheless depends to a great extent on the will of the workers' state. Consequently, as we have already indicated, a rightly applied system of foreign trade will be of exceptional importance, and the function of the concessions policy of the workers' state will increase in importance in connection with this.

Of course it will be impossible to exhaust this subject here. Our task now is merely to formulate the question, which may be divided into two sections: (1) By what methods and to what extent will the planning and guidance of the workers' state be capable of protecting our economy against the influence of the fluctuations of the capitalist market; and (2) to what extent and by what methods may the workers' state protect the future development of the socialist tendencies of our economy against the capitalist pitfalls of the world market?

These two questions were also faced within the limits of the "isolated" economy. But they attain a new and increased importance in the larger arena of the world market. In both arenas, the element of planning in the economy is now attaining an incomparably greater significance than in the preceding period. The market would unquestionably subject us to its rule if we were fighting the market alone, for the world market is stronger than we. It would weaken us by its acute economic fluctuations, and once having weakened us it would coerce us with the quantitative and qualitative superiority of its mass of commodities.

We know that an ordinary capitalist trust is at pains to protect itself against the influence of acute fluctuations in supply and demand. Even a trust that is practically a monopoly does not aim to fill the market completely with its products at any given moment. In a period of emphatic prosperity, the trusts quite frequently tolerate the existence of nontrustified enterprises, permitting the latter to cover the surplus demand, and thus freeing themselves from risky investments of new 'capital. These nontrustified enterprises then fall victim to an ensuing crisis, after which they are frequently bought up for a song by the big trusts. The next boom is now faced by the trust with larger productive forces. When the demand again exceeds its own production, the trust again resorts to the same game. In other words, the capitalist trusts aim to cover only an absolutely assured demand, and to expand only with the assured expansion of the demand, assigning, as far as possible, all risk associated with fluctuations of economic conditions to weaker and temporary organizations which play, as it were, the role of a reserve army in production. Of course, this outline has not been followed in every case and in all places, but it is nevertheless a typical process and may therefore serve as an illustration of our thought.

Socialist industry is a "trust of all trusts." This gigantic producing body can afford even far less than a specific capitalist trust to undertake to follow all the curves of market demand. Trustified state industry must attempt to cover a demand that is assured on the basis of the entire preceding development, making use, as far as possible, of the private capitalist reserve army in order to cover the momentary surplus demand, which may be followed by a new constriction of the market. The function of such a reserve army is discharged by our domestic private industry, including the concessions industries, and by the world market's aggregate of commodities. This was what we had in mind above when we spoke of the significance of the domestic trade system and the concessions policy as a regulator.

The state imports such instruments of production, such raw materials, such articles of consumption, as are absolutely necessary for the maintenance, improvement, and planned expansion of the production process. Simplifying the extremely complicated mutual relations into a crude outline, the matter assumes the following aspect. In boom periods in foreign trade and in world industry, our exports will increase by an additional amount, but the purchasing power of the population will also increase. It is therefore quite clear that should our industry at once expend all its financial resources in order to import machines and raw materials for the expansion of the branches of industry concerned, the next world crisis, which would involve a reduction of our economic resources, would condemn those branches of industry that had ventured too far out—and simultaneously, to a certain extent, *all* our industry—to a crisis. Of course, such phenomena are inevitable to a certain extent. The peasant economy on the one hand, and the world market on the other hand—these are the two sources of crisis-creating fluctuations. But the art of economic policy will consist in covering any powerful increase of domestic demand only in its assured portion out of state production; and on the other hand, in covering the momentary excess demand by importing finished products at the appropriate time and involving private capital. Under such circumstances, a momentary depression in world conditions cannot have a very great effect on our nationalized industry.

The peasant economy constitutes an extremely important—in some cases, even decisive—factor in this entire work of regulation. We learn from this fact alone how great a significance is attached to such forms of organization as the cooperatives and an elastic state commercial apparatus, if the isolated small peasant economy should continue. These organizations will make it possible to calculate and predict the fluctuations in the supply and demand of commodities in the village.

But does not the process of our "growing into" the world market involve still greater dangers? Are we not threatened with the severing of numerous threads of life in case of war or blockade? It must not be forgotten that the capitalist world is our mortal enemy, etc., etc. This thought harasses the brains of many. You will find among those in charge of production quite a number of unconscious or semiconscious adherents of an "isolated" economy. We must also devote a few words to this question. Of course, both the loans and the concessions, as well as the greater dependence on our exports and imports, involve certain dangers. It follows that we may not go to excess in any of these directions. But there is also an opposite and by no means smaller danger. It consists in delaying our economic progress, in retarding the speed of its advance; this danger is not less than that involved in an active utilization of all the possibilities of world relations. But we have no choice in the selection of our rate of development, living and growing, as we are, under the pressure of world economy!

The argument as to the dangers of war or blockade after we have "grown into" the world market might perhaps seem somewhat farfetched and abstract. For, in strengthening us economically, the international exchange in all its forms also strengthens us for the eventuality of a blockade or a war. There is no doubt that our enemies may still desire to put us to this test. But, on the one hand, the more varied our international economic relations become, the more difficult our potential enemies will find it to disrupt these relations. And, on the other hand, if this thing should nevertheless come to pass, we shall give a far better account of ourselves than would be possible in the case of an isolated and therefore retarded development.

We may learn a little in this connection from the historical experience of bourgeois countries. Germany had developed a tremendous industry by the end of the nineteenth and the beginning of the twentieth century, and became an extremely active force in the world economy by reason of this industry. Its foreign trade and its relations with foreign—including overseas—markets developed to huge proportions within a short period. The war put an abrupt end to this situation. By reason of its geographic position, Germany was forced into an almost complete economic isolation from the first day of the war. And yet the entire world was then made to understand the extraordinary vitality and endurance of this highly industrialized country. The preceding struggle for sales markets had developed an unusual elasticity in Gemany's productive apparatus, which it then proceeded—during the war—to utilize, in the now constricted national field, to the last penny.

The universal division of labor is not a circumstance that we can afford to ignore. We can only accelerate our own development in all fields by expediently utilizing the means arising from it.

Conclusion

In my whole presentation thus far I have kept to the base of the economic process and its logical evolution, so to speak. In this manner I have consciously kept out of the field almost all other factors, which not only influence economic development but may possibly impart an entirely opposite direction to it. Such a one-sided economic analysis is perfectly justified and necessary, from a methodological standpoint, in a bird's-eye view of an extremely complicated process, extending over a great number of years. The practical solutions of the moment must in each case be found, as far as possible, by considering *all* the factors as they are juxtaposed at present. But in taking a general view of economic development over a long period, the "superstructural" factors must be eliminated, in particular the factor of politics. A war, for example, might exercise a decisive influence on our development in one direction, while a victorious European revolution would tend to affect it in the opposite direction. And this is true not only of events coming from without. Our internal economic processes produce a complicated political reflex action, which in turn may develop into a factor of very great importance. The economic differentiation of the village—which, as we have already shown, by no means involves any direct *economic* dangers, i.e., dangers of a rapid increase of the capitalist tendencies at the expense of the socialist tendencies—may nevertheless under certain circumstances produce *political* tendencies having an unfavorable influence on socialist development.

Political conditions, domestic as well as international, constitute a complicated concatenation of problems, each of which needs to be considered alone—of course, in close connection with the economic situation. Such an analysis was not essential to the tasks of this book. An outline of the fundamental tendencies of the development of the economic base, of course, is not meant to furnish a perfect explanation of all the alterations in the political superstructure, which has its own internal logic as well as its own tasks and difficulties. A general economic orientation will not take the place of a political orientation, but will merely facilitate it.

We have, therefore, in the course of our analysis, entirely neglected the question of the possible duration of the capitalist order, the alterations it will encounter, and the direction of its development. A number of variants are possible in this field, and while it is not our intention to discuss them in these concluding lines, we shall nevertheless indicate their outline. Perhaps we may have occasion in some later book to touch upon this problem again.

The question of the victory of socialism will attain its most simple solution if the proletarian revolution should develop in Europe during the next few years. This "variant" is by no means the most improbable. But from the point of view of socialist prognosis, this situation would constitute no difficulty for us. It is obvious that a merging of the economy of the Soviet Union with the economy of a Soviet Europe would victoriously solve the question of the comparative coefficients of socialist and capitalist production, however great might be the resistance offered by America. And it may be doubted whether this resistance would be of long duration.

The question becomes extremely complicated if we provisionally assume that the capitalist world that surrounds us is still to endure for a number of decades. But such a presupposition would be perfectly without meaning per se, unless we rendered it more concrete by means of a number of other presuppositions. What is to become, given this variant, of the European proletariat, and of course the American proletariat? What will be the productive forces of capital? If the decades conditionally assumed by us should be decades of stormy ebb and flow, of cruel civil war, of economic stagnation or even decay, i.e., a long drawn-out labor preceding the birth of socialism, it is obvious that our economy would attain a predominant strength in this transition period, if only by reason of the incomparably greater stability of our economic foundations.

But if we assume that in the course of the next few decades a new dynamic equilibrium will take shape on the world market, let us say of the type of expanded reproduction represented by the period from 1871 to 1914, the question will assume an entirely different form. Such an "equilibrium" as that assumed here would be equivalent to a new unfolding of the productive forces; for the relative "love of peace" on the part of the bourgeoisie and the proletariat, and the opportunistic readjustment of the Socialist parties and the trade unions in the period preceding the world war were possible enough by reason of an immense boom in industry. It is perfectly clear that the improbable will become real if the impossible becomes possible. If world capitalism, and more specifically European capital, should find a new dynamic equilibrium (not for its unstable government combinations but for its productive forces); if capitalist production in the next few years or decades should experience a new great rebirth; this would put us, the socialist state, in the peculiar position of being obliged—though already engaged in changing from our slow freight train to the faster passenger train—to catch up with a first-class express. Putting the matter more simply, this would mean that we were mistaken in our fundamental historical judgments. It would mean that capitalism has not yet exhausted its historic "mission," and that the imperialist phase now unfolding before us does not constitute a phase of capitalist disintegration, its death struggle, but rather the necessary precondition for a new period of prosperity.

It is clear that under the conditions of a new capitalist rebirth in Europe and in the whole world, possibly enduring for many years, socialism in a backward country would find itself eye to eye with colossal dangers. What would be the nature of these dangers? They might be the dangers involved in a new war, a war which the European proletariat, "pacified" anew by prosperous conditions, would again be unable to prevent, and in which our enemy would have a colossal technical advantage over us. Or they might take the form of a deluge of capitalist goods produced far better and more cheaply than our own goods, which might smash our foreign trade monopoly and together with it the other bases of our socialist economy. This is at bottom a question of minor importance. But it is absolutely clear to all Marxists that socialism in a backward country would be hard pressed if capitalism should again be given an opportunity not just to vegetate but to develop the productive forces of the most advanced countries for a long period of years.

But the reasons adduced in favor of this second variant are by no means serious reasons, and it would therefore be idiotic to develop a perspective extremely favorable to the capitalist world and then break our heads over the methods of counteracting this fictitious situation. The European economic system and the world economic system at present represent such a mass of contradictions—contradictions which, far from favoring the course of its development, undermine this process at every step— that history will offer us in the next few years a sufficient opportunity for the achievement of an accelerated growth rate, provided only that we utilize all the resources of our own economic system and the world economic system. Needless to say, it is our object to do this. Parallel with this, European development will also, in the meantime, shift the "coefficient" of *political* power in the direction of the revolutionary proletariat, though it be with delays and minor deviations. In general, it must be assumed that the historical balance sheet will turn out more than favorable to us.

Table 1

CONTROL FIGURES OF THE NATIONAL ECONOMY, 1925-26.

General Table of the Control Figures for the National Economy of the Union of Socialist Soviet Republics for 1925-26.

	In pre-war prices (In millions of rubles)			Present prices in Commodity rubles		Present prices in Chervonets rubles		As a percentage of 1913 — In pre-war prices		As a percentage of 1913 — Present prices in Commodity rubles		As a percentage of the preceding year — In pre-war prices		As a percentage of the preceding year — Present prices in Commodity rubles		As a percentage of the preceding year — Present prices in Chervonets rubles	
	1913	1924-25	1925-26	1924-25	1925-26	1924-25	1925-26	1924-25	1925-26	1924-25	1925-26	1924-25	1925-26	1924-25	1925-26	1924-25	1925-26
I.—Production																	
A—Agriculture																	
Farming (and stock raising)	11,782	8,106	10,236	7,620	9,720	13,273	16,019	69	87	65	82	102	126	121	128	121	121
Forestry, fisheries, game.	1,044	1,044	1,200	980	1,140	1,767	1,878	100	115	94	109	101	115	121	116	120	106
Total for agriculture...	12,826	9,150	11,436	8,600	10,860	15,490	17,897	71	89	67	85	102	125	121	126	121	116
B—Industry																	
Nationalized large-scale industry	5,621	3,950	5,280	4,190	5,540	7,520	9,150	70	94	75	99	154	134	129	132	136	122
Small industry	1,390	1,050	1,370	1,110	1,440	2,000	2,370	76	99	80	104	130	130	108	130	114	119
Total for industry	7,011	5,000	6,650	5,300	6,980	9,520	11,520	71	95	76	100	148	133	124	132	131	121
Total of production ...	19,837	14,150	18,086	13,900	17,840	25,010	29,417	71	91	70	90	114	128	122	128	124	118
II.—Total Marketable Commodities																	
A—Agriculture (Including commodities exchanged within agricultural domain)																	
Farming (and stock raising)	3,988	2,537	3,139	2,385	2,982	4,295	4,913	64	79	60	75		124		125		114
Forestry, fisheries, game.	510	320	500	300	475	542	783	63	98	59	93		156		158		144
Total for agriculture ..	4,498	2,857	3,639	2,685	3,457	4,837	5,696	64	81	60	77		127		129		118
B—Industry																	
Large-scale industry	5,261	3,400	4,140	3,600	4,350	6,480	7,170	65	79	68	83	153	122		121		111
Small industry	1,390	1,050	1,370	1,110	1,440	2,000	2,370	76	99	80	104	130	130		130		119
Total for industry ...	7,011	4,450	5,510	4,710	5,790	8,480	9,540	63	79	67	83	147	124	122	123	130	113

Table 1, continued.

In millions of rubles (columns under "In pre-war prices", "Present prices in Commodity rubles", "Present prices in Chervonets rubles"); *As a percentage of 1913*; *As a percentage of the preceding year.*

	In pre-war prices 1913	In pre-war prices 1924-25	In pre-war prices 1925-26	Present prices in Commodity rubles 1924-25	Present prices in Commodity rubles 1925-26	Present prices in Chervonets rubles 1924-25	Present prices in Chervonets rubles 1925-26	% 1913: pre-war 1924-25	% 1913: pre-war 1925-26	% 1913: Commodity 1924-25	% 1913: Commodity 1925-26	% prec. yr: pre-war 1924-25	% prec. yr: pre-war 1925-26	% prec. yr: Commodity 1924-25	% prec. yr: Commodity 1925-26	% prec. yr: Chervonets 1924-25	% prec. yr: Chervonets 1925-26
Total domestic commodities	11,509	7,307	9,149	7,395	9,247	13,317	15,236	63	79	64	80		125		125		114
Total domestic commodities, including imports:																	
Agriculture	4,795	3,002	3,828			5,092	6,171	63	80				128				121
Industry	7,721	4,644	5,839			8,821	10,015	60	76				126				114
Total commodities	12,516	7,646	9,667			13,913	16,186	61	77				126				110
III.—Foreign Trade (Over the European frontier)																	
Exports																	
Agriculture	927	204	559			354	950	22	60				274				268
Industry	378	66	121			108	150	17	32				183				139
Total exports	1,305	270	680			462	1,100	21	52				252				238
Imports																	
Agriculture	297	145	189			255	475	49	64				130				186
Industry	710	194	329			341	475	27	46				170				139
Total imports	1,007	339	518			596	950	34	51				153				159
IV.—Stocks of Money																	
At the beginning of the year	2,041	379	693	379	693	623	1,157	19	34	19	34		183		183		186
At the end of the year	2,076	693	1,261	693	1,261	1,157	1,973	33	61	33	61		182		182		171
Average for the year	2,058	496	950	496	950	890	1,565	24	46	24	46		192		192		176
V.—Wholesale Price Index of the State Planning Commission																	

THE NATIONAL ECONOMY, 1925-26.

Item	(1)	(2)	(3)	Index A	Index B	(6)	(7)	(8)	(9)	(10)	(11)
Prices of Agricultural Products											
At the beginning of the year	1.000	0.83	0.93	1.359	1.524	83	93	140	112	155	112
At the end of the year	1.000	0.93	0.93	1.576	1.460	93	93	111	100	112	93
Average for the year...	1.000	0.94	0.95	1.693	1.565	94	95	119	101	126	92
Prices of Industrial Products											
At the beginning of the year	1.000	1.21	1.08	1.984	1.778	121	108	113	89	79	90
At the end of the year	1.000	1.07	1.07	1.809	1.678	107	107	90	100	91	93
Average for the year...	1.000	1.06	1.05	1.905	1.733	106	105	83	99	88	91
General Commodity Price Index											
At the beginning of the year	1.000	1.00	1.00	1.642	1.646	100	100	100	100	110	100
At the end of the year	1.000	1.00	1.00	1.689	1.565	100	100	100	100	101	93
Average for the year...	1.000	1.00	1.00	1.796	1.647	100	100	100	100	106	92
For domestic commodities, total	1.000	1.00		1.822	1.665	100		100			91
For commodities, including imports, total	1.000	1.00		1.820	1.674	100		100			92
VI.—Deposit and Current Accounts											
At the beginning of the year	3,844	337	640	554	1,067	17	9	17	190	190	193
At the end of the year	4,214	640	1,534	1,067	2,400	36	15	36	240	240	225
Average for the year...	3,956	452	1,052	811	1,733	27	11	27	233	233	214
VII.—Loan and Discount Operations, including Long-term Credits											
At the beginning of the year	4,400	572	1,139	940	1,900	26	13	26	199	199	202
At the end of the year	4,800	1,139	2,428	1,900	3,800	51	24	51	213	213	200
Average for the year...	4,500	791	1,730	1,420	2,850	38	18	38	219	219	201
VIII.—Budget*	2,919	1,392	2,064	2,500	3,400	71	48	71	148	148	136

* Not including the following: Transfers to local budgets; cost of newly-coined money; the amount of the peasant loan bonds that were turned into the national treasury in payment of taxes.

Table 2

MONTHLY WAGES OF WORKERS IN LARGE SCALE INDUSTRY

Branches of Industry	1913	1923-24	1924-25 The full year	1924-25 Second half of year	1925-26	1924-25	1925-26
			(Nominal) wages in rubles (In Chervonets gold rubles beginning with 1923-24)			The same figures in percentages of preceding year	
1. Mining	33.0	32.8	36.8	38.7	45.1*	112.2	122.5
Including:							
Coal	34.4	32.5	36.1	38.0	43.1	111.1	119.4
Petroleum	30.5	33.9	40.8	45.2	45.1	120.4	110.5
2. Metallurgy	35.4	39.4	48.7	51.5	57.7	123.6	118.5
3. Textiles	17.0	32.1	36.4	37.8	40.8	113.4	112.1
Including:							
Cotton	17.3	33.0	37.4	38.8	41.8	113.3	111.8
4. Chemical Industries	20.0	35.9	41.1	41.1	43.1	114.5	104.9
Including:							
Matches †	14.3	25.5	28.8	28.8	31.8	112.9	110.4
Rubber †	30.0	55.2	68.0	68.0	71.0	123.2	104.4
5. Foodstuffs	16.0	46.9	55.1	55.1	58.1	117.5	105.4
6. Woodworking Industries	22.0	45.6	44.1	44.1	47.1	96.7	106.8
7. Paper	18.0	36.6	39.9	39.9	42.9	109.0	107.5
8. Graphic Arts	32.0	66.7	69.2	69.2	72.2	103.7	104.3
9. Leather	25.0	48.3	54.0	54.0	57.0	111.8	105.6
10. Needle Industries	......	41.0	54.0	54.0	57.0	131.7	105.6
Average	25.0	35.2	41.5	43.5	48.0‡	117.9	115.7
Real wages	25.0	16.8	20.7	21.0	25.0§	123.2	120.8
As a percentage of 1913	100	67.2	82.8	84.0	100	......	......

* The average wage is being increased in 1925-26 owing to the addition of ore-mining establishments to this group.
† Pre-war figures for the match and rubber industries were calculated on the basis of the movement of the industries within the last years and on the assumption that at the end of the projected period wages would attain the pre-war level.
‡ Wages for labour in 1925-26 include a three-ruble allowance for rent.
§ In calculating real wages, the rent allowance is *not* included (being a supplementary item for a fixed and definite purpose).

Table 3

CAPITAL FUNDS OF THE UNION OF SOCIALIST
SOVIET REPUBLICS* AS OF OCTOBER 1, 1924

(In millions of Chervonets rubles.)

Class of Funds	State	Cooper-ative	Total	Private	Grand Total
1. Agriculture:					
(a) Livestock, etc.	45	5	50	4,891	4,941
(b) Implements and other working inventory	13	2	15	1,571	1,586
Total	58	7	65	6,462	6,527
2. Transportation	6,050	......	6,050	......	6,050
3. Large scale industry	4.572	87	4,659	33	4,692
4. Small industry	14	86	100	544	644
5. Public buildings, works, etc.	338	......	338	......	338
6. Dwellings	6,422	153	6,575	13,017	19,592
7. Trade and commerce	669	384	1,053	419	1,472
Total of 1-7	18,123	717	18,840	20,475	39,315
Percentages	46.1	1.8	47.9	52.1	100
Total (1-7) without dwellings	11,701	564	12,265	7,458	19,723
Percentages	59.3	2.9	62.2	37.8	100
1. The Country:					
Means of agricultural production	58	7	65	6,462	6,527
Small industry	......	......	......	430	430
Public buildings, works, etc.	38	......	38	......	38
Dwellings	258	28	286	9,720	10,006
Trade and commerce	66	142	208	209	417
Total	420	177	597	16,821	17,418
Not including dwellings	162	149	311	7,101	7,412
2. The City:					
Large scale industry	4,572	87	4,659	33	4,692
Small industry	14	86	100	114	214
Transportation	6,050	......	6,050	......	6,050
Dwellings	6,164	125	6,289	3,297	9,586
Public buildings, works, etc.	300	......	300	......	300
Trade and commerce	603	242	845	210	1,055
Total	17,703	540	18,243	3,654	21,897
Not including dwellings	11,539	415	11,954	357	12,311

* Prepared from the (incomplete) calculations of the Central Statistical
Department, with corrections and additions by the State Planning
Commission.

Table 4

CONCENTRATION OF WORKERS IN LARGE SCALE INDUSTRY IN THE UNION OF SOCIALIST SOVIET REPUBLICS AND IN THE UNITED STATES

Size of establishment according to number of workers	Union of Socialist Soviet Republics (Factories, mills, mines and smelters)						U.S.A. Manufactures (Establishments of more than 21 workers)					
	Number of establishments			Number of workers			Number of establishments			Number of workers		
	1901	1911	1925	1901	1911	1925	1909	1919	1923	1909	1919	1923
Absolute fixtures:												
1. Up to 50 workers	14,354	11,754	3,723	287,264	269,626	92,300	23,544	25,379	25,253	764,408	829,301	818,403
2. From 51 to 500 workers	5,667	5,553	2,971	802,772	848,169	459,200	21,985	26,072	26,195	3,047,394	3,720,982	3,790,090
3. Over 500 workers	874	995	681	1,179,893	1,424,040	1,212,700	1,763	2,770	2,756	1,850,747	3,603,223	3,335,994
Total	20,895	18,302	7,375	2,269,929	2,541,835	1,764,200	47,292	54,221	54,204	5,662,549	8,153,506	7,944,487
The Same in Percentages:												
1. Up to 50 workers	68.7	64.2	50.5	12.7	10.6	5.2	49.8	46.8	46.6	13.5	10.1	10.3
2. From 51 to 500 workers	27.1	30.3	40.3	35.3	33.4	26.0	46.5	48.1	48.3	53.8	46.5	47.7
3. Over 500 workers	4.2	5.5	9.2	52.0	56.0	68.8	3.7	5.1	5.1	32.7	44.3	42.0
Total	100.0	100.0	100.0	100.0	100.0	100.0	100.0	100.0	100.0	100.0	100.0	100.0
Average number of workers per single establishment	……	……	……	108.7	139	239	……	……	……	120	151	147

A SPLIT IN THE TRIUMVIRATE

NOTE: The disunity within the triumvirate culminated in an open split at the Fourteenth Party Congress (December 18-31, 1925), where Zinoviev and Kamenev denounced socialism in one country, the lack of planned industrialization, and the course Stalin and Bukharin were following toward the peasant. Although he apparently was aware before the congress of the differences within the triumvirate, Trotsky underestimated their scope and their importance. Preoccupied with his duties in the Supreme Council of the National Economy, he had not been following the growth of dissent in the Politburo; and he was especially disarmed to see that it was Zinoviev, who had been the most vicious member of the triumvirate and the most outspoken representative of its policies, who was mobilizing his followers in the Leningrad party organization and leading them in a retreat from the right-wing program. When the discussion came into the open at the congress, Trotsky did not participate. He regarded it initially as an intrabureaucratic squabble. Then his illness recurred. It was not until the spring of 1926 that he would meet with Zinoviev and Kamenev to form the United Opposition; by that time the strength of the Leningrad Opposition had been broken and its leadership dispersed.

"A 'Bloc' with Zinoviev (For a Diary)," translated by Marilyn Vogt, and "An Analysis of the Slogans and Differences," translated by Pat Galligan and George Saunders, were written before the congress. "On the Leningrad Opposition," translated by Marilyn Vogt, was written during the congress. All three translations were made for this volume from copies in the open section of the Trotsky archives, by permission of the Harvard College Library. None of the notes was ever published. They all appear to have been written for Trotsky's own use in attempting to figure out what was developing. It was only some months later that he decided on forming a bloc.—Ed.

A 'Bloc' with Zinoviev (For a Diary)

December 9, 1925

I. The Sources of the Present Discussion and Its Methods

1. The party discussion which is now unfolding between the Leningrad organization and the Central Committee, and which is becoming more and more heated, has its social roots in the relations between the proletariat and the peasantry under conditions of capitalist encirclement. Neither side has made any specific, practical proposals that would alter in one way or another the economic and political relationship of forces between the proletariat and the peasantry. The legalization of the leasing of land and the hiring of farm labor were carried out, to the best of the party's knowledge, without any internal struggle. The reduction of the agricultural tax went through in the same way. When measures for the grain collection campaign were being worked out there was no noticeable division within the Central Committee between supporters of high prices and supporters of low prices. The same is true of the decision on the size of wage increases. There was no evidence of differences either, as far as the party could tell, when the national budget for 1925-26 was being drawn up. In other words, on all the questions that directly or indirectly determine the scope and tempo of development in industry and in its different branches, the amount of assistance to the peasant economy by way of its various layers; or on questions that directly or indirectly determine the share of the working class (wages, etc.) in the wealth produced by the economy as a whole; there has been no indication of disagreements between the Central Committee majority and its minority, based on the Leningrad organization. Finally, the resolutions of the October plenum, which drew the balance sheet on all the work indicated above, and which formed the basis of the resolution that the Central Committee is presenting to the congress, were unanimously adopted.

2. Nevertheless, the struggle surrounding the unanimously adopted resolutions is becoming more and more heated, though primarily organizational in character and reflected only partly and rather formlessly in the press and in the discussion. The party, or rather, the party's higher, better-informed ranks, have

become witnesses to, and semi-passive participants in, an extremely ferocious apparatus struggle over key questions of the relations between the proletariat and the peasantry; yet no specific legislative proposals or counterproposals are made and no platforms clarifying the opposing principles are presented.

3. As far as the essence of the differences is concerned, it undoubtedly arises, as has already been said, from the general orientation of the two fundamental classes—from their desire to establish, or to define more precisely, their relationship to one another in the present, new stage of development, from their apprehensions about the future, etc. As for the forms and methods of the dispute, they result entirely from the party regime as it has taken shape over the past two or three years.

4. The extraordinary difficulty, at least at the present stage, in determining the real class essence of the differences is engendered by the absolutely unprecedented role of the party apparatus; in this respect it has gone far beyond what existed even a year ago. One need only consider the significance of the fact that in Leningrad a resolution directed against the Central Committee was adopted unanimously or virtually unanimously at the same time that the Moscow organization unanimously—without a single abstention—adopted a resolution directed against Leningrad. It is quite obvious that local circumstances, rooted in the composition and work of the apparatus of party secretaries, and not in the life of the masses themselves, played a decisive role in this striking phenomenon. Certain mass moods, which have no chance of being represented at all accurately through the mass organizations, trade unions, or party, make their way through to the upper party circles by obscure and roundabout means or by open disturbances (strikes), thus setting into motion certain lines of thinking and subsequently either gaining a firm foothold or not, depending on the wishes of the apparatus in charge of a particular area.

II. The Essence of the Differences

5. Nevertheless, it is no accident that Leningrad ended up as the site of the apparatus's opposition to the Central Committee. The party's complicated and protracted maneuvers with respect to the countryside, the growth of the economic and political weight of the rural areas in the overall life of the country, the increasing stratification in the countryside, the failure of industry to keep up with the demands of the market, the appearance of one or another discrepancy in the economy, the

relatively slow rise of wages, the pressure of rural unemployment—all this put together cannot help but give rise to anxieties about the future among precisely the most thoughtful elements of the proletariat. Regardless of whether this or that discrepancy results from mistakes in foresight and leadership or from objective factors (in reality, of course, both occur), facts are still facts, and since these problems are not thrashed out in systematic public and party discussions, they do from time to time become the source of moods of alarm that in turn lead to fits of panic in the apparatus, as undoubtedly is occurring in Leningrad.

6. While dismissing all the demagogy, the search for popular slogans, the defense mechanisms of the apparatus, etc., one must still say that the position taken by the upper circles in Leningrad is a bureaucratically distorted expression of the political anxiety felt by the most advanced section of the proletariat over the course of our economic development as a whole and over the fate of the dictatorship of the proletariat.*

Of course, what has been said does not mean that workers in other parts of the country do not share this anxiety or that in Leningrad it has spread to the entire working class. The question of where and how these moods find expression depends to an enormous degree on the apparatus of party secretaries.

7. The character of the struggle—muffled and confined for the time being to the top circles—results in an extremely schematic, doctrinaire, and even scholastic character in the ideological reflections that have appeared. Suppressed and stifled by the unanimity of the apparatus, party thought, when it encounters new

---

*References to the fact that Comrade Sokolnikov—who in all instances counterposes his misinterpretation of the interests of the countryside and the private trading sector to the vital interests of industry—is in a bloc with the leaders of the Leningrad organization is by no means an argument against the above characterization of the function and meaning of the Leningrad Opposition. The muffled apparatus struggle inevitably results in the intertwining and mixing together of conflicting tendencies which are sure to assume their rightful places as the struggle develops further. But it is absolutely clear that Comrade Sokolnikov's position, his readiness to sacrifice the interests of industry and the monopoly of foreign trade for the sake of revitalizing commodity circulation in general, does not alter the nature of the Leningrad Opposition, which is a bureaucratic and demagogic adaptation of the apparatus higher-ups to the anxiety of the advanced section of the working class over the general course of our development.—L.T.

questions or dangers, makes its way by circuitous paths and gets lost in abstractions, reminiscences, and innumerable quotations. At this time, it seems, the official press is trying to focus the party's attention on the theoretical definition of our regime as a whole.

III. State Capitalism and Socialism

8. In 1921, during the transition to the NEP, Lenin was particularly insistent on defining the overall economic regime taking shape in our country as state capitalism. At that time, when industry was in a state of complete paralysis, there were many reasons to think that its development would proceed chiefly by way of mixed companies, attracting foreign capital, granting concessions, leasing, etc.—i.e., by way of capitalist and semicapitalist forms, controlled and directed by the proletarian state. Under these conditions, cooperative organizations were to become the distributors of goods produced by state-capitalist industry, and consequently they were to become a constituent part of the state-capitalist economic apparatus linking industry with the peasantry.

The actual course of development, however, followed more favorable lines. State industry took the decisive position. By comparison, not only the mixed companies, concessions, and leased enterprises, but even cottage industry took an insignificant share of the market. The cooperatives distributed goods obtained chiefly through the state trusts, i.e., through the basic units of the socialist economy under construction. This gives the cooperatives themselves a different character, despite the fact that at their lowest level they rest on a fragmented commodity-producing peasant economy. The cooperatives are becoming part and parcel not of a state-capitalist but of a socialist economic apparatus in the process of formation, and are an arena for the struggle of this apparatus against capitalist tendencies.

It is absolutely clear that a general definition of our economic regime as "state capitalism" becomes meaningless under these conditions; neither state industry nor the peasant economy fits this definition. To define the whole system on the basis of its least significant components (the mixed companies, concessions, leasing, etc.) would be an appalling violation of all proportions.

One could easily show that during the 1923 discussion the term "state capitalism" was applied indiscriminately to our system as a whole, including even the state-owned trusts, in obvious violation of the meaning Lenin gave to that concept when he outlined a less favorable line of development, with a weak role for the purely state-owned industries and a large role for private, particularly foreign, capital in the first years.

9. Leaving aside, however, the past confusion surrounding this question—confusion resulting from the fact that an uncritical selection of quotations has been substituted for a living Leninist analysis—it is possible to say with certainty that the present dispute over the term "state capitalism," though doctrinaire in form, reflects the desire of thoughtful party members to reexamine the question of relations between industry and agriculture, in view of the unsatisfactory way in which this question has been formulated in recent years.

10. In the fall of 1923, the official thinking of the party was that the main danger lay in an overly rapid development of industry, for which there would be no real market. The main slogan with respect to industry was, Don't run ahead. The correlation between industry and agriculture was understood and interpreted statistically but not dynamically, i.e., no recognition at all was given to the idea that industry is a leading principle; that precisely for that reason industry must "outstrip" agriculture in order to lead it forward; and that with correct leadership such a relationship can greatly speed up the overall tempo of economic growth. The entire economic orientation was given a minimalistic tone. As a result, five-year plans and other programs for industry, transport, credit, and so forth were played down to the point of becoming caricatures. An entire stage of economic and political development has been colored by a passive reverence for the conditions of the peasant market; and every particular phase has been marked by underestimation or misunderstanding of the role of industry as an economic principle that does not passively adapt itself to the conditions of the market, but dynamically shapes and expands the market.

To assert now, after the fact, that the warnings and exhortations of 1923 concerning agriculture and industry were warranted is to fly in the face of the actual course of developments of the past two and a half years. Long-term projections and programs bearing the mark of timidity and pettiness invariably had to be revised upward under the direct pressure of demand from quarter to quarter and often from month to month, with the inevitable loss not only of the possibility of forecasting but even of maintaining day-to-day control.

11. We are now living in a period of queues. The shortage of industrial goods has created the gravest difficulties in the export-

ing of goods, which, in turn, strikes a blow at industry. It goes without saying that today's queues are fundamentally different from the queues of the first years of Soviet power; those were the product of a steady economic decline; the queues of today are a result of expansion. But they are the clearest expression of the fact that in evaluating perspectives for economic development, official thought was stricken with indecision, minimalism, and an underestimation of the real potential.

12. The glaring discrepancy between the forecast and the actual development could not help but give rise to anxiety and doubt among the most thoughtful layers of the working class. The forecast ran: Don't go to extremes, don't rush ahead, so as to avoid creating a breach with the countryside. But reality showed at every step that industry was lagging terribly behind and that hasty improvising in the sphere of industrial planning was needed. The culmination of all this is the queues.

13. With respect to so-called goods intervention, the same picture is evident. The call for "goods intervention," i.e., the suggestion that we not forget about the international division of labor and the world market and about the need to take advantage of its resources to regulate the domestic market and hasten our own economic development—was declared to be a concession to the kulak. This orientation fed on a passive and fearful attitude toward the world market, and in its conclusions stumbled headlong over the theory of a self-contained national economy. Reality has totally refuted this way of looking at the problem. "Goods intervention" was imposed upon us by the expansion of our own economy. It has shown itself to be a powerful instrument for accelerating the development of state-owned industry. Its negative consequences have made themselves felt only insofar as it was put into effect as a hasty improvisation—in disregard of all forecasts and plans.

14. It has become increasingly and strikingly clear that planning is not a passive coordination of departmental plans—the limits of which have been set by the Commissariat of Finance—with the economic processes in the private sector, which are guessed at or anticipated on the basis of statistics. Planning by a state based on a powerful complex of industry, transport, commerce, and credit, is the conscious setting of great economic tasks and the creation of conditions for their fulfillment. Minimalism or Menshevism exists as a way of approaching tasks and possibilities. And it exists not only in politics but also in economics, especially since nine-tenths of politics today lies in the solving of

economic problems. Minimalism in regard to production is a result of underestimation, on the one hand, of the leading role of state industry, and on the other hand, of the resources and methods at the disposal of the workers' state.

The party needs a new orientation on this fundamental question. State industry must become the backbone of economic planning, based on the firm and effective coordination of the constituent units of the state-owned and socially owned sectors of the economy, both in their internal relations with one another and in their relations with the private sector.

An Analysis of the Slogans and Differences

December 14, 1925

Neither classes nor parties can be judged by what they say about themselves or by the slogans they raise at a given moment. This fully applies to groupings within a political party as well. Slogans must be taken, not in isolation, but in relation to all their surroundings, and especially in relation to the history of a particular grouping, its traditions, the selection of human material within it, etc.

This does not mean, however, that slogans have no meaning. Although they do not fully determine the political complexion of a grouping, they do constitute one of its component elements. Let us try to analyze the key slogans in and of themselves, and then evaluate them within the framework of the existing political situation.

To have the question of differentiation within the peasantry posed sharply is, undoubtedly, a positive and important development, if only because it brings us back from the purely abstract concept of the "cooperatization" of the middle peasant to the reality of the economic process. Focusing the party's attention on differentiation within the peasantry forces it to understand that there is and can be no way out, toward socialism, through the resources existing in the village alone. Hence the shift in the position of Kamenev, who now counters Bukharin's concept, that "socialism is Soviet power plus the cooperatives," with something more complex, namely: "Soviet power, plus electrification, plus the cooperatives," in which electrification should be understood as industrial technology in general. Such a formulation of the question, in comparison with the 1923 position, which was one of the reasons for the systematic lagging behind of industry, is unquestionably a step forward. If one is to carry the thought through to its conclusion, then it should be formulated roughly as follows:

Cooperatization can have either a socialist or a capitalist character. If the economic process in the countryside is left to itself, then cooperatization will undoubtedly proceed in a capitalist direction, i.e., it will become an instrument in the hands of the kulaks. Only on the basis of new technology, i.e., on the basis of the increasing predominance of industry over agriculture, can the cooperatization of the poor and middle peasants ensure an advancement toward socialism. The faster the tempo of industry and the sooner it achieves predominance over agriculture, the more confidently one can expect a delay in the process of differentiation within the peasantry, a safeguard for the mass of middle peasants against pauperization, etc.

But at the same time that Kamenev counterposes industry as a motive force to Bukharin's agrarian-cooperative perspective, Bukharin comes out against Kamenev on the question of how to evaluate the social nature of industry itself. Kamenev, Zinoviev, and the others still consider industry a component part of the system of state capitalism. They held this point of view in common two or three years ago, and advanced it in an especially persistent fashion during the 1923–24 discussion. The essence of this point of view is that industry is one of the subordinate parts of a system that includes peasant economy, finance, cooperatives, state-regulated privately owned enterprises, etc. All these economic processes, regulated and controlled by the state, constitute the system of state capitalism, which is supposed to lead to socialism through a series of stages.

In this schema, the leading role of industry completely vanishes. The planning principle is almost entirely pushed aside by credit-finance regulation, which assumed the role of an intermediary between the peasant economy and state industry, regarding them as two parties in a lawsuit. It is precisely from this schema that there arose the concept of agrarian-cooperative socialism, against which Kamenev correctly comes forward. But from this very schema also arose a characterization of state industry not as the key factor of socialism but as a subordinate component of state capitalism, against which Bukharin now correctly comes forward. We see here that each side has partly liquidated the position held in common in 1923, a position which led, on the one hand, to industry's lagging behind agriculture and, on the other, to Bukharin's middle-peasant cooperative schema, expressed in the by no means accidental slogan "Enrich yourselves."

The 1923 position should be liquidated not in part, but completely. One must state firmly and distinctly that the essence of the question lies not in the present level of differentiation in the countryside, nor even in the rate of differentiation, but in the rate of industrial development, which alone has the capacity to bring about qualitative changes in the basic process of economic development in the countryside. From this it follows further that "Face to the countryside" means, first of all, "Face to industry." From this it also follows that planning is not an intermediary between industry and peasant economy, but the object of the state's economic activity, which is accomplished first and foremost through industry. The axis of planning can and should be a program of industrial development. Planning, set apart from industry, inevitably degenerates into petty niggling, making a correction here or there, and attempting to coordinate from one case to the next. This also applies to Gosplan as well as to the Council of Labor and Defense. To the extent that planning has become semipassive mediation between state industry—which has lagged behind the market—and the peasant economy, the Commissariat of Finance has naturally pushed Gosplan aside because finance was found to be a more direct and practical means of intermediary regulation than the statistical compilations of Gosplan. But credit-finance regulation in and of itself does not include any principle of planning at all, and while it gives sustenance to the whole economic process, it does not and cannot contain any inherent guarantee of an advance toward socialism.

At the dawn of our economic work Lenin advanced the idea of electrification as the basis for an economic plan. Electrification is a highly developed expression of the industrial principle. Formally, electrification has continued to be acknowledged as a leading idea. In practice, it has occupied a relatively smaller and smaller place in the general development of the economy. Electrification was intimately linked with the concept of an economic plan. Here we find the very first expression of the idea that the economy can be planned in a socialist way only through industrial technology. Without closely linking Gosplan with the Supreme Council of the National Economy, we will not have either a properly integrated program of industrial development or practical, purposeful, and active economic planning, implemented primarily through industry. For agriculture, transport, and even the stability of the chervonets depend on the character and rate of industrial development. In the overall chain of the economy, industry is the basic and decisive link.

On the Leningrad Opposition

December 22, 1925

Pravda and the speakers for the congress majority characterize the Leningrad Opposition as the continuation and development of the 1923-24 Opposition. We must admit frankly that this equation is not merely a polemical device but contains an element of truth. It is only necessary to correctly specify what that element is.

The central theme of the Leningrad Opposition is to blame the official policy, or its right-wing manifestation, for the fact that the peasantry is beginning to push the proletariat into the background, and for the fact that within the ranks of the peasantry the kulak is edging out the middle peasant and the middle peasant is edging out the poor peasant.

At the present time there can be no doubt that the so-called pro-kulak deviation has received a very big push forward since the Twelfth and, particularly, the Thirteenth Congress. The main line pursued in the struggle against Trotskyism has been the charge of underestimating the peasantry. What was this charge based on? On the fact that the Opposition considers industry and its development to be of paramount importance and demands that the tempo of industrial development be accelerated, i.e., demands the corresponding reallocation of industrial capital, the introduction of the planning principle in industry, etc. This position was declared to be a revision of Leninism, and the principal elements of the latter were proclaimed to be the *smychka,* the alliance of the workers with the peasants, etc. Among the older generation, which had not forgotten the experience of past decades, these simplified formulas at least came on top of the experience accumulated in the struggle against the Narodnik movement and for a proletarian class policy. But as for the broad layers of the youth—who have not been tempered in the class struggle—in their eyes the discussion of recent years, minus all the intricacies and distortions, appeared as follows: On the one hand, recognition of the "dictatorship of industry" and the uninterrupted development of the international revolution; on the other, the *smychka* with the peasantry, the alliance with the middle peasant, the cooperatives as an *alternative* course for development, etc.

In essence, the young generation, which has not been tempered in the class struggle, has been molded on the basis of this polemic. It is safe to say that by such a process a very wide and fertile base was created for the development of a peasant deviation. That the country's entire public life, given the delay in the world revolution and the lag in industrial development, has created favorable material preconditions for this deviation—of this there cannot be the slightest doubt. Thus, under the banner of a struggle against the Opposition, elements of a Soviet Narodnik movement were taking shape especially within the younger generation of the party and in the Communist Youth. This elemental movement only awaited its official theoretical expression. Bukharin's school, albeit in a very timid and half-hearted fashion, provided this.

It is not at all accidental that the Leningrad organization turned out to be the most sensitive to the voices of warning, just as it is no accident that the leaders of that opposition were forced, in the struggle for self-preservation, to adapt themselves to the class sensitivity of the Leningrad proletariat. The result of this is a paradox, quite shocking on the surface but at the same time totally in accord with the underlying forces at work: The Leningrad organization—having gone to the farthest extent in its struggle against the Opposition, having inveighed against the underestimation of the peasantry, and having raised the slogan "Face to the countryside" loudest of all—was the first to recoil from the consequences of the noticeable turnabout that has occurred in the party, the ideological source of which was the struggle against so-called Trotskyism.

As for the incessant cries about underestimating the peasantry, the demand to turn our "Face to the countryside," the advancement of the idea of a closed national economy and a closed construction of socialism—as early as 1923-24 the Opposition warned that such an ideological orientation in the party could lay the groundwork for and facilitate a gradual backsliding into a Thermidor of a peasant variety. And now we hear the Leningraders warn of that very same danger, although their leaders played a key role in paving the way for it ideologically.

That the Leningrad methods of party and economic leadership, the shrill agitational style, the regional arrogance, etc., built up an enormous amount of dissatisfaction with the ruling group in Leningrad; and that the intense resentment against the Leningrad regime felt by many, many hundreds of workers who have at one time or another been thrown out of Leningrad and dispersed throughout the country, has added to this dissatisfaction—these facts are absolutely incontestable and their importance must not be underestimated. In this sense, the replacement of the top ranks in Leningrad and the Leningrad organization's adoption of a less arrogant tone toward the party as a whole are unquestionably positive factors.

But it would be blindness to overlook the fact that at the Fourteenth Congress, behind the hostility toward the specific features and manners of the Leningrad leaders, appeared sentiments of hostility toward the ideological dictatorship of the city over the countryside. The centers have too large a budget, they have the industry, the press, the strongest organizations, and ideological supremacy; they don't give up enough for the good of the countryside, instead deafening it with empty slogans—these are the themes that in a very, very faint way were echoed in many of the speeches at the congress. Today it is Leningrad's turn; tomorrow it may be Moscow's. Moscow and Leningrad's attacks on one another facilitate the possibility. The provinces have grabbed Leningrad by the throat for its opposition to Moscow in order to prepare a blow against the cities in general. Of course, what we have here only foreshadows a process that as it develops can become fatal for the role of the proletariat.

The fact that today Sokolnikov appears as one of the leaders of the Leningrad Opposition is unprincipled politics of a purely personal kind and at the same time it is a great curiosity. He was and remains the theoretician of the economic disarmament of the proletariat in relation to the countryside.

One cannot fail to take into account the provinces of Tambov or Voronezh, or Georgia. The peasant deviation results from the objective necessity for the party to pay attention to the peasantry. But it is entirely a matter of degree and of having an active counterweight. The most effective possible counterweight to the countryside would be to have energetic and powerful proletarian organizations in the industrial centers, i.e., in Leningrad and Moscow. Democratization of the internal life of these organizations is a necessary precondition if they are to energetically and successfully counteract the peasant deviation. In fact, we have seen the opposite happen. The apparatus regime has been deadening the consciousness of both these organizations. Any demand for a relaxation of regimentation is branded as a capitulation to petty-bourgeois amorphousness, etc., etc. Held tightly in the grip of the apparatus regime, Leningrad served the cause of the struggle against the Opposition 100 percent under the slogan "Face to the countryside" and thus helped the tendencies toward a national and rural perspective to develop and gain sufficiently vivid expression even at the present party congress. Although formally no one agrees with the "extremes" of the Bukharin school of thought, actually all the "fire" is being directed the other way—at Leningrad.

Appendix A
THE PLATFORM OF THE FORTY-SIX

October 15, 1923

NOTE: Reprinted with permission of Macmillan Publishing Co., Inc., from The Interregnum (History of Soviet Russia, *Volume 4*), *by E.H. Carr. Copyright 1954 by Edward Hallett Carr.—Ed.*

To the Politburo of the Central Committee of the Russian Communist Party

Secret

The extreme seriousness of the position compels us (in the interests of our party, in the interests of the working class) to state openly that a continuation of the policy of the majority of the Politburo threatens grievous disasters for the whole party. The economic and financial crisis beginning at the end of July of the present year, with all the political, including internal party, consequences resulting from it, has inexorably revealed the inadequacy of the leadership of the party, both in the economic domain, and especially in the domain of internal party relations.

The casual, unconsidered, and unsystematic character of the decisions of the Central Committee, which has failed to make ends meet in the economic domain, has led to a position where, for all the undoubted great successes in the domain of industry, agriculture, finance, and transport—successes achieved by the economy of the country spontaneously and not thanks to, but in spite of the inadequacy of, the leadership or, rather, the absence of all leadership—we face not only the prospect of a cessation of these successes, but also a grave economic crisis.

We face the approaching breakdown of the chervonets currency, which has spontaneously been transformed into a basic currency before the liquidation of the budget deficit; a credit crisis in which Gosbank [the State Bank] can no longer without risk of a serious collapse finance either industry or trade in industrial goods or even the purchase of grain for export; a cessation of the sale of industrial goods as a result of high prices, which are explained on the one hand by the absence of planned organizational leadership in industry, and on the other hand by an incorrect credit policy; the impossibility of carrying out the program of grain exports as a result of inability to purchase grain; extremely low prices for food products, which are damaging to the peasantry and threaten a mass contraction of agricultural production; inequalities in wage payments which provoke natural dissatisfaction among the workers with the budgetary chaos, which indirectly produces chaos in the state apparatus. "Revolutionary" methods of making reductions in drawing up the budget, and new and obvious reductions in carrying it out, have ceased to be transitional measures and become a regular phenomenon which constantly disturbs the state apparatus and, as a result of the absence of plan in the reductions affected, disturbs it in a casual and spontaneous manner.

These are some of the elements of the economic, credit, and financial crisis which has already begun. If extensive, well-considered, planned, and energetic measures are not taken forthwith, if the present absence of leadership continues, we face the possibility of an extremely acute economic breakdown, which will inevitably involve internal political complications and a complete paralysis of our external effectiveness and capacity for action. And this last, as everyone will understand, is more necessary to us now than ever; on it depends the fate of the world revolution and of the working class of all countries.

Similarly in the domain of internal party relations we see the same incorrect leadership paralyzing and breaking up the party; this appears particularly clearly in the period of crisis through which we are passing.

We explain this not by the political incapacity of the present leaders of the party; on the contrary, however much we differ from them in our estimate of the position and in the choice of means to alter it, we assume that the present leaders could not in any conditions fail to be appointed by the party to the outstanding posts in the workers' dictatorship. We explain it by the fact that beneath the external form of official unity we have in practice a one-sided recruitment of individuals, and a direction of affairs which is one-sided and adapted to the views and sympathies of a narrow circle. As the result of a party leadership distorted by such narrow considerations, the party is to a considerable extent ceasing to be that living independent collectivity which sensitively seizes living reality because it is bound to this reality with a thousand threads. Instead of this we observe the ever increasing, and now scarcely concealed, division of the party between a secretarial hierarchy and "quiet folk," between professional party officials recruited from above and the general mass of the party which does not participate in the common life.

This is a fact which is known to every member of the party. Members of the party who are dissatisfied with this or that decision of the Central Committee or even of a provincial committee, who have this or that doubt on their minds, who privately note this or that error, irregularity, or disorder, are afraid to speak about it at party meetings, and are even afraid to talk about it in conversation, unless the partner in the conversation is thoroughly reliable from the point of view of "discretion"; free discussion within the party has practically vanished; the public opinion of the party is stifled. Nowadays it is not the party, not its broad masses, who promote and choose members of the province committees and of the Central Committee of the RCP. On the contrary, the secretarial hierarchy of the party to an ever greater extent recruits the membership of conferences and congresses, which are becoming to an ever greater extent the executive assemblies of this hierarchy.

The regime established within the party is completely intolerable; it destroys the independence of the party, replacing the party by a recruited bureaucratic apparatus which acts without objection in normal times, but which inevitably fails in moments of crisis, and which threatens to become completely ineffective in the face of the serious events now impending.

The position which has been created is explained by the fact that the regime of the dictatorship of a faction within the party, which was in fact created after the Tenth Congress, has outlived itself. Many of us consciously accepted submission to such a regime. The turn of policy in the year 1921, and after that the illness of comrade Lenin, demanded in the opinion of some of us a dictatorship within the party as a temporary measure. Other comrades from the very beginning adopted a skeptical or negative attitude towards it. However that may have been, by the time of the Twelfth Congress of the party this regime had outlived itself. It had begun to display its reverse side. Links within the party began to weaken. The party began to die away. Extreme and obviously morbid movements of opposition within the party began to acquire an anti-party character, since there was no comradely discussion of inflamed questions. Such discussion would without difficulty have revealed the morbid character of these movements both to the mass of the party and to the majority of those participating in them. The results have been illegal movements which draw members of the party outside the limits of the party, and a divorce of the party from the working masses.

Should the position thus created not be radically changed in the immediate future, the economic crisis in Soviet Russia and the crisis of the factional dictatorship in the party will deal heavy blows at the workers' dictatorship in Russia and the Russian Communist Party. With such a load on its shoulders, the dictatorship of the proletariat in Russia and its leader the RCP cannot enter the phase of impending new worldwide disturbances except with the prospect of defeats on the whole front of the proletarian struggle. Of course it would be at first sight most simple to settle the question by deciding that at this moment, in view of all the circumstances, there is not and cannot be any room to raise the question of a change in the party course, to put on the agenda new and complicated tasks, etc., etc. But it is perfectly apparent that such a point of view would amount to an attitude of officially shutting one's eyes to the real position, since the whole danger resides in the fact that there is no real unity in thought or in action in face of an extremely complicated internal and foreign situation.

The struggle that is being waged in the party is all the more bitter the more silently and secretly it proceeds. If we put this question to the Central Committee, it is precisely in order to bring about the most rapid and least painful issue from the contradictions which are tearing the party asunder and set the party without delay on a healthy foundation. Real unity in opinions and in actions is indispensable. The impending difficulties demand united, fraternal, fully conscious, extremely vigorous, extremely concentrated action by all members of our party. The factional regime must be abolished, and this must be done in the first instance by those who have created it; it must be replaced by a regime of comradely unity and internal party democracy.

In order to realize what has been set forth above and to take the measures indispensable for an issue from the economic, political, and party crisis, we propose to the Central Committee as a first and urgent step to call a conference of members of the Central Committee with the most prominent and active party workers, providing that the list of those invited should include a number of comrades holding views on the situation different from the views of the majority of the Central Committee.

Signatures to the Declaration to the Politburo of the Central Committee of the RCP on the Internal Party Situation of October 15, 1923*

E. Preobrazhensky, B. Breslav, L. Serebriakov

Not being in agreement with some of the points of this letter explaining the causes of the situation which has been created, but considering that the party is immediately confronted with questions which cannot be wholly resolved by the methods hitherto practiced, I fully associate myself with the final conclusion of the present letter.

A. Beloborodov

With the proposals I am in full agreement, though I differ from certain points in the motivation.

A. Rosengolts, M. Alsky

In essentials I share the views of this appeal. The demand for a direct and sincere approach to all our ills has become so urgent that I entirely support the proposal to call the conference suggested in order to lay down practical ways of escape from the accumulation of difficulties.

Antonov-Ovseenko, A. Benediktov, I. N. Smirnov, Yu. Pyatakov, V. Obolensky (Osinsky), N. Muralov, T. Sapronov

The position in the party and the international position is such that it demands, more than ever before, an unusual exertion and concentration of party forces. I associate myself with the declaration and regard it *exclusively* as an attempt to restore unity in the

---

*The signatures are so arranged in the copy from which this translation has been made that it is impossible to be certain that the original order has been preserved.—E.H.C.

party and to prepare it for impending events. It is natural that at the present moment there can be no question of a struggle within the party in any form whatever. It is essential that the Central Committee should assess the position soberly and take urgent measures to remove the dissatisfaction within the party and also in the nonparty masses.

A. Goltsman, V. Maksimovsky, D. Sosnovsky, Danishevsky, O. Shmidel, N. Vaganyan, I. Stukov, A. Lobanov, Rafail, S. Vasilchenko, Mikh. Zhakov, A. M. Puzakov, N. Nikolaev

Since I have recently been somewhat aloof from the work of the party centers I abstain from judgment on the first two paragraphs in the introductory section; for the rest I am in agreement.

Averin

I am in agreement with the exposition, in the first part, of the economic and political situation of the country. I consider that in the part describing the internal party situation a certain exaggeration has crept in. It is completely indispensable to take measures *immediately* to preserve the unity of the party.

I. Bogoslavsky, P. Mesyatsev, T. Khorechko

I am not in agreement with a number of opinions in the first part of the declaration; I am not in agreement with a number of the characterizations of the internal party situation. At the same time I am profoundly convinced that the condition of the party demands the taking of radical measures since the condition in the party at the present time is not healthy. I entirely share the practical proposal.

A. Bubnov, A. Voronsky, V. Smirnov, E. Bosh, E. Byk, V. Kosior, F. Lokatskov

With the assessment of the economic position I am in complete agreement. I consider a weakening of the political dictatorship at the present moment dangerous, but an elucidation is indispensable. I find a conference completely indispensable.

Kaganovich, Drobnis, P. Kovalenko, A. E. Minkin, V. Yakovleva

With the practical proposal I am in full agreement.

B. Elstin

I sign with the same reservations as Comrade Bubnov.

L. Levitin

I sign with the same reserves as Bubnov, though I do not endorse either the form or the tone, the character of which persuades me all the more to agree with the practical part of the declaration.

L. Palydov

I am not in full agreement with the first part which speaks of the economic condition of the country; this is really very serious and demands extremely attentive consideration, but the party has not hitherto produced men who would lead it better than those who are hitherto leading it. On the question of the internal party situation I consider that there is a substantial element of truth in all that is said, and consider it essential to take urgent measures.

F. Sudnik

Appendix B
THE NEW COURSE RESOLUTION

December 5, 1923

NOTE: The "Resolution of the Central Committee and of the Central Control Commission Concerning Party Structure" was adopted unanimously at the joint session of the Politburo of the Central Committee of the Communist Party and the Presidium of the Central Control Commission on December 5, 1923. It was published in English in Inprecorr, January 29, 1924.—*Ed.*

1. The Party During the New Economic Policy

a. The New Economic Policy, which has caused a growth of the productive forces, has proved itself to be a necessary stage on the long-protracted transitional road from capitalism to socialism. It has contributed to the revival of the national economy in general, and of state industry, state commerce, and the cooperatives in particular. We have witnessed a gradual increase in the rate of wages, a return of qualified workers to the towns, a raising of the level of culture among the broad proletarian masses and, in particular, the formation of new ranks of proletarian and peasant intellectuals, thanks to the systematic instruction imparted to the workers and peasants in the higher educational establishments.

b. The Twelfth Congress of the party, while taking note of the revival of the economic life of the country, has at the same time pointed out the necessity of evaluating every stage of economic development from the point of view of socialist construction. The dictatorship of the proletariat, which cannot be consolidated and developed without an increase in material prosperity, could not even have maintained itself if this increase in material prosperity had created a preponderance of private capital over state capital.

The extraordinary difficulties facing the economy of the country at the present moment are mainly expressed in the fact that the products of our state industry do not find a sufficient market. If during the last year the disposal of our products has met with ever-increasing difficulties, this is to a very great extent attributable to the extraordinarily high *cost of production,* the exceedingly high *trading expenses,* and in addition, the unjustifiable methods of setting prices at an *exaggeratedly high level* at the expense of the consumer. The underlying causes of these difficulties are the low productivity and the lack of coordination in the various sectors of the state economy, whether among themselves individually or between themselves as a whole and the market; the irrational or insufficiently rational way of organizing industrial and commercial enterprises and conducting their operations, in particular the inability of our still bureaucratic commercial and cooperative organizations to find their way to the peasant market.

The central task remains, as heretofore, to link up state industry with the peasant economy, i.e., in the first place, the establishment of proper proportions between the productivity of our state industry on the one hand and the size and requirements of our mainly peasant market on the other. This task can be carried out to the extent that the various factors and sectors of state industry are appropriately and systematically linked with each other.

From all this the party—from its highest to its lowest ranks—must draw the conclusion that further economic revival, which will enable us to overcome the existing crisis within the more or less near future, can serve the cause of *socialist* construction only to the extent that we learn to coordinate the sectors of the national economy in their constant interaction with one another and with the market generally.

From this arises the exceptional importance of Gosplan, the economic general staff of the socialist state, and all the economic planning organizations at the local level. It is necessary to guarantee them in practice the role indicated in the resolution of the Twelfth Congress.

The measures adopted in recent times to reduce the prices of manufactured goods and to promote the export of 'grain have already led to a certain recovery in the volume of trade and to an increase in the price of grain. However, the struggle against the fundamental causes of the marketing crisis demands from the party a complex and systematic effort to carry out the measures indicated by the Twelfth Congress regarding the concentration of industry, proper organization of the apparatus of trade and industry, the promotion of agriculture, the raising of its technical level, and its adaptation to the struggle on the world market by various means, including the extension of agricultural credit, etc. These tasks are squarely confronting the party in the most urgent manner. There is no doubt that the party will concentrate all its forces in order to carry them out effectively.

c. The present stage of the transitional period contains objective contradictions, which result from the simultaneous existence of the most varied economic forms, from the prevailing market relations, from the necessity for the state institutions to employ capitalist forms and methods of work, from the necessity of relying for support upon a staff which is still alien to the proletariat, etc.—these contradictions find their expression in a whole series of negative tendencies, the fight against which must be placed on the agenda. Among these tendencies may be mentioned: striking disparities in the material living standards of party members, determined by their differing functions and by the practice of so-called "wasteful expenditures"; the growth of connections with bourgeois elements and the ideological influence of the latter; a departmentalized narrowing of intellectual horizons among officials (which must be distinguished from necessary specialization); and as a result of this, the weakening of the connections between communists working in different sectors; the danger of a loss of the perspective of socialist construction as a whole and of world revolution; the danger, already indicated by the congress, of the "NEP degeneration" of a layer of functionaries who, owing to the nature of their activity, come most into contact with bourgeois elements; the process of bureaucratization that can be observed in the party apparatus; and the resulting threat of the party becoming separated from the masses.

2. The Party and the Working Masses

The confidence of the proletarian masses in the party has increased. This finds its expression in the Soviet elections, in the collapse of the Menshevik and SR parties, and in the formation of a body of nonparty workers who are actively supporting the party. At the same time the active communist workers, who of course should form the connecting link between the party and the nonparty masses, are almost entirely absorbed in administrative and economic work and thereby unavoidably lose contact with the work of production. In this connection, therefore, the fundamental task is the recruiting of new party members from the ranks of the workers at the bench. It is the task of the party organizations to devote special attention to such party workers, to do everything possible in order to prevent them from being divorced from the work of production, to help them raise their cultural level, and to use every means to make it easier for them to play a real role in all party affairs. The effort to enlarge the proletarian core of the party must be seen as one of the most important tasks facing all party organizations in the months ahead. The initiative of certain organizations which have already oriented their activities in this direction must be supported by all the organizations of our party in industry. The party must facilitate the influx of new industrial worker cadres into the party organizations and their promotion from candidates to party members. In the same way it is necessary to give increased attention to work among the rising generation of proletarian youth.

Regarding the *peasantry,* among whom proletarian and semi-proletarian strata are again appearing, it is necessary to improve by every means the qualitative composition of the cells, to direct their work into the channel of cultural and political activity, in particular to intensify their work of helping to spread knowledge of scientific agricultural methods, and also their work in the cooperative field, in the organization of agricultural credits, etc. Along with this the village proletariat (especially the committees of landless peasants in the Ukraine) must be given every support, and the proletarian elements must be drawn into our party organizations as well as into the All-Russian Confederation of Agricultural and Forestry Workers.

Among the *intelligentsia,* as a result of general causes as well as the improvement of their position in our country, at the very time when the middle classes of Germany are being pauperized, there is to be noted a general swing of opinion in favor of Soviet power. Of special importance is this turn of opinion among the rural teachers and agricultural instructors, who can be considered among the most important connecting links between town and country. This turn of opinion among broad strata of the intelligentsia in favor of Soviet power, in itself an outstanding positive phenomenon, can, however, also have consequences of a negative character, as it increases the danger that the communists will be ideologically surrounded.

The struggle for the ideological purity of our party against petty-bourgeois and *smenovekhi* obscurantism is therefore an equally important task of the party.

3. The Party and Workers' Democracy

The negative phenomena of the last few months in the life of the working class as a whole, as well as within the party, led to the inescapable conclusion that the interests of the party, both for its successful struggle against influences generated by the NEP and to enhance its fighting capacity in all areas of work, demand a serious change in the party's course in the sense of an active and systematic implementation of the principles of workers' democracy. In view of this, the October joint plenum of the Central Committee and the Central Control Commission decided as follows:

"The plenums of the Central Committee and of the Central Control Commission entirely approve the policy in the direction of democracy which was recently adopted by the Political Bureau, and they also approve of the intensification of the struggle against "wasteful expenditures" and against the corrupting influence of the NEP upon certain elements of the party, as proposed by the Political Bureau."

Workers' democracy means the liberty of frank discussion of the most important questions of party life by all members, and the election of all leading party functionaries and commissions by those bodies immediately under them. It does not, however, imply the freedom to form factional groupings, which are extremely dangerous for the ruling party, since they always threaten to split or fragment the government and the state apparatus as a whole.

Within a party, which represents a voluntary union of people on the basis of definite ideals and practice, it is obvious that there can be no toleration of the formation of groupings whose ideological content is directed against the party as a whole and against the dictatorship of the proletariat, as for instance the Workers' Truth and Workers' Group.

Only a constant, vital ideological life can maintain the character of the party as it was before and during the revolution, with the constant scrutiny of its past, the correction of its mistakes, and the collective discussion of the most important problems. Only these methods can provide effective guarantees that episodic disagreements will not lead to the formation of factional groupings with all the above-indicated consequences.

In order to avert this, the leading party bodies must heed the voices of the broad party masses and must not consider every criticism a manifestation of factionalism and thereby cause conscientious and disciplined party members to withdraw into closed circles and fall into factionalism.

Under no circumstances can the party be regarded as a mere institution or bureaucratic department, but at the same time it cannot be considered a debating society for every tendency. The Tenth Congress laid down the principles of workers' democracy, but the same Tenth Congress, and afterwards the Eleventh and Twelfth Congresses, also laid down a series of limitations as to the exercise of these principles of proletarian democracy: forbidding factions (see the resolution of the Tenth Congress, "On Party Unity," and the corresponding resolution of the Twelfth Congress); purging the party; limiting the admission of nonproletarian elements to party membership; laying down certain lengths of membership as necessary qualifications for holding certain offices in the party; confirming secretaries by the superior party authority (see party statutes). While it will be unavoidably necessary, because of NEP conditions, to continue to maintain certain limitations in the future also, there must at the same time be a reexamination of the appropriateness of some of these limitations based on the experience already acquired (particularly by the local organizations)—for instance, the right of the higher authorities to confirm secretaries. In no circumstances can the right to confirm secretaries be converted into the right to appoint them in practice.

4. *Immediate Measures for Realizing Workers' Democracy*

In order to prevent the line of the party from being diverted, to really put workers' democracy into practice, and to secure for the entire mass of party members the opportunity to systematically influence the direction of all party policy, the following measures must first be put into effect:

a. Strict examination of the qualifications of candidates, with the limitations mentioned above; it shall be regarded as inadmissible to impose such candidates against the will of an organization; in particular there must be a strict examination of the eligibility of cell secretaries.

b. It shall be obligatory to submit all essential questions of party policy, insofar as exceptional circumstances shall not render this impossible, for discussion by the party cells and the party masses as a whole; the number of party discussion clubs shall be extended; unjustifiable appeals shall not be made to "party discipline" when it is a matter of the right and duty of party members to discuss questions in which they are interested and to adopt decisions regarding them.

c. Attention must be paid to the task of promoting new functionaries from the rank and file, in the first place from among the workers.

d. Special attention must be paid to having the correct party policy understood by the cadres who are in closest contact with the masses of the party.

e. It shall become required procedure for the party organizations to report back to the bodies that elected them and to the broad party masses.

f. There must be an increase in the educational work of the party—at the same time carefully avoiding all bureaucratic ways of approaching it, both among the mass of the party as a whole and, in particular, among the Communist Youth and the women.

g. Attention must be paid to the mutual exchange of experience by functionaries in various fields of work; compulsory conferences shall be periodically convened by the Central Committee, as well as by the region, province, and district committees, to be attended by the responsible functionaries in all fields of work.

h. Party members shall be kept more fully informed by means of the press and by visits to various localities by members of the Central Committee, the Central Control Commission, the region and province committees, and by members of the collegiums of the commissariats.

i. In the press the columns devoted to party life must be increased.

j. At the next party congress a proposal must be submitted regarding the convocation of province and all-Russian party conferences twice a year.

In order to secure the effective implementation of all the measures mentioned above regarding the realization of workers' democracy, it is necessary to pass from words to deeds by proposing to the local cells, the district, region, and province party conferences, to systematically renew the party apparatus from the bottom up at the regular party elections, by promoting to responsible posts such functionaries as are in fact able to ensure democracy within the party.

5. On the Control Commissions

a. The most important tasks in the improvement of the party apparatus have already been put before the party. This work needs much time in order to yield effective and perceptible results.

The basic condition for successful work on the part of the Control Commission and the Workers and Peasants Inspection regarding the improvement and purification of the state apparatus, is that they be supported by the whole party and all its organizations, and that the working masses be drawn into this work. There must be a closer connection between the control commissions and the corresponding party committees; every means must be used to increase the interest of the public opinion of both the party and the working masses in the activity of the control commissions and the Workers and Peasants Inspection.

b. The experience of the last months has shown that, besides the Central Control Commission, questions of the state apparatus must also be dealt with by the local, province, and region control commissions, and that the problem of extending the functions of the subordinate control commissions must therefore receive attention.

c. As one way of attracting the working masses to the study and improvement of the state apparatus, auxiliary cells may be included in the shops and state institutions—these cells to be set up by the Control Commission and by the Workers and Peasants Inspection along with the trade unions. The party cells in the shops must work closely with the auxiliary cells of the Workers and Peasants Inspection and supervise their work through the shop committees.

d. A particularly important task of the control commissions at the present moment is to fight against the bureaucratic perversion of the party apparatus and of party practice, and to call to account those party functionaries who prevent the principle of workers' democracy from being put into practice in the day-to-day work of the party organizations (restricting the liberty of expression at party gatherings, arbitrarily limiting the number of elective offices when not required to by party rules, etc.).

e. Of special importance at the present juncture is the fight of the control commissions against the so-called "wasteful expenditures" in the state apparatus and on the part of certain of its officials. The corrupting influence of the negative aspects of the NEP upon members of our party, and in particular upon certain responsible functionaries, must be energetically counteracted by the entire party.

f. There must be a more careful employment of extreme disciplinary measures (expulsion from the party). The greatest leniency must be accorded industrial workers at the bench, and the most drastic measures (expulsion from the party) must be employed here only where circumstances make it unavoidable, i.e., where all other means at the disposal of the party have been exhausted.

Finally, those who have been previously expelled from the party, in particular industrial workers, must be accorded really comradely treatment when they express a desire to reenter the party and when in such cases there is good reason to believe that they will properly fulfill the demands the party places upon them.

6. Party Organization and Work in the Economic Sphere

One of the greatest and most valuable of our advantages is that we have participants in all spheres of economic work within the ranks of our party, from the simplest proletarians at the bench right up to the most responsible administrators. All of this varied personnel must, and by a proper arrangement of the work can, contribute their extraordinarily many-sided collective economic experience toward the creation of a real party management of work in the economic sphere. Workers in the economic sphere must be accorded in their work a sufficient degree of independence and initiative, together with the full support of the party. Systematic leadership by the party must not by any means permit hairsplitting discussions over every casual and secondary matter.

For this purpose it is necessary to bring the communist cells into contact with production; accounts and reports must be regularly given by the communist workers in the economic spheres; the essentials of the reports must be discussed; it is necessary to arrange regular meetings of the communists in the cells of those shops which, taken together, form an economic unit (for instance, a trust), and also party economic conferences; cell representatives are obliged to deliver reports to their respective cells regarding these conferences. It is necessary to disseminate much more systematically the experiences and suggestions of the local cells.

7. Work Among the Masses and Drawing the Masses into Practical Constructive Work

The work of attracting the masses into practical construction must be intensified, particularly in view of the danger of the state apparatus becoming separated from the masses. For this reason the responsibility to report back, which was imposed on functionaries in the economic sphere, must be extended to include the masses (general meetings of workers and their delegates, shop committees, conferences of nonparty workers and peasants, and the like).

Special attention must also be paid to bringing the trade unions into contact with production. The actual influence of the trade unions in selecting and promoting new candidates for economic positions, and in controlling the work of economic organizations, must be increased (of very great importance also is control of punctual and proper payment of wages, etc.); the trade unions must convene conferences dealing with the question of production by trusts, attended by representatives of the shop committees and of the administrators of enterprises; the trade unions must submit reports on their work to the trade union press, which must be improved and made more efficient.

Every means must be employed to increase the efficiency of the institution of worker-correspondents, carefully preserving it from all bureaucracy and red tape. The party and the Soviet press must give the greatest and most considerate attention to demands and proposals emanating from the masses.

In the elections to the workers' and peasants' soviets, attention must be paid to the candidacy of new people; besides party workers, active nonparty workers must also be selected and drawn into active work (in the departments of local soviets, meetings of the departments and executive committees with the representatives of the workers and peasants and of the auxiliary cells of the Workers and Peasants Inspection, etc.).

To extend the practice of holding large-scale conferences of nonparty workers and peasants; to facilitate the growth of all kinds of voluntary, self-governing organizations, cultural, educational, athletic, and the like; especially those which touch the family and social life of the working masses (communal kitchens, etc.), securing for them the possibility of proper development.

The practice of holding open meetings of the cells must be extended, and based on the experience of these open meetings, nonparty workers and peasants who are to become active helpers of our party must be selected.

NOTES

1. In his report on party organization to the Twelfth Party Congress (April 1923) Stalin called for "drawing into the work of the Central Committee new, fresh workers, and . . . bringing to the top the most capable and independent." In practice, of course, this meant independence not from manipulations by the party center, but from the control of the rank and file members over whom the new party functionaries were appointed.

2. Although Trotsky prevented the addition of Stalin to the Revolutionary Military Committee, Stalin's follower Voroshilov and Zinoviev's follower Lashevich were in fact added at that meeting of the Central Committee. The campaign against the Ukrainian Council of People's Commissars had occurred during the summer of 1923, as part of Stalin's effort to win approval for a draft constitution of the USSR in which non-Russian nationalities held a subordinate position. The opposition of the Ukrainians and others to this effort was met by punitive transfers and personnel reorganization.

3. **Valerian Kuibyshev** (1888-1935) was head of the Central Control Commission and of the Workers and Peasants Inspection, and a candidate member of the Politburo. In 1926 he became chairman of the Supreme Council of National Economy, and in 1927 a full member of the Politburo.

4. Lenin's **Theses** of April 4, 1917 ("The Tasks of the Proletariat in the Present Revolution") precipitated a crisis in the Bolshevik Party. Newly arrived from Switzerland, Lenin condemned the Provisional Government that had been established by the February revolution, called for an end to the war, and defined the task of the Bolsheviks as preparing the soviets to take full power and establish a workers' state. In his call for a dictatorship of the proletariat, Lenin was initially opposed by virtually the entire Bolshevik leadership. The April Theses are in English in Lenin's **Collected Works,** Vol. 24.

5. **G.I. Myasnikov** (1889-1946) was expelled from the CP in 1923 for violating party discipline in his leadership of the Workers Group.

6. The opposition of Zinoviev and Kamenev to the seizure of power in October 1917 is described in detail in "Lessons of October," in the chapter entitled "On the Eve of the October Revolution; the Aftermath—" (see below, p. 227).

7. **Brest-Litovsk** was a town on the Russo-Polish border where a treaty ending hostilities between Russia and Germany was signed in March 1918. The Central Committee of the Bolshevik Party was sharply divided on whether to sign the treaty. Lenin called for signing immediately on German terms. Trotsky argued for declaring the state of war at an end but against signing, and for prolonging the negotiations in the hope of a revolutionary insurrection in Germany. Bukharin led a group of "left communists" opposed in principle to signing the treaty, and called for organizing a revolutionary war against Germany. The left communist faction controlled the Moscow party organization and issued their own periodicals assailing Lenin and the Central Committee. When the German army resumed its attack on Russia as a result of the deadlock in negotiations, Trotsky deliberately abstained from voting within the Central Committee in order to give Lenin's position a majority. The November 1918 revolution in Germany and the German defeat in World War I enabled the Soviet government to recover most of the territory it lost through the treaty.

8. During the civil war, the Russian Tenth Army, under the influence of Stalin and Voroshilov, became the seat of the **"military opposition,"** which opposed the use of military specialists from the tsarist army and resisted the centralization of the Red Army under a unified command. The Eighth Party Congress in March 1919 reaffirmed the military policy that Trotsky, as head of the Red Army, had been implementing. Others in the "military opposition" included V.M. Smirnov, Safarov, Pyatakov, and Frunze.

9. Disagreements over the role of the **trade unions** caused bitter debate in the Bolshevik Party between 1920 and 1921. Several groupings were formed before the question was resolved at the Tenth Party Congress (March 1921) by the inauguration of the New Economic Policy.

10. **The Workers' Opposition,** led by Kollontai and Shlyapnikov, called for transferring all control and direction of the national economy to the trade unions. The Workers' Opposition was expelled from the party at the Tenth Congress.

11. In 1920, after Soviet forces drove an invading Polish army out of Soviet Russia, a debate broke out within the Central Committee over whether to pursue the retreating Poles all the way to Warsaw. Lenin, Zinoviev, and the Central Committee majority favored an offensive as a prelude to a revolutionary upsurge in Poland. Trotsky and Radek opposed the attempt to march on Warsaw on the basis that the majority was overestimating the revolutionary situation in Poland. The Russian offensive was defeated and and rolled back.

12. The **otsovists** ("recallists") were a group of Bolsheviks after the revolution of 1905 who advocated the "recall" or withdrawal of the social democratic deputies elected to the Duma (parliament) on the grounds of the Duma's extremely reactionary character.

13. In 1922-23, Lenin launched a struggle within the leadership of the party against Stalin, Dzerzhinsky, and Ordzhonikidze, because of their repeated violations in Soviet Georgia of the party's traditional policy

supporting the right of self-determination for non-Russian nationalities within the Soviet Union. Himself confined to bed, Lenin appealed to Trotsky to lead the struggle against them. This development is documented in **Lenin's Fight Against Stalinism** and in **The Stalin School of Falsification.**

14. The directing "Centers" of production, during the period of war communism, were quasi-military boards in full charge of the various industries in Russia, each functioning in its own sphere without much concern or coordination with the other spheres. The attempt to organize production on this basis was abandoned in 1921 with the introduction of the NEP.

15. Zinoviev was the first to charge that Trotsky had disrupted the transportation system by issuing Order No. 1042, which is described below. Stalin, Yaroslavsky, and Rudzutak repeated the charge.

16. The attack on Trotsky's record in connection with Order No. 1042 aimed, among other things, at covering up the records of other leaders who had acquired immunity from criticism by their support of the triumvirate. Among them was A.I. Rykov, who had been head of the Council of National Economy and was at that time one of the most prominent partisans of the triumvirate's campaign against Trotsky. By analyzing the real role of the Council during the period of the restoration of the transportation system, Trotsky is striking back at such hidden opponents as Rykov.

17. As opposed to Trotsky's insistence upon the central importance of developing Soviet industry, the supporters of the triumvirate tended to emphasize the importance of financial policy in bringing the economy out of crisis; they also maintained that financial policy, and credit in particular, could not be subjected to planning. Sokolnikov, the commissar of finance, was the chief representative of this theory and put great stock in the beneficial effect of currency stabilization.

18. Liebknecht, Bebel, Singer, Kautsky, and Bernstein were the founders and builders of the German social democracy, Adler of the Austrian movement, and Lafargue and Guesde of the French movement. In almost every case, the old orthodox Marxist leaders retreated from their original revolutionary views. Trotsky's suggestion that the Bolshevik "Old Guard" was not immune from a similar degeneration was violently rejected by the leaders of the party bureaucracy and denounced as slander.

19. **Fyodor Dan and V.M. Chernov** were leaders of the Menshevik and Social Revolutionary parties, respectively, in 1917. They were hostile to the Bolsheviks and to the October Revolution, and continued to oppose the Soviet Republic from exile by exploiting differences among the Bolsheviks.

20. **Famusov** is a character in Griboyedov's play **The Folly of Being Wise** (1824). He is a high official who is obsequious to higher officials and lives in dread of endangering his comfortable position.

21. The proponents of an **"active balance of trade"** argued that a surplus in the balance of payments was needed to provide the gold reserve

that would stabilize the gold-backed ruble (chervonets). Trotsky and the Opposition had urged that such a surplus be spent on purchases of machinery or otherwise invested in industry. This was another example of the tension between the proindustrialization tendency and the supporters of the "dictatorship of finance." By **"goods intervention"** was meant the importation of foreign commodities that were cheaper than analogous commodities produced in Russia. The sale of these imports would subsidize the sale of the Russian product at a lowered cost. Both the active balance and goods intervention had become issues in a counterresolution presented by four Oppositionists at a meeting of Moscow party workers on December 29, 1923, in reply to a speech by Rykov.

22. In June 1923 the Bulgarian government of the peasant leader Stambulisky was overthrown by reactionary forces. The Communist Party remained neutral, but the victorious reaction subjected the communists to ferocious persecution, forcing them underground. The Bulgarian communists denied they had suffered any defeat and in September attempted to retrieve themselves by a putsch which was doomed to defeat in advance.

23. The **Kazan events** were a crucial turning point in the Russian civil war. At Kazan and nearby Svyazhsk in August-September 1918, partisan detachments under Trotsky's direct leadership stood firm against the invading Czechoslovak White Army; in the process they were organized by Trotsky into an arm of the Red Army.

24. The **Emancipation of Labor** group was founded by Plekhanov together with other Russian emigres in Switzerland after their break with populism in 1883. Its founding marks the beginning of a Russian Marxist movement. It was dissolved when the Russian Social Democratic Labor Party was formed in 1898.

25. **Dual power** occurs in the course of a revolutionary or prerevolutionary situation when there arises, alongside the ruling class state institutions, a parallel "government" regarded by the insurgent masses as the real government, while the government of the ruling class loses its authority in their eyes. Such a situation is unstable and short-lived, and is resolved either by the recovery of the ruling class and the crushing of the insurrection, or by the victorious seizure of power by the workers.

26. The **July days** of 1917 in Petrograd were a period of spontaneous upsurges and bloody repression. The Bolsheviks were declared responsible, their leaders arrested, and their papers shut down.

27. **Defensism** is a term applied to the political support of a bourgeois government's war. After the February revolution a large part of the Bolshevik Party supported the Provisional Government's policy of continuing the war. Lenin proposed a policy of revolutionary defeatism toward what remained an imperialist war being waged by a bourgeois government. **Pravda**, with Stalin as one of its editors, had adopted a defensist position before Lenin returned to Russia.

28. The **April Conference** formally endorsed Lenin's April Theses after heated debate.

29. **Economism** was a Russian variant of syndicalism. It held that the economic struggle of the workers was sufficient to develop a mass movement, political consciousness, and an active leadership. Lenin devoted much of his pamphlet **What Is To Be Done?** to attacking Economism as a dangerous tendency that glorified the backwardness of the working class, evaded political issues, and downplayed the revolutionary party.

30. **Blanquism,** after Louis-Auguste Blanqui (1805-1881), is the theory of armed insurrection by small groups of selected and trained conspirators, as opposed to the Marxist concept of mass action.

31. The **Cadets,** or Constitutional Democrats, were the liberal party favoring a constitutional monarchy in Russia or even ultimately a republic. It was a party of progressive landlords, middle bourgeois, and bourgeois intellectuals.

32. In the summer of 1917, a joint committee of the Scandinavian Socialist parties invited the Executive Committee of the Soviets to attend an **international peace conference in Stockholm.** The Mensheviks and SRs accepted, but the April Conference of the Bolsheviks rejected the invitation on Lenin's ground that it was a political maneuver of German imperialism, working through the government socialists to feel out the most advantageous terms of peace. Only Kamenev supported the idea of participation.

33. **General Lavr G. Kornilov** (1870-1918) became Kerensky's commander in chief in July 1917 and led a counterrevolutionary putsch against Kerensky in September 1917. His defeat by the armed masses of Petrograd boosted the prestige of the Bolsheviks.

34. The **Democratic Conference** was an attempt by the Mensheviks to impede the growth of the Bolsheviks and their struggle for Soviet power, and to try to create an alternative to the soviets. The conference appointed a permanent body to constitute a **Pre-Parliament** until the Constituent Assembly convened. Trotksy proposed boycott of the Pre-Parliament, but was voted down. Lenin shared his view but was absent. The Bolsheviks finally withdrew after reading a declaration.

35. The letter of Kamenev and Zinoviev, dated October 11, 1917, and entitled "On the Current Situation," is available in English in Lenin's **Collected Works** (New York: International Publishers, 1929), Vol. XXI, book 2, pp. 328-31.

36. The **Mezhrayontsi** (Inter-District Organization) had consistently maintained an internationalist opposition to the imperialist war and opposed the Provisional Government. It merged with the Bolsheviks in August 1917. The name of its journal in 1917 was **Vperyod** (Forward).

37. **M.S. Glazman** had been the head of Trotsky's secretariat during the civil war. Hounded out of the party by the Stalinists because of his adherence to the Left Opposition, he committed suicide in 1924.

38. The 1909 article Trotsky refers to is also entitled "Our Differences," and is published in English as Chapter 25 of **1905** (New York: Random House, 1972).

39. **A.L. Parvus** (1869-1924) was a prominent Marxist propagandist

and theoretician in the period before World War I. Trotsky broke with him in 1914 when he became one of the leaders in the prowar wing of the German social democracy.

40. **Lieberdans** was a nickname that stuck to the Menshevik leaders Lieber and Dan and their followers; it was coined by Demyan Bedny in August 1917.

41. Trotsky's memoirs of Lenin are available in English as **Lenin: Notes for a Biographer** (New York: G.P. Putnam's Sons, 1971).

42. **Sukharevka** was the largest and best known of Moscow's black markets.

43. **Smena Vekh** (Changing Landmarks) was the name of a journal published by a group of emigre Russian intellectuals in Prague from 1921; they expressed sympathy with the Soviet government to the extent that it departed from the ideals of Bolshevism and appeared to be moving toward capitalism.

44. Charles Dawes (1865-1951), the Republican vice-president of the United States (1925-29), developed the **Dawes Plan** to ameliorate the economic crisis in Germany in 1923 by stabilizing the currency and balancing the budget.

Abbreviations and Russian Expressions

The **Bolsheviks** and the **Mensheviks** were formed through a split in the Russian Social Democratic Labor Party in 1903. The Bolsheviks believed that the workers had to unite with the poor peasants, taking the lead in a struggle against the bourgeoisie. They led the soviets to power in October 1917. **Old Bolsheviks** were those who joined the party before 1917, that is, members of the party's **Old Guard.** The Mensheviks were a moderate socialist party claiming allegiance to Karl Marx but believing that the working class must combine with the liberal bourgeoisie to overthrow tsarism and establish a democratic republic. In 1918 the Bolshevik Party changed its name to **Communist Party.**

Gosplan—the State Planning Commission, created in 1921.

NEP—the New Economic Policy, instituted in 1921 to allow the forces of the capitalist market to assist Russia's economic recovery.

Politburo—the Political Bureau was the ruling body of the Russian Communist Party, although it was ostensibly subordinated to the Central Committee.

Rabkrin—the Workers and Peasants Inspection, a commissariat designed to oversee the functioning of the other government departments. It was headed by Stalin from its beginning until 1922.

smychka—"link," or "bond," between workers and peasants or, more broadly, between industry and agriculture.

Social Revolutionary Party (SRs)— founded in Russia in 1900, emerging in 1902-03 as the political expression of all the earlier populist currents. It had the most influence among the peasantry before the revolution of 1917. Its right wing was led by Kerensky after February 1917; its left wing blocked with the Bolsheviks until the signing of the Brest-Litovsk treaty.

War communism—the sytem of subordinating economic life to the needs of the front, prevailed during the civil war. It was replaced by the NEP in 1921.

Further Reading

The following works contain articles or speeches by Trotsky during the period covered by this volume, and relating directly or indirectly to the beginning of the Left Opposition's struggle:

Europe and America: Two Speeches on Imperialism. New York: Pathfinder Press, 1971.
The First Five Years of the Communist International (2 vols.). Second edition. New York: Monad Press, 1972.
Lenin: Notes for a Biographer. New York: G.P. Putnam's Sons, 1971.
Leon Trotsky on Britain. Monad Press, 1973.
Leon Trotsky on Literature and Art. Pathfinder Press, 1970.
Problems of Everyday Life and Other Writings on Culture and Science. Monad Press, 1973.
Women and the Family. Second edition. Pathfinder Press, 1973.

The following works were written later but contain important material about the Left Opposition of 1923-25:

My Life. Second edition. Pathfinder Press, 1970.
The Permanent Revolution and Results and Prospects. Third edition. Pathfinder Press, 1969.
The Revolution Betrayed. Fifth edition. Pathfinder Press, 1972.
The Stalin School of Falsification. Third edition. Pathfinder Press, 1972.
The Third International After Lenin. Third edition. Pathfinder Press, 1972.

Other works that were consulted in the preparation of this volume and provide extensive information on the subject are as follows:

Broue, Pierre. *Le Parti Bolchevique: Histoire du P.C. de l'U.R.S.S.* Second edition. Paris: Les Editions de Minuit, 1963-71.

Carr, E.H. *A History of Soviet Russia.* 7 vols. Incl. Vol. 1-3, *The Bolshevik Revolution (1917-1923);* Vol. 4, *The Interregnum (1923-1924);* Vol. 5-7, *Socialism in One Country (1924-1926);* with R.W. Davies, Vol. 8-9, *Foundations of a Planned Economy (1926-1929).* New York: The Macmillan Company, 1951-1971.

Daniels, R.V. *The Conscience of the Revolution: Communist Opposition in Soviet Russia.* New York: Simon and Schuster, 1969.

Day, R.B. *Leon Trotsky and the Politics of Economic Isolation.* Cambridge: Cambridge University Press, 1973.

Deutscher, Isaac. *The Prophet Armed (Trotsky: 1879-1921); The Prophet Unarmed (Trotsky: 1921-1929); The Prophet Outcast (Trotsky: 1929-1940).* New York: Vintage Books, 1965.

Eastman, Max. *Since Lenin Died.* London: The Labour Publishing Co. Ltd., 1925.

Lenin, V.I. *Collected Works.* 45 vols. Fourth edition. Moscow: Progress Publishers, 1960-1970.

———, and Trotsky. *Lenin's Fight Against Stalin.* Pathfinder Press, 1975.

Lewin, Moshe. *Lenin's Last Struggle.* New York: Pantheon Books, 1968.

Rosmer, Alfred. *Moscow Under Lenin.* New York and London: Monthly Review Press, 1972.

Shapiro, Leonard. *The Communist Party of the Soviet Union.* New York: Random House, 1959.

INDEX

Palydov, I., 403
Paris Commune (1871), 176, 202
Party, role of, 165-67, 168, 170, 173, 185, 201, 203-05, 249-56, 268-74; democracy in, *see* Workers' democracy
Parvus, A.L., 44n, 278, 418-19n
Peasantry, 19-20, 21-22, 30, 35, 46, 50, 53, 54, 135-41, 320-22, 337-39, 384-90, 390-91, 393-95, 407; course toward, 46-47, 50, 383, 384, 393; "underestimation" of, 63, 101-09, 228-29, 297-300, 302-03, 305, 393, 394; *see also* Agrarian policy, Kulaks, *and* New Economic Policy
"Peasants, enrich yourselves," 35, 392
Peasant War in Germany (Engels), 206
Permanent revolution, 42-44, 101-03, 277-78, 298-99, 305
Peshekhonov, 257-58
Planning, 24-25, 35, 46, 47, 53, 54, 60, 65, 109-23, 155-59, 332, 383, 389-90, 391-92, 393
Poland, 20, 21; invasion of, 84, 415n
Pravda, use of, as factional weapon, 37, 37-38n, 41, 393
Preobrazhensky, E., 24, 36, 401
Pre-Parliament, 212, 223, 224, 226, 227, 228, 236, 243, 244, 285, 418n
Provisional Government, 43, 213, 214, 216, 217, 218, 223, 241, 242, 243, 245, 285
Puzakov, A., 402
Pyatakov, G., 24, 36, 38n, 52, 401, 415n

Rabkrin, *see* Workers and Peasants Inspection
Radek, K., 28, 36, 38n
Rafail, 402
Rakovsky, C., 36
Red Army, 130-35, 192
Revolutionary Military Committee, 44-45, 57, 227, 240-41, 280, 306, 308, 414n

Revolution proletarienne (Paris), 310, 316-17, 318
Romania, 20
Rosengolts, A., 401
Rosmer, A., 310, 316-18
Rovensky, 258
Ruhr, invasion of (1923), 26, 94, 165, 168, 170
Rumer, I., 258
Rykov, A., 23, 35, 47, 52, 62, 121, 416n

Safarov, 415n
Saltykov, 134
Sapronov, T., 38n, 401
"Scissors" effect, 23, 50, 53, 54, 91, 121-22, 137
Second International, 93, 125, 204, 222-23
Seeckt, H. von, 94
Serebriakov, L., 401
Shlyapnikov, A., 415n
Shmidel, O., 402
Since Lenin Died (Eastman), 309-15
Singer, P., 125-26, 416n
Skobelev, M., 242
Smena Vekh (Changing Landmarks), 329, 407, 419n
Smirnov, I.N., 401
Smirnov, V., 402, 415n
Smychka (alliance of workers and peasants), 20, 21-22, 30, 42, 43, 52, 54, 88, 118-19, 120, 135-41, 299-302, 393-94, 405, 420n
Socialism in one country, 42, 44, 47, 383
Social Revolutionaries (SRs), 30, 32, 43, 103, 105, 107, 148, 172, 207, 208, 220, 223, 228, 235, 236, 245, 249, 258, 283, 285, 406, 420n
Sokolnikov, G., 23, 386n, 395, 416n, 419n
Sorin, 257
Sosnovsky, D., 402
Sotsialistichesky Vestnik (Socialist Messenger, Berlin), 38n, 51, 295, 313

BOOKS AND PAMPHLETS BY LEON TROTSKY*

Against Individual Terrorism

The Age of Permanent Revolution

The Basic Writings of Trotsky

Between Red and White

The Bolsheviki and World Peace (War and the International)

The Case of Leon Trotsky

The Challenge of the Left Opposition (1923-25) (incl. Lessons of October, The New Course, Problems of Civil War, and Toward Capitalism or Socialism?)

The Chinese Revolution: Problems and Perspectives

Europe and America: Two Speeches on Imperialism

Fascism: What It Is and How to Fight It

The First Five Years of the Communist International (2 vols.)

The History of the Russian Revolution (3 vols.)

In Defense of Marxism

Lenin: Notes for a Biographer

Lenin's Fight Against Stalinism (with V.I. Lenin; incl. On the Suppressed Testament of Lenin)

Leon Trotsky Speaks

Literature and Revolution

Marxism in Our Time

Military Writings

My Life

1905

On Black Nationalism and Self-Determination

On Britain (incl. Where Is Britain Going?)

On Engels and Kautsky

On the Jewish Question

On Literature and Art

On the Paris Commune

On the Suppressed Testament of Lenin

On the Trade Unions

Our Revolution

The Permanent Revolution and Results and Prospects

Problems of the Chinese Revolution

Problems of Everyday Life and Other Writings on Culture and Science

The Revolution Betrayed

The Spanish Revolution (1931-39)

Stalin

The Stalin School of Falsification

The Struggle Against Fascism in Germany

Terrorism and Communism

Their Morals and Ours (with essays by John Dewey and George Novack)

The Third International After Lenin

The Transitional Program for Socialist Revolution (incl. The Death Agony of Capitalism and the Tasks of the Fourth International and On the Labor Party in the U.S.)

Trotsky's Diary in Exile, 1935

Women and the Family

Writings of Leon Trotsky (1929-40) (12 vols., to be completed in 1976)

The Young Lenin

In preparation:

The Challenge of the Left Opposition (1926-29) (incl. The Platform of the Opposition)

On China

On France (incl. Whither France?)

Political Portraits

The War Correspondence of Leon Trotsky

---

*This list includes all books and pamphlets by Leon Trotsky published in the United States and in print as of 1975.